Patrolling
Chaos

Patrolling
Chaos

The U.S. Border Patrol
in Deep South Texas

Robert Lee Maril

Texas Tech University Press

Lyrics from "All Along the Watchtower" by Bob Dylan. Copyright © 1968 by Dwarf Music All rights Reserved. International copyright secured. Reprinted by permission.

This book is typeset in Times Roman. The paper used in this book meets the minimum requirements of ANSI/NISO Z39.48–1992 (R1997). ∞

Library of Congress Cataloging-in-Publication Data
Maril, Robert Lee.
   Patrolling chaos : the U.S. Border Patrol in deep South
Texas / Robert Lee Maril.
      p.   cm.
   Includes bibliographical references.
   ISBN 0-89672-537-5 (cloth : alk. paper)
     1. United States. Immigration Border Patrol. 2. Border patrols—
Mexican-American Border Region. I. Title.
   JV6483.M298 2004
   363.28'5'097644—dc22

                                                  2004009454

Printed in the United States of America

04 05 06 07 08 09 10 11 12 / 9 8 7 6 5 4 3 2 1

Texas Tech University Press
Box 41037
Lubbock, Texas 79409–1037 USA
800.832.4042
www.ttup.ttu.edu

In Memory of
Lynn Elizabeth Maril
Marie Maril

Contents

Contents

Part Three: The Substance of Chaos

Acknowledgments

I would like to acknowledge the support of my colleagues Elena Bastida, Ronald Thrasher, Josiah Heyman, and Dan Dearth. I have greatly benefited from ongoing conversations with Genaro Gonzalez, Edzel Cardena, Molly Sheridan, and Rene Garza. Cynthia Garza greatly facilitated the completion of this research. Thomas Cleary researched articles I otherwise would have missed. I am particularly indebted to Ronald Thrasher for his intellectual guidance and friendship throughout this project. My wife, Dindy Reich, consistently encouraged and supported me during the most challenging of times. I could not have completed this project without her.

My graduate seminar in the Sociology of Immigration and Immigration Policy at the University of Texas–Pan American was particularly beneficial in clarifying issues of importance to new illegal immigrants. I personally want to thank Jesus Garcia, Marta Garcia, Rodrigo Guzman, Felipe Hinojosa, Larry Molina, Caprica Neal, Christopher Omar Park, Ernesto Ramirez, John Rodriguez, and Mark Williams for sharing their ideas and experiences.

At Thomas Harriot College of Arts and Sciences at East Carolina University I especially have leaned on the expertise of David Griffith and Jeff Johnson. Betty Lou White ably served as my administrative assistant through crucial parts of the writing and editing of the manuscript. Dan Haught worked on the endnote citations and bibliography and deserves thanks for his efforts. The

Acknowledgments

students in my graduate seminar on qualitative methods were extremely helpful in raising methodological concerns I might otherwise have diminished.
I am very grateful for the support of Dean Keats Sparrow. I also want to
acknowledge the comments of two anonymous reviewers.

Finally my deepest gratitude goes to the men and women of the United
States Border Patrol who of necessity must remain nameless, but without
whom this book would not have been possible.

There must be some way out of here said the
    Joker to the Thief
There's too much confusion I can't get no relief
Businessmen they drink my wine, plowmen
    dig my earth
None of them along the line know what any
    of it is worth.

—BOB DYLAN

On the street the poor rock and sway, like burying
parties. Their eyes are ice.

—MARTIN AMIS

A disorganized society cannot generate conceptions
of its alternative futures or act on them.
Organization is power, a power essential to a
vigorous democracy. Disorganization is surrender to
drift, to accident, to fate.

—CORNEL WEST

One

All Along the Watchtower

The Agent and the River

Hanging by one lone hinge, the door of the '85 Econoline van creaks forlornly in the soft, tropical breeze of Deep South Texas, the January air a crazy blend of paloverde, mesquite, and huisache crossed with acrid toxicity from the putrid waters of the Rio Grande running just below the twenty-foot bluff. Jack Spurrier, supervisor for the United States Border Patrol based at the McAllen Station on Old Military Highway, brakes his brand-new Ford Expedition before warily approaching the vehicle sitting on the northern bank of the river. The carcass of the van is covered with mud, its Mexican plates barely visible; beneath, faded gray paint peels in swatches from the van's exterior. Hammered back into form countless times, the sheet metal is a terrain of minute hills and dales punctuated with mesas of vestal Detroit steel, while the windows, the work of an unskilled painter in a big hurry, are the color of Texas crude. Although it is impossible to see through the glass, the open double doors at the rear reveal a ratty scarlet carpet hugging a floor covered by a large piece of dirty cardboard. Skinned to the puffy yellow foam revealing the naked wire of the springs, only the front two seats remain.

Smugglers abandoned this Econoline the night before, left it on the low bluff above the river that now forms a visual oddity amid the carrizo cane, the scorched, brittle brush, crumbled buffalo grass, retama, and proud native sabal palms. Faded and tattered green garbage bags cover the sandy banks, along with plastic gallon bottles, ragged clothes, and other belongings carried by illegal aliens as they crossed from the state of Tamaulipas into the state of Texas. Cautiously casting their eyes north, America's newest illegal immigrants soon realize their journey has only really just begun: having crossed without legal documents, *sin papeles,* into the lower Rio Grande valley of Texas, they stand five hundred miles due south of Dallas.[1]

Not yet sensing the need to draw his .40-caliber Beretta, Border Patrol Agent Jack Spurrier, fourteen years of service under his belt, approaches the Econoline with caution. Right hand resting on his holster, Agent Spurrier knows his service weapon holds eleven rounds in the magazine, one in the chamber, and that his gun has no safety. An agent must always be ready for the unexpected. There may be no microsecond to snap off the safety with the index finger before squeezing the trigger. Human life ebbs and flows in South Texas, the pendulum swinging back and forth in sluggish parabolas of time or as quickly as dry lightning.

Waiting and listening, the only sound the soft breeze blowing gently through the cane and the trees that line the riverbank, Jack Spurrier decides that the smugglers have, at least for now, departed this peaceful scene. Only then does his surprising tenor voice break the quiet of the morning. Above his placid face, his brown hair is cut tightly in a military haircut; his broad forehead is overcome by wrinkles of thought. A thick South Texas accent covers all his words with drops of honey and chunks of hot peppers.

"See the footprints. They had a mechanical problem. See where they been working on the engine. It's all messed up. You can tell they had some problems, tried to get it running again, but then gave up and just left it there. Look at it. It's a piece of crap."

Searching for any piece of information that might prove useful, Jack Spurrier rummages through the detritus in the spacious cargo area emptied of rear seats. When he finally digs under the front seat, a smile slowly lights up his boyish face as he pulls a license tag from beneath the rotting foam. He holds up the tag like a trophy tarpon netted forty land miles due east in the Gulf of Mexico.

"Texas plate," he grins as he walks back to his new Expedition, one of the few perks of wearing the two gold supervisor bars on the epaulets of his uniform. Green and gold seals against a field of white on both front doors of his

Expedition read, "United States Department of Justice United States Border Patrol." The Border Patrol, for the majority of its history the official enforcement arm of the Immigration and Naturalization Service, is now part of U.S. Customs and Border Protection, falling under the new Department of Homeland Security. Jack calls in the plate to the dispatcher, then returns to the van to complete his inspection.

"What are they smuggling?" he is asked. Cocaine? Illegal aliens?[2] Machine guns and rocket propelled grenades bound for guerillas hunkered down in tropical jungles? Laundered drug money?

As a flock of turkey vultures eyes the agent from the limbs of a dead mesquite tree, Jack Spurrier takes time to answer the question. There is no reason to rush. Out here on the quiet bluffs overlooking the putrid waters of the Rio Grande, out here where the historical past and present collide in a tangle of sweat, greed, and human desperation, the Econoline could have been loaded with almost anything. From cruel, outlandish violence to small, unexpected gifts of personal compassion, Jack Spurrier has been a witness to the gamut of human actions.

"*Ropa usada,*" says Jack Spurrier, still keeping a wary eye on the edge of the sandy bluff. *Ropa usada.* Old, rumpled, filthy clothes that few Americans would look at twice. Clothes the Salvation Army rejected. Clothes so tightly bound together in heavy, rectangular bundles they seem to explode when the ropes are severed. In the dark of night and the panic of quick decisions the problem is that *ropa usada* is easily mistaken for burlap bags filled with bricks of marijuana or cocaine.

Last night, just before the sun could rise once more over lands subdued by four years of drought, men smuggled used clothes *from* the United States *into* Mexico. Maybe there was drug money stuffed between the layers of used clothes. Who knows? It all depends.

It could be cocaine one night, workers from Mexico, Bosnia, Brazil, or China the next. Or guns bound for a revolutionary Latin American force. Or a ton of avocados headed north to Dallas. Or nothing at all.

There is an elusive carnival of humanity along the banks of the Rio Grande in Deep South Texas: bailouts, fresh tube, Waylon and Willie, M&Ms armed with .50-caliber machine guns, river divers, *federales,* Benny *el elefantino,* gotaways and turnbacks, cannibals, Grupo Beta, and Nature Boy. Many others remain faceless and nameless as they disappear into the night shadows, their only memory half a footprint in the dust, a broken blade of grass, or a castoff garment.

A silky, indigo snake, the Rio Grande, the Big River, is a fierce force of nature set adrift in an ocean of stone and rock where even spiny cacti find a hard welcome. It commences as an insignificant stream in the San Juan Mountains of southern Colorado just a few miles from the Continental Divide. Fed by mountain springs, snow melt, and other smaller rivers along its way, the broad, crystal cold waters cut through the mountain ranges and mesas of northern New Mexico heading toward the Gulf of Mexico. Running west of the Sangre de Christo Mountains, the river at every twist and turn leaves behind small settlements and villages perched a cautious distance from its flood-prone banks. Farmers and ranchers siphon off water into ancient and intricate irrigation systems as the Rio Grande speeds toward Albuquerque; these agriculturists, nurturing a river culture that has endured in one form or another for centuries, transform raw desert into orchards of peach and plum and cherry and narrow fields of tall corn.[3]

Not far from Taos, pale August tourists covered in catalog gear dip their hands into its waters, moan at its frigid temperature, then lie back in rubber rafts to let their grateful bunions dangle in the refreshing cold. Anyone can see the rocky bottom four feet down, feel the stiff current, decipher the outlines of the brown trout painstakingly hatched by Ph.D.s from New Mexico State University. The trout, both those raised from hatchlings and the infrequent indigenous fish, carefully avoid the currents by passing their time in the shadows of the trees and the boulders that line and fill the river. Although often hidden beneath a thick cover of snow, the frigid waters, in winter as throughout the year, relentlessly continue marching toward a tepid Texas sea.

Separating the richest and most powerful country in the world from an exploding third-world population with little on its plate but hope, the Rio Grande becomes an international border as it leaves southern New Mexico. Mexicans named this same river the *Río Bravo,* Fierce River. From a car window on Interstate 10 East, the twin cities of El Paso and Ciudad Juárez resemble Pittsburgh before steel moved offshore. On a bad day pollution covers every particle of air with a high yellow sheen. Adobe shacks with metal roofs line the low hills of Juárez; not the fake adobe of the new Santa Fe, but real adobe bricks fabricated from the surrounding high plains desert.

The Rio Grande/Río Bravo is slam dunked by the effluvia of both El Paso and Juárez, each city transforming a roaring Colorado mountain river into a sluggish, gray stream. Rated one of the most toxic rivers in the United States, the river miraculously redefines itself as it cuts through the high canyon walls of Big Bend National Park 200 miles southeast of El Paso/Juárez.[4]

At the tiny village of Ciudad Carmen a man asks for an American dollar before he drags you and, at most, one other person from the shores of the United States to Mexico by way of a six-foot, dented metal skiff. Here, where there is no bridge to span the river, he accomplishes this feat in less than three minutes. Here, too, there is no port of entry, no wall or fence, no razor wire, no lights. And no border guards. With any luck a man on the Mexican banks of the river appears to offer a ride on his scrawny mule to a small outdoor restaurant in the village. Gorging on cold chicken tacos and lukewarm Coca Cola, the occasional tourists stare at the imprint of glass Coke bottles *hecho en Mexico,* made in Mexico.

By the time the Rio Grande reaches Amistad, friendship, Reservoir, which stalls and drains the river to form a sprawling, immense lake that covers both sides of the border, it has finally been defeated. Once a wild-running, frigid river, it becomes a polluted, docile body of water as it staggers past the twin cities of Del Rio/Ciudad Acuña, Eagle Pass/Piedras Negras, Laredo/Nuevo Laredo and other communities too small to find on many maps. Each human settlement depends on the river for its lifeblood, for water to sustain the farms, the livestock, and the crops, and for the residents themselves.

Evidence of the unremitting Texas drought, a drought plaguing much of the Southwest, is never more evident than in the tiny tourist town of Zapata, which supplies bait, refreshments, and lodging to recreational fishermen from Dallas, Houston, and Monterrey, Mexico. Because of the drought, fishing piers and boat docks on Amistad stand high and dry hundreds of yards from the water's edge. The ghosts of Old Guerrero, a Mexican town built long before the waters of Falcon Dam in the 1950s erased its memory, have reemerged, the walls of the old plaza and the spires of the cathedral standing bare and deserted except for a wayward tourist with camera.

McAllen, Texas, population 106,414, and its twin city, Reynosa, Tamaulipas, estimated at 450,000 residents, lie one hundred land miles farther southeast of the ghosts of Old Guerrero, past a host of tiny ranching communities and old river towns on both banks—communities such as Rio Grande City, settled by Spanish colonists before the Pilgrims landed at Plymouth Rock.[5] Large metal pipes transport river water to quench the thirst of the residents of Los Ebanos, La Joya, Abram, Granjeno, Madero, Palmview, Havana, and Mission. Pump stations fill the concrete and earthen irrigation ditches feeding the orchards of orange and grapefruit and nourishing the vast fields of onions, carrots, cabbage, melon, and sugar cane.

Mission, immediately to the west along the rail line, is a small town besieged by new housing developments transforming citrus groves into acres of commuters, but its history mirrors that of McAllen and other Valley communities. Although the Hayes-Sammons Chemical Company, makers of a portion of the pesticides used by Valley farmers over the years, closed its doors in the 1950s, it was not designated a toxic Superfund site by the Environmental Protection Agency until 1987.[6] Despite its new role as a bedroom community, Mission annually pays tribute to, among others, "the Duchess of Star Ruby Grapefruit, the Duchess of Rio Red Grapefruit, Queen Citriana, the Duchess of Marsh White Seedless Grapefruit, the Duchess of Pink Grapefruit, the Duchess of Ruby Red Grapefruit, and the Duchess of Honey Dew Melon."[7]

At first glance these small communities along the banks of the north side of the Rio Grande, all in Hidalgo County, appear deeply entrenched in the same poverty that pervades the region. Nationally seven out of the top ten poorest small municipalities are located in this area, and McAllen holds the title of the poorest city, out of two hundred, in all the United States.[8] A closer inspection reveals pockets of large homes hidden behind cinder-block walls covered by flowering bougainvillea, poinsettia, and hibiscus and topped by broken glass bottles. Behind these walls are compounds of affluence and wealth. A study in contrasts, Cameron and Hidalgo Counties are undergoing rapid economic change as a result of the North American Free Trade Agreement passed by Congress in 1994. These compounds are also clues to what economists euphemistically refer to as an "alternative economy."[9] Alongside legitimate business development is a rigid, highly structured industry and culture based upon illegal smuggling.[10] One writer aptly labeled McAllen a "hot zone of growth."[11]

The call comes back on the Texas plate. The van once belonged to a woman from the town of Missouri, Texas. "Probably sold it to these guys and they kept the plate for some reason. Doesn't help much, I guess." Jack Spurrier nods to himself, makes a mental note of the plate, then climbs back into the front seat of the Ford Expedition.

Agent Spurrier continues to patrol the river looking for illegal aliens, drugs, or anything else blatantly against the law he is sworn to uphold. He guides his cumbersome two-ton vehicle along the narrow track of sand and clay that bends its way through the Santa Anna National Wildlife Reserve. Every few minutes he stops to cut sign as he checks for footprints, tire tracks, or any other evidence of human activity. He eyes the dirt paths that lead from river landings across the narrow road, then northward into the thick brush, prickly pear, yucca, retama, and stunted mesquites. Providing excellent cover for new immigrant workers or drug traffickers, fifteen-foot-high carrizo cane covers the riverbanks in thick foliage and shadow.

It is the job of Jack Spurrier to recognize who has come to the northern banks of the Rio Grande, why they have come, and where they now are. Most of the time it is illegal aliens. Sometimes it is drugs. But he can never be sure what he might encounter. He brakes, jumps out to cut sign, then returns.

"They've been using a new landing to bring it in," he says. "It" is illegal drugs. "You can see where they pulled their trucks around to load up. See those tracks?"

Hauling an extra twenty-five pounds into the front seat of the Expedition, Jack swears, starting next week, he will lose weight. He adjusts his equipment belt to fit behind the wheel. On it he carries the standard tools of his trade: besides his holstered .40-caliber Beretta automatic there are two extra ammo magazines, pepper spray, an Asp collapsible metal baton, handcuffs, and clasp knife.

"I'm usually in better shape," he admits defensively. "But I got married again three months ago. My wife is Mexican American.[12] Very traditional. She's a heck of a good cook. I'm going to lose weight as soon as this gringo can find the time to work out. You know, they don't pay us like they do the DEA to work out. They pay those guys. It's considered part of their job. Can you believe that?"

For too many years after his first wife left him, Jack was the single parent of his two young girls. Now his girls have a new mother, and he has a new stepson. Things are looking up.

Coded talk from the dispatcher to other agents in the field, as well as talk between agents, filters through on his radio, a series of numbers to the uninitiated. Jack listens intently as he steers the Expedition along the narrow dirt path.

"I'll tell you straight up the way it is. It's slow for January. Nothing much happening. But it's going to pick up. All the Mexicans are going to go back to work after Christmas vacation. They have to. When it happens, it's going to happen real fast. You don't have time to think. You got to react, just rely on your training and your experience."

A perfunctory voice comes over his radio. "We got four OTMs. Father, mother, two children. Correct that. One baby. Father wearing a red shirt. Guatemalans." OTM stands for Other Than Mexican. Most agents hate OTMs. Not because they dislike foreigners, but because each OTM represents an hour or more of mind-numbing paper work back at the station on Old Military Highway. If you are sitting at a work station filling out page after page of government forms, you cannot, by definition, catch a load of dope or round up a group of illegal aliens.

Far off in Washington, D.C., a world away from Agent Jack Spurrier in his little corner of Deep South Texas, Linda Chavez gives a press conference to the national media surrounded by five former illegal aliens she has "helped" in recent years. Nominated for secretary of labor by President George W. Bush, she has been dogged by critics who charge that she knowingly harbored Marta Mercado in her home from late 1991 to 1993. Marta was an illegal alien at that time, the same status as the family just apprehended by the Border Patrol. Both Marta and the family of four, including the baby, also have something else in common: they were born in Guatemala.[13]

Chavez, fast on her way to becoming a footnote to the first term of George W. Bush, will soon succumb to her critics and withdraw her nomination as secretary of labor. Sooner still the Guatemalan family, who just minutes before crossed the Río Bravo, will be interviewed by patrol agents at the McAllen Station on Old Military Highway, then released. It will take the Guatemalan family two hours and forty-one minutes at the station, during which time they stand patiently against a pale green cinder-block wall, answer a series of questions, are fingerprinted, sign their names on different government forms, and gulp down salami sandwiches made with Wonder Bread. They will finally set off by foot for the new McAllen International Bus Station four miles north of the McAllen Border Patrol Station in downtown McAllen. Although they are ordered to report May 7, 2001, to the INS in Houston, Texas, for a hearing on their status, it is highly unlikely this Guatemalan family will ever be seen again by the INS or the Border Patrol unless by chance they are apprehended once more as they illegally cross the river.[14]

As the newest of illegal immigrants silently trudge along the cracked side-walks of downtown McAllen past an assortment of retail establishments with bright signs in Spanish, they are surrounded by the squawk and shriek of hun-dreds of tropical green parrots. The Valley is home to more than 150 species of birds found nowhere else in the United States. Each day at sunset in McAllen flocks of parrots search for a roost as they soar with the air currents, briefly covering up the noise from the busy traffic in the streets with an impervious wall of sound.[15]

Although the Guatemalans will be listed as another statistical "apprehen-sion" by the Border Patrol, the truth is that they were never really apprehended in the first place, at least not in the sense that most Americans understand the word "apprehended." A more accurate description is that, with the help of a *coyote,* they waded across the Río Bravo, sighted the border patrol vehicle at the top of the levee, then walked over to it to voluntarily surrender themselves into the custody of the agent behind the wheel.

This Guatemalan family, like many other OTMs, knows INS policy back-ward and forward. The scenario is this: We're here, we are illegal because we are here, so please arrest us right now. We know you define us as a "family unit" and, as such, we know you will not separate us and will, in fact, soon set us free after we pay a bond. At that time we are off to work anywhere in the United States. Maybe we will go to Dallas, maybe to Chicago, Atlanta, Des Moines, or New York City. It all depends.

Guatemalans, like many other illegal immigrants entering the United States from the Mexican border, may possess little formal education, but they are not necessarily completely naïve about the immigration system they encounter. Many, but certainly not all, are experienced transnational players, or come with experienced relatives or friends who, as border crossers, know the rules. To consider them anything else is to risk stealing their humanity by denying their intelligence and experience or, worse still, romanticizing their plight in a booming global economy that requires thousands upon thousands of low-wage workers. The vast majority of illegal immigrants leave their home countries to work hard, save their money, then return to their homeland. Some in this complex pattern of migration become full-time illegal residents in the United States. The victim of exaggeration and stereotype, immigrant behavior is diverse and broad. But one thing is very clear: these individuals do not travel their difficult and dangerous journeys searching for a welfare handout; they immigrate to work.[16] Just like Chavez's "friend."

Although a vital part of this nation's economy, illegal immigrant workers remain vulnerable to every kind of exploitation. U.S. immigration laws and policy, which may sound rational and pristine within the confines of Washington's inner beltway, blow hollow and vapid along the Rio Grande in Deep South Texas.

The INS estimates that there are 7 million undocumented workers residing in the United States; 350,000 illegal aliens a year came to this country between 1990 and 2000.[17] Regardless of the exact numbers, undocumented workers employed in a wide variety of industries are, and have been, a vital component of the American labor force.[18] Some illegal workers came to this country a hundred years ago or more, some future Americans last night.[19]

Just as ephemeral, the figures for illegal drugs, including marijuana and cocaine, are iridescent numbers that lose their luminosity when examined against any objective criteria. One estimate suggests that the Mexican marijuana and cocaine industries generate $3 billion a year.[20] Producing and distributing illegal drugs creates more revenue for Mexico than oil exports. Whether drug profits are in fact $5 billion or $2 billion, these thriving but illegal industries have profoundly and fundamentally changed Mexican society even as the core of America from the streets of the inner cities to the suburban malls has been shaken to its very roots.

For many years Deep South Texas has been one of the major transportation routes for illegal drugs. For example, along the Mexican border from October 2001 to July 2002 the Border Patrol seized a total $352.7 million worth of cocaine. More than half, 55 percent, of these cocaine seizures took place in Deep South Texas.[21] During one typical weekend three separate shipments of cocaine and marijuana with a street value of $5.8 million were intercepted by the Border Patrol not far from the city of McAllen.[22] Drug smugglers transport cocaine and marijuana by the ton across the Rio Grande in Deep South Texas, then the drugs are distributed to other points throughout the United States. Although largely unpublicized, drug-related violence in Deep South Texas and on the southern banks of the Río Bravo is out of control, as terrifying and disruptive to the region's law-abiding residents as it is in any metropolitan area in the United States and Mexico.[23]

Jack Spurrier works to stop the illegal aliens and the illegal drugs, but he knows that most Americans neither know nor care much about the realities of the Mexican border, of illegal aliens, or the transportation of illegal drugs into the United States. Or about the work he does each day as a border agent. Except when a big load is confiscated or an agent is charged with brutalizing an undocumented worker, news of the Border Patrol rarely appears in American media. There have been, of course, a few throwaway movies about the Border Patrol with actor studs like Jack Nicholson romancing beautiful actresses. But these movies were as unrealistic as scenes with ex-karate champ Chuck Norris of *Walker: Texas Ranger* roaring through the streets of Houston in his macho black truck with oversized tires. More recently the movie *Traffic* temporarily grabbed the public's attention, but Jack Spurrier hated its depiction of the illegal drug trade because he and other agents never appeared along the 2,000-mile Mexican border. In this film it was if the thousands of men and women who work in the U.S. Border Patrol never existed.

Jack does not like any of this. Not some Washington bureaucrat who wants to be the newest secretary of labor, or Chuck Norris's uncanny ability to keep his black Stetson atop his head when performing those fantastic karate kicks in slow-mo, or an award-winning acting performance by the cast of *Traffic,* or the apprehension of four Guatemalans by agents downriver, or, least of all, the American penchant to reduce complex policy to media sound bites.

Pale river clay swirls around the drain as he washes his Expedition in the big lot behind the McAllen Station. Jack waves to fellow agents as they come and go through one of the steel doors at the south end of the station, then heads for his locker with other things on his mind.

Soon he is driving his own truck toward home, thinking about his three kids as he heads down Old Military Highway. About how his two daughters will look when he comes through the front door and about how good it feels to have a stepson. And the gaze of his new wife when he comes home dead tired after a long shift, when all he wants is a shower and a cold beer.

Jack Spurrier works as hard as any agent of the U.S. Border Patrol and may be in line for one last promotion before retirement. In the meantime his personal goal is to be a damn good agent as he patrols the banks of the Rio Grande. Whatever it takes, Jack Spurrier is equally determined to be a good husband and father.

Purpose

Agents like Jack Spurrier spend day after day, week after week, and year after year along the banks of the Rio Grande. When they finally retire from the ranks of the Border Patrol, they have collected twenty years or more of unique, first-hand experiences. My primary intention in this book is to understand agents like Jack Spurrier, men and women who know the U.S.-Mexico border far better than anyone else. My goal is to comprehend what they know, to describe and explain their deep knowledge of the border.[24]

Agents of the U.S. Border Patrol have rarely been asked about their understanding of their work environment. Or if they have, it has been collapsed into a ten-second sound bite on the local news or a quotable sentence in a 750-word newspaper story. Academics have only occasionally bothered to study them; one notable exception is the work of Josiah Heyman, who has closely scrutinized the parent agency of the Border Patrol, the Immigration and Naturalization Service.[25]

Unlike, then, other works that may portray the border through the macro-level eyes of social scientists and policy makers, or the micro-level perspective of new immigrants who cross the Río Bravo, or those with journalistic or literary leanings, all very valid points of inquiry, viewpoint, and understanding, my major purpose here is to explore and understand those who maintain a rich and often complex knowledge of the people who live on the northern side of the Rio Grande, the people who quickly pass through it, the dynamics of the physical landscape itself, and the daily implications of certain public and national policies.[26]

My account of the world of agents of the U.S. Border Patrol describes and defines a rarely documented viewpoint that may contribute to a more diverse and comprehensive understanding of our border with Mexico, the people and the resources of the borderlands, the constant flows of illegal immigrants and illegal drugs, and new challenges confronting the enforcement of laws and policy in light of international terrorism.

Methodology

My focus is always on, and constantly returns to, what agents do. I do not dismiss lightly the interests of all others, including illegal immigrants who are most endangered along the Mexican border, but their stories have already been well documented. Neither do I take a specific political or ideological position based upon previous bias. I come to this task with a critical, inductive eye to all the stereotypes that prevail along the Rio Grande, false images not only of illegal immigrants and the process of immigration, but also others who frequent this region: many residents of McAllen, along with other Americans, hold very strong negative attitudes about the U.S. Border Patrol.

Having systematically collected rich and detailed data from the agents themselves, I then compared these data to what I had myself observed, to interviews conducted with those inside and outside the Border Patrol, and to the relevant research literature. This research approach, participant-observation, was particularly well-suited, because the majority of the work that agents engaged in along the Rio Grande was, by definition, far from the sight of the public and also subject to controversy. My research was necessarily exploratory, inductive in approach, and informed by my own previous experiences along the border.[27]

From January 1, 2000, to January 1, 2002, I rode with agents in their trucks during their ten-hour shifts in Deep South Texas whenever my class schedule and administrative duties allowed, a total of approximately sixty shifts. I followed agents on these ride-alongs as they chased undocumented workers through forests of prickly pear, I rode shotgun as they pursued drug traffickers along narrow dirt roads, I hid with them as they waited for *coyotes* or mules to appear with their cargo, I hugged the bows of their boats at night as they patrolled the waters of the Rio Grande, and I sat in the cabs of their scope trucks for long hours watching the thermal images of illegal immigrants on tiny green screens.

In addition I observed agents at the McAllen Border Patrol Station as they processed the men, women, and children they apprehended. I drank coffee with agents at their designated tables at local restaurants, and I drank beer with them at their hangouts, parties, and celebrations. I stood next to them at McAllen's Miller International Airport as they asked, "Are you a citizen of the United States?" carefully observing those who were questioned as they struggled, out of a combination of anger, fear, and anxiety, to voice their answers. I sat next to agents as they waited to testify in court or as they gave a press conference announcing construction bids for new buildings. I politely asked agents to clarify a point when they lectured in my university classes and I demanded, on more than one occasion, bug repellent when I had forgotten my own—infestations of mosquitoes and insects, along with the other wildlife along the Rio Grande, were no laughing matter.

Approximately 300 men and women staffed the McAllen Border Patrol Station, a majority of whom were patrol agents responsible for guarding about forty-five miles of the Rio Grande. This station was one of nine forming the McAllen Sector, which patrols 17,000 square miles of Deep South Texas extending into eighteen Texas counties. Sector headquarters was located in McAllen.[28]

After the first few months, the majority of the men and women at the McAllen Station paid little attention to my presence although the supes and other managers regularly announced my purpose among them and I repeatedly clarified my intentions. At the beginning of each shift I would tell the agent behind the wheel who I was and how I was conducting my research although everyone soon knew me. Agents often referred to me as "the professor from the university."

In this methodological approach I sought always to better understand their world and their perspective as an insider, but certainly not to accept it blindly. For this reason I constantly compared and contrasted what I was told to what I saw, to other legal, community, and societal standards and expectations, and to other law enforcement organizations, all within the parameters of my professional and personal experiences and the relevant research literature.

Under a scorching desert sun and in the dead of night along the banks of the Rio Grande, I asked these men and women what they knew, what they had seen, and what they thought. In no uncertain terms and with direct, sometimes alarming honesty, they told me.

I firmly believe that these agents, with few exceptions, were open and honest with me not just because they came to trust me, but because few, if any, had ever been asked about their work as agents and the wealth of experience and knowledge bound up in years of patrolling the banks of the Rio Grande. They were anxious to talk and to show me what they knew.

As their trucks stopped bouncing over the bumpy dirt paths following the

Rio Grande, or when they went for a coffee break at the Whataburger, or when they stopped to talk with one of their supes alongside a dusty back road, I wrote down both what they told me and what I observed. Sometimes their answers to my questions and my observations were identical, sometimes not. My notes, by the end of it, covered the front and back of hundreds of checks from my bank at that time, Lone Star National Bank of Texas. For several years I have used my checkbook as a convenient and unobtrusive notepad. A day or two after a shift ended, as soon as I could find the time and the energy, I transcribed and edited these field notes into a more coherent narrative on my laptop. As the pages of this text grew in number, I realized I may have missed or misplaced sentences, thoughts, and ideas through human error. I know for a hard fact, however, that I always collected the direct sense and meaning of what they told me and recorded my observations with a consistent diligence.

I tried to capture the way agents told me their stories, although I have intentionally left out much of the Spanish that was commonly used in their conversations, judging that the average English-speaking reader would find it distracting. Just to be sure, I regularly asked agents to repeat themselves. Originally I had planned to end the ride-alongs after twelve months, but the events of September 11, 2001, and the response of the Border Patrol to these events convinced me to continue for an additional year. By the fall of the second year of ride-alongs I had reached a saturation point—I was learning very little that was new from the agents. I slowly ended this phase of the project.

After transcribing the field notes into a narrative, I compared what the agents told me to what their supes and other managers told me. I maintained a professional working relationship with managers throughout this research both to facilitate the research and to learn as much as possible about this group of organizational leaders. Also, management had invited me to work on a specific project that involved a presentation designed to inform and persuade the public of the need for new facilities for the Border Patrol. This two-month project provided me an insightful view of managers including their leadership styles as well as the opportunity to learn more about the nature of their relationship to agents in the field.

I then compared what agents told me to written public policies and relevant documents that describe and govern this agency, to the relevant extant literature on law enforcement, and to my own twenty-five years of experience as a researcher along the United States–Mexico border.[29]

All Along the Watchtower

At the same time I attempted to place the group of agents I was studying within a larger historical framework and context. Not only did I collect individual histories of agents whenever possible, but I analyzed institutional data provided me by managers. These data as well as national data from the U.S. Border Patrol and other sources suggested significant historical patterns and trends.

As I began to learn about the work of agents in specific and concrete ways, I constantly discussed my experiences with professional colleagues, close personal friends, and my wife. All of these individuals helped keep me embedded in my own life as a university professor, administrator, husband, and father even as I learned more and more about a way of life far different from my own.

From one day to the next I could never fully control or influence events that unfolded during a work shift. Throughout this period of time I remained, as I was trained, as objective as humanly possible and in the background. The circumstances of these ride-alongs also demanded, for the personal safety of both the agent and me, that when necessary I actively participate in some of the same policing techniques and procedures that I was observing. Often having no time to consider or weigh the ethical efficacy of my specific actions, I made pragmatic decisions based upon my best professional and personal judgment. It could be fairly argued that some objectivity might be lost in this necessary practice, but I came away with a much broader understanding of the work that agents perform, allowing me to question certain fundamental assumptions held by agents, managers, and the general public.

To protect the privacy and confidentiality of agents, other law enforcement personnel, and others in this study, I have assigned fictitious names and, when necessary, disguised identities in other ways. This does not diminish either my observations about their work, the analysis of the data, nor conclusions and policy implications drawn from this study.

After returning home from his ten-hour shift, U.S. Border Patrol Agent Jack Spurrier, like most of the other 106,414 residents of McAllen, Texas, sleeps soundly. While he sleeps, the Rio Grande/Río Bravo sweeps sluggishly past the drug landings at Miller's Farm, Mac 40 Pump, Harper's, Bull's Balls, Hoagies, Los Ebanos, and a hundred others, past where men, women, and children remove their wet clothes at Sector 306, Chimney Park, Cavazos Beach, and Anzalduas Park in absolute, dead silence.

Powerful beams cut tensile pathways through the shadows to reveal forms and textures caught under the exacting microscopes of trained and experienced officers of federal law enforcement. Precise procedures and strategies must be followed. Then the headlights are switched off to avoid detection; only when the agents tap their brakes to slow their speed do rear brake lights give away their positions to those who are watching. They are always watching.

Within the steel confines of the truck cabs, regulations and policies pervade: orders to be followed; forms to be filled out; precision communication and sensor technology tested and utilized. Agent Spurrier stirs in his sleep as this small armada of agents, each truck on its own tack, moves in fits and starts down the long drag roads that follow the Rio Grande. Brake lights, like errant, red lightning bugs at a Fourth of July picnic, sporadically dot the immense darkness along the border in Deep South Texas separating the United States of America from the Republic of Mexico. As utter night takes over, the river throbs and inundates with human silence, the essence of darkness only broken by the occasional, lone lights of seventeen Ford Expeditions from the midnight shift at the McAllen Station.

Targets

Two nights later, as the citizens of McAllen slumbered in their beds, Border Patrol Agent Fernando Rodriguez stared bleary eyed at Supervisor Jack Spurrier sitting behind two end-to-end tables at the McAllen Station on Old Military Highway. To the left of Jack Spurrier at muster, facing the five rows of agents fidgeting on old metal chairs, sat Supe Billy Villareal, and to his left Supe Mira. Leaning against the cinder-block wall at the back of the windowless room, Field Operation Supervisor Jose Monteverde eyed the thirty-five agents, thirty-two men and three women. FOS Monteverde was a small, unimposing man with intelligent, bright eyes who listened intently to each of the supes as they made their announcements.

Without thinking Agent Rodriguez drank big gulps of lukewarm station coffee from his own personal mug. A large dose of caffeine was one way to start the midnight shift at the station, or mids, as it was called. Maybe it was the only way to survive mids because mids began at 10:00 P.M. sharp with the required briefing at muster and ended, after the optional two hours of overtime, at eight the next morning.

Jack Spurrier read the daily intelligence from the Drug Enforcement Agency. Only a few agents paid him much mind because DEA intel was shaky at best. Maria Contreras, striking even in the standard Border Patrol uniform, was one of a handful of agents who seemed to listen to Jack Spurrier with any intensity or focus. At worst the intel was a total waste of time, but agents could never tell. Just when they were ready to write it off, a choice nugget came along that could lead to a bust.

After Jack Spurrier finished reading the DEA intel, one of the other supes at the table stood up to read intel from the FBI, normally only slightly more helpful than DEA Pablum. But tonight most of the agents at muster struggled to pay attention to what the supe was telling them. "Dragon's Breath," a new kind of shotgun shell on the market, was field tested at the FBI lab after it was found in the possession of a two-time felon in the act of making it three. Draping a standard bulletproof vest over the target, FBI agents fired the shell from a 12-gauge shotgun at twenty feet. "The result being," droned the supe, "that a large incendiary flame shot up from the manikin ten feet or more. The vest melted."

"Always nice to hear good news at the start of mids," mumbled one agent loud enough from behind his mug of station coffee so that everyone in the room could hear. Unconsciously shifting in their Kevlar vests, four recruits on the last row of metal chairs, all recently minted from the training academy, stirred uneasily. The older, experienced agents were as likely to use their Kevlar as back rests in their Expeditions as they were to wear them while on duty, but the new recruits were wedded to their life-saving equipment after five months of academy training. For them Kevlar was a second skin; for others it was just another inconvenience.

"Who said that?" joked Supe Billy Villareal, suddenly a high school English teacher. Most of the agents laughed at Billy's attempt to lighten the mood. Those that did not were busy chasing away the fog inside their heads. Tonight was a double-back, the time at the end of each month when agents ended up working two shifts in twenty-four hours with a few hours in between to catch a quick nap. For security reasons, the four units changed shifts every month. This unit, Unit One, had worked the morning shift from 6 A.M. to 4 P.M., and was now beginning the start of their second shift in one day.

"I got some news for you guys," said Supe Billy Villareal, not missing a beat after the laughter subsided. "Those convicts that escaped from the prison up near Kenedy were spotted at a convenience store not far from here in Sharyland. The sighting has not been confirmed yet by the FBI, but, guys, this is a wake-up call. Be careful out there."

All Along the Watchtower

That got everyone's attention in the room. All of the agents sat up a little straighter in the metal chairs. The so-called "Texas Seven" had escaped by killing a prison guard and now represented the worst nightmare of every law enforcer in the country: all convicted murderers or rapists with nothing to lose, they had robbed a sporting goods store and were armed to the teeth with stolen weapons.[1] News seemed scarce in the first weeks after the New Year marking the millennium, and the national media, quicker than anyone could remember, had turned the Texas Seven into the modern-day equivalent of the James Gang. Reaching for their ballpoint pens en masse, the men and women wrote in their notebooks or on the backs of their hands the radio frequencies used by the escaped convicts.

The muster broke up at 10:14, one group of agents rushing forward to grab the keys to their assigned vehicles in the parking lot, another heading for the line that was forming at the door of the armory. While they waited in line to pick up their Night Vision Goggles (NVGs), shotguns and, for those who were qualified, M-4 machine guns, they traded stories and jokes.

Rodriguez swapped lies with the rest of them as he passed back through the muster room after accidentally rubbing his shoulder against a poster taped to the green wall. The two- by three-foot poster displayed the back of a male patrol agent in black with a circle reaching from one broad shoulder to the other.

"Remember: You are a Target" read the poster. Most of the agents, including Rodriguez, did not need reminding.

After checking the assignment sheet once more to determine who was working the Rio Grande on either side of him, Rodriguez passed by FOS Jose Monteverde's tiny office just in front of the rear steel door exit to the parking lot. The field operation supervisor's office was not more than eight by eight, windowless, and crammed with a desk, two chairs, and piles of files. FOS Monteverde was already leaning over a pile of papers.

Rodriguez's reputation was simple. He did his job. Other agents could count on him in a pinch. He kept his mouth shut. Rodriguez was a popular guy, and popular guys joked with and were kidded by everyone. Every step of the way to the parking lot Rodriguez was shaking hands with bros he encountered. Everybody knew him, and everybody liked him.

Grabbing his gear from the cab of his six-year-old truck, he stopped to admire a new Ford F-150. It seemed to Rodriguez as if every new recruit bought a new truck the first month he or she arrived at the McAllen Station direct from the training academy. Some even purchased one of the top-of-the-line four-wheel drives that hovered in the $30,000 price range.

"I got bills to pay," Rodriguez said, hefting his bulk into the front seat of his assigned Expedition. Most of the weight was muscle, including his thick neck and massive shoulders. From a distance he looked like a Texas high school fullback, but up close he had lost a few yards to Father Time. Rodriguez hated the extra weight because it aggravated an injury to his right knee. One night he had been chasing a group of illegals across a cotton field when his knee buckled under him. Now the doctor was telling him he needed it scoped, but Rodriguez kept putting off the inevitable.

"I got a new house to show for my time," Rodriguez continued. "These recruits, they spend half of their paycheck on truck payments and the rest of it on a lease at one of those new apartments. The minute they drive that truck off the lot, they've lost 20 percent of what they paid. But you can't tell them that." Then he added, "Throwing your money away on rent never made much sense to me."

Rodriguez carefully aimed the Expedition through the narrow automatic security gate on the south side of the parking lot, then turned west, a right, onto Old Military Highway. Rodriguez and other patrol agents based at the McAllen Station were responsible for patrolling more than forty miles of the Rio Grande. Situated on a perfectly flat parcel of land surrounded by flat land as far as the eye could fathom, the one-story, tan brick building with a blue tile stripe around its girth looked better suited to serve as a library than home to 300 patrol agents. Back in 1973 when the station was originally constructed, only 70 men were assigned to the building. That was long before NAFTA, long before the construction of huge metal warehouses and plants that catered to it, structures that surrounded and dwarfed the McAllen Border Patrol Station, which had once stood squarely between the banks of the Rio Grande and the city of McAllen.

Now it seemed as if a new group of academy graduates arrived weekly, forced to run a customary gauntlet of questions from experienced agents who wanted to know more about the kind of men and women on whom their lives depended.

"Where are you from?" was what they heard at their first muster. Then, "What did you do before you went to the academy?" Recruits trained either at

All Along the Watchtower

Charleston, South Carolina, or Glenco, Georgia. When they arrived at the McAllen Station they were green, nervous, and on probation until they successfully completed a series of written tests and evaluations.

If an agent at muster did not like the answers he or she was hearing, the rogue interview might continue for several minutes while the old-timers, shaking their heads, remembered the way things used to be: when they knew every agent's name, the name of his wife, and his kids' names, too. Back when all the agents were men, long before the compulsory workshops on sexual harassment. The Border Patrol was one big family in those good old days—at least the way the old-timers told it.

After seven years in the Border Patrol, Rodriguez was a seasoned veteran. Agents either knew the ropes by then or they moved on to some other kind of work. At first for Rodriguez it was about the steady paycheck and the job security. A federal job was a big deal in Rodriguez's family. No one had ever held that kind of job security or earned that kind of paycheck. Not to mention the guaranteed retirement money.

Rodriguez had married after his junior year at the University of Texas at El Paso, then started having a family. A biology degree in hand soon after, he found work in El Paso as a lab technician for a large drug company. But the job had no future to it so he quit after a year.

"We tested various kits they assembled for industry. The kits were first aid kits for special situations. Like in labs and in factories and things like that. I didn't mind the work, but when I heard about the pay in the Border Patrol and the other benefits, I signed up. Then I waited for two years. Back then you waited. You expected it. Some of the guys waited three years, and I heard of others who waited even longer."

The McAllen Station became a distant speck in the rearview mirror as Agent Rodriguez headed for his assignment on the banks of the Rio Grande. While the rest of the United States endured bitter ice storms and power outages, the temperature hovered at a pleasant fifty-five degrees outside the windows of his vehicle. Rodriguez knew and appreciated that winter tourists to the area, called snowbirds, drove a thousand miles or more to soak up the sunny days in Deep South Texas before returning in April to their homes in Iowa, Wisconsin, Minnesota, Indiana, Illinois, and Missouri.

A bull at rest, Rodriguez switched off his headlights before swinging onto a dirt road that swept past a field of eight-foot-tall sugar cane. After pasting a strip of tape over the greenish hues of light emanating from the digital clock on the dash, the agent became even less visible to those who watched him.

And they were watching him. Of that he had not the slightest doubt.

While Supe Jack Spurrier monitored communication between agents from his desk in the operations room, and FOS Jose Monteverde tackled another stack of time sheets with bureaucratic gusto, Agent Rodriguez gazed up at the scattered clouds that partially hid a full moon. As the clouds began to dissipate in the sky, Agent Rodriguez, his Expedition visible from a half a mile away in the strengthening moonlight, became a sitting duck.

In complete deference to his situation, Rodriguez sipped more raw station coffee from his mug. He knew they were watching him, listening to him, perhaps had him in their night scope as he placed his coffee mug in its crude holder formed of thin sheet metal.

The scouts for the *narcotraficantes* were always out there, paid scouts who worked for the drug smugglers from behind forests of prickly pear or at the edge of the vast fields of sugar cane. Or they knelt on one knee at the side of the levees, their right hands glued to their cell phones. Behind every stunted tree, crouched low on every rise in these flat lands, they waited for Agent Rodriguez and the other agents of the McAllen Station to appear.

Or the scouts were in rusted pickups and four-door gas guzzlers traveling up and down the back county roads adjacent to the river. From behind their illegally tinted windows they made their calls whenever they spotted the Border Patrol. Or in full view they sat casually at wooden picnic benches in the fenced front yards of their shotgun houses on Old Military Highway, or on rotting metal chairs to the side of mom-and-pop convenience stores that were the only signs of commerce once outside the city limits of McAllen. They sat on those benches and those metal chairs, day and night, cell phones palmed discreetly in their right hands, and waited for the parade of Expeditions. Then they made their calls.

While Rodriguez patrolled the Rio Grande, the scouts for the *narcotraficantes* patrolled him.

About the only thing Rodriguez could do was to listen to them watching him. Clipped to his sun visor was a Radio Shack portable scanner that tracked their conversations, in Spanish, as they waited for Rodriguez and the other agents to make their expected appearance after muster.

The *narcotraficantes* initiated this dance, picked the time, the place, and the means of transporting the load of dope across the Río Bravo and to the waiting safe houses. It was only then that Rodriguez and the other agents had a small window of opportunity to interrupt the billion-dollar flow of illegal drugs to the United States. Only during this small moment of time did the drug smugglers give up, however briefly, their overwhelming superiority and control.

Static garbage floated across Rodriguez's scanner, a piece of equipment he had purchased at his own expense.

"It's the bad guys," said Rodriguez quietly. "It's encrypted. I can't touch it."

Encryption was American technology at its finest. Only under this full moon Mexican drug smugglers employed the sophisticated communications system to conduct their criminal business. As Rodriguez sat uneasily in the driver's seat of his Expedition, the richest and most powerful nation on the planet was outgunned by a group of international crooks fed constant information by their scouts. Or if they were not discussing their next shipment, and besides themselves only God knew the substance of their real discourse, they might just be trashtalking about the Giants against the Colts in the Super Bowl five days hence. Mexicans fans throughout the State of Tamaulipas followed the Dallas Cowboys and always anticipated the premier NFL game of the year in January, *El Super Tazon,* the Super Bowl.

Rodriguez had no idea what they were saying and could not do a thing about it. He knew that the supes back at the McAllen Station were well aware of the use of encrypted communications between the *narcotraficantes.* FOS Jose Monteverde, the station chief, and the sector chief also had to know about it. And there had to be some team of federalized snoopers listening to the conversation from Washington, D.C., or the nearby environs. But none of that mattered to Agent Rodriguez one iota because no one on his side was telling him what the hell was going on.

At the beginning of the twenty-first century, Agent Rodriguez daily battled with drug organizations capable of spending millions on whatever technology, fire power, legal advice, transportation needs, or labor was necessary. Rodriguez, in contrast, could do nothing but rely on one of his own horse-and-buggy plans: patrolling the line for sign, he would pray the scouts would call him out. They would radio each other and their boss to relay that he had been spotted. Then, and only then, Rodriguez could conclude by pure seat-of-the-pants deduction that he had been seen and that a possible drug load was about to cross the Rio Grande somewhere close by. Otherwise there would be no reason for the scouts to be there or to communicate with each other.

The calling out was a grain of information in a sea of doubt, a clue that eventually brought eight agents from Unit One to the asphalt parking lot behind Mission Junior High School at 1:15 A.M. The glare of lights from the nearby all-night Circle K convenience store silhouetted eight agents, four Mexican Americans and four Anglos, as they stood in a crude circle next to their vehicles. Spanish and English were passed around the circle, the Anglos joking and occasionally cursing in the same colloquial Tex-Mex as their brother agents. Because in the Valley Anglos were historically a minority who were required to know Spanish, it was nothing new to hear Anglos and Mexican Americans switching back and forth from one language to another as they conducted their business.[2]

Slouched next to Rodriguez in the circle of agents, Noe Escondido, two inches taller than his fellow agent but giving up more than a hundred pounds, had weathered fourteen years along the banks of the Rio Grande. Bar none he was the best sign cutter at the McAllen Station and, because of it, caught more drug loads every year than any four agents put together. The other seven agents respected Noe not just because he was the senior agent among them, but because he was The Man.

Rodriguez grumbled, "Since yesterday I got an hour and a half of sleep. You know," he said to no one in particular, "the really tough part is not tonight but tomorrow night. Tonight we got adrenaline to carry us, but tomorrow night we don't have nothing." No one in the circle disagreed.

Noe Escondido stood there nodding as the cumbersome plan took shape, then altered just like the circle of agents. It was then that his partner Paco, a small, bald man resembling a beanie bear, began donning his full gear. Paco changed his appearance at least every six months going from bald to a military cut to a full mustache to goatee to bald again. As the agents made their plan under Noe's watchful eye, Paco donned his Kevlar, his standard issue jacket, and then began stuffing his pockets with extra ammunition, mosquito repellent, cell phone, camouflage hat with flaps, NVGs, and binoculars. Last was his M-4 along with a tin of smokeless chewing tobacco.

All Along the Watchtower

As he readied himself for battle, tiny Paco admitted that he had collapsed on the couch at the party the night before. The party was the monthly celebration of the shift change when the agents got together to cook fajitas, drink beer, and talk shop. His confession received a guffaw or two, but then it was back to business while Paco, using the side-mounted mirror from his Expedition, expertly applied camouflage paint to his face and neck.

By the end of it Noe had signed off on a plan of action with a final nod, everyone in the circle knowing his assignment.

Adrenaline marching through their veins, Agents Noe Escondido and Paco locked their truck and jumped in the rear steel cage of Rodriguez's Expedition, and the other agents took up their positions. Rodriguez's job was to drop off the two agents in the brush near the suspected drug landing that the scouts may have been watching and talking about in their encrypted dialogues. Although there were several possible drug landings of choice along this particular stretch of the Rio Grande, the encrypted chatter between scouts should intensify when Rodriguez passed by the landing where the drugs would be crossed during the night or early morning. Rodriguez would radio Noe and Paco, the two agents would position themselves to keep the area under surveillance and, when the bad guys finally showed up, Noe would call for all the troops to converge for the bust.

With any luck they would nail the smugglers between the banks of the Rio Grande and Old Military Highway. Once the crooks reached a mile north of the river, station policy required agents to end their pursuit and to hand the case over to local law enforcement or the Texas Department of Public Safety.

Rodriguez and the other agents knew that the chances of a bust were small. But what else were they going to do?

After dropping off Noe and Paco, who were now geared up and armed to the teeth, Rodriguez took forty-five minutes to complete his patrol of his assigned area along the drag that followed the bends and twists of the river. No one called him out. As the night wore on his scanner remained eerily quiet.

Noe, from his position in the tick-infested brush near the suspected drug landing, radioed his feelings to all the agents as well as the supe back at the McAllen Station who was listening in.

"*Chingalo.*" Translation: "Fuck it."

The scouts had disappeared. Maybe they had been spooked. Maybe they had caught sight of the agents' confab behind Mission Junior High School. Maybe from the start the real action was at another landing, and the scouts had been a temporary diversion. Maybe there never was a drug load, the electronic chatter Rodriguez intercepted on his scanner only bored scouts discussing the best fishing holes in the nearby Laguna Madre Bay. Whatever the situation, Noe was steamed enough to let every agent on mids, not to mention management back in the ops room, know his sentiments. Radioing his location to Rodriguez using the number of the closest sensor (sensor numbers matched specific locations only agents knew about), Noe and Paco waited impatiently for Agent Rodriguez to pick them up.

The full moon had disappeared as the night dragged on and the two men in full camouflage opened the rear door to Rodriguez's Expedition before Rodriguez ever saw them. When Rodriguez pulled into the back of the Mission Junior High School parking lot, Noe jumped out without a word, slamming the door and stalking off to his truck. Noe hated to lose. Paco followed him, giving the senior agent plenty of space.

Two minutes later Agent Rodriguez was standing at the front counter of the Circle K in Mission while he purchased batteries for his Radio Shack scanner. Two Mexican American teenagers entered the store, saw Rodriguez, then carefully backtracked without another glance in Rodriguez's direction. Rodriguez, his Kevlar vest inflating his normal bulk, appeared nothing short of ominous as he stood at the counter. Whatever the teenagers had in mind, the sight of Rodriguez and the bad vibes that hung over him led to a quick retreat. By the time Rodriguez returned to his Expedition, the night's frustrations were beginning to overwhelm him.

"I can't believe it," Rodriguez said as he climbed into the driver's seat. "That jerk in there wanted a dollar for one battery. That's robbery. They don't even sell them in a three-pack. Just singles with no wrapping. I could go to Wal-Mart and get three batteries for less than what he wants for one." Rodriguez, who hated losing to the bad guys as much as Noe did, could not let go of the previous two hours.

All that was left for Rodriguez was to respond to the sensors as he patrolled the banks of the Rio Grande. A group of agents on special duty at the McAllen Station placed sensors at likely landing spots all along the banks of the river. Hidden beneath the sandy clay, or carefully located at trailheads or foot bridges spanning irrigation channels, the devices, once tripped, sent a signal back to the McAllen Station by way of an attached antenna that resembled a single blade of grass. The dispatcher at the station, in turn, reported each sensor response, or hit, to all vehicles in the field by the number of the sensor and the number of hits it received. So you would hear, "The 305 has five hits."

"This radio frequency is supposed to be for us alone. If you are a civilian, you are not supposed to be able to listen to our communication," explained Rodriguez. "But any idiot in the country can walk into a Radio Shack, purchase a special chip for his radio, install it, and right away he's got access to our system. See, it's not against the law to buy the chip, but it is against the law to use it. I'm asking you a simple question: does that make sense to you?"

The sensors could not distinguish between a man carrying a one-hundred-pound bag of marijuana on his back or a herd of grazing cattle, or javelinas, the wild hogs that roamed freely throughout Deep South Texas, or the nine-banded armadillo, striped skunk, bobcat, raccoon, coyote, wild dog, deer, *el tigre chiquito,* ocelot, endangered jaguarundi, long-tailed weasel, badger, and omni-present possum. Or the *irrigadores,* the irrigators, who carefully tended the water systems, or farmworkers, or the local tick rider from the U.S. Department of Agriculture charged with checking for Mexican livestock that strayed from the banks of the Río Bravo. Or whoever else might be there, for whatever reason: lovers, drinkers, kids fishing with their fathers, families on a picnic, a young man sighting his .22-caliber rifle, tricksters from *el otro lado*—from the other side—with nothing better to do than play games with the Border Patrol. There were too many possibilities.

Less than two miles from the south side of the city of McAllen, Agent Rodriguez parked his unit under the unyielding branches of a mesquite tree, then edged quietly out of the front seat careful to close his door without a sound. The area was known as Miller's Farm and was a popular landing spot for loads of marijuana and cocaine. It was 3 A.M.

One knee in the dirt, Agent Rodriguez waited for ten minutes in the silence. A coyote howled off in the distance; another responded. The wind picked up a notch while the agent crouched in the dirt, but nothing happened along the tree line fronting the banks of the river. Nothing until a small cloud of mosquitoes found him there, dive bombed his neck, then attacked the thin material of his uniform covering his broad back. Rodriguez swatted furiously as he remained on one knee. Defeated for the moment by the Kevlar vest underneath his shirt—Rodriguez had chosen this night to keep the vest on since the earlier failed surveillance—the mosquitoes finally retreated.

"I forgot the damn spray," Rodriguez whispered. Then the mosquitoes, as if on cue, attacked again, this time going for his hands. They worked his knuckles over pretty good, then aimed once more for his bare neck.

"I should have brought the spray," he said, scratching the backs of his hands as he slowly rose to his feet to make his way back to his truck. Can of bug repellent in hand, he sprayed himself from the toes of his Timberline boots to the top of his head with the preferred stock of McAllen agents: Deep Woods Off. Agents swore by the stuff. The mosquitoes left him alone for another ten minutes, then dived in, buzzed around his head, but did not bite.

So it went for the next hour and the next, each segment of time an exact replica of that which preceded it. The gangly sugar cane waved quietly in the light breeze, and the fields of stubby cabbage, broccoli, and onions rested under a star-filled night. Waiting and watching for undocumented workers who never appeared and for drug smugglers busy somewhere else, Agent Rodriguez was left with little to fill the broad chasm of time but stories about the Rio Grande and the intersection of this same lore with his own life. After being stationed with the Border Patrol in Santa Theresa, New Mexico, Agent Rodriguez grabbed at the chance to move to the McAllen Station. By the time he moved to the Valley, Rodriguez had been promoted to a GS-11, which meant that with overtime he grossed close to $55,000 a year. His wife, who first worked as a social worker before becoming a schoolteacher, earned about half that much, so they were able between the two of them to pay off their old debts and buy a new house. For the first time they could also think about the future, about a time when Rodriguez retired from the Border Patrol to start a new life. Rodriguez considered numerous options, but none included returning for more education. The agent could not see himself listening to some professor with a fancy degree pontificating in the classroom. Rodriguez had real doubts and fears about what the future held for him, but for the first time in his life his troubles were not about money.

After so much time patrolling the banks of the Rio Grande, Rodriguez was not sure what else he was good for.

Before the long hours melted into dawn Rodriguez gave up his sweet spot at Miller's Farm to inch along the single-lane drag road in the Expedition. All he saw were paraques, big, languid birds with yellow eyes and brains the size of a pea. The night birds lined both sides of the narrow lane and stood in the dust until the front bumper of the Expedition almost grazed their feathers before finally taking to flight.

Rodriguez handled this part of mids with one hand glued tightly to the steering wheel, the other to the radio mike, which linked him to his bros all along the river. They talked about anything and everything to keep themselves alert. When their voices fell silent, Rodriguez found a rollicking cumbia to comfort him in the deepest interiors of the night. Now it was just about staying awake, fighting through the nanoseconds that lie like tidal pools before the light of dawn. Time was as thick and slow as the Rio Grande below Falcon Dam, as the waves of super-heated air that would soon appear in Deep South Texas and never seem to go away.

Scanning the banks of the river through the optical wizardry of the NVGs, Rodriguez saw the world as a fluttering, deep emerald sea, the river a shimmering highway of iridescent light sandwiched between huisache, mesquite, and stately sabal palms. In this desert the McAllen Chamber of Commerce liked to call the "Magic Valley," water was both illusion and dream, solace and threat. When the rains finally came, they were likely to bring with them high winds and flooding. Torrential rains spawned flash floods in the Magic Valley as common as the nopal buds on the spring foliage of the prickly pear that, with eggs, were a popular Lenten dish.

Rodriguez's world of sight, sound, and sense was shattered at 5:34 A.M. by the heavy breathing of a predator tracking prey.

"They're out of my sight," came the disembodied voice as it breathlessly penetrated the radio ether. "They dropped into a line of brush near the levee. Hold it. I've got them again. They're coming out. No problem."

The ether reabsorbed the lone human voice only for it to reemerge.

"Shit. Lost them." Then, "I got 'em back. The scope should be picking them up by now. They're crossing a big cabbage field." The "scope" was the scope truck, a rare and fragile $100,000 piece of modern technology that appeared, at first glance, to be nothing more than a pickup with a camper in the back but, in a matter of thirty seconds, was transformed into a remote infrared camera atop a ten-foot scissor-jack platform. At the screen in the cab of the scope truck sat Agent Herman Morningside.

As usual, Morningside tossed in his unsolicited two cents. "I can't see a thing." Morningside hated this duty. He would switch places with Rodriguez or any other agent in a second if given the chance. But this night, like many others, he was stuck operating the scope truck while the other agents had all the fun. It was not fair but Morningside was keeping quiet about it, because yet again he was in trouble with the supes. Working the scope truck was designed to keep Morningside out of more trouble.

Rodriguez roared into full-tilt action, pushing the Expedition to eighty miles per hour as he sped along narrow, two-lane caliche back roads to reach the illegal aliens who had tripped a sensor near the Hidalgo International Bridge. With any luck he would be able to assist the other agents before the illegals got away.

"You should be seeing them by now if they're coming your way," came from a nameless agent over the radio. So there were at least two agents following the sign not far from where the international bridge crossed the river into the dark streets of Reynosa.

"I can't see a thing on my screen," Agent Morningside repeated. "They could be taking the ditch at the far southwest corner of that field. If they did that I can't see them until they reach the road."

Agent Rodriguez parked his Expedition behind the scope truck sitting on one of the fifteen-foot earthen levees adjacent to the Hidalgo International Bridge. Perched high atop the bed was the infrared camera. From this vantage point Agent Morningside had a broad field of vision to the south toward Mexico. After a brief conversation with Morningside, although it was almost impossible to keep any communication with Morningside really brief, Rodriguez roared off along a one-lane dirt track that skirted empty cotton fields and cabbage soon ready to harvest. As he neared the banks of the river, he switched off his headlights, steering by the powerful bridge lights and his familiarity with the area. As the citizens of McAllen grabbed a few more precious moments of sleep before the first light of dawn, Rodriguez closed the trap on four illusive pixels on an infrared camera monitor.

"I can't see them," said Morningside, watching the screen from the cramped front seat of the scope truck. "Want me to give Fox Two a call?" Fox Two was the Border Patrol helicopter.

"Negative," came the reply from one of the pursuing agents. Rodriguez swung his truck to avoid a small, dry irrigation ditch before he finally spotted gray human forms walking directly toward him. The illegal workers had been apprehended less than two hundred yards from Old Military Highway.

All Along the Watchtower

Two hundred yards short of their dream. The dream of a father, twenty-eight, his wife, the same age, and their nine-year-old daughter. And another man. The father and the mother were dressed in old jeans and dark blue sweatshirts. The lower halves of their torsos were still soaked from their crossing, and they shivered in the slight breeze even though they had another layer of clothes beneath the outer layer. The father carried $100 in fives and tens in the front pocket of his jeans. One of the agents counted it, then returned it to him. The illegal immigrant acted surprised to see his money again.

Their daughter wore a pink, sleeveless party dress over a black sweatshirt, along with white socks and black party shoes polished to a high shine. The outfit, a mixture of celebration and practicality, was not what I expected an immigrant child to wear crossing an international frontier in the middle of the night. Because she was not drenched from the river, the girl had probably made the trip to the United States on top of an old inner tube or *una balsa,* a small, inflatable raft.

Rodriguez was the father of two girls, so he had no doubt that the child was frightened as she sat separated from her parents, who were being questioned by the side of the cotton field. He approached the vehicle where she had been placed, bent on one knee, and asked a few questions to try to put her at ease.

Later he admitted, "You know that Guatemalan family from two days ago? Well, I took them a Happy Meal when they were back at the station." He shrugged, not expecting a response.

While Rodriguez calmed the little girl—I could not hear his exact words—one of the agents quizzed her father. As the sun rose a few degrees in the east casting sharp rays across this living tableau, another agent unceremoniously pulled the other adult male behind one of the Expeditions. This man, well dressed and in his early thirties, was not related to the family, nor was he their friend, nor a fellow immigrant. This man, the agents knew, was a *coyote* in the flesh, as utterly confident as the little girl was confused and scared. So familiar with the routine that lay before him, the *coyote* spoke without the slightest hesitation.

"I'm a diamond and gold seller," he said unasked, explaining away the gold jewelry covering his neck, wrists, and fingers. "I'm going to find work in a mall. One of those shops where they sell chains and necklaces. It's my trade. I went to technological school in Guadalajara, and it's how I make my living. I'm a businessman."

Exhausted from the double-back mids, the agent was beyond dubious. It never failed. All the action invariably came at the end of a shift. "You got a trade?" he asked the *coyote* without any expectation of hearing the truth. "You say you're on your way to work in some mall?"

The *coyote* smiled, revealing a bright gold tooth. He was a thin, almost gaunt man who made an excellent livelihood crossing illegal aliens. The Río Bravo bandits *en el otro lado* must have known him well enough to leave him and his gold jewelry alone. He must have paid a sizable *mordida,* the bite or bribe, to Mexican authorities so that any of the *bandidos* stupid enough to harass him on the south side of the river would pay for it dearly.

This time the Border Patrol caught the *coyote.* Usually he got away. But whether the newest illegal immigrants were apprehended or reached their destination the *coyote* win or lose kept the $300 he charged each member of this family. The *coyote*'s money was safe back in Reynosa: $900 total for the husband, wife, and child.

Coyotes were in big demand at the bus stations in Reynosa, on the streets, and in many of the *colonias* where new immigrants congregated. New immigrants from the interior knew two things if they had never crossed the frontier into the United States: the Río Bravo was a dangerous river; and the Patrullas Fronterizas, the Border Patrol, would beat them and steal their money if they were caught. Or worse. The new immigrants from the interior had heard the stories. The Mexican undocumented workers who daily crossed from Reynosa and environs knew far better, of course, based upon their own experiences.

"I know my rights," said the *coyote* in a defiant voice. He did not want to anger the agents, but he wanted them to know he was a Mexican with *cojones*—with balls—and they should not mess with him. If they did, he would have an American lawyer, an *abogado,* on them before they could get him back to the station.

"You know your rights?" said the agent, not amused but just very tired. "What are they?"

"I know my rights," the *coyote* repeated but this time in a calmer voice. No use making the agent angry. He backed off a little as his tone softened. "I can demand to see a judge if I want to."

"Yeah, you can do that," Agent Rodriguez said, coming up from his blind side. "But that judge is going to throw you back across the river so fast you won't be able to blink an eye. Or maybe you're a known criminal who'll show up on our computer back at the station. Then you get to stay in one of our finest prisons."

"Oh, no," said the *coyote* quickly. Perhaps he had pushed them a little too hard. "I have a trade. I sell gold and diamonds. I work all over the United States. That's where I learned my good English."

Sick to death of the man, and exhausted by mids, the agent gave the *coyote* a piece of paper and a pen to sign it. It was the easiest way. This guy was a *coyote,* but the family would not identify him as such. No witnesses, no case. He quickly signed a statement that he was in the United States illegally, that he gave up his right to a formal hearing before an INS judge, and that he agreed to be summarily returned to Mexico. Mr. Gold and Diamonds was going to be VRed, voluntarily returned, to his country of origin. Two minutes after signing the document, the gaunt *coyote* sat in the cage in a nearby Expedition. Fifteen minutes later he was handed over to a Mexican officer who accompanied him and the others back across the Río Bravo.

The *coyote* had been caught and temporarily detained by the Border Patrol, and within less than an hour he was back on the streets of Reynosa $900 the richer.

After signing the same form as the *coyote,* the little girl and her parents were VRed in the same vehicle as the *coyote.* Right back where they started from that same evening, worse for the wear and minus most of their total assets, they wondered, as they walked back across the Río Bravo, if they would ever see, despite his promises, the *coyote* again. He had told them he would meet them the next night and take them across again.

Agent Rodriguez was climbing back into the front seat when a call came over the radio. Ten minutes later he was roaring west along Old Military Highway toward Prietas, a river village within shouting distance of McAllen. There was not another vehicle on the pavement at that time of the early morning, the sun now rising above the table top horizon as full, unimpeded rays drove countless shadows back into the dense thickets and stands of sugar cane. Rodriguez parked near a white planked, austere church set back from the road. Thriving St. Augustine grass fronted the church, but behind it dense vegetation led to the banks of the Rio Grande.

Responding to the directions from his earphone Rodriguez, a big, black flashlight in his left hand, hid behind a squat ebony tree to one side of the church yard. Then, with a burst of energy summoned from deep within, he suddenly broke off at a steady trot in the direction of the prickly pear and other cactus that formed an almost impenetrable jungle behind the church. A flashlight signaled him from that direction, then another.

"I got you," Rodriguez spoke into the mike pinned to his right shoulder, picking up the pace from a jog to a gallop as he lumbered along in the early morning light. In the weakening shadows cast by the cactus and mesquite Rodriguez could barely discern the figures approaching him. There were nine of them, nine illegal aliens, all dressed in dark pants and cotton sweatshirts with Harvard University logos. Ragged, wet sneakers covered their feet. An agent senior to Rodriguez whom he knew well walked in front, but at the end of the ragtag line came another agent whom Rodriguez did not recognize, one of the newest of the recruits from the academy.

The aliens made no attempt to flee. They could have escaped in nine different directions back to the banks of the Rio Grande or north toward Old Military Highway. If they had wanted to. But these men and women were bone tired, their faces in the emerging light smudged with dirt and sweat from their ordeal. When first spotted a few steps from the banks of the river, the *coyote* abandoned them to dive into the Río Bravo. With never a glance back at those he had left to their own fate, the *coyote* reached the banks of *el otro lado* and disappeared into the brush. His human cargo, at $200 a head, was left to panic in all directions, running blindly through the dense vegetation, stumbling, falling, stumbling again, then hiding under fallen trees or tunneling into the thick brush. Their fear, their labored breathing, and the sign they left gave them away. They were tracked down one by one until all nine were rounded up and led to the church parking lot.

One at a time the undocumented workers allowed themselves to be searched, then were herded into a transport van for which Rodriguez had called. The agents never pulled their guns because the immigrants, once captured, were as passive as lambs.

When the seven men and two women were placed in the back of the transport van, they smiled and talked animatedly to each other about what had happened to them when spotted by the agents. It was bad luck. That was all. But except for a few cuts and bruises, they were no worse off than before except the *coyote* had most of their money. In short, they were tired but alive and well.

A few still had money in their pockets. One man even mumbled about finding the *coyote* again and recrossing the Río Bravo. But most were tired and thirsty and just wanted to sleep.

Rodriguez had held back one of the men before he had slipped into the back of the van with the others. This man stood out from the rest but he was not a *coyote*. He handed Rodriguez his ID when asked, confirming that he was Mexican born. But Rodriguez knew differently.

In the blink of an eye Agent Rodriguez, just like the Border Patrol's scope truck, morphed into another form. He grew very loud, an obnoxious soldier determined to please his superiors. Chest puffed out, he yelled to the senior agent in charge, "You want me to break him, sir? You want me to break him?"

The senior agent nodded. Rodriguez grabbed the illegal alien by the elbow and pulled him over to the far side of the transport van where he was temporarily out of sight of the other illegals. In a voice all could clearly hear, Rodriguez grilled the alien with question after question in rapid-fire Spanish. First he asked where the man lived in Mexico. When the alien stammered, Agent Rodriguez yelled at him, calling him a cowardly liar and worse. Rodriguez challenged the immigrant to act like a real man by telling the truth. Thrown completely on the defensive, not knowing what to expect next, the man shrank back from his interrogator. He could not think clearly nor fast enough to satisfy the probes hidden amid the insults. He faltered, grew quiet, then hung his head in defeat.

"This guy is not from Mexico," Rodriguez concluded loudly in Spanish to the senior agent. "Ecuador maybe. But not Mexico. Look at this ID. It's a joke. Brand new plastic. He probably bought it ten minutes before he crossed the river. It says he was born in Guadalajara, but you heard him. He doesn't know shit about Guadalajara."

They placed the OTM in the transport van along with the others. The Mexican workers greeted him with smiles, but all the OTM could summon, looking around at them, was a painful grimace. He was too tired, had been through too much, and now he knew he was in more hot water.

A sudden noise came from the thick brush that backed the church, a rustling of branches and vines as if someone had stumbled or fallen. Without a moment's hesitation, Rodriguez and another agent disappeared into the hostile undergrowth.

Rodriguez was gone for twenty minutes. When he finally emerged, he brought with him another illegal immigrant with his hands cuffed behind him. The other agent appeared a few moments later leading eight men behind him. Rodriguez had one alien, plus eight more, plus the nine already in the van. That made eighteen. There was no way that the van could safely carry that many immigrants to the McAllen Station. They called for another transport van.

"Another sensor just went off," Rodriguez said matter-of-factly as he got the news through his earphone. "There are more of them out there." Neither of the other agents moved. They had had enough of it. It was the end of mids, they were still looking at at least an hour of paperwork on the OTM, and they were, like the aliens, dead tired.

Rodriguez alone went back into the dense thicket of yucca and prickly pear.

It was creepy in there. Although the sun was already climbing in the broad Texas sky, he could not see more than ten feet in any direction. Dark shadows covered every inch of this hostile undergrowth where hanging vines with sharp thorns and prickly pear ruled. Rodriguez used his flashlight to navigate. When he fell—and everyone fell in this jungle mess—he fell on cactus and thorns. On horse cripplers or barrel cactus the size of a fist. Or the other ten kinds of cactus that covered every square inch of ground. Getting lost was too easy even with the flashlight. The parched and cracked pale earth smelled of sage and animal urine.

Rodriguez searched for another half hour but flushed out no other undocumented workers. They might have been there, but Rodriguez could not find them. Swatting his way through the vines, he carefully circumvented ten-foot-high stands of prickly pear grown together into a solid, living mass. Rodriguez finally gave up. Not surprised to find the transport vans and the other agents long gone with their human cargo, he walked slowly back to his own truck, checked his wristwatch, then stopped, rolled up his pants leg, and began probing his shin with a special pair of Leatherman tweezers he always carried with him.

One by one he removed the thorns from his hide, commenting about the size of each thorn as he flicked it aside. It was tedious work because many of the thorns that had managed to pierce his uniform were silky smooth and so thin that they were almost impossible to see. Once he finished his right leg, he started on his left.

"I got less than thirty minutes to get back to the station. After the overtime is over, you don't get paid for any extra you put in unless you cleared it first with the supe. If I really haul it, I can catch my girls before they leave for school. But usually they are long gone by the time I do the paperwork, get cleaned up, and finally get out of there.

"I got most of them. The others will pop out in a day or two. You got to get at them right away or they work their way deeper into you. One of the liabilities of the job, I guess. You'd be surprised how much trouble these little things cause you if you don't pay attention to them."

On the way back to the McAllen Station, the lines of exhaustion wearing on his face, Rodriguez smiled several times when asked to recall the highlights of his shift.

"Morningside in the scope truck?" he said, unable to stifle his own chuckle. "I'm not going to say anything about that man. I'm not about to judge him. You got to reach your own conclusions about Morningside."

Agent Fernando Rodriguez quickly and efficiently hosed off his Expedition in the rear parking lot at the McAllen Station, stopping once more to work on the thorns in his right kneecap. After he completed his paperwork, he walked swiftly to his own truck before speeding home to see his girls. He missed them by twenty-five minutes.

Gumbys

A **gent** Herman Morningside sat in the driver's seat of the scope truck looking forlornly at the wrong end of another midnight shift, the hours lying before him like an endless list of high school homework assignments before the big date on Saturday night. Formal education, including homework, had never been one of Herman's strong points although he longed to learn the slightest tidbit about his penultimate passion of choice: ornamentals. As in plants, bushes, trees, flowers, and indigenous cacti. Especially cacti. Cacti from Arizona, New Mexico, and the other western states were prime if not always legal for the taking, but Herman would do almost anything to get his hands on indigenous cacti.

It was two days after the double-back mids, but Herman was still assigned to the scope truck. He hated mids, but mids in the scope truck were especially deplorable. He felt chained up by the supes while memoranda clearing his good name made their way up the chain of command. Memos Herman painstakingly wrote because he once more had blundered. Not a career-ending blunder, but one that could not be ignored. Misfortune during a shift that could happen to anyone, but seemed to happen only to Herman.

Herman turned on the overhead light in the scope truck, stretched both legs carefully—there was not much spare room for his six-foot, two-inch frame—then ran through the prescribed steps of raising the infrared camera. After doing penance on scope truck duty more times than he could remember, Herman knew the procedure backward and forward. It involved cautiously climbing out of the cab, lowering the tailgate, and proceeding number by number through the weathered directions, which any idiot could follow, printed in bright orange letters affixed to the surface of the tailgate. Everyone had to follow the directions in the Border Patrol. There was a right way to do things and a wrong way. Unfortunately there had been far too many accidents with this delicate piece of equipment, rumored to cost more than $100,000. Whatever the actual price, even minor repairs took weeks, weeks that the scope truck was sorely missed.

At the pace of a wedding march, a hydraulic scissors jack levitated from the truck bed with a remote camera welded to a small platform at the very top. As the advanced optics reached their zenith, Herman shook himself all over like a big bear coming out of a mountain stream then, uttering an involuntary groan, climbed back into the front cab. He would have denied the groan if asked about it.

Mac 40 Dump was one of a list of place names known only to the agents of the McAllen Station, an unlikely outcropping of naked rock and gravel near the city water pumping station. It, like much of Hidalgo County, bore the embarrassment of an impromptu garbage dump. Piles of rotting wallboard littered the ground along with glass shards, the unrecognizable carcasses of threadbare convertible sofas; and trash bags of decaying palm fronds and grass clippings from McAllen lawns. There was, surprisingly, no stench.

Another crazy loop and turn of the Rio Grande coursed by lazily less than a half mile distant; the night air was broken by the bark of a large dog protecting its turf. With a grand altitude of fifteen feet above the rest of the flat terrain, not counting the full height of the narrow platform that supported it, the scope truck's remote camera had an unobstructed 240-degree view of the bending river, which allowed it to spot illegal immigrants soon after they had crossed the boundary between northern Mexico and Deep South Texas.

As the valves of the truck's diesel engine hummed a rough but merry tune, Herman adjusted a variety of knobs and switches on the viewing screen next to his right knee. The screen was a mighty eight inches square, a minute tapestry of virtual green that was a born eyeball wrecker. Sighing time and again, Herman tapped the side of the screen to hasten the imaging, then stated with a great degree of confidence, "If there is anything out there tonight, I'm going to see it." Resembling more a college professor than an agent of the U.S. Border Patrol, Herman readjusted his heavy, black bifocals on his broad, sun-baked nose and once more jiggled the lever to trigger the remote camera as it scanned the night horizon.

Back at the McAllen Station a nervous supe called Herman on his cell phone. All the supes had Herman's cell phone number because they always needed to call Herman. The two-way truck radio was useless for this kind of dialogue because every sound broadcast between the station and agents in the field was recorded for posterity. What the supes had to say to Morningside usually was not something they wanted documented for eternity or plaintiff's lawyers.

Morningside answered his cell clipped to the sun visor.[1] "No problem," he said. "No, sir, my plan is to stay right here with the truck all night." Then, "Yes, sir, I will." The supes could fret and worry all they wanted at the McAllen Station, but the raw truth was this: Agent Herman Morningside was their worst nightmare, a walking reprimand, a memo magnet that attracted piles of paperwork like honey to a killer bee.

There was the time Agent Herman Morningside tracked a van full of illegal aliens as they left their hiding place on the far west side of the McAllen International Bridge. Herman, working line watch without a partner, pulled the vehicle over and cautiously approached it. At the wheel was a short, stout woman in her forties who immediately demanded in a nasty way to know why he had pulled her over. What, she said, was the problem? Herman replied that the problem was the five illegals sitting like statues in the back of her van.

Herman asked the woman to get out of her vehicle. She refused. He asked her again. She again refused. Herman called for backup, then stepped back and ordered the woman out of the vehicle. Reluctantly she opened the van door, climbed out, and stood squarely facing the much taller agent. Then, without another word, she turned her back on Agent Morningside and headed down the road at a brisk pace.

Staring at the receding figure Herman, dumbfounded, recovered from the shock to run after the woman, who was not only disobeying his order but also fleeing the crime scene. As he grabbed her left shoulder to turn her toward him, the woman, barely five feet tall, pivoted on her left leg and, with the full force of her twisting body and two hundred pounds behind it, slammed her right fist into his *cojones,* testicles.

Herman fell to the ground like a redwood in a deathly silent forest. Then, the pain still battering his brain, he staggered to his feet. The suspect, now a hundred yards down the road, was proceeding rapidly while the five silent spectators in the van watched this drama unfold, not daring to move.

Act Two. Herman reached the woman again, grabbed her roughly by the back of her shoulder and, to his eternal surprise, received the same treatment.

"I couldn't believe it," he admitted much later. "Not once, but twice she hits me in the balls." Herman spared no force in taking her to the ground, handcuffed her as the nausea refused to subside, then waited for backup. The backup, in the form of a police unit from Palmview, population 4,107, asked Herman the particulars. Escorting the handcuffed smuggler to their car, they Mirandized her and carefully placed her under arrest.

"I told them what she'd done to me," he said. "I warned them. They led her to their vehicle, opened the door, and started to put her in the vehicle. It was the strangest thing I ever saw."

Act Three. "She did the full splits, one leg against each side of the door. There was no way they could get her into the back seat. It was like she was possessed! Two grown men are pushing but she's holding them off doing the splits with her legs. Absolutely one of the weirdest things I ever saw." Herman watched as, finally, they managed with their full weight to leverage her into the backseat and close the door on her before she could jump out.

"I figure she had to be on some heavy drugs to do that kind of shit. The next day the police said she didn't remember a thing."

Herman spent half of his next shift writing that one up for the supe.

Or this time: Herman got into an argument with a man and his son who were suspected of using their trailer home as a safe house for drugs. Herman assumed his loud voice, a voice aggravating enough to rile a nun deep in prayer, and the son, who was just a kid, hammered Herman squarely on the chin. Herman, who never saw it coming, again took the big fall.

"To tell you the truth, it completely surprised me. A boy like that. I wasn't expecting it." Another five hours of paperwork back at the station.

In the end, of course, they all called the station to complain about Agent Herman Morningside. The ones with little justification and the ones who had a real bone to pick. That included Hispanics who felt intimidated by the large, Anglo agent with a booming voice. At times it seemed to the station supes that the lines were jammed with complaints, any one of which could form the core of a potential lawsuit. All the callers wanted to know what the supe was going to do about the big gringo agent with the social skills of a mutant bear in a china shop.

There was another side to Agent Herman Morningside.

Like the time, Herman related, "when I was driving around here one morning in a regular unit, must have been just about light. And I'm driving down the drag in the middle of nowhere, maybe I was a half mile from the river, and I see this guy walking along the side of the road. So I figure he's got to be illegal because he's got no other reason to be out that time of day in that place. I stop the truck and get out. The guy looks like shit. He's walking along crying his eyes out. He's in his early twenties, maybe younger. Hungry, tired, cut-up, looks like he's been through a war. He'd been lost for three days. Three days, bro! Didn't know where the heck he was or where he was going.

"See, he thinks he's going to die out there. He's out of food and water, getting weak, and has no idea where he is. He finally gets himself composed and tells me his story. He decided to cross the river by himself. Didn't have the money to pay a *coyote*. Doesn't know where the river is but finally finds it and swims across. But when he reaches this side there are no lights or towns and he doesn't have any idea which way to head. After a day of walking in circles he starts to think he's going to die. He's got a wife and daughter back home, and he is thinking he will never see them again. By the time I catch sight of him, he has given up hope.

"So I think to myself, 'After all this guy has been through, am I just going to process him and send him back across the river? No. The right thing to do is to cut the guy some slack.' I take him to the Whataburger in Mission right there on Old Military because it's open twenty-four/seven, feed him a Whataburger with cheese and some fries, give him ten bucks, then drive back to the bridge as a VR. I admit this guy got to me. Now, some of the other agents would get on my case because I'm buying a illegal food and giving him money, but what else was I supposed to do? He's a human being just like everyone else. All he's trying to do is find a decent job. All of us have hearts out here."

As Herman talked—and he liked to talk—the night hours grew deeper and melted softly one into the other. Agent Morningside rambled through story after story in the early morning hours by the banks of the Rio Grande, all the while expertly manipulating the camera in grand sweeps of the riverscape that lay in absolute darkness. The camera, sensitive only to thermal heat, worked on a totally different principle than the NVGs, which reacted to light. What showed up on the tiny screen as dark greens, grays, and indigoes was cold and dead, while life in any shape or form appeared in pure white light.

"See that there?" he asked. "It's something lying down. Some kind of an animal. Maybe a cow or something. No, look, it's a dog. See how it walks and the legs? Definitely a dog." The outline of a white dog pixel smelled its way across the screen.

"There's a jackrabbit there. See. It's frozen in front of the dog. As soon as the dog goes by, that rabbit is going to take off." It did, pixel ears flopping across the green screen until it all at once disappeared.

"It's behind a rock or something. Just wait. It'll probably come out again."

Herman, in spite of the talk, was bored. Tonight only he and two other units including Agent Fernando Rodriguez patrolled a thirty-mile stretch of the Rio Grande. All the other agents on mids were hunkered down a few miles upriver because DEA intel promised a shipment of cocaine would cross between 1:00 and 4 A.M. Herman Morningside gambled that the hot spot would be near the area where he had set up the scope truck. So far he had lost his roll of the dice. All total there had been one dumb dog and one smart rabbit.

Adjusting his bifocals yet again, Herman said with a hint of anticipation in his deep voice, "What the heck is that?" He rescanned the area the remote had covered, then sat back in the driver's seat of the scope truck as his right hand unconsciously sought the radio mike.

"We got one, no, two, no, three, four, five," Herman began to count the outlines on the screen with his index finger as adrenaline sampled the blood in his veins. "We got six, seven, eight, nine, ten, eleven, no, twelve." Excitement rose in Herman's voice as he lightly touched the figures on the screen with his left hand to be sure of their exact number. "Fifteen, sixteen—there's seventeen of them there," he said finally, relaying the information to the two backup units and the supe who would be listening at the station. White, Gumby-like human figures crossed the green screen before coming to a dark solid swath of gray that was in actuality a narrow lane less than a quarter of a mile due south of the scope truck. Small boulders and dense brush lay on both sides of the dirt path. Along this particular section of the river the rocky soil supported only prickly pear, purple sage, and a few stunted wild olive trees.

The terrain was rough going for the nameless Gumbys guided by their pixel *coyote* under a moonless sky. With great effort they navigated rock outcroppings and stands of prickly pear reaching fifteen feet high and covered with thorns capable of mutilating human skin.

Back at the McAllen Station the supe listened to the animated talk between Morningside and the other two units. With any luck, the supe prayed, Morningside would not screw up. With any luck, maybe the station would soon be filled with Mexicans. No OTMs, of course. No one wanted to see OTMs and the paperwork that came with them.

Outside the station where the supe sat sweating bullets, powerful lights on new utility poles lit up every square inch of Border Patrol property, providing a corridor of security around the building. The wide, concrete streets that framed the station and its outer buildings were, in contrast, buried in dark shadow, but even at this late hour the highways and roads were alive with a heavy stream of tractor-trailers taken through their gears amid the noisy clanks and thumps from open-air sheds, warehouses, and plants.

There had always been two sides to the city of McAllen: one north of the railroad tracks, one south. Until the early 1950s Anglos lived only on the north side of McAllen along with a handful of affluent Mexican Americans. The south side was reserved for the majority of the city's population, poor Hispanics, many of them farmworkers and day laborers who just barely survived on dirt-poor wages. In Mission and towns throughout the Valley the south side of the tracks was "Mexican" and the north side "American."[2] Belt-high chain-link fences, thick poinsettias, hibiscus, and ivy hid a dismal poverty with no future. Behind eight-foot plastered and painted cinder-block walls of gated communities with grand entrances watched over by security guards were million-dollar houses sheltering a small but wealthy class of McAllenites who had little time for anything but the enhancement of their own welfare.

The McAllen Border Patrol Station was constructed in the early 1970s on the far south side of the city amid cotton fields and orange groves that in the 1980s became the McAllen Foreign Trade Zone. Now the trade zone, prospering since NAFTA in 1994, was itself under attack from urban sprawl including tract houses and two-story apartments.[3] But the vast majority of south side McAllen residents, even amid all the obvious rapid economic development and growth, remained surprisingly and abysmally poor, disenfranchised, and Hispanic even as the trade zone boomed.

And boom it did. The trade zone was filled with warehouses holding thousands of tons of NAFTA-regulated products headed south to Mexico, fast becoming the United States' most important partner in trade, and north to all parts of the United States. The trade zone's fresh produce center occupied more than half a square mile of land, five huge sheds painted in tropical pink and mauve, each with concrete loading docks nursing the eighteen-wheelers that flooded the trade zone constantly with hundreds of tons of fresh vegetables and fruits. Panasonic assembled electrical components next to plants manufacturing plastic moldings, metal bolts and screws, and medical supplies. The bulk of the maquiladoras, however, were located across the river at the Reynosa industrial park. The McAllen Foreign Trade Zone was, in effect, a giant warehouse storing the bounty of maquiladoras from Reynosa and the interior of Mexico, until the goods could be shipped north.

Each of these out-of-scale buildings was the same configuration of acres of sheet-metal roofs atop steel beams covering a vast concrete floor.[4] The only difference between the warehouses, besides the color of their three-story sheet-metal walls, was the company logo that fronted Old Military Highway. Frequent cascading tile fountains seemed some architect's failed attempt to beautify the bare industrial sites on a limited budget, not unlike Lady Bird Johnson's campaign in the 1970s to improve the visual attractiveness of Texas rural and urban landscapes by shielding junkyards with wooden fences.

A few steps from the McAllen Economic Development Council, which facilitated this economic juggernaut of trade zone and twin plants, across Old Military Highway from a satellite branch of South Texas Community College, where they specialized in instructing students how to drive the big truck rigs that transported NAFTA goods, the flags of the three countries of NAFTA, Canada, the United States, and Mexico, wafted lazily in the night breeze.

A new four-lane highway ran from the trade zone south to Reynosa and north to the rest of the North American continent. All along the concrete was a hodgepodge of used car lots, auto parts stores, junkyards, auto glass repair shops, bargain-priced Mexican ceramics, tortilla factories, car mechanics, and a variety of mom-and-pop operations catering to the large number of poor Hispanics living in South McAllen. Signs outside the businesses were as likely to be in Spanish as English. In front of one convenience store a sign attempted to mimic those observed in the more affluent neighborhoods on the north side of the city: "Convenient Store." Nearby was a rent-to-own tire business.

Miller International Airport also lay just south of the railroad tracks, its name belying the fact that only two of its four gates were actually used by fliers. The last Continental flight from Houston had landed on time at 10:35 P.M., so the airport had long since grown quiet. Its glass front doors remained unlocked, however, a magnet to undocumented workers who regularly gathered in the airport restrooms across from gates one and two, holding tickets purchased by a *coyote*, before attempting to rush aboard the 6:05 A.M. Continental flight back to Houston. It was an old trick that never worked.

McAllen's only mall, La Plaza Mall, was just down the street from the airport, a mecca to shoppers from both sides of the McAllen tracks and a popular attraction to shoppers from Reynosa and Monterrey, Nuevo Leon, Mexico's third-largest city. Billboards advertising La Plaza Mall decorated the streets of both Reynosa and Monterrey, luring scores of Mexican shoppers to the mall parking lots during both the Christmas holidays and Mexico's national week of vacation preceding Easter, *Semana Santa.*

To the west Business 83, which bisected the Valley from east to west from South Padre to Rio Grande City, connected a succession of communities grown fat with rapid population growth. Some towns along this corridor, like Pharr and Weslaco, more than doubled in size within the last decade and were still growing, a far cry from the villages laid out at the turn of the century by the railroad. These towns were originally intended as modestly sized communities serving as minor agricultural hubs for the groves and farmland that were created out of the thick mesquite and impenetrable brush that once covered every inch of the Valley.[5]

The key to this early development at the start of the twentieth century was the precious commodity of water from the Rio Grande. To the west of McAllen, Mission, La Joya, Los Ebanos, Sullivan City, and La Grulla were established upon this same model, but a handful of communities had never been touched by the railroad—*ranchitos* first settled by the Spanish three centuries earlier. Tightly hugging the bends and twists of the Rio Grande, these settlements were so small and unknown that they rarely made it into print on most maps and, to a great degree, neither did they find a place on the cognitive maps of most Valley residents.

The settlements along the river, with the exception of Brownsville far downstream, withered and were lost to common consciousness while the agricultural communities along Business 83 swelled with a population spurred by NAFTA and one of the highest birthrates in the nation.[6]

All Along the Watchtower

Here in one of these *ranchitos* that only state historians could accurately name, here where the dim lights of two nearby houses barely illuminated the scope truck, the dwellings on land now technically incorporated within the McAllen city limits, Agent Herman Morningside frenetically fiddled with the knobs and switches of the little green screen. Attempting in vain to keep the Gumbys under surveillance, Agent Morningside ignored the only outside sound penetrating the cab, the howling of a pack of coyotes. Back at the station, the supe reached for his coffee and wished he had a cigarette.

"Whoooaaah there. What is this?" said Herman. More Gumby figures appeared as if from nowhere. This was not the first group of seventeen, but a second group with their own *coyote* leading the way. Herman counted twelve of them. That made twenty-nine in two different groups.

Herman radioed Fox One, the helicopter that was in the air. Fox Two was not working this shift. Both flew out of a special hangar at Miller International Airport. The news from the pilot was not good.

"I'm near Kingsville," the pilot said. "I'm low so I got to refuel, then I'll head your way. I'd say forty minutes tops."

Kingsville was seventy air miles north of Herman's location by the Rio Grande. In forty minutes the illegal aliens could reach a safe house in nearby Peñitas or, equally plausible, recross the Rio Grande.

Herman passed on the info to the four agents in the two units. Agent Fernando Rodriguez was mapping out their strategy in one Expedition, Agent Reynaldo Guerra giving him his opinion from the cab of the other. Between them they decided to outflank the illegal aliens or, at worst, herd them north toward Old Military Highway. Images of Gumbys appeared on the screen, faded into empty pixels, then morphed into human shapes under the thermal lens of the remote camera. The screen revealed long lines of Gumbys, gender impossible to denote, all jogging rapidly along the narrow trails behind the lead *coyote* only to disappear behind rock formations, dense brush, or stands of yucca. When Agents Rodriguez and Guerra along with their partners arrived at the scene, they joined the parade of humanity transformed by the thermal-sensing unit into white stick figures against a backdrop of moss.

Under the direction of Herman Morningside ensconced in the scope truck, four agents challenged the expertise of two *coyotes* guiding twenty-seven illegal aliens. After fifteen minutes it was clear that the U.S. Border Patrol, notwithstanding their technological superiority in this particular instance, was losing the game of hide-and-seek played out on a square mile of turf in Deep South Texas. The first group of undocumented workers disappeared, no longer anywhere on the screen. Maybe their *coyote,* NVGs in hand, had spotted the scope truck atop the dump. It would not be the first time. As if in answer, the first group suddenly reappeared heading due south to recross the Río Bravo. Individuals in this line of humanity ran, stumbled, fell, then regained their footing as they made their way across the challenging terrain. Then they disappeared. A minute later they were back on the screen running west at full speed along the dirt trail. During this dodge in the dark they came within twenty-five yards of Agent Reynaldo Guerra. But in this terrain twenty-five yards was as good as a mile; the agent never saw them.

Blindly following Herman's commands from the scope truck, the four agents gave chase to the twenty-nine figures on the screen but never established contact.

"Okay, guys, a little north, then west. I saw them about a hundred yards, maybe a little less, from your position two minutes ago. Then I lost sight of them. No, there they are again, up and moving fast."

Fox One was twenty minutes away and closing.

"What?" Herman said to himself in some amazement as he stared at the screen. "What the heck is going on here?" Gumby figures were once more situated on the dirt trail but this time their bodies were forged so closely together in a chain of human flesh that it was impossible to count them. Was it one of the two groups or a new group? The reflection from the screen cast a pale light on Herman's high forehead making him look every one of his forty-eight years.

In the right circumstances Herman could be a patient man. He had waited eight years in the early 1980s to join the Border Patrol, working as a landsman for an Oklahoma oil company. Although today the Border Patrol aggressively recruits for hundreds of new positions, back then the only way to get a position was for another agent to retire or die.

"That's not the same group," Herman concluded. "Okay, what we got out there is *three* groups. I'm not sure how many I saw just now. Maybe twenty. At least twenty. They were so close together I couldn't get a good count. So we got fifty of them out there. Maybe more."

Morningside and the other agents knew that the terrain was riddled with ravines. If the illegals reached those ravines, they could follow them straight north to outflank the scope truck, then reach the caliche and gravel quarries that led by numerous trails to Old Military Highway. Once at the highway, they were long gone.

"We got a small problem here. If that first group makes it to the base of this rock I'm sitting on, they can come around immediately behind me." Herman then considered the logical conclusion to his broadcasted observation. The group of seventeen illegals—and that was just an estimate—would be within clear sight of his truck. If they did not see the scope truck, they would hear the Expedition's oversized engine running.

Herman had his service handgun in his holster but for some unexplainable reason the M-4 from the station armory he was qualified to carry was nowhere in sight, nor the standard-issue 12-gauge shotgun. The undocumented workers were most likely harmless men and women looking for jobs in the United States. But along the Rio Grande agents were forced to minimize their personal risk by assuming a worst-case scenario. These Gumbys on the screen could be seventeen armed and dangerous Mexican criminals. Or they might not be undocumented workers at all but drug smugglers, or M&Ms, Mexican soldiers.

"We stay in this truck," Herman said too loudly for my taste as he laughed at the uncomfortable truth of the situation. Even in his prime Herman Morningside would have been no match for seventeen undocumented workers. Or whatever they were. His years of experience did not bestow upon him the powers of a Hollywood superhero. In a fight, Herman's bifocals were not an advantage, nor his game right knee, which had evoked involuntary groans as he climbed into the truck cab. After seventeen years chasing illegal immigrants, Herman had suffered through two surgeries and still had the nagging pain in his right leg. In three years' time Agent Herman Morningside could retire to a life governed by the growth cycle of household plants, shrubs, trees, and the holy cacti.

So these days Herman at least tried to play it safe. He had his new family to think of, including the son he had always dreamed about. "You know, I found out what they say about children is true. They are very special. I am very blessed to have a son like mine." For the sake of his family, Herman took extra care not to put himself in harm's way. He had heard about the agent based in Harlingen who, in the middle of mids, had parked the scope truck on railroad tracks. When the train came barreling down the tracks, the agent just barely made it out of the scope truck before the crash. The near tragedy had been a palpable warning to Herman and other agents bound to the green screen during mids.

We waited. Nothing happened.

Fox One, running lights blackened to avoid detection from the ground, suddenly hovered over the scope truck. The sound was deafening. Behind the pilot in a cramped seat, the copilot scanned the terrain with an infrared detector similar to Herman's. No pixels of life illuminated either screen.

"Don't see a thing," radioed Fox One. The copter began to fly large concentric circles near where the illegal aliens were last spotted while on the ground the four agents waited for directions.

"Okay, I got 'em," the pilot confirmed just a few minutes later. "You've got to come a hundred yards northwest from where you are located. There are maybe ten of them hunkered down in there."

The four agents each came at the undocumented workers hiding in the thick brush from a different direction but at a point less than ten yards from their hiding place still had established no visual contact.

"You're right on top of them," said the pilot. "A few more feet to the southwest." The agents still could not see a damn thing as they picked their way slowly and carefully through the rough land.

"You're on top of them right now," said the pilot, his frustration mounting. On duty for the last seven hours, fatigue was beginning to drain his patience. An hour piloting the craft through the lenses of the NVGs was the equivalent of at least two normal flight hours. Nevertheless Fox One would not be returning to the tarmac until the illegal aliens had been apprehended.

"We got 'em," came the agent's voice a few seconds later. Discovered, the Gumbys on the screen crawled out one by one, hands raised into the air. They formed a line behind one of the agents as they were led to a waiting Expedition.

"I counted eleven," said the pilot. "I'm going to find the others." The copter veered out of its hover to continue its systematic sweeping of the area covered in rocks and dense vegetation.

The thickets and strips of forest along the banks of the Rio Grande were among the last remnants of the original indigenous environment prior to European contact. When Anglo developers in the early 1900s ordered the land to be cleared for plowing, crews of Mexican and Mexican American workers labored for years to remove the impenetrable blanket of vegetation criss-crossed only by narrow horse trails. They built enormous stacks of limbs, trunks, and foliage, then set them afire. The fires burned for years, covering the Valley sky with thick clouds of smoke.[7]

With little more than machetes and oxcarts, the Hispanic labor force, working for pennies a day, constructed the system of irrigation channels and dikes that bring water to Valley lands miles from the banks of the Rio Grande. In less than two decades the workers turned raw ranchland into one of the most productive agricultural regions in the United States. Workers were paid $1.25 a day or less for this grueling effort, which even by the standard of the times was barely enough to keep them alive.[8]

At first the virgin Valley farmland was a tough sell to potential farmers who lived in the Midwest. Valley developers built model farms to lure these outsider buyers to the Valley, then chartered trains to bring farmers from as far away as Illinois. The pitch was simple: this new land came with two growing seasons and an unlimited supply of local labor who worked for next to nothing. Cotton was king and the economics of it were simple enough to understand. Fifteen short years later the best Valley land was owned and farmed by midwesterners who hired Mexicans and Mexican Americans to till their land, plant their crops, harvest their bounty, then pack it for market in large metal packing sheds one hundred feet from the rail line. Through it all the Mexican and Mexican American *irrigadores,* the irrigators, constantly monitored and watered the fields from the irrigation canals and ditches.

Without the water from the Rio Grande, the Valley was nothing more than flat, arid land covered in thick brush and short grasses. Only along the banks of the Rio Grande did the tall palms grow along with other tropical trees. The first Spaniards to explore the region had, in fact, named the river *Rio de las Palmas,* River of Palms.[9] In a good year the Valley received barely twenty inches of rainfall, the majority arriving in the late summer and early fall along with the tropical storms and hurricanes that plagued the region.[10]

Anglo developers had fabricated a magnificent dream by the 1920s, a dream predicated upon abundant water and cheap labor from Mexico. Those farmers and growers who owned generous water rights, strictly regulated by the water masters from each water district, thrived over the years, while those depending on natural rainfall to sustain their crops inevitably failed. Most ranchers struggled except for operations that were immense even by Texas standards, such as the King Ranch, upon which oil and gas were eventually discovered.[11]

Prosperous farmers, growers, and ranchers formed a small class of Anglo rural and town elite who presided, sometimes ruthlessly, over the majority of poor Valley Mexicans and Mexican Americans. As the Valley population increased, there was never enough work. Mexicans in growing numbers were recruited to labor on Valley farms and ranches. In this manner wages were kept low by landowners, and many residents struggled to survive. Valley farmworkers were eventually forced to migrate each spring to work the fields in the Midwest; by the 1970s the Valley had become the permanent home for hundreds of thousands of migrant farmworkers who composed a majority of the local labor force. In spite of its transition to a major agricultural producer, Deep South Texas remained mired in abject poverty.

Hispanics historically were, in short, a vital but sorely mistreated part of the Anglo dream of prosperity for the lower Rio Grande valley of Texas. Shunted to live on the south sides of the railroad tracks in McAllen, Mission, Pharr, Weslaco, La Feria, Harlingen, San Juan, Mercedes, La Joya, and Alamo, the same story was repeated each decade: poor Mexicans and Mexican Americans were educated in public schools with few resources, then actively discouraged from continuing their formal education past elementary school; lack of education led to exclusion at the ballot box under laws enforced by Anglos; Anglos, although the minority in Deep South Texas, governed the majority of Hispanics through personal intimidation, institutional racism, and manipulation of the political and legal systems.[12]

Although Herman Morningside knew little of this history, he grasped enough based on observation. Still, he was a practical man who knew his place in life and, at this late date in his Border Patrol career, was not about to stir up the natural order as he defined it. Ignoring the rooster that announced its presence at just after 4 A.M., Herman scanned the tiny green screen in vain. Somewhere out there in the one square mile of Valley land forty illegal aliens still hid behind cactus, sedimentary rock, and stunted mesquite.

"They got to be pretty beat up by now," he said staring at the screen. "They've been running around in that prickly pear for two hours so they got to be tired and they got to be cut up some. Just look at what they been running through," he said, shining his black Mag flashlight on a nearby cactus half as high as the infrared camera on its perch. "They probably would like to give up and try again after a few days' rest. They got to be demoralized."

Reaching for his Thermos of hot coffee, Herman fondly remembered two full-time crooks from his time in the Valley: Waylon and Willie. "They were a pair," Herman said. "They lived right down there by the river in the town of Peñitas. They were a royal pain. Especially Waylon. They called him Waylon for Waylon Jennings. Willie was for Willie Nelson. Waylon was the grandson of an old woman who lived in a little farmhouse which was on some land that bordered the river. Waylon decided to rent out the land to some drug smugglers and, of course, right away they started bringing in the dope across her property. Did it at night. The little old lady lived all alone in that house. I think she was eighty-eight, maybe older. She had no intention of going to a nursing home, which is what her kids wanted her to do. They worried about her because she was all alone and it was getting worse each day.

"One Sunday afternoon her kids were sitting out there on the front porch and they see the smugglers come walking right across the property from the river with a load of drugs. Right there in the daylight! The oldest son, without thinking, goes right up to one of the smugglers and says, 'You got no right being here on my grandma's land.' But the doper says, 'Sure we do. We rent this land from the old woman's grandson.' So they could see what was going on. Waylon was getting rich off a deal he cut with the dopers, and their mother was in grave danger.

"Her kids got real mad at the situation so they decided to build a big chain-link fence all around her house to keep the smugglers out. But it didn't work. The smugglers cut holes in it with wire cutters and pulled it down. They even tried burning it."

Herman decided one day to tell her that the Border Patrol was keeping a special eye on her in case she needed help. "She met me at the door and started yelling at me that I had no right to be there, and I'd better leave or she'd call the police. At eighty-eight she is doing this! If you ask me, it was pretty damn brave for an old lady."

A week later he was passing by on line watch. "She invited me in and was as nice as could be. We sat at a small table for two. She was almost blind but she kept the house real clean. She served me some tea and told me that she didn't want to go to a nursing home because of no drug smugglers." She told

Herman she wanted to die in her own bed in her own house, not a nursing home in McAllen.

The Border Patrol eventually caught Waylon with a load of drugs. Waylon did his time in prison, then returned to Hidalgo County. "He swore," said Herman, "that he wasn't smuggling. I saw him a few weeks ago. Said he was living on welfare and just barely making it. But you can't trust a snake like that."

Willie was different from Waylon, an aging Dead Head, high on grass all day and night. The agents called him Willie after Texas' own Willie Nelson. The problem was that the Valley Waylon and Willie hated each other with a passion. Representing rival drug smuggling organizations, they thrived on reporting each other's activities to the authorities. So the Border Patrol got tips about Waylon's drug smuggling from Willie, and tips about Willie's drug smuggling from Waylon. They finally took Willie down on a tip from Waylon. Willie, when he was released from prison, kept a low profile. At least for a while.

"They would've kept feuding," Herman summed up. But then Willie ran over a guy with his vehicle and hid his car in his garage, but could not lie his way out of the fragments of skin and bone police found on the front bumper. So Willie went back to prison, this time for a longer spell.

"What keeps me going is my Airodyne," Herman said, shifting conversational gears as the first pale light of dawn shone upon the tops of the yucca and the prickly pear. "That's the reason I'm in as good a shape as I am. Five days a week I do thirty to forty minutes on my Airodyne. You know the one I'm talking about? The one that Paul Harvey recommends on the radio. It's a good workout and easy on my bad knees. I went to the doctor and he flat out told me to stop jogging. I haven't been running for five years. I have the Airodyne to thank. It's a stress buster. That's what it is. A stress buster. I get stressed in this job, but I get on that bike and forty minutes later I'm as good as new. I recommend you consider buying one. They're expensive, but just figure out how much a health club is going to cost you."

Fox One found the third group of aliens and pinpointed them for the agents on the ground. Agents Rodriguez and Flora counted eight men and two women before the transport van hauled them to the McAllen Station for processing. The supe who had been listening to Herman's chatter on the radio finally heaved a huge sigh of relief. No new memos on this shift.

Not at all like the time Herman and his trainee Borg, who was behind the wheel, were traveling along Old Military Highway in the middle of mids. There was a sharp curve and railroad track not far from La Joya, but Herman never told the rookie to be extra alert. They took the curve at forty; the trainee lost control of the vehicle as it rounded the hairpin turn. The vehicle took flight, then finally came to rest on its side in the brush. Luckily neither agent sustained even a scratch. The same could not be said for the Chevrolet Tahoe. Herman and Borg filled out forms for the next several days attempting to explain why they had knowingly destroyed property belonging to the U.S. government. Since the accident, agents had called the site "Borg's Curve," though it should probably be named in honor of Agent Herman Morningside.

They never found the last group of new immigrants. The agent had spotted at least fifty of them at one point, but only about half ended up processed at the McAllen Station. Where did they go? No one knew. Odds were that they had circled the scope truck, then reached the trails leading to Old Military Highway and a quick ride to a safe house.

Herman Morningside was more exhausted from mids than he realized. Slowly and carefully following the narrow road from the dump, he suddenly slammed on the brakes.

"Oh, shit!" he yelled, sweat popping out on his forehead. "Oh, shit. Oh, shit. I forgot to take down the scope!" He jumped out of the cab, eyed the platform wobbling precariously fifteen feet above the bed of the truck, and then carefully lowered the mechanism.

"It's okay. Now that would be a heck of an ending, wouldn't it? Wrecking the infrared camera on an electrical pole." The supes sipping their last round of station coffee were oblivious that they had just dodged a bucket of memos from Agent Herman Morningside.

Herman quickly put the miscue behind him as he easily switched to his favorite topic besides his beloved family. He had recently started his own nursery business. Herman planned to go into the ornamental business full time after he retired from the Border Patrol.

As the truck sped west along Old Military Highway, a stream of commuters already beginning to clog its lanes, Herman looked over at me as I wearily rested my head against the dusty window glass of the scope truck.

"You ever considered how important root bags are?" he asked.

Cavazos Beach

For families who enjoyed fishing and boating on the river, picnicking at concrete tables and barbecues, and playing softball, Frisbee, or soccer on the grassy fields, Anzalduas Park at $5 a carload was a choice destination. Directly adjacent to the Hidalgo County park was a large rookery that attracted various species of migratory birds throughout the year as well as birders trooping after them. Anzalduas was, unfortunately, also a popular landing for bales of Mexican marijuana and undocumented workers from around the globe.

This particular night in January the honest citizens of McAllen had returned home, leaving Anzalduas to the business of the *coyotes* and drug smugglers. The park was veiled in silence but for the rustling of feathers, cackles, and random honking from the rookery, the predictable sounds of the Border Patrol Expeditions along the drag road, the sure footfalls of the smugglers on reconnaissance, and the soggy squish of immigrants' clothes dropping to the riverbank as they undressed in a desperate rush against time.

Intent on adding a number of species to their list of sightings, the birders who arrived the next morning for the chartered boat trip were from all parts of the United States, Europe, and Japan. Among the serious birders were snowbirds, blue-collar retirees from Minnesota, Iowa, Missouri, Illinois, and other midwestern states. They annually spent the six coldest months of the year in the tropical Valley climate attending square dances, playing shuffleboard, and shopping the aisles of Sam's Club for specials. Counting their blessings in the early morning chill as they left the warmth of their trailers and mobile homes, they had grabbed for their binoculars as an afterthought when carefully selecting their red and blue winter parkas with ruffled, fake fur collars and hoods. In contrast the serious birders delicately carried in their hands sophisticated optical tools with compound lenses fashioned from space-age plastics with a price that would cover the monthly bills of a south side McAllen family. To ward off the damp and the chill, their backs were covered with mail-order outer shells, hoods, and jackets crammed with enough Thinsulate to keep the entire population of Montana warm and dry for the winter.

None of the serious birders perched on the second tier of the imitation paddle-wheel steamboat was very pleased to see Agents Rochester, Plovic, and Contreras as they unceremoniously roared by, the rough-running Johnson engine propelling the seventeen-foot BayMaster at just more than thirty knots. Their wake was substantial enough when it hit the faux steamboat that many of the elderly passengers reached for the railing in modest desperation.

The agents on board the BayMaster did not so much resemble border guards as large, overstuffed baked potatoes, layer upon layer of vestments distorting their true forms. They sported bulky bulletproof vests atop their uniforms, followed by standard-issue green jackets and puffy, required life preservers, all crowned with M16s.

Canada geese, ducks, herons, egrets, white pelicans, and other species rose up from the patches of fog along the river in random cyclones of wings as Agent Rochester, the captain of the BayMaster, pushed the Johnson up a notch. Then the birds, gathering themselves as one but not yet ready for full flight, resettled behind the disappearing wake of the boat.

Ever mindful of the importance of public relations, the three agents awkwardly tipped their heads in the direction of the tourist boat wallowing in their wake. No reason to be rude to the members of the public—all civilians were taxpayers. The professional and the amateur birders emitted a communal groan, however, as a hundred yards farther up the Rio Grande three white pelicans preening in the first warm sunlight of the day took flight to avoid the Bay-Master bearing down on them. The serious birders who had traveled a great distance to the Rio Grande shot quick photos of the pelicans as they skimmed the waters on their takeoff, while several snowbirds aimed their throwaway cameras at the Border Patrol boat. In this fashion the serious birders recorded what they assumed to be yet another disturbance of pristine bird habitat by agents of the federal government, while the former midwestern firefighters, welders, postal workers, administrative assistants, and managers of burger franchises documented for the folks back home how rules along an international border were enforced.[1]

The sensor at Cavazos Beach, just around the bend from Anzalduas Park, had taken three hits. Agents Rochester, Contreras, and Plovic arrived at the same time Fox One appeared from out of nowhere in the sky. Ignoring this mechanical beast as it circled Cavazos Beach, flocks of egrets, terns, and herons chose to remain in the shallows close to the banks until the sun chased away the patches of fog and dried their feathers.

It was only fifty degrees on the river, but the windchill was cold enough to remind Steve Plovic of his childhood in Buffalo, New York. All three agents, regardless of their layers of cloth and gear, were chilled to the bone. Steve had been staring at the back of Maria Contreras's graceful neck since she had first climbed on board. He had hoped to catch a glimpse of her eyes. Large, dark brown eyes that sparkled in the early morning sun's reflection off the water, intelligent eyes that hid behind them thoughts he could not fathom.

Maria was not officially assigned to the boat, but she had seen little action on her line watch throughout the early morning hours and was bored to death. So they had agreed to pick her up at a designated landing. She said that she wanted to see the river at dawn. She knew that Steve Plovic could not take his eyes off her. That was his problem, not hers. Although they had begun a relationship in November, Maria was already unsure after only two months whether it was worth continuing. It was no one's business but their own, but everyone at the McAllen Station knew what was going on. This morning she ignored Steve less out of ego or frivolity than because she intended to enjoy the beauty of the early morning fog and the patches of shadow hugging the banks. All the while she pretended that she did not know what went on in the dense vegetation lining both sides of the river. It was better that way.[2]

Maria felt far colder than she would reveal to Plovic and Rochester. She felt the ice in her veins as she held the aluminum bow rail but turned it into a slight pain she chose to ignore and then tried to ignore it. The men would take it as a female weakness if she complained. In fact, she was miserably cold simply because she had been born and raised in Pharr, a city a mere fifteen miles from their position on the river. Like anyone born in the tropical climate of Deep South Texas, she would always feel this cold, the windchill below twenty degrees when the BayMaster skimmed the top of the river.

Yet again she reviewed exactly why she was standing on the back of the BayMaster dressed as an agent of the U.S. Border Patrol. She had never planned it that way. Certainly it was not what her parents wanted for her. She had returned home to Pharr from Austin with an undergraduate degree in history, no job, and significant loans crying to be paid off. She had promised her parents she would return to the Valley after she graduated, but she did so more to assuage their doubts about her leaving home than to fulfill a part of any career plan. Her school debts were not that substantial, especially not compared to some of her friends', but she needed a real job. Looking back, she knew that she had stuck out her neck when she had left home for Austin, when she had chosen not to get married out of high school like many of her childhood friends or to sign up for courses at UTPA in Edinburg or South Texas Community College in McAllen.

Maria had not known exactly what she wanted to do in college, but she did know that she had to get out of the Valley. She had heard too much from her sisters who like her had left home as soon as they had the chance. The real shock came when she went job hunting, history degree in hand. After three months of fruitless searching, all she could find was a minimum-wage job at Wal-Mart, which she eventually traded for a secretary's position at a retail business not too far from her parents' house in Pharr.[3] Suffering in silence the slights from her boss and coworkers, who ridiculed her fancy college degree, Maria held that worthless job for almost a year as she rebuffed the advances from a host of males who found reasons to walk by her desk each day seeking the favors of a local girl who was beautiful but full of crazy ideas.

Maria thought little of her good looks and valued even less those who were blinded by them. She spent her free time working out at the gym. She enjoyed weight training with men who were not intimidated by her, and she discovered that the more time she spent at the gym, the more she felt in control of her life.

Maria had not considered a career in the Border Patrol, but after enough abuse as a secretary to last a lifetime she was ready to sign up for an annual salary that could erase her school debts. Excelling at the academy where the physical training, language skills, and immigration law came almost too easy for her, she had surprised herself. She had not been the world's greatest student in Austin, where she had spent more than her share of time partying instead of studying. The proof was her 2.5 GPA, which while not outstandingly bad kept her dreams of graduate school at bay. She was, behind the shiny black hair, the flawless skin, and a smile to die for, an intelligent young woman who sought more from life than a husband to love and protect her. Maria did not want to be protected, and at this point of her life she was not sure she was looking for a lifelong lover. Maybe she did not know exactly what her dream in life was, but she damn sure knew what it was not.

"We got a vehicle on the drag," said Plovic scanning the north bank. The BayMaster roared up to the bank, and Plovic jumped into the brush like some big cat. Rochester, in the meantime, took the BayMaster out to midstream to get a better angle at Plovic as he easily scaled the top of the bluff and disappeared into the carrizo cane.

Maria appreciated his athleticism. She was not so sure about his shaved head, or the broken nose, or the pale eyes. He was so Anglo. Plovic had been a star linebacker in high school, then had won a scholarship to SUNY-Cortland not far from his hometown. When the coach asked him his senior year to move to the defensive line, he had put on an extra forty pounds. With his height and frame he could handle the weight, and at 260 he had held his own on the Division Three team. But the first thing he did after football season ended was lose the weight. He had been in the gym ever since. That was a part of the tangible bond he and Maria shared. They liked to work out together; they both tolerated the price of the effort and pain in return for the feeling of fitness and the sense of well-being. What Plovic did not seem to understand was that the gym was even more important for Maria than for him. For Maria it was about carrying both literally and figuratively her share of the load as an agent. It was about equality.

After a long minute Steve Plovic fought his way out of the carrizo cane at the top of the river bluff where, with a big smile, he gave a double thumbs-up hand signal that everything checked out. It was impossible to communicate any other way because of the din created by Fox One hovering directly overhead, the deafening shockwaves of air bending and flattening the cane and the branches of a nearby mesquite. Satisfied that there was no further need for him, Fox One veered downriver and became a speck in the air. A temporary sanity and calm returned to the riverbanks.

"It's an old man," Plovic explained as he reboarded. "He's cutting grass at the end of this field. That's his truck on the drag over there. That's what set the sensor off."

Agent Rochester shoved the Johnson into reverse, then headed back downriver in the direction of the Gulf of Mexico. Rochester was feeling edgy. The physical limitations of the boat defined the available policing strategies on the river. "We can only do so much with what we have," he said. "We can patrol the river slowly, or we can rev it up and get there fast. We try to vary our speed to confuse the bad guys."

Agents Rochester, Plovic, and Contreras were all true believers in their mission: to deter aliens from crossing the river and the trafficking of illegal drugs. Perhaps to varying degrees based upon their experience—Rochester had six years on Plovic and Contreras—these agents of the U.S. Border Patrol also believed in the rightness of their cause.

"The second thing we can do because of the situation we are in at the present time," Rochester explained, "is we can double back on them real fast. Then maybe we catch them because they're waiting for us to pass by before they make their move. We can come out of nowhere to nail them good. Surprise them." He quickly told a story to validate this strategy. They had nabbed two men in tubes who had reached the middle of the river and, at the same time, forced the other eight hiding in the brush to run away. This strategy was called "deterrence."

"If we had more boats, we could do a heck of a better job," he ended. He nodded to affirm himself. "Guy from Washington came down about six months ago. We showed him what we do. Then we showed him Cavazos Beach. He says to us, 'You'll get your boats,' and sure enough three months later we got three more boats. But you can't cover forty miles of river twenty-four/seven with four boats. For one thing, we don't have the manpower. We don't even have a separate unit for the boats. Not even like the bike patrol. But we got the boats. That was a start. We're here for deterrence. Just like the units pulling X's on the levees.[4] It's all about deterrence."

"Right there," Rochester said, pointing at a thumb of sandy land jutting into the Rio Grande. "That's what we call Cavazos Beach." Five black tire tubes floated lazily among the cane on the south side of the river in a stew of dead moss, plastic bottles, faded green garbage bags, and Coke cans. At first the small stretch of sandy beach on the north side of the Rio Grande resembled the south side, but upon closer inspection as the BayMaster nudged toward the shore the ground turned the color of pea soup. Faded garbage bags in various stages of decay from exposure to the elements covered almost every inch of the banks. Cavazos Beach was a quagmire of decaying plastic.

Agents Plovic and Contreras jumped onto the bank with equal grace, their booted feet digging into a thick, mushy carpet the color of green vomit. Beneath the garbage bags lay other garbage bags in deeper decay, hundreds, no, thousands of individual garbage bags. Each individual bag had once been filled with a change of clothes for the new immigrant along with other sparse personal belongings, then floated diligently across the river on an old tire tube. As soon as the new immigrants reached the northern shore, the garbage bags were no longer of any use. Emptied and abandoned, the plastic jetsam baked under the Texas sun and was transformed into a subterranean fungus, a sinking mound of polymer fibers at once both a tribute to human ingenuity and a squalid dump.

Behind a stunted line of scrub mesquite, a larger stretch of beach reached for more than one hundred yards. Here the plastic, shredded by the elements, fluttered noisily in the breeze as it endured the inevitable decay. Here also were moldy shoes, boots, sneakers, jockey shorts, boxers, panties, bras, plastic water bottles, one pants leg of a pair of jeans, children's shorts, a tattered woman's purple skirt, more unmatched shoes and sneakers, and a gimme cap faded to dirty gray. Farther up the trail that led from Cavazos Beach to the drag road, green garbage bags hung from the limbs of huisache and covered the trunks of the mesquite and a lone sabal palm.

"What they do," said Plovic unasked, "is they float over from the other side on all those tire tubes or, if they're very lucky, a small wooden boat. They stuff everything they own into the garbage bags. They are in a big hurry and they can't see what they are doing. They left all this stuff behind. We find billfolds and purses and IDs. These empty bottles they use for floats if they can't find a tube. They tie a bunch of them together and that gives them just enough flota-tion to cross over."

Agent Plovic dug his heel into a woman's purse at the base of a paloverde. Inside he found a photo ID and an address book with phone numbers. The smiling, posed photo identified a certain woman from El Salvador in her early twenties with long hair combed to one side.

All Along the Watchtower

"They come from everywhere," offered Plovic. "The public thinks it's just Mexicans, but it could be anyone. Remember that group of Bosnians we caught four months back?" he asked Maria.

Maria turned back to nod. "Yeah," she said, "we thought they were from Guatemala or were maybe Iranians. Then they turn out to be from Bosnia. Fifteen of them."

"Nothing new here," Plovic concluded after spending little time searching for new sign. "You should have seen the face on that guy from Washington when we brought him here. He freaked out. Told us he'd never seen anything like it in all his years along the Mexican border. He came back with a video camera, and they made a movie for INS. Later we got three new boats. Three boats for this whole section of the river. I guess it's better than just one boat. But we've been short of manpower, and most of the time at least one of the new boats just sits there. Or they're getting repaired. The way our system works, the boats are getting repaired a lot of the time."

The day warmed. Back at the McAllen Station only the supes and the staff, including the secretaries, radio dispatchers, and janitors, occupied the rooms. It was a slow January. Usually by now the undocumented workers were returning to their jobs on the north side of the river after a month-long break at Christmas. FOS Jose Monteverde sat staring at the pile of paperwork on his metal desk by the back door to the station. He put his coffee cup down for a moment, pushed the day schedules around on his desk, then tried not to think about what was really bugging him. One of his duties when he left the checkpoint at Falfurrias, eighty miles north of McAllen on Highway 281, was to teach ethics training, an annual requirement of all agents. Every agent got eight hours of the do's and don'ts of the U.S. Border Patrol as interpreted by Jose Monteverde, a tough-as-nails former supe and agent who disallowed moral ambiguities.

Jose Monteverde would not, therefore, have approved of the way agents Rochester, Plovic, and Contreras were discussing illegal immigrants and drugs as they cruised the Rio Grande. Jose Monteverde contended that there was the Border Patrol's way of doing things and there was the wrong way. The color gray did not exist. As the embodiment of the law who spoke not only for the McAllen Station but the entire sector, Jose Monteverde simply did not tolerate those who broke the rules.

It was to be expected, then, that the case of Agent Wayne Thornton, set to go to trial in less than one month, was eating at him. A witness called by the prosecution, FOS Jose Monteverde would tell the truth on the stand as he knew it. He just wished that someone else had been on duty when the incident had occurred. If only Wayne had managed to keep his anger to himself. Everyone at the station had known that the man had a big temper and that he might eventually explode. Guys like him always lost it sooner or later. As far as Jose Monteverde was concerned, Wayne Thornton had sealed his fate by striking the old man a second time. The second time was inexcusable and before a judge and jury indefensible. One shot could be attributed to the stress of the situation. A judge and a jury would say, "Well, we don't like it that he hit this old man, but we can maybe give him the benefit of the doubt. After all, the man is an employee of a federal law enforcement agency just doing his job in a dangerous situation." They would cut him loose, the Valley newspapers would kill the story, and in a short time it would all be forgotten. But not a second shot to the head. And certainly not a third. Not with the weight of Thornton's heavy Mag flashlight against an old man's fragile skull. At that point the average citizen smelled brutality. If only it had been some other field operation supervisor on the shift, Jose would have been spared the public testimony against one of his own. He hated doing it but had no choice. Management would understand his dilemma and so would most of the other agents in the field. They would say, "Monteverde did what he had to do" and leave it at that.

FOS Jose Monteverde would not have liked my observing what transpired an hour later on the Rio Grande. It brought up questions best left unasked. A young M&M, a Mexican soldier, clearly identifiable by his uniform and standard-issue rifle, was surprised by Agents Rochester, Plovic, and Contreras as they rounded a bend. Filling his canteen with river water, the soldier was crouching at the bank when the agents flew by in the BayMaster. The Mexican soldier had his orders from his sergeant not to be seen, let alone photographed, by the U.S. Border Patrol. Only after the BayMaster zoomed by the exact spot where he sat on his heels did he rise. He was no older than sixteen with eyes wide in shock. Agent Rochester never had a chance to catch him with his camera, the soldier visible for just a fraction of a second, then nothing but a blur as he dived into a nearby bush. No instant replay in the reality of this moment. Instead there was the clear image on the retina reminiscent of an old Marx

Brothers movie in which Harpo or Groucho, to avoid detection by a jealous matron's husband, leaped squarely into a hedge.

The agents laughed at the sight.

Rochester, perhaps remembering one of Jose Monteverde's rules from the ethics workshop then said in an offhanded manner, "I could tell you some stories that would freak you out." But instead of saying more, he stared off into the distance. Plovic and Maria, following Rochester's lead, remained silent.

Then Rochester seemingly forgot all about FOS Jose Monteverde and his moral legalisms.

"You tell me," proposed Rochester, "what the heck is the Mexican army doing out here in the middle of nowhere? What are they guarding? You tell me. What could they have to do out here on the river?"

"I seen 'em everywhere in their Hummers with their .50-caliber machine guns," he continued, talking more to himself than anyone. "We see them all the time. Am I right?" he said in Plovic's direction.

"Yes, sir," said Plovic, not missing a beat. As quickly as it had been raised the topic was dropped.

The hours passed slowly as the BayMaster and its crew patrolled the waters of the Rio Grande. The sun climbed in the broad sky, and the temperature peaked at sixty-eight degrees. The birders' boat ride had long since ended, and soon they would be lunching at Luby's, Furr's, the Golden Corral, or the twenty-five Chinese restaurants in McAllen offering low-priced buffets to snowbirds.

When Agent Steve Plovic could tolerate Agent Maria Contreras's inattention no longer, he had tickled her ear with a leafy twig. Maria, believing the annoyance to be an insect, absent-mindedly brushed it aside. Steve persisted. When she turned the second time to give Plovic a piercing look, he posed as the innocent and hid the evidence behind his back. Agent Rochester, observing this play between two second graders, chuckled to himself but kept his eyes tuned to the open waters before him. Having dug himself a hole, Steve Plovic could not quietly retreat without a third attempt. Maria grabbed the twig in one quick motion, twisting it and tossing it over the railing into the river.

Now full in the sky, the sun shone flatly on the multicolored chemical sheen that rode atop the stratified layers of slow current. The energy from the sun heated up the sludge that was a part of the river's integral core and that lined the riverbanks on both sides. The stench rose into the air along the twisting river, an undeniable blend of postmodern millennial chemistry, old world rotting river jetsam, and excrement.[5]

With one eye on a Ford Fairlane on the Mexican side of the river, Agent Rochester slowly approached the concrete boat ramp at Anzalduas Park as their shift ended. Along with Crown Vics, Ford Fairlanes with their large trunks and spacious rear seats were drug smugglers' vehicle of choice. Nine young men stood passing the time around the car's open trunk. The men, no poles or bait buckets in sight, did not seem interested in fishing. They began to laugh theatrically when they spotted the patrol boat and realized they were being watched through binoculars. Then their laughter turned to strings of obscenities shouted in the direction of the patrol boat.

Studiously avoiding Agent Rochester's gaze, two of their colleagues sat in a small aluminum boat twenty feet from the Mexican shore smoking cigarettes in an exaggerated fashion. As soon as one cigarette was finished, another was lit. The two men also did not carry any fishing equipment with them.

"They look guilty as sin," said Rochester, "but it's hard to say what's going down." Then he observed four teenagers on a bench not far from the boat ramp. The teenagers were also smoking. Three guys and a young girl. Agent Rochester, like most cops, never believed in coincidences.

"Gang bangers," said Rochester.

The Mexicans on the banks of the Río Bravo continued to shout, point, and laugh at the agents, but they seemed to be getting tired of the ruse. Finally they stopped, turned their backs to the Río Bravo as if it did not exist, and began the waiting game.

"Can't arrest them for laughing at us," said Rochester. "Especially not when they are on the other side of the river. Any idiot can see they're going to commit a criminal act. Probably with those teenagers over there. But at this exact moment no laws are being broken. They'll wait until we leave, then do what they're going to do. I'd guess, just from looking it over, they are getting ready to bring someone across. Maybe a friend of those gang bangers. Or maybe it's a small load. Hard to tell. For sure they're not here to fish."

Agents Plovic and Contreras jumped off the boat onto the concrete dock and went for the boat trailer parked in the space reserved for the Border Patrol. Two older couples who could have easily fit in with the crowd of snowbirds earlier touring the river strolled arm and arm along the asphalt road that wove its way through Anzalduas Park. Smells from the barbecue pits of fajitas, hamburgers, and charcoal wafted lazily in the air. No one on the north side of the Rio Grande, with the exception of the chain-smoking teenagers, seemed to care the slightest about the activity on *el otro lado,* as if what took place across a fifty-yard expanse of ambulating water could have no possible meaning, value, or significance in the lives of those in Anzalduas Park.

While Agents Plovic and Contreras maneuvered the BayMaster onto the trailer, Rochester checked out the teenagers.

"They seemed okay," he said, swaggering back to the boat. A big, beefy man with a thin moustache and a shaved head like Plovic's, Rochester at thirty-five was still intent on proving himself to the supe. "Could be just a coincidence." he said, not believing it. After a ceremony in body language demonstrating maximum indifference to their surroundings, the four teens climbed into their Camaro and punctuated their exit by laying down a track of rubber on the asphalt.

"I'd say it's drugs," pronounced Rochester with some finality. "But it isn't going to happen until we leave."

Plovic and Contreras yanked the BayMaster out of the Rio Grande, lashed it to the trailer, then secured the gear for the ride back to the McAllen Station. Behind them, as they slowly motored away, they left thousands of garbage bags rotting at Cavazos Beach. Tonight, new immigrants crossing the Rio Grande would add their personal contribution to the ever-growing dump.

On a low bluff a quarter of a mile downriver from Cavazos Beach four M&Ms knelt on one knee to survey the river that lay before them. Rochester had pointed them out with a slight nod of his head as the BayMaster swept past their position, the M&Ms believing they had gone undetected. When the BayMaster had cleared the next bend in the Rio Grande, the M&Ms returned to their work at hand. Just like the nine men by the Ford Fairlane across from Anzalduas Park, once the Border Patrol's boat was a distant sound the M&Ms did what they were going to do.

Back at the McAllen Station the three agents, after picking up Maria's vehicle along the way, meticulously washed the boat, stored the life vests and the other special gear in one of the Quonset huts behind the parking lot at the south end of the station, then entered through the hallway that ran directly by the office of FOS Jose Monteverde. Jose paid them little attention, but when he did look up, he frowned at the thought of agents patrolling the line by boat. There were too many ways agents could get into big trouble on the river, too many ways that did not, might not, fit into the antiseptic legal categories of right and wrong. Although Jose, along with upper management, believed the boats provided a legitimate deterrence to aliens and drugs, he did not believe that the exposure of agents could be logically justified. Only a few days before, someone had strung a line of one-inch steel fish hooks across the river from the south bank and then tied it off around a tree on the north bank. Head-high over the river, the hooks could seriously wound or even kill unsuspecting agents onboard as they responded to a sensor or spotted illegal aliens. They had taken photos of the lethal rig before they cut down the line, and then dutifully sent the photographs, along with the appropriate forms, up the chain of command.

Jose had long since worked through the female agent issue and did not pay special attention to Agent Maria Contreras. He had come to terms with it, which was not easy for a man of his generation and training. He did not like it, but that was the new way, the accepted way. It was the law. Maria was, in his opinion, no better or worse than male agents and as long as she did her job, there was no problem. The law was the law. But like most male agents at the McAllen Station he worried about what might happen if Maria or any other female agent were placed in a high-risk situation. Could Agent Maria Contreras be counted on, law or no law, when her life and the lives of other agents were at stake?

If only all the agents at the McAllen Station, both female and male, were like Noe Escondido. Noe was one hell of an agent. Old School. Did his job and knew his place. At a party the week before FOS Jose Monteverde, with his wife by his side, had once again admired how Noe handled himself. The man had class. Flooded with contentment as he sat in his plastic lawn chair after digesting a plate full of beef fajitas, corn tortillas, refried beans, and pico de gallo, all prepared and cooked just the way he liked them, Jose looked up just in time to see Noe Escondido make one of his patented grand entrances. Agents, spouses, girlfriends, and boyfriends were eating first-class South Texas barbecue and drinking beer by the pool at FOS Quiones's new home in Mission. Nice house on a full acre of land with water rights so the grass was green as a Christmas tree in spite of the drought. Jose was wondering how Quiones could afford that kind of house—the rumor was that his brother-in-law was a home builder and cut him a sweet deal—when Noe made his entrance. As Noe ambled down the cement sidewalk of Quiones's lush St. Augustine backyard, all the other agents looked up from their conversations and smiled broadly with respect that money could not buy. Noe, taking it all in, shook each hand as he warmly greeted his bros.

Yes, sir, he was one hell of an agent. If only they were all like Noe Escondido.

Noe Escondido

At first I was worried about what my father would think when I joined the Border Patrol. Him being from Mexico." Noe Escondido adjusted the brim of his straw hat, climbed in his unit, then thought back to the days when he was one of eleven scrawny kids who traveled every summer with their parents to pick vegetables in the fields of southern Colorado. Noe's family worked the northern crops during the hottest months of the year, then each fall and spring picked Valley tomatoes, carrots, cabbage, lettuce, and spinach.

Because he had to help support his family Noe, like many other migrant kids, could not and did not spend much time in the classroom. He managed to graduate from high school, but it never entered his mind to continue his formal education. It was his duty to work with his family and, when the time came, start his own.

Noe's father was born and raised in Mexico. During World War II he crossed the Río Bravo as a bracero in the Bracero Program.[1] Like many former citizens of Mexico who were now American citizens, Noe's father despised the Border Patrol. In the "old days," as a handful of the agents at the McAllen Station remembered because either they had been there or had worked with other agents who had experienced them, some agents would as soon beat undocumented workers on the head as look at them. Some agents then boasted about the aliens they had humiliated. But those were the "old days." All the agents at the McAllen Station agreed that those days were long gone. Also gone were the kinds of agents and culture that permitted if not encouraged the abuse of undocumented workers.

Mexicans and Mexican Americans in the Valley who suffered at the hands of agents of the U.S. Border Patrol, however, did not forget what they had endured.[2] They could not ignore the history. Many Hispanic residents of McAllen neither trusted nor respected the Border Patrol and never would. In their opinion the Border Patrol had not changed one iota from the 1940s. So when Noe first signed up for a career in the Border Patrol, he was not sure how his father would react. Would he disown Noe or celebrate him?

"My father told me, 'Being in the Border Patrol is a federal job that is reliable. Something you can raise a family on. It's nothing to be ashamed of.' So after that I knew my father approved of what I did for a living." Because Noe was a member of the Border Patrol, his own family would never have to migrate to find work in the fields. No shanty towns, or living out of the back of a pickup, or exposure to pesticides, or dealings with exploitative growers who refused to pay after he had finished harvesting their crops.[3]

Although Noe's father and the rest of his family saw nothing wrong with Noe's wearing the uniform of the U.S. Border Patrol, others in McAllen and the surrounding Valley communities shunned him. Cops and other agents of law enforcement were clannish anyway, prone to hang with their own. However, in the Valley at times the agents of the Border Patrol were even more socially isolated from their community, including their next-door neighbors, because of a disdain bordering on hatred. Agents and their families had to endure snubbing and dirty looks. Ironically most agents considered the Valley an excellent posting, because they had been treated much worse in other places in Texas, New Mexico, Arizona, and California. At least in McAllen *some* members of the public respected the Border Patrol and treated its agents well. Often in border communities the majority of residents regarded them as hired scum.

Noe did not start out as an agent. First he worked for the McAllen Police Department in 1984, only a few years after the notorious C Shift, the graveyard shift, had made national news by systematically brutalizing suspects who were poor Mexican Americans. The scandal led to the dismantling of the force, then the careful reconstruction of the entire police department. Just after the dust from the criminal indictments and the civil lawsuits finally settled Noe, fresh out of high school and a tour of military duty, submitted his application.[4]

"What did I know?" he said. "I should have researched them and the Border Patrol too." Noe not only had not heard about the notorious C Shift when he joined the McAllen PD, but he also was misinformed about the minimum requirements to qualify for the Border Patrol. He thought that he had to work with a law enforcement agency a minimum of three years before applying. After a year in the McAllen PD, he learned from a buddy that the three-year requirement for the Border Patrol was bad intel. He immediately signed up.

Noe never regretted his decision. In his fourteenth year, Noe was hands down the best agent in the McAllen Station. Others like Supe Mira came close, but Noe Escondido was The Man.

"What I like doing is thinking how they think. You think like them, then figure out what they're going to do. You have to analyze a particular place, then walk out the trails to find out where they lead. You got to think. It's not about running around in the dark chasing shadows." Or it should not be, not if agents watched Noe in action.

Noe had volunteered for sensor duty in January 2000 and was only now, a year later, returning to line watch. He would never have volunteered for sensor duty if the sensors had not been in such poor shape. Sensor duty meant digging holes under a hot sun, clearing brush, and then tinkering with delicate mechanisms. All on a shoestring budget. For Noe sensor duty was much more, both a craft and an intellectual exercise that called upon his years of experience chasing undocumented workers and drug smugglers.

"I'll tell you how bad a shape we were in with the sensors. The paperwork had not been getting done on the sensors so we didn't even know where some of them were! They were lost. It all happened when a certain agent took over. He dropped the ball. That's what he did. It took me and some other agents almost a year, but I can tell you honestly that the system is working again at this time, and it's working good."[5]

The entire U.S.-Mexican border was planted with electronic sensors from Brownsville to San Diego. All along the Rio Grande in Deep South Texas, McAllen Station agents had placed sensors at popular landings, trailheads, anywhere and everywhere that illegal aliens and drug smugglers congregated. The sensors sounded an alarm, the dispatcher radioed the news to the agents, and the agents nabbed the perps. That, at least in theory, was the way the sensor system was supposed to work.

In practice there were problems. Even when the sensors were finally back in full service, the biggest flaw in the system involved the way in which agents responded to a hit. Noe made it his life work to teach and train agents what to do when the sensors sounded the alarm. It was an uphill battle.

"I'd have to say," Noe confided as he drove west along Old Military Highway, "that the new guys from the academy drive me nuts when it comes to the sensors. They don't get it." Noe braked to a stop, spread his hands, palms up, then shrugged his narrow shoulders. He was not a big man, and many other agents cut a finer figure in uniform. At thirty-eight Noe sported a jaunty mustache underneath a sunburned visage; a small potbelly stretched the creases in his ironed shirt. He was a short, nondescript man with a large head.

Many of the newer agents did not understand that by the time the dispatcher recorded a hit on the sensor five or more minutes had passed. The time delay was the result of dispatchers who had multiple responsibilities: they relayed messages, checked for stolen autos on the state system, monitored other law enforcement agencies, and were responsible for a number of other duties, all of them time-consuming.

Noe often lectured those smart enough to listen to him that whoever set off the sensor was not going to wait patiently for agents of the U.S. Border Patrol to make an appearance. Whether a group of honest undocumented workers headed for Dallas or a mule carrying eighty pounds of cocaine on his back, they would hide, run, dodge, and deceive to avoid arrest. Therefore the most difficult dilemma for any agent was to analyze which way they would head. Where will they be after the dispatcher reports the hit?

Once workers or smugglers eluded the Border Patrol outside of the zone of apprehension, approximately one mile distant from the banks of the Rio Grande, they were virtually free to roam anywhere in the United States. The policy of the McAllen Station, preached constantly by the supes at muster, was not to pursue or apprehend anyone who walked, ran, crawled, or was carried more than a few hundred yards north of Old Military Highway. *Them's the rules, like it or not.* Most of the agents of course hated the rules but still followed station policy. The checkpoints at Falfurrias and Sarita functioned as the Border Patrol's last effort at stopping illegals or contraband.

Year after year Noe taught agents how to outguess the nighttime shadows and daytime ghosts. Noe found it idiotically simple: determine the destination of those in flight, arrive before they do, then select a position to give them a big surprise when they walk into the trap. According to Noe's bible, if agents worked it right the illegals would walk close enough to smell their breath. Then all the agents had to do was corral them before leading them in single file toward the waiting transport. Alternative strategies—and Noe had seen them all—led to the same result: the illegal aliens panicked, fled into the brush, and were difficult if not impossible to catch again.

However, many new recruits proved unteachable; they already knew it all. They rushed the sensor as soon as the hit was announced, then scratched their heads after twenty minutes of waiting for Godot.

"I tell them a thousand times, 'Go to where the illegals are going, not where they've been.' But they don't get it. Then they ask me after a shift how come I apprehended five times what they caught. *Chingalo,*" Noe said, shaking his head slowly and a little sadly.

Like the agents themselves, some illegal aliens and smugglers were smart; some, dumb; and the rest, average. The dumb ones stomped on the sensors, then spent too much time changing into their dry clothes. Even the slowest agent, new recruit or old timer, nabbed these workers. The most inadequate of agents, all things being equal, got some apprehensions on any given shift. Add luck to the mix and maybe a new recruit on one shift might come near to matching Noe's body count. But Noe consistently apprehended workers and smugglers like no one else on duty. Except maybe Supe Mira who had recently been slowed down because he was management.

Noe Escondido was king along this stretch of the Rio Grande because he knew that the *coyotes* who led groups of undocumented workers, as well as the aliens who were without a guide, followed various favorite trails through the rough and diverse terrain. He had to keep on top of those trails and know when they abandoned one for another. Noe learned their habits from sign cutting, then used his knowledge against them.

"You watch them carefully," he said in a classroom voice. "You have to be willing to cut sign." The new recruits and many of the experienced agents were frequently unwilling to learn and practice the craft of sign cutting.

"140 has seven hits," came the dispatcher's voice. The sensor, less than two miles from Noe's position on Old Military Highway on the west side of the Reynosa Bridge, was a popular landing for illegal workers.

All Along the Watchtower

"Okay," said Noe, again lecturing as if he were at the academy, "This is what's going to happen. That traffic is always good. They hit the sensor, and they come out near Stewart Road not far from the highway. I've cut that sign a hundred times. There is only one way this is going to go down."

Noe called for backup, then headed for Stewart Road. Parking his vehicle in the evening shadows along the side of a dirt path, he reached for the machete that he always kept by his left foot. The grass trail was narrow and worn, first leading along a four-strand wire fence, then taking a turn around an impenetrable cluster of prickly pear. Noe hurled himself down the trail at full throttle and did not stop until two hundred yards farther he eyeballed a small, abandoned stock shed, its raw wood rotting slowly. A rusty metal roof covered a three-sided enclosure meant to provide shelter for cattle long since slaughtered at market. Pieces of metal roofing lay scattered on the ground, short tufts of buffalo grass, horse cripplers, and other vines and vegetation slowly engulfing them.

It rained for two days during the third week of February. Moisture in the Valley was always a scarcity. The previous year less than seventeen inches of rain had fallen on Hidalgo County and this year had started no better. Desert plants thrived from the sudden downpours as they added awkward new growth. Sporting pods the color of fresh-cut green beans, the prickly pear readied their blooms in time for Lent.

Just a few feet from the cow shed out of place colors covered the ground where the horse cripplers, barrel cactus, and thorny vines thrived. Primary colors dominated the sandy loam infiltrated by fragments of seashells. Noe, reading the significance of the red and blue and yellow streaks like a road map, yelled in Spanish, "Get up! Let's get going. Come on. Get up." The colors stirred, became pants legs and shirts, then under Noe's commands gained height, weight, and true humanoid form. The undocumented workers formed, with no hesitation, a crude line in the middle of nowhere. Machete in his left hand, Noe led them silently back to the dirt road as he cleared a vine or a tree branch from the trail with a sharp stroke of his machete.

Noe always carried his machete with him. He used it, he admitted, to intimidate the illegal workers. Simple as that. They saw his machete and they knew, right away, not to mess with this agent in spite of his unimposing stature. The message, ten times more distinct than the Beretta on his hip, was communicated wordlessly from a second-generation American citizen to new but illegal immigrants.

Over the years they had followed Noe and his machete by the hundreds. By the thousands.

"You can't leave yourself open out here," Noe explained. "We've got a lot of critics but they don't get it. If you get jumped out here, what are you going to do? Call 911? By the time another agent gets to you, you got a lump on your head or worse. And the illegals are swimming back across the river."

Noe recognized that the majority of undocumented workers were honest men and women. Fourteen years as an agent had taught him that they were generally not thinking about ways to kill him. They wanted jobs. But Noe had also processed hardened criminals with crude prison tats oozing up the backs of their necks. Not many—but enough to remind him that only foolish agents would drop their guard. All it would take would be one bad decision to make his wife a widow and leave his kids without a father. Reasonable agents had to make reasonable choices along the Rio Grande or face even greater risks than the job normally required.

After Noe and his line of four young undocumented workers met up with Noe's backup, two fellow agents, Noe once again drove back down the trail. He was positive that there were more of them when he heard through his earpiece that an agent working the river not far from the sensor spotted a group of possibly fifteen or more. Noe never found the others himself, but by thrashing around in the brush he helped drive five men and two women into the waiting arms of other agents positioned a few hundred yards north of his position.

That made eleven workers for his shift, but Noe was less than satisfied. For another half hour he tirelessly searched the surrounding area before finally calling it quits.

"I hate to lose," he said as he climbed back into his truck. "Man, I just hate to lose. Drives me nuts. Maybe the rest of them doubled back. Or maybe the agent counted them wrong by the river."

The academy did not teach sign cutting. Agents who wanted to learn how to cut sign had to study how Noe or one of the other older agents did it. It was a matter of practice, effort, and hard work. All things that the best agents considered requirements of the job.

Noe was so old school that he preferred regular binocs over NVGs. Noe also favored narrow-brim cowboy hats over the more popular gimme caps, black cowboy boots to Thinsulate footwear, and chewing tobacco to nicotine patches.

Transport took its time as Noe and two other agents waited with the eleven illegal workers under an old mesquite tree on Stewart Road. In the dusk drivers stopped to rubberneck, then sped up when one of the agents waved his hand in their direction. Noe, who always liked talking with the men and women he captured, was accustomed to asking them where they were headed and what kind of work they hoped to find. Searching for clues in their responses, he filed the info away for another day.

"All I am now," said one man about fifty years of age in slow, precise Spanish, "is tired. I just want to sleep." He confessed to Noe that he was headed for a job in Houston when fate led him down the wrong trail. Exhausted from the chase, dirty and still soaking wet from crossing the Río Bravo, he had hit rock bottom. He knew how the system worked. All he wanted to do was get VRed back to Reynosa.

Two young women in their twenties, equally fatigued, huddled in silence a few feet from the other men. Eyes on the ground, they sat on the freshly mowed grass just off the shoulder of the road and wished that they were somewhere else. In another few moments three of the men fell into a deep slumber. Another man asked for water.

A Border Patrol agent turned ballistic. "Why should I give him water?" he asked. "That guy spends all this time running around in the brush while we're chasing him, then he has the balls to ask for water? I don't have any water, and if I did he's the last guy in the world that would get it." Reining in his anger, he told the man in Spanish that he would have to wait for a drink until they returned to the station.

But the agent was not through grumbling at the injustice of it. "Does he think I'm his babysitter? Can you believe these guys?"

Transport finally appeared as two headlights far down the straight and narrow stretch of pavement and potholes. Noe, searching for some levity to lighten the immigrant's load, joked to the undocumented worker headed for Houston, "Here comes the bus for Houston."

But the man was far past laughing at his own misery. In perfect English he said, as he slowly climbed into the van, "Fuck Houston."

Noe nodded in agreement then returned to the problem he had been mulling as he waited for transport. What if four more illegals were still out there? Four more illegal immigrants who had eluded his search and were hunkered down waiting for total darkness or a shift change or the honk of a car horn before they made their move. Even though another agent had retraced the trail left by the immigrants from the riverbank where they had landed, Noe decided to take another shot at it.

Atop the levee in his Tahoe on his way to the trailhead, he spotted an adult male walking across the manmade flood plain that lay between the Rio Grande and the forest of brush where the first group of illegals had been captured.

The man saw Noe's Border Patrol vehicle and began flailing his arms wildly. The new immigrant wanted to be noticed and apprehended to save himself the trouble of recrossing the tricky Río Bravo. Noe radioed Agents Wilson and Cooler, who soon escorted the man into the rear cage of their vehicle. He was so glad to see the U.S. Border Patrol that he did not stop talking to them the entire time they were searching him. The illegal immigrant wanted sympathy and affirmation from the same men who had hunted down his friends. The agents could not give it. To them he was just another apprehension, another statistic.

Wilson and Cooler released the man from the cage when Noe decided to talk to him. The two agents stood off to the side of their truck smoking cigarettes as Noc spoke with the man. Still out of breath from his earlier flight from the border agents, wiping the sweat from his brow with the sleeve of his shirt, he immediately showed interest in Noe's machete. He talked freely in Spanish about what constituted a good machete. "*El machete de mi abuelo, el papa de mi papa . . .*" he began, the machete of my grandfather, the father of my father. That machete without doubt, he told Noe, was the most beautiful machete he had ever seen.

Noe was having none of this attempt at one-upmanship played out atop a dirt and gravel levee on a February night. "No," he told the man, "that one wasn't the best. I have a machete that my uncle gave me. It has a pearl handle. It's all steel. *Puro.* It's a work of art sharper than any other machete ever made. The best."

The man, with all due respect, did not agree. He had seen others that could cut through hard metal as easily as a knife through cake. Noe expressed disbelief. Huge white clouds appeared from nowhere as a half moon rose in the sky. The light of the half moon gave the mosquitoes sight; the two men and the other two agents swatted against the onslaught on their necks and backs.

Finally Noe turned to the two other agents, Wilson and Cooler, and announced that more illegals remained in the brush. Noe pointed with his machete toward the tree line that bordered the levee just south of them.

Another half mile down the levee Noe stopped in front of Border Patrol Agent Tom Clark. Clark stood leaning against the driver's side door smoking a filtered cigarette as he listened to his favorite country station. Humming along with a tune, he tipped his hat at Noe.

"How many we got?" he asked Noe between songs.

"Eleven, plus four, plus that fat guy I spotted. So sixteen."

After grabbing his machete, Noe slid down the embankment and easily, born of years of experience, crossed over the barbed-wire fence. Agent Clark, sitting on the levee still smoking, nodded again as Noe disappeared into a twenty-acre tract of woods directly bordering the Rio Grande. The last thing Noe heard was a taunt about his growing waistline.

"Hey, bro, you oughta go easy on them enchiladas and tacos."

The illegal aliens, all lying flat against the ground, were just ten feet inside the fence. They were not asleep, but their faces were turned down so they would not see Noe as he approached. They hoped beyond hope that since they could not see Noe, then he could not, would not, see them. Hearing Noe sear off the limb of a nearby ebony tree with his machete, the four young men rose to their feet without a word to form a line behind the agent.

"Well, what do you know about that," said Agent Tom Clark as the short parade emerged from the woods. It was not lost on Agent Clark that while he had been smoking cigarettes to his favorite tunes, four illegal workers hid under his very nose. Noe called for transport over his radio while Agent Clark searched each man before placing him in the back of his Tahoe, one of the last in the motor pool.

Already past dinnertime, Noe was arranging a meeting with two other agents at the local Burger King when the dispatcher dropped a bombshell. Just a few brief words, but every on-duty Border Patrol agent within listening distance gave the communication their undivided attention.

"Possible 10-46 at Pepe's. Dark blue van."

A 10-46 was law enforcement talk for illegal drugs. Pepe's Riverside Fiesta Club was a popular bar and dance hangout south of Mission where smugglers liked to off-load shipments of drugs at the dock adjacent to the large parking lot. They sped up to the dock in an eye-popping power boat, off-loaded the bales of marijuana into a truck, van, Crown Vic, or LTD, then the driver drove like a bat out of hell toward Old Military Highway. Because a number of county roads led northward from there, smugglers making it that far could start counting their profits. Or they could hide the bales in a nearby safe house. The smugglers knew that once the Border Patrol had chased them as far as Old Military Highway, agents were required to end their pursuit and call the local police department or other law enforcement including the troopers of the Texas Department of Public Safety. Frequently the chase ended with the drug smugglers' escape because local law enforcement showed up too late.

His ears still ringing after two-stepping the night away to oldies like Hank Williams's "Your Cheating Heart," an old man from Iowa, who was just another snowbird killing time at Pepe's Riverside Fiesta Club, was climbing into his car when he had seen the boat zoom up to the dock. Four men tossed the bales into the back of the dark blue van. The whole thing took less than thirty seconds. The old man went back inside Pepe's to make the call from the pay phone. Info from snowbirds—unlike that from many other sources—was as reliable as their pacemakers.

No Border Patrol units were at the scene, but every unit within a radius of ten miles headed for Pepe's Riverside Fiesta Club. Agent Charlie Ashton just happened to be at the right place at the right time.

"I got a dark blue van coming this way," he radioed within sixty seconds of the dispatcher's call. Then, "I got him," unmistakable excitement in the voice of a former campus cop. Within three short years Agent Ashton had established a reputation as one of the most gung ho agents at the McAllen Station. As he gripped the wheel of his Expedition against the jolt of adrenaline, he found himself shouting through the ether, "They spotted me! They definitely spotted me!" The dark blue van, to no one's surprise, headed due north toward Old Military Highway with Charlie Ashton, driving without a partner, hanging loose behind the van's rear bumper.

Noe knew all the risks. "Fall back," he advised Charlie. "Give them plenty of room."

"I'm falling back. They have all the room in the world," Charlie responded, sounding a little hurt. He was a professional and wanted to be treated as such. Especially by someone he respected as much as Noe Escondido.

Like an NFL quarterback setting up the big play with the score tied in the fourth quarter, Noe directed units to take up different positions. He sealed off all the escape routes, then asked a question everyone had failed to consider.

"Has anybody checked for a second van?" No one answered. "One of you guys needs to check the parking lot at Pepe's for a second load." Finally, after sixty seconds of dead air, a unit responded that it was en route.

Charlie came back on. "Oh, boy. This guy is mixed up. He can't make up his mind where the fuck he's going. I'm giving him plenty of room. If he wants to bail, he's got all the room in the world."

Charlie, as well as every other agent who patrolled the line in Deep South Texas, had memorized their chief's pursuit policy. With all the supes huddled in the ops room back at the McAllen Station listening to his every utterance, Charlie bore no illusions about what they expected of him. To avoid endangering the taxpaying public, not to mention the possibilities of impending lawsuits from said public, agents were never allowed to stop a vehicle being pursued. At no time were agents encouraged to erect roadblocks, shoot out tires, or place sharpened nails or other obstructions in the vehicle's path. Their strict orders were to follow the load until it reached a few blocks past Old Military Highway, at which time other law enforcement agencies were empowered to give chase. The problem, from the point of view of the Border Patrol, was that these same agencies then took credit for the bust even though they were not involved in the original surveillance, providing the intel, or other basic police work.

Most often the pursuit led directly to a "bailout." After the Border Patrol had blocked all paths of escape, the smugglers slowed to twenty-five miles an hour or less, then exited the car—jumped out of a moving vehicle. Then they ran like hell for the Río Bravo. Sometimes they drove their trucks, vans, or cars *into* the Rio Grande. The agents, not unreasonably, called them "bailouts" if they occurred on land and "river divers" if the vehicle ended up immersed in the Rio Grande.

Noe caught his first sight of Charlie as he rounded a curve in Old Military Highway at ninety miles per hour, braked hard, then once again pounded the accelerator. Noe also saw the van make a sloppy U to double back toward the river just as Charlie, his voice a notch above shrill, radioed, "He's heading south again. He's heading back for Pepe's."

Noe backed off from the chase as he instinctively swung his Tahoe around to block the blue van from reaching the Rio Grande. He worried that the panicked and desperate smuggler was going to become a river diver. It had happened too many times. In the Hollywood version the driver and vehicle careen off a scenic cliff in slow-mo, the driver escaping to live another day after smacking into the water. River diving in Deep South Texas was not the work of Hollywood stunt drivers but real human beings who could maim or kill themselves or anyone unlucky enough to get in their way.

Sitting behind the wheel of the van was a young Hispanic male high on alcohol, weed, or cocaine. Or maybe crank (methamphetamine), which was becoming ever more popular because it was so cheap. This was not Hollywood.

"Give him room," Noe cautioned once more.

"Affirmative. He's got plenty of room. I'm just begging him to bail out. He doesn't know what the shit he wants to do."

Cut off from the Río Bravo, surrounded by U.S. Border Patrol units with their racks of lights ablaze in the night, the driver bailed out in an empty cotton field near Harper's Farm. Within seconds five units besides Charlie Ashton were on the scene. By the time Noe pulled up behind his unit, Charlie was already counting the bales in the rear of the van. Noe directed four new recruits to track down the driver, then joined Charlie at the rear of the dark blue van. The new agents, as they made their way to the banks of the river, sank to their calves in the freshly tilled, black delta soil. A blind man could have followed the sign, but walking through this field was about as easy as snowshoeing across the parking lot of McAllen's La Plaza Mall.

"Looks good," said Charlie. "Looks good." Sky-high, he was riding the adrenaline wave. This was what the Border Patrol was supposed to be all about, why he had signed up, endured the rigors of the academy, and moved his family to Deep South Texas from the known world of a Pennsylvania college town.

The driver's door was ajar. Noe glanced inside to check for weapons, gave further orders to secure the area, then turned to Charlie.

"You got the keys?" Charlie nodded. "Okay, that unit over there will follow you back to the station. Let's get out of here." It was Border Patrol policy never to leave an agent alone with a load. Even for a minute. Marijuana was valued by the Border Patrol at $800 a pound on the streets of McAllen; cocaine, $32,000.[6]

Charlie and the other agents who had participated in the pursuit took a few fast trophy pics at the rear of the van before they returned to the station with the drug load. The bales, stuffed quickly into the back of the van at the dock near Pepe's, were wrapped in clear plastic and bound with cheap twine. Back at McAllen Station Ashton would weigh each of the bales to the ounce on the scales next to the steel evidence locker, total the weight for all the bales, then spend the next two hours writing a detailed report. All through the process fellow agents who had heard the good news would shake Ashton's hand or pound him on the back.

As the camera's flash lit up the empty cotton field, the agents posed stiffly and sternly at the rear of the van. Agents at either end of the small group framed the photo cradling their M16s while Ashton, holding the place of honor at the center because he was the primary on the bust, looked as proud as any peacock. (Noe asked me to stand in with the others who had been involved in the pursuit.) These trophy shots, not unlike those taken of serious offshore fishermen onboard their Bertrams at South Padre Island, were of prime importance, visual proof to Charlie and his bros that they had indeed done some serious damage to the bad guys and had helped to stem the flow of illegal drugs into the United States. With this load of marijuana, a prize catch, agents scored a point for those who continued to fight the Drug War. At the same time, a drug bust looked good on their work records when they were evaluated annually by their supes. Charlie had his own scrapbook of pics lying on the coffee table back at his apartment.

In another five minutes the cotton field near Harper's Farm lay empty under the night stars, the pungent, overwhelming smell of a ton of marijuana crowding the air with its unmistakable aroma.

Noe knew from experience that the faster they got out of that field, the safer it was for all the agents.

"Agent Cooler and I got shot at two years ago. Guy with a rifle on the Mexican side of the river. We could hear the bullets coming in over our head. We're sitting ducks in this field. Not to mention that agent who was chasing a doper up near El Paso a few years back when the doper turned on him, pulls out a small-caliber handgun, and shoots him dead. They say the bullet went in just above his collarbone right where your vest doesn't protect you," he pointed to his collarbone, "then ricocheted off the bone into his heart."

They never found the bailout. One of the new agents who was chasing him hyperextended his right knee. They took the agent to the emergency room at Rio Grande Regional Hospital in Edinburg where he had to wait for seven hours before the doctors treated him. Charlie and another agent got solid looks at the driver who finally disappeared into the Río Bravo. Much older than the usual driver in his teens, the driver wore a big cowboy hat, long sideburns, and a bushy moustache. Their chances of running into him again were small, but they never knew.

Even if the new recruits had nabbed the bailout, Hidalgo and Cameron County district attorneys would not have taken the case to trial or pled it out. Because of a serious overload of drug cases in the Valley, DAs were reluctant to take on any new drug cases. Although possession of ten pounds of marijuana, or even much less, guaranteed a convicted offender jail time in most parts of the United States, Valley district attorneys turned up their noses at anything less than a suspect caught red-handed with at least a thousand pounds of grass or more depending on the particular court and its backlog of drug cases.

The case overload had become so catastrophic that a group of border district attorneys finally announced before the start of the New Year that they would no longer accept any drug cases until their court dockets were cleared of the backlog. As the DAs and judges pleaded in the local media for state and federal funds to staff additional courts, smugglers and *coyotes* knew that the chances of doing serious jail or prison time were remote.[7]

At about the same time that Charlie Ashton finished weighing bales of marijuana at the McAllen Station—the total came to 1,543 pounds—Noe returned to the drag road to track aliens. The street value, announced Charlie, who worked the calculator awkwardly, came to $1,227,200. It was a modest load by Valley standards and would not make the first section of the McAllen newspaper, if at all. Charlie Ashton luxuriated in the praise and admiration of other agents at the station. ("This is what makes the job worthwhile," he kept saying to those who listened.) Meanwhile, Noe huffed and puffed along a narrow trail.

Following the trail northward a few minutes later to the point where the new workers to the United States had scattered to avoid capture, Noe read the sign, then estimated that only one or two had escaped capture. Illegal immigrants who were observed but escaped apprehension by agents were called "gotaways." Noe knew that tonight two illegal immigrants at the most had managed to escape the best efforts of the U.S. Border Patrol.

"I hate losing those two gotaways," Noe said begrudgingly. "It happens. But I had me an okay shift. What was it now?" he said, although he knew the figures. "Sixteen illegals, no, it was seventeen, and a load of dope." Fifteen minutes later he fruitlessly chased two ghosts dressed in black across a grassy field in Anzalduas Park. The figures disappeared into the night. After searching for them for thirty more minutes, Noe finally gave up. Two more gotaways.

Noe was simply the best. The other agents told stories about Noe's ability to track sign even across rock and gravel terrain. One time Noe followed four undocumented workers for miles through land that carried no visible sign. Noe tracked the men to within ten feet of where they stood. "Well done," they told him in Spanish, betraying a respect few held for the Patrullas Fronterizas. "Well done."

Noe was the best damn tracker in Deep South Texas.

"I'd say I had myself an okay shift," Noe once more announced in the cab of his Border Patrol truck as the clock struck midnight. The gross understatement bounced around the small, confined space. Rebuking himself in silence was no longer an option. Something was eating at Noe, eating at him hard.

The Mole

The Rio Grande commenced as an insignificant stream in the San Juan Mountains of southern Colorado just a few miles from the Continental Divide before quickly cutting its way through massive mountain ranges, mesas, and desert. The cities of Albuquerque, El Paso, and Juárez staggered the mighty river, but it continued its journey through Deep South Texas before finally slouching into the warm and salty waters of the Gulf of Mexico.[1]

For the first time in recorded history, in the first week of February 2001, the waters of the Rio Grande fell short, forming moss-covered pools a few hundred yards from its mouth. Siphoned off by urban dwellers and farmers, slowed by a five-year regional drought, the mighty river was finally brought to its knees by hydrilla, a plant originally imported to Florida from Southern Asia as an aquarium decoration.[2] Hydrilla has no known predators in Deep South Texas, where it flourishes in a tropical climate with few frosts or freezes. The aggressive plant has fat green leaves, purple flowers, and long stalks that root on the river bottom and overwhelm the weakened river.

Cutting hydrilla into tiny pieces with a machete only helps it propagate, while resorting to chemicals poisons the water for humans, animals, and domestic crops.[3] The only proven way to rid the Rio Grande of the noxious weed is to yank it out by hand one plant at a time, an arduous, impossible task without thousands of workers and as many boats. Even then it is a race against time, a race to eliminate the plant in one section of the river before it over-comes another.[4]

The natural action of wind and wave drove sand and silt into the empty riverbed, further blocking the waters of the Rio Grande from reaching the Gulf of Mexico.[5] A bulldozer dug a small channel through the sandbar, but the channel quickly silted up again. Governmental agencies on both sides of the Rio Grande at first ignored the situation. A growing stretch of sand and sedi-ment now connected the two countries. Anyone could walk from one nation to the next in thirty seconds or less. In a half-hearted effort to provide some sem-blance of international security as well as normalcy, the Border Patrol erected a rickety four-foot fence made of webbed plastic and placed warning signs in strategic locations.

Forty miles upriver from this true anomaly, turkey vultures near Peñitas cast their shadows on the blackened sugar cane stubble that bordered the river-banks as a half moon, flaring burnt orange an inch above the horizon, rose regally in the broad South Texas sky. When stirred, the turkey vultures spread their wings to appear even more ominous, then returned to their gorging.

The Mole, at the west side of this field of cane, crouched on the back of his boot heels in an empty irrigation ditch. Paco hid behind a tree fifty yards down a dirt trail from the Mole while a new recruit, Agent Sandra Aldrete, buried herself in dense vegetation a hundred yards farther on. Agonizing over a piece of gear he had forgotten to toss into one of his duffel bags, Agent Shuman stood in the shadows a few yards distant from Agent Aldrete.

The four agents, Reynaldo Guerra, alias the Mole, Paco, Aldrete, and Shu-man, all stared with different degrees of patience and intent at the dirt path that passed along the irrigation ditch fronting the sugar cane field.

The sugar cane had been burned then harvested the night before using huge, rumbling machines resembling wheat combines. Long into that night and this the turkey vultures gorged on the carbonized remains of panicked rab-bits, birds, and other wild creatures caught in the maelstrom of fire set by the crew. A slow breeze from Mexico ruffled the tops of the stale winter grasses that bordered the field, and for a brief moment the tops of the ebony trees repeated a slow, melodic dirge.

Because field crews annually burned the sugar cane that provided choice cover and hiding places for undocumented workers and drug smugglers, the agents of the Border Patrol looked forward to February and early March.[6] Field after field was burned along the banks of the Rio Grande, forcing immigrants and smugglers to find new trails and escape routes along the tree lines, irrigation ditches, and other manmade cover. From the perspective of agents, the playing field was at least temporarily leveled when the cane was burned each year. The cane, in the meantime, soon began growing again from out of the havoc, a perennial crop requiring only irrigation to thrive in Deep South Texas.

No sane agent ever liked going into a sugar cane field after an illegal alien, not when the cane had grown seven to ten feet in height and might hide a few undocumented workers having lunch or a load of cocaine guarded by a band of heavily armed men. It was not worth the effort or the risk. The cane cut arms, necks, and faces—agents frequently emerged looking as if they had lost a cat-fight—and more than one agent at the McAllen Station had come very close to losing an eye. The cane shredded shirts and pants like a Veg-O-Matic, which was no laughing matter; uniforms were expensive.

In the cane it was dense, a claustrophobic cave filled with a jungle of plant matter in which there were infinite places to hide. Other minor irritants included the infestations of fleas, ticks, and poisonous spiders along with an occasional poisonous snake. But the biggest reason agents never volunteered to go after a suspect in a sugar cane field was the mind-boggling disorientation and confusion of searching for human beings in a hundred acres of ten-foot-tall sugar cane. Compass or no compass, night or day, hot or cold, most agents avoided the sugar cane like the plague.

"Shit," the Mole breathed as he crawled deeper into the ditch, his back gingerly pressing against the far bank. Fresh moonlight began to backlight his chunky figure, exposing him to anyone who walked along the path. The last thing in the world that the Mole wanted was to be visible to the naked eye or to NVGs like those cradled with care by Agent Shuman. He pressed harder against the bank of the ditch and partially disappeared into the shadows.

The other agents called Reynaldo Guerra the Mole because one midnight shift an agent working the scope truck not far from Miller's Farm was staring blankly at the screen, trying to ward off sleep, when he spied a relatively large thermal image working like crazy with a shovel. The agent downed another gulp of coffee from his Thermos, then reconsidered what he saw. After the frantic digging ceased, the creature had disappeared into the earth. The agent phoned his supe. Describing what he had witnessed, the supe checked the assignment chart for mids, then radioed the agent in the scope truck not to worry. It was just Reynaldo Guerra on surveillance for dopers. But that did not fool the agent. He knew what he had seen, and what he had seen was a giant mole tunneling into Valley clay.

The Mole, 250 pounds of mostly muscle, readjusted his feet beneath him, exhaled slowly, then whispered, "This is either going to happen in thirty minutes, or we are wasting our friggin' time."

It had been a long, frustrating shift for the Mole and the other agents at the McAllen Station. The trial of Border Patrol Agent Wayne Thornton was in its sixth day, and the testimony presented to the jury was fast sealing the fate of the defendant. The trial in the courtroom on the tenth floor of Bentsen Tower, one of McAllen's two high-rise structures, was nothing less than a barrage of witnesses for the prosecution. The jury, half Mexican American and half Anglo, pieced together the evidence in their own minds, then grew restive and in the end angry as credible witnesses revealed the story from different viewpoints. Agent Wayne Thornton's attorney, Jack Wolf, could do little during his cross-examinations of the long and persuasive parade.

Agent Roberta Alanis was Wayne's partner that night, but her testimony, which might have cast a modicum of doubt on previous statements by other witnesses, was of little aid to the defense, because she had remained in their unit at the time of the alleged assault. At the last minute the batteries in their portable radios had failed, so Agent Alanis had stayed behind in the Expedition. She could only affirm that by the time she reached the scene of the alleged crime, a man lay bleeding on the ground. Blood covered the back of his neck and head; however, that had not drawn her immediate attention. Instead her eyes were riveted to the man's limbs. The man on the ground had no right arm. Agent Alanis immediately radioed the status of the injured suspect to the supe at the station, who in turn passed the information to the on-duty field operation supervisor. Fifteen minutes later, FOS Jose Monteverde arrived at the scene to assume command of the initial investigation.

Outside the courtroom doors Jose Monteverde paced the hallway before retreating to the witness room. A few minutes later he resumed his pacing, finally sitting in a chair in the witness room. Clasping his hands before him, he had a good idea of the way the testimony must be going. FOS Monteverde had completed his investigation by the book and had filed his report to his supervisor, Assistant Chief Bill Valdez. Jose had no doubt that the witnesses who were digging the hole deeper for Wayne Thornton were agents who either had been at the scene immediately after the alleged attack or had talked with Thornton at the McAllen Station later that night. Worse still, civilians had heard Agent Thornton brag about his actions the next day at South Texas Community College on Walnut Street in McAllen, where the agent was taking classes to finish his associate's degree.

The Mole did not sympathize with Agent Wayne Thornton. Many of the other agents felt the same way, although Wayne did have his supporters. Agents at the station seemed to agree on one thing: Even if the jury found Wayne Thornton guilty he should be spared the ignominy of prison because of his family. Wayne might have been unpopular among the agents, might have been thought by many to be a blowhard with a short fuse, but his wife and kids should not have to suffer for his actions. It was enough, according to the station consensus, that Wayne should lose his job as a Border Patrol agent. If found guilty of the charges, he would become a convicted felon. Wayne could never again hold a job in law enforcement, nor could he expect to land a good-paying position, because of the felony record. But, for the sake of the economic hardships his family would face, he should not have to go to prison.

The agents also knew that a guilty verdict would symbolize another black mark on the already tarnished reputation of the Border Patrol. It only took one agent to ruin it for the hundreds of others.

The victim of Wayne's attack, according to the station scuttlebutt, was a local scumbag who, when he was not crossing dope or immigrants, busied himself with other avenues of crime. Few had sympathy for this known offender who had been bloodied in a criminal act. Although Wayne had allegedly bludgeoned a one-armed, fifty-year-old man, a fact not ignored by the local media, many agents held that the man got what he had coming. Sure, they agreed that Wayne went too far, but when were the bigwigs from Washington, D.C., the policy-makers who had never spent thirty minutes of their valuable time on line watch, the same decision-makers who sent two high-powered attorneys to prosecute the case at taxpayers' expense, going to cut them some slack? This viewpoint maintained that because there would always be rotten apples like Agent Thornton in every law enforcement organization, the feds should give equal time to the quagmire that agents faced daily and nightly.

All Along the Watchtower

Agent Shuman—alias Inspector Gadget because of his love for the two thirty-pound bags of gear he hauled everywhere with him ("Bro, I got to be prepared for any contingency")—tiptoed to where the Mole sat on his heels. The two of them discussed the predicament, both agreeing to give it another fifteen minutes. Either the group of twenty illegal aliens came down this trail they were watching, or they had headed off God knows where. The Mole reminded Inspector Gadget that there was only one logical way to hike from the landing zone by the Rio Grande. With any luck, they would be calling for extra transport vans within the hour.

The Mole, content for the moment to pass the time, considered Agents Paco and Inspector Gadget, choosing his whispered words carefully as the turkey vultures feasted under the rising orange moon. The breeze had calmed in anticipation of a blue norther set to arrive by dawn. The Valley's weather forecasters at Channels 4 and 5, the local CBS and ABC affiliates, always seemed to get it wrong, terribly wrong, as if they never bothered to consult the wire reports or look outside the broadcast studio door.[7]

But for the rustling of vulture wings, a complete stillness had fallen upon the sugar cane field.

Breaking the stillness, the Mole nodded in the direction of Paco and Inspector Gadget, "Those two are what I call Rambos. You know, guys out to make a name for themselves. The only way to do it in this organization is to concentrate on drug busts. It's all about drugs these days. The younger guys, that's all they are interested in. I can't blame them. They're going for the glory."

Paco was the first to call it quits. He never complained about the mosquitoes, but the chiggers from the previous night's shift were driving him crazy. At Tío Pico's on Old Military Highway he had argued with Inspector Gadget about the best way to treat chigger bites. Inspector Gadget's girlfriend of the moment had researched the best cure for chigger bites on the internet. The number one remedy was an over-the-counter anti-itch ointment. The website claimed that home remedies such as nail polish were useless. Paco informed the group sitting around the small table with a red-checkered, plastic tablecloth that the cyber crap was all bullshit, because he used nail polish on his chigger bites and it worked every time. Except this time. Inspector Gadget countered that the rum and Cokes Paco frequently consumed were the real problem.

The Mole was beginning to see Paco's side of it. The illegals should have been there by now. Because he was senior agent, it was the Mole's call. The Mole knew that there was no way the group would have gone east or west. Their info was from a reliable sensor. "You tell me," he said as the group gathered around him. Maybe they had been tricked.

"Could have been the locals," offered another agent who showed up late, the smoke from his cigarette hanging over him like a halo. "Remember it was the local PD that gave us the intel. They could be diverting us while a load comes in somewhere else. Remember there were two of them in the car. How often do you see two of them riding around together? They looked real anxious to talk to us."

"Could be," said the Mole, but not committing himself to it. "Could be bad intel. They get it just like we do."

"Anybody hear about the Thornton thing today?" asked the agent with the cigarette.

Every agent there knew it looked bad for Thornton. Thornton could not keep his mouth shut. He had told anyone who would listen what had happened that shift, then resumed his bragging the next day at the community college. Instead of keeping it to himself, he had turned everyone he talked to into a potential witness.

When FOS Jose Monteverde finally took the stand, he told the jury and the judge what every agent called as a witness already had told them. Wayne Thornton carried a Stinger flashlight that was twice as large as the other agents'. It was his own personal gear, not standard issue, and it was as big and hard as any wooden baton or club.

Attorney Jack Wolfe, noting the way the jury was soaking in this inflammatory piece of information, tried to turn the testimony to benefit his client. He asked FOS Jose Monteverde if a large flashlight with a powerful beam constituted a necessary piece of equipment when patrolling the river at night. Wolfe implied that the monster flashlight that Wayne had used as a weapon against the one-armed man was in fact a necessity to protect agents from harm's way.

FOS Jose Monteverde did not hold back. Right was right. The ethics instructor must set an example. "I've never seen a flashlight like that one," he said looking straight ahead.

There was no way Jack Wolfe could spin it, so he acted as if Monteverde's response was just what he had expected and quickly asked another unrelated question.

Jose Monteverde was on the stand for less than twenty minutes. Afterward, standing rigidly by the water fountain as if before a hostile crowd of reporters, he said quietly, "This is a low day for the Border Patrol."

Then he was gone, back to the station to mull over his testimony and the certain conviction of Wayne Thornton.

Three students from South Texas Community College followed Jose Monteverde on the stand. They gave identical testimony. While smoking a cigarette during a break between classes, Wayne Thornton had joked about hitting an illegal alien with his flashlight, continually referring to his alleged victim as a "tonk."

"Tonk" got Judge Ricardo Hinojosa's fullest attention. A no-nonsense jurist, he interrupted the testimony with a rare note of naïveté in his firm voice. "What's a tonk?" Judge Hinojosa knew what a tonk was, as did the Hispanic jurors sitting in the jury box. The Valley Anglos, on the other hand, were clueless.

"He told us a tonk," said the student, as if forced to repeat a dirty story to his mother, "is the sound an alien makes when you hit him over the head with a flashlight."

"What?" asked the judge, as if not hearing right. "Why would he say that?" The witness repeated his testimony.

"Then," continued the witness, "he says it was him that should be upset because his flashlight might have broke."

Wayne Thornton listened quietly without expression from the defense table. He was a lean young man with a military haircut who appeared attentive and well-mannered throughout his trial. Across the aisle from Wayne sat the two legal gunslingers from Washington, D.C. Next to them was their case manager, a special agent from the Department of Justice. Five feet behind Wayne and his attorney sat Wayne's pretty blond wife with two other family members. Except for Wayne's family, there was no one else in the courtroom but the bailiff. No friends, no supporters, no other family in sight. At the break immediately after FOS Jose Monteverde's testimony and the damning testimony from the three college students, Wayne Thornton rose, turned, then spoke quietly with his wife across the waist-high wooden railing. She stood, too, absent-mindedly reaching to straighten his tie, a usually normal act between wife and husband now discordant because of the ten-year prison term and $250,000 fine hanging over Wayne Thornton's head.

Only some McAllen citizens bothered to read the small article on the trial in the next morning's *The Monitor.* The newspapers were tossed on their front lawns just a few hours after the Mole and the other three agents broke off their surveillance next to the cane field where the vultures feasted. What caught the public's eye was not the brief description of the trial but the news from Matamoros that had taken three days to travel seventy miles to McAllen. Saul Antonio Martinez Gutierrez, deputy editor of the paper *El Imparcial,* was found shot to death in his SUV near La Soledad, a small community on the south side of the Río Bravo twenty-eight miles east of the city. *El Imparcial* had taken a strong position in its news coverage and editorials against illegal drugs in Tamaulipas. In the past two months Martinez, thirty-eight, had received repeated death threats because of his critical stance against the drug traffickers. During that same time, "The paper's offices were shot into three different times," according to Francisco Cayuela Villarreal, director of the Tamaulipas State Police task force investigating the murder. Martinez died from four 9mm bullets to the head.[8]

It had been slow going in the first months for Mexico's new president, Vicente Fox, who surprisingly won the election from the PRI candidate. Fox ran on a reform platform dedicated to eradicating the *narcotraficantes* from Mexican society, but Martinez's murder was one more sign that those who dared to criticize the powerful drug cartels should watch their backs. Martinez joined a growing list of Mexican journalists who had been assassinated for voicing their opinions.[9]

After wasting almost an hour next to the field of vultures, the Mole, Paco, Aldrete, and Inspector Gadget returned to their units. The Mole remained keenly positive, preferring to sustain a broader perspective about his duties patrolling the line rather than to let the last two hours drag him under. October, November, and December were always slow times of the year for apprehending aliens. Mexicans workers usually returned home for Christmas, then after the holidays traditionally recrossed the Río Bravo as they headed back to their jobs in Dallas, Detroit, Kansas City, and all points in between. January had been unusually slow for the McAllen agents, the numbers of apprehensions substantially lower than those of the previous year.[10]

Then, as the first days of February unfolded, the floodgates began to give way. Nightly, large groups were seen crossing the Rio Grande then escaping into the brush, mesquite, and huisache. Some were caught, but most were not. One measure of the huge number who escaped was the number of apprehensions at the two northern Valley checkpoints near Falfurrias and Sarita. On February 5, ninety-nine illegal immigrants were discovered waiting for rides in an old motel in the town of Falfurrias, ninety miles north of McAllen. Another fifty were found locked in an eighteen-wheeler at the Falfurrias checkpoint a few days later, followed by seventy-eight undocumented workers discovered on March 7 at the Sarita checkpoint located on Highway 177 in the middle of the King Ranch. Agents soon after uncovered forty-one immigrants in the backs of two semis stopped at the Sarita checkpoint.[11]

A month later the Border Patrol's intelligence unit flipped a Brazilian *coyote.* The *coyote,* upon promises made in return for his complete cooperation, showed agents his favorite landing places along the Rio Grande where he had personally smuggled more than ninety groups of undocumented Brazilians into Deep South Texas over a three-month period. Not ninety illegals, but ninety *groups* of illegals.

Apprehensions dramatically increased in February and March, helping to boost morale at the McAllen Station. Agents were now up to their ears in illegal immigrants. Yet any agent would admit that it was far better to be too busy than to spend ten hours a day waiting for something, anything, to happen.

Before the Mole got a hundred feet in his truck he received a call from his supe directing him to assist the DPS. There had been a bailout three miles north of the small community of San Miguel on Highway 281. Possible fatality.

"Shit," said the Mole. Not because of the orders from his supe, but because late on a Friday night highway traffic in the Valley could be treacherous. He wheeled the Expedition onto the four lanes of Highway 83 in south McAllen, found the ramp to Highway 281 North, then switched on his Christmas tree. As the traffic cleared before him, he observed with some satisfaction, "No problem now because it's a little early for the drunks to be out. They usually come out about midnight after the convenience stores stop selling beer."

The Mole, one hand on the wheel, fastened his seat belt, then pushed the truck up to ninety. At close to one hundred miles per hour the engine governor kicked in with a whirl and a swoosh as the truck's powerful engine automatically decelerated.

"They don't let us go very fast in these units," said the Mole. Far down the pavement flashing lights penetrated the clear tropical night. The Mole braked hard as he slowed to seventy-five, then eased down the speedometer as he neared the scene. Cars headed north were being diverted into the far left lane by three DPS officers standing in the middle of the road surrounded by flares and highway cones. In the center grassy median six DPS units and an ambulance surrounded a late model red Pontiac Trans-Am.

The Mole climbed gingerly out of his unit to jog across to the center median, where three DPS officers stood at the rear of the red Trans-Am. One of the troopers rested his hand on the trunk lid. When the Mole was within ten feet, the trooper, with a grand, sweeping gesture in deference to the arrival of the Border Patrol, popped the lid of the trunk.

The small trunk was crammed with humanity. Stunned, the DPS trooper stepped back, then recovered as he shone his flashlight on human forms clasped in fetal positions. Charlie and a new recruit appeared at the side of the vehicle. The body closest to the license plate stirred first, then, one limb at a time, unfolded carefully, finally swinging its legs up and over the edge of the trunk. It appeared to be a practiced motion. What had first resembled a polyester sack of potatoes became a frightened man in his early twenties. Two others painstakingly followed the first man. The DPS officers handcuffed them as they emerged, questioned them in Spanish about their nation of origin, and told them to stand at the side of the car.

Charlie, ignoring the human sardines packed in the trunk, admired the car with a professional's eye. "See where they've reinforced the suspension? Those springs there. You can't have three or four hundred pounds in your trunk without it sagging, but the way they've fixed it with this heavy-duty suspension, you can't tell the difference. Nice job."

The troopers had established that the Mexicans had entered the United States illegally and were anxious to hand them over to the Border Patrol. But first they wanted the men to identify the body.

The Mole asked the troopers what they knew.

"We're not sure yet," said one of the officers from beneath the wide brim of his cowboy hat. "We spot the aliens and we tail them. There were three cars. We decide to take the lead car on the theory that that's where the *coyote* is. They see us. Then the driver of the lead vehicle, the Trans-Am, decides to bail out. So he bails and the other passengers are left hanging. We're not sure how many of them there were in the car. They all jump and one of them doesn't make it. See that gray car over there on the far side of the highway? That woman was driving behind us, and when the passengers bailed, one of them crossed the lane directly in front of her. She never saw him and couldn't have stopped if she had."

The Mole also wanted to see the body. The trooper pointed to the San Manuel fire engine parked on the grassy shoulder with its diesel still rumbling. The agent recrossed the highway carefully, silently circumventing the gray car. In the back seat an elderly woman with gray hair tied in a tight bun sat alone, arms folded tightly across her chest. The windshield of her car bore deep cracks from the impact, but the safety glass had not shattered.

"It's got to be tough on her," said the Mole as he headed toward the fire engine. "She's driving along and before she knows it a body hits her windshield out of nowhere. It's not her fault."

Before he reached the fire engine, the EMT from San Manuel cheerfully pointed the Mole to the objects on the highway pavement. Seemingly untouched, a lone tennis shoe lay on the asphalt shoulder of Highway 281 North just outside the painted white line marking the far right lane. When the elderly lady in the gray car hit the undocumented worker, he was literally knocked out of one of his shoes.

The force of the impact, of the car's metal against human flesh, blew the dental plate out of the victim's mouth before flinging him fifty feet into the tall grass. The dental plate was not more than three feet from the tennis shoe. An upper dental plate, intact and flawless under the moonlight.

While the Mole examined the shoe and the dental plate, the troopers escorted the handcuffed former trunk passengers to the tall grass at the side of the highway, pulled back the space-age silver blanket that covered the body, and insisted that each immigrant identify the corpse. The victim, between forty and fifty years of age, lay on his back, arms and legs askew. Although the body was badly mangled, his dark, wavy hair remained combed and in place. Congealed blood covered the man's chin and neck. His moustache was long and thick, the lower lip thin.

Each of the handcuffed men denied knowing the victim as he made the sign of the cross. Charlie, taking custody of the illegal immigrants, marched them back to his transport van, searched them for weapons, then removed their cuffs as he shepherded them into the vehicle. After their confinement in the trunk, even the steel cage was a welcome improvement. The men jumped into the back seat of the Border Patrol van as if they were boarding a train bound for New York City. The first man into the van sat down quickly on the bench seat, tightened and fastened his seat belt, then grinned broadly.

He had good reason to grin. After the driverless car came to a stop a few feet onto the grassy highway median, a quick-thinking trooper had pushed it a few extra, crucial feet from the busy highway. Otherwise the Trans-Am could have been rear-ended by an eighteen-wheeler and the three men still hidden in the trunk killed instantly. Crossing themselves again, the workers from Mexico knew that they were very lucky.

A woman had been riding in the front seat of the red Trans-Am. She wore a fancy, dark-colored dress and four-inch heels. When the driver bailed out and the others followed, she headed for the fence line that bordered the highway. But just one look at the dense brush and cactus convinced her that she was going nowhere in her short dress and shoes. The troopers found her there, staring at the four strands of barbed wire that separated the state highway from an immense cultivated field bordered with thick vegetation, which soon gave way to isolated ranches stretching for nearly seventy miles.

The woman refused to talk, refused to tell the troopers how many workers were in the car, which way they were headed, or their names. Not a word. The troopers were beginning to think that they would never know the full story. The victim could not talk, the woman would not talk, and the three men in the trunk had not seen a thing. All the others had disappeared.

The Mole reached for his NVGs in his bag of gear in the back seat of his unit, then admitted, "It's a long shot. But we're going to give it a try."

Charlie concurred. "We should do it," he said, psyching himself up for a pointless search. "We should give it an honest shot. We don't know crap about how long a lead they have on us, but we should give it our best."

The new recruit was assigned to keep a watchful eye on the three Mexicans in the transport. The Mole, carefully straddling the top strand of the barbed-wire fence, jumped blindly into the thick shadows and landed with a loud thump. The first thing he bumped into was a head-high prickly pear.

"Oh, shit," swore the Mole. "Now I'm really screwed." He flexed his leg in the dark, felt the pain, then gingerly, step by step, made his way through the cactus and mesquite. Although barely a hundred feet from the busy highway, this was a desolate place. The highway noises were blocked and filtered by a corridor of vegetation, a jungle of spikes and thorns that raked human skin raw. The darkened parabolas manufactured by the Mole's flashlight hid rattlesnakes, poisonous spiders, fire ants, and other creatures best left undisturbed.

Slowly, carefully, the Mole and Charlie searched the area. Once through the vegetation line that bordered the fence, they crossed a wide expanse of field freshly plowed and waiting for seed. The field stretched for a mile or more until it reached another tree line in the distance. The Mole and Charlie scanned the field carefully with their NVGs, listened intently for signs of life, then began a systematic sweep for fresh sign. At one point, after twenty-five minutes passed in complete silence, the Mole yelled out to Charlie, "What did you find?"

Charlie shouted back from the shadows, "Absolutely nothing."

For a half hour more the two agents searched for the *coyote* and the other passengers of the Trans-Am. Charlie finally found fresh sign, but, after they tracked it for a quarter of a mile northward, it disappeared. It could have been tracks of the driver of the car or sign from other immigrants making their way toward the checkpoint at Falfurrias. Charlie also found a major trail heading due north toward the Falfurrias checkpoint along with several resting spots filled with empty plastic water bottles, sandwich wrappers, and other evidence. The trail, two to three feet wide through the brush and low grasses bordering the fields, had been beaten down by the feet of thousands of illegal aliens.

In some ways this trail resembled a smaller version of Cavazos Beach, with washouts protected by stunted trees overrun with faded green garbage bags, jeans, T-shirts, socks, and underwear rotting in air laden with the humidity of the Gulf of Mexico. However, this trail lined with throwaway junk was not on the banks of the Rio Grande but twenty miles north of McAllen.

The Mole, ignoring the pain in his leg, waxed theoretical. "The way I see it," he said, now a disembodied voice in this confusing night terrain, "the driver and the woman were going to pose as a married couple at the checkpoint. They'd keep the guys in the trunk but drop the others off south of the checkpoint, then arrange to meet them on the other side. Only they never got that far."

The Mole and Charlie kept searching for no other reason than their pride. The *coyote,* undoubtedly a seasoned professional, had most likely used his cell phone to call for a ride as soon as he had abandoned the new illegal immigrants. Even now he could be tossing down a cold beer in a McAllen bar while celebrating his escape from the hands of the DPS and the Border Patrol. He could have been long gone, in fact, even before the ambulance and the fire engine left the station house at San Manuel.

The immigrants who fled—if they were experienced—should have headed north toward Falfurrias. But they may have panicked under the circumstances, might already be lost in the brushlands. They would be fortunate to find water at a stock tank and might eventually make it to Corpus Christi.

By the time the Mole and Charlie returned to their vehicles, the DPS troopers had departed along with the fire truck, the ambulance, the medical examiner in his white pickup truck, and the other law enforcement personnel. The flares had been heaved into the buffalo grass. The troopers took with them the traffic cones, tennis shoe, and dental plate.

Neither the next day nor in the following days did local television, radio news, or Valley newspapers mention the bailout or the fatality. From the vantage point of the media, nothing had happened on Highway 281 near the town of San Manuel.

While Charlie and his partner transported the three illegal immigrants to the McAllen Station for processing, the Mole pulled out his faithful Leatherman tool and, after rolling up his pants cuff, inventoried the damage. He used the tool to remove the prickly pear thorns one by one. It took him twenty minutes.

"Handy little thing," he said, as he went about his task with workmanlike precision. He knew his knee was going to swell up within a few hours. It always did. The Mole had no hard scientific proof, but he firmly believed that there was a toxin in the thorns of the prickly pear. "Hey, bro," he said, "Remember, I know what I'm talking about. I was a biology major in college."

The Mole limped back to his truck and on a hunch drove to check out the convenience store two miles south of the bailout. A pimply clerk ran out when he noticed the Border Patrol unit by the gas pump.

"I'm real glad you came by," he said holding three crunched Coke cans in his left hand. Two Hispanic males had just come by. One was in a Toyota truck; the other, a blue Tercel. "I didn't like the way they were looking at me. I know what to look for. You work out here long enough, like I have, and you can tell the good people from the bad."

The store clerk was convinced that the two men meant to rob him as soon as he closed up for the night. "I'm alone out here. My wife is visiting my mother a couple of miles down the road. You mind waiting another thirty minutes until closing time? Just in case they decide to come back?"

The Mole did not mind one bit, but he had to clear it with the supe first. He made the call, received clearance, then sat eating his dinner of a baloney sandwich with mustard. While he chewed, the Mole thought about the cedar fence for his new house. The estimate had come in at just under $3,000.

The clerk turned off the lights at the convenience store in the middle of nowhere and walked over to thank the Mole. Then he forced a can of Coke on the Mole, who finally took it to avoid hurting his feelings. Half an hour later the Mole was at the scope truck atop the levee east of Peñitas. The diesel hummed loudly as the camera scanned the fields and the brush lines north of the Rio Grande.

Five agents from the midnight shift gathered around the scope truck, each sharing with the others what had transpired since muster at 10 P.M. When it came round to the Mole, he simply said, "I was working a bailout on Highway 281 near San Miguel. One fatality and four apprehensions, including a woman. Charlie and I searched the area for an hour but couldn't find a thing."

Inspector Gadget then bragged about the nine apps he and his partner, Agent Sandra Aldrete, had tallied near Pepe's Fiesta Restaurant. Sandra Aldrete accepted the praise from her fellow agents in the form of brief nods of her head. Then it was the next agent's turn.

By chance, three days later, agents nabbed a seventeen-year-old Guatemalan boy as he tried to circumvent the Sarita checkpoint on Highway 177 North—seventy miles as the crow flies from the site of the bailout. The first thing he asked the agents when he was apprehended was, "Was my father hurt when he jumped out of the car?"

And so the whole story finally emerged. When the *coyote* bailed out on State Highway 281 there were, in addition to the three Mexicans in the trunk and the woman sitting in the front passenger seat, four Guatemalans in the back seat. The men included the fifty-year-old father, who was killed; his son, apprehended near Sarita; and two acquaintances from a nearby Guatemalan village. The four Guatemalans had paid another *coyote,* not the driver of the Trans-Am, $1,500 each for the trip to the United States. But the *coyote* who had profited by a total of $6,000 had abandoned them on the banks of the Río Bravo. With no money and no food, the Guatemalans spent two hard days in the brush along the river. They did not know how to swim the Río Bravo, which to them seemed as wide as the Mississippi River during flood stage. Finally they met up with a group of fifteen Mexican workers. They followed the more experienced immigrants and waded across a narrow bend in the river.

While waiting to find a guide who would take them to Houston, the Guatemalans spent another three days on the north side of the river hiding in the brush. They met several *coyotes* but could not afford the $500 price tag demanded for each of them.

They finally found a *coyote*—the one who drove the red Trans-Am—on their third night in the United States. Without payment up front, he agreed to take them to Houston. He would hide them in a safe house in Houston, he promised them, but then they had to repay him as soon as they found jobs. If they did not repay him his money in a week, $500 per person, the *coyote* would report them to the INS, which he assured them would deport them back to Guatemala. Half-starved and weary, they accepted the offer.

Two weeks later the Catholic Church in San Manuel published two sentences in their monthly church newsletter about the death of a Guatemalan man in a traffic accident on Highway 281. Prayers were offered in his memory.

The Mole, with still five hours of mids before him, climbed slowly back into his Expedition to consider how he would best spend the remaining time on his shift. Making his decision for him, the dispatcher at the McAllen Station broke the momentary quiet in the Mole's cab.

"We have an armed robbery at the convenience store in Peñitas. Hispanic male, dark hair, five six, approximately twenty years old. Suspect entered the store and demanded cash. He is armed with a big rock. Any units in the area?"

Spring

No one, including the new recruits, denied that academy standards were slipping. At one time applicants had to wait two to three years for an opening in the U.S. Border Patrol, only to confront an academy instructor who was determined to flush them out in record time. New recruits were once required to have time in the military, a few years in the local police department, or both. These were young but experienced individuals.

Halfway through the muster before mids, Supe Mira announced that six recruits were joining the McAllen Station.

Juan Jose Galvan was the first new agent Supe Mira recognized. "Mr. Galvan, where are you from?" asked Supe Mira, a cordial note in his welcome.

"From McAllen, sir," said Juan Jose Galvan, who wore a rough military cut to make himself appear a few years older. He was visibly uncomfortable as the other agents in the room turned to eyeball him.

Agent Herman Morningside wasted no time in beginning the impromptu interview. "What did you used to do?"

"Real estate," replied Juan Jose Galvan quickly. Morningside, shifting his bulk awkwardly in the metal chair, immediately turned to Agent Rodriguez, who was sitting a few feet to his left. Morningside mouthed the words "Real estate?" in Agent Rodriguez's direction. Rodriguez nodded.

Every agent in the room with more than six years of experience recognized that Galvan was a product of the new Border Patrol, an agency many believed was growing too fast for its own good. Since 1995 the Border Patrol had more than doubled in size to its current ten thousand agents. Recruiters had been hitting high schools and college campuses and, along with the media play, were attracting a new kind of recruit to the academy. The pitch was simple. If you liked being outdoors, if you liked excitement and action, then the Border Patrol was just the ticket. The big sign outside Sector Headquarters across from Miller International Airport read, "A Job with No Borders and No Boundaries."

Most of the older agents strongly believed that academy standards were sacrificed to allow thousands of new recruits an opportunity to wear the uniform. No experienced agent would trust Juan Jose Galvan until he had demonstrated his abilities on line watch. All new recruits from the academy were increasingly suspect. Working behind a desk five days a week and pitching properties to buyers did not prepare an agent to make the right decision in a high-risk situation. Besides Galvan the new recruits included two retail salesmen, a lab tech, and a former Valley police officer. None among them had military experience except the cop.

Agent Shuman, alias Inspector Gadget, was a Rambo who, to his credit, worked his shifts as hard as any agent at the station. But language requirements at the academy were a slippery slope, and more than one experienced agent had noticed that the new academy graduates did not seem to know their Spanish. Inspector Gadget's Spanish, in fact, was worse than terrible. Entering the academy not knowing a word of Spanish, he passed all the language tests but still could not speak Spanish worth a hoot. Sure, he passed the written language test, but in the field what came out of Inspector Gadget's mouth was anybody's guess.[1]

In his third month in uniform Inspector Gadget collared several immigrant workers; he strutted into the McAllen Station processing room with his three apprehensions trailing him. He instructed the men to stand against the green cinder-block wall and, after seating himself behind one of the computers, called the first illegal alien to sit in the chair opposite him.

"*Sientese,*" sit down, he said to the eighteen-year-old, who was not at all intimidated by the surroundings or the routine. He had crossed the Río Bravo numerous times and had been arrested more than once by the Border Patrol.

All Along the Watchtower

He seated himself comfortably in front of Inspector Gadget and prepared to answer the simple questions he knew were coming.

"Como me llamo?" asked Inspector Gadget, ready to enter the young man's name into the data file. But he had asked what is *my* name, not *como se llama,* what is *your* name.

The puzzled immigrant shrugged his shoulders. He did not know the name of this gringo who had nabbed him on the top of the levee near the Río Bravo. Why should he?

Inspector Gadget stiffened in the swivel chair. This was an easy question. He had three illegal aliens to process and no time to waste. Why was the man across from him being such a hard case? So he asked again, this time in a louder voice, *"Como me llamo?"*

Once more the undocumented worker shrugged his shoulders. He turned the palms of his hands up to indicate that he did not know the name of this agent of the U.S. Border Patrol. Was this some kind of new trick to get money from him? A gringo *mordida,* a bribe, that he was expected to pay? He was very confused.

"Listen, I'm asking you one last time," Inspector Gadget spoke slowly in English, his voice loud enough for all the other agents in processing to hear. *"Como me llamo?"*

Guffaws from the other agents careened around the bare walls of the processing room, but the amusement masked a serious concern. How could Inspector Gadget interrogate or investigate suspects in the field if he could not communicate with them in Spanish? Of equal importance, how could he make crucial decisions on line watch based upon the answers and comments of those he apprehended?

While Juan Jose Galvan and the other new recruits during mids nervously shifted and swayed in their boots as the interrogation continued, signs of spring were everywhere to be seen on the other side of the station's cinder-block walls. Fields of carefully tended aloe vera bloomed in unison just a few short miles from Old Military Highway. First the plants sent up long and improbable stamens, miniature versions of the hydraulic scope truck that supported the thermal-sensitive camera. Then the stark, symmetrical rows of aloe vera, which in parts of the Valley stretched to the horizon, revealed their blooms as one. Never mind that the blooms were something of a minor disappointment, a paltry white against the green, waxy outspread arms of the squat, dreary plant. The thick liquid within, a vital ingredient in cosmetics and shampoos, was also highly prized for its capacity to soothe and heal burns.

The blooms of the omnipresent prickly pear cactus were, of course, the traditional harbinger of spring in Deep South Texas. Just before blooming the buds were harvested carefully by hand and cooked in a variety of Lenten foods, including scrambled eggs. Because there were many more indigenous prickly pears throughout the Valley than fanciers of nopal, the cactus flashed these bland desert lands with brief but splashy eye candy witnessed only by new illegal immigrants trekking through the countryside or by agents of the Border Patrol chasing after them.

In McAllen, where prickly pear carried the same status as any other noxious bush or tree, the blooms of multitudes of acacia, poinsettia, mimosa, hyacinth, citrus, and other flowering trees, bushes, and plants filled the night air with a thick, lavish perfume during the brief spring. City blocks were covered with the molecules of the rich, blooming citrus along with the juices of the fruit of date palms and other non-native palms smashed to pulp by possums on their night forages. Unattended oranges, lemons, grapefruit, and limes fell to the earth in the backyards of the rich and the poor in McAllen, then, if not collected, quickly rotted in the thick humidity from the Gulf of Mexico.

The possums and the alley rats grew fat on the citrus and the other fruits and seeds. So did the starving feral cats and dogs, which were periodically rounded up and transported to the Humane Society on Trenton Road in northeastern McAllen.

Six-inch geckos and chameleons lay flat as pancakes under porch lights waiting for mosquitoes and other nighttime insects. Until attacked they seemed languid and disinterested. Across the freshly tended lawns of St. Augustine grass in the affluent McAllen suburbs, flying cockroaches the size of silver dollars buzzed here and there, at times swarming as thick as bees around street lights. Venturing from their hidey-holes, hairy brown tarantulas paraded unafraid along city sidewalks with creepy but purposeful strides. The tarantulas were driven by the random spring rain, which dampened their nests even as it turned the drag roads along the Rio Grande into a mudfest that agents avoided. No agent ever wanted to call for a tow truck because he or she had become stuck in spring mud. Yet the rain and the mud did not stop either the undocumented workers or the drug smugglers. Nothing seemed to stop them.

All Along the Watchtower

The admixture of fecundity, along with the odor of diesel fuel from Mexico, hung like a fog near the stinking Rio Grande while often seeping into the skin pores and the clothing fibers of both illegal aliens and federal agents.

Residents of the Valley knew what was soon coming—knew that spring was nothing but a bluff. As if on cue, the winds began to swing from the northwest to the southeast, steamy winds conceived in weather events in the Yucatan Peninsula of Mexico and Central America. During the days the winds played hotter and hotter from the southwest, but at night they calmed, at least in the last week of spring, and the midnight air was pleasantly cool, the skies cloudless, the stars bright and hard as diamonds when the moon descended.

During March 2001, 180,000 college students from Texas, Oklahoma, Louisiana, Kansas, Iowa, Nebraska, and Illinois, marketed to death by MTV and the major beer companies, headed for the beaches of South Padre Island in Deep South Texas. Along the way a handful fell asleep at the wheel, killing themselves and others in senseless pileups on the interstates. When the hordes finally reached South Padre Island after fifteen to twenty hours of driving, they binged on cheep beer and tequila, ogled each other on the sand, and, one special night, tossed furniture out the windows of the Radisson Hotel when the power mysteriously went off. A few unlucky ones were thrown into jail by the *federales* in Matamoros or died in car accidents on the way back to the beach from the Mexican bars in Matamoros. The smarter ones, those who knew after a night of drinking that they could no more steer a car than ride a live bull, boarded buses that picked them up in front of their hotels and deposited them at the Mexican bars and clubs. Most years one or more college students drank so much booze or ingested so much ecstasy that they thought they could fly from the balcony of their ten-story condo.[2] A decade earlier the cannibals had picked them off one at a time. Now car accidents and drugs proved most deadly.[3]

Agent Taylor, a member of the Border Patrol for less than eighteen months, was the same age as the college students who roamed the beaches of South Padre Island looking for frenzied fun before returning to campus for the last months of the semester. Along with Agent Negrete, twenty-two, he had spent two hours tracking a group of illegal workers hours after muster ended at the McAllen Station and the new recruits had weathered the agents' cross-examination. Now, as dawn broke the horizon in Deep South Texas, the new immigrants were once again ready to make their move.

A sensor near the river had received fifteen hits. Agents Taylor and Negrete figured that the aliens would move north along a trail that placed them not too far from the entrance to the Santa Ana Wildlife Refuge. But first the immigrants had to cross a single lane of asphalt bordering a burned cane field. Agent Taylor lay in ambush across the top of a levee a third of a mile from the spot the illegals must cross if they were to gain their freedom in the USA. Agent Negrete took up a position on the trail behind the illegals so that if and when they decided to retrace their steps back to the Rio Grande, he would be waiting to arrest them.

It was a good plan, a plan both Taylor and Negrete borrowed from senior agents. Because the academy did not teach this kind of thinking, new McAllen Station recruits were first teamed with senior agents who showed them the ropes of line watch. Sometimes this worked; sometimes the relationship between the two agents failed miserably, and the new recruit learned little.

Agents Taylor and Negrete were not Rambos, but they daily put some effort and energy into their jobs. They did not simply show up like a few of the worst agents. But theirs was not the maximum effort of Noe Escondido or Charlie. Far from slouches, Agents Taylor and Negrete were typical in some ways of the new recruits, a generation of agents who did not buy into the program. Ten years earlier Agents Taylor and Negrete may not have made it through the academy.

"I see them," said Agent Taylor, shifting his equipment belt for comfort. "Just off to the side of the road there. Two of them so far." He sneaked another peek as the sun's rays stretched lazily across the horizon. Silently he pulled himself into a crouching position for a better look through the binocs, first scanning the terrain to the left of his position, a line of brush and prickly pear in full bloom, and then to the right, the field of cane stubble.

"Okay, I still got them. They're coming this way. What we do is let them get about halfway here, far enough so they are out in the open with nowhere to run. Then we rush them in my truck. Get ready."

A few minutes staggered by before Agent Taylor took another peek to mark the progress of the aliens. This time he was less committed.

"I don't know. They're still there in the same spot. I thought they were moving, but they're still in the same spot. Maybe I'm seeing things because I'm looking too hard at them."

Another few moments passed and with it the surface bravado of Agent

Taylor. A local boy from the Valley, Taylor was educated at the University of Texas–Pan American. To him, the Border Patrol was about making good money. Little else had attracted him to the job in spite of the media hype. He did not picture a future with the Border Patrol, not like Noe and the other lifers who lived and breathed the agency. Taylor, a handsome man with short, dark hair, took yet another look. "Could be them. Hard to tell. I don't know. Maybe it's the wind. It's been picking up a little. That could explain it. But whatever it is, it looks human to me. Let's give them a little more time," said Agent Taylor. Humberto Taylor. Valley Hispanics had intermarried with Anglos since the eighteenth century.[4] Taylor identified himself as Mexican American regardless of his name and was very forthright about his Hispanic heritage.

Then, in a voice grown a tad defensive, Agent Taylor said, "I guess it could be a bush."

Belly crawling back to his unit, we jumped in, careful to mute the doors, and Agent Taylor gunned the Expedition up over the levee and down the narrow asphalt road. Slamming on the brakes at the edge of an irrigation canal near a trailhead that eventually led to a grass landing along the banks of the Rio Grande, we jumped out of the Expedition to stare dully at a green bush with two limbs fluttering head high in a nascent spring wind. It was easy to understand how from more than a third of a mile away, after nine hours of night work on the line, this plant could be mistaken for two undocumented workers standing by the road.

But it was still a bush, not two Mexican immigrants ready to start looking for jobs at a meat packing plant in Nebraska.

"Guess I'm looking pretty bad right now," said Agent Taylor, a pleasant smile crossing his handsome face. Without waiting for an answer, he radioed his friend Negrete the bad news.

"I usually catch my share," Agent Taylor said. "Every shift for the last two weeks I've brought in at least one illegal alien."

Agents Taylor and Negrete were not quitters. They had another hour left on their shift, and they intended to work it. Ten minutes later another sensor went off on a nature trail in the Santa Ana Wildlife Refuge. A haven for birds and birders, the area was not known for its criminal activity. Unlike some of the other refuges and parks that bordered the Rio Grande, such as Anzalduas and Bentsen, dopers and illegal aliens rarely crossed here, because although the park tightly hugged a bend in the river, the native vegetation along the river-banks was virtually impenetrable.

Swatting at the mosquitoes that attacked him in spite of the thick layers of spray covering his exposed skin, Humberto Taylor knelt to hide behind a bush to the side of the nature trail that snaked through the park. Agent Negrete found a hiding place farther up the trail deep among the moss-covered branches of the weathered trees.

But no one came along the trail. No drug traffickers. No aliens.

"This is frustrating," Agent Taylor muttered to himself as he climbed back into the Expedition. The mosquitoes followed him into his vehicle, and he took another five minutes to smash them systematically between his hands and various parts of the cab. Finally underway, he opened the power windows to allow the wind to suck the remaining insects into the new spring morning.

A plea for help came over his radio. "I'm going to need some medical backup. I got a Brazilian here who is having difficulty. He's looking dehydrated. I need some medical backup quick. I'm next to the water tower."

Taylor was there in five minutes, Agent Guarjardo not far behind him. The water tower was a landmark located in a small neighborhood of battered, World War II–vintage trailers in South McAllen just a few steps from the bridge to Reynosa. One of the trailers, a rusting washing machine a few feet from its door, was a known haven for dopers. Last week Charlie caught a 220-pound load of marijuana not five feet from the trailer's front door.

By the time Taylor drove up, the ambulance was already headed for the hospital with the ailing Brazilian. Four other agents stood around their Expeditions as big and burly Agent Gretsky, first on the scene, relayed the story. The trailer was under surveillance by two agents. Because of the neighborhood and its criminal history, at first they thought they were onto a load of dope. A suspect popped his head out of the brush that fronts the trailer court, then disappeared only to return to survey the area. Then he disappeared again, but when he once more reappeared he was with four other men. With no heavy bags weighing from their shoulders, these were undocumented aliens, not mules, as first believed.

When the two agents busted the five illegal aliens, the aliens did not passively submit as expected; they instead ran in all directions. The agents were able to catch only one man.

"The guy starts saying he's 'desperate,'" says Gretsky. "That he needs water. Then he starts panting like he can't get enough air. Same thing happened with that Brazilian last year. Remember that? So that's when they call for backup. Maybe it's a part of Brazilian culture or something.

"Then the McAllen PD gets a call that the driver of a late-model van has been attacked by four men just down the street from here. It had to be the same four guys. The driver in the van comes to a stop when he sees the four Brazilians. They start yelling at him, then try to break his windows. Then they start rocking the van, all the time yelling at him that they are desperate and need help. The driver thought it was a carjacking."

After thinking the situation over for a minute, Agent Taylor said, "I don't like the idea of those four Brazilians running around here crazy as hell." The other agents concurred, but there was little they could do. The four men belonged to the McAllen PD. After the lone Brazilian was released by the hospital, he would be processed at the McAllen Station. He would probably be sent to the detention center near Los Fresnos for a hearing before an INS judge. It could take two weeks, two months, or longer depending on how busy it was at the detention center. There were even times when they were completely filled up and Brazilians, as well as other OTMs, were simply VRed back to Reynosa because the INS system was overtaxed.

With less than a half hour left in his shift, Agent Taylor spent his last minutes checking the trail that led to the trailer court. Fresh sign was everywhere, but no one was in sight. After he received word from the dispatcher that the next shift was officially on duty, he headed back down the levee toward the McAllen Station.

Braking hard atop the gravel, the Expedition skidded more than a few feet on the roadbed before Agent Taylor shifted the vehicle into reverse.

"I just saw the biggest tarantula I ever saw in my life," he said as he got out of the cab.

Oblivious to any vulnerability, a dark brown tarantula bigger than a man's fist walked along the gravel lane atop the levee. Agent Taylor pinned the huge spider with the heel of his boot, then thought better about his prize. If he took it home, it might bite one of his two sons. It was not worth the gamble.

"They say they have the bite of a wasp. I don't know for sure. It's what I've heard. I've seen black widows and brown recluses out here. They're really poisonous. One of the agents in Brownsville, I don't remember his name, has a chunk missing out of his right arm where a spider got to him. I saw a black widow on one of the gate locks a few months ago. I don't know. I guess I just don't like the idea of all these spiders. You know, like you're laying in at night waiting for some doper and all of a sudden you feel this thing on you."

Agent Taylor released the tarantula, and it promptly set off once more along the one-lane levee road a stone's throw from the Rio Grande.

It takes all kinds of men and women to staff a law enforcement agency, whether a local police department or federal program, whether five police officers at the Palmview Police Department or three hundred federal agents at the McAllen Station. Were Agents Taylor and Negrete, or any of the other new recruits, so different from others throughout the United States sworn to uphold the law? Different from Agents Jack Spurrier, Rodriguez, Reynaldo Guerra (the Mole), Herman Morningside, Charlie, Maria Contreras, Noe Escondido, Paco, Roberta Alanis, Sandra Aldrete, Cooler, Wilson, Tom Clark, and Shuman (Inspector Gadget), or Supes Mira and Billy Villareal, or FOS Jose Monteverde? Or any of the other men and women at the McAllen Station?

Husbands and wives, fathers and mothers, sons and daughters, all the agents at the McAllen Station were fallible human beings. Some were strong of character, some not, some responsible, some immature, but all were vulnerable men and women thrust into an environment of policies and rules that made their best sense under the fluorescent office lights of men like FOS Jose Monteverde. In a small, cramped office at the rear of the McAllen Border Patrol station, logical and exacting questions could be asked and correct responses received according to the rules of management and the dictates of the federal employees union. Time was abundant under those fluorescent lights—time to consider the ethical ramifications of various issues and, most importantly, to weigh each dictum against the other until the correct legal, procedural, and moral action rose like cream to the top of the churn.

While pundits inside and outside the government debated, all along this Deep South Texas watchtower, agents of the U.S. Border Patrol searched frantically for the legal, appropriate, and moral course of action. Their incessant predicaments were tangible, intractable, and frequently mundane. At times it was impossible to tell who was Dylan's Joker, who the Thief, or for that matter who the perpetrator and who the victim. Even when legal, procedural, policy, and moral distinctions could be made, at times it did not seem to matter to anyone except the agents and those directly involved.

Agents in the field apprehended, as mandated by law, undocumented workers who crossed the Rio Grande by the thousands, while tens of thousands admittedly escaped. Agents in the field confiscated tons of marijuana and cocaine, again mandated by law, but agents would affirm, based on their own experience, that the vast majority of drugs slipped by.

The men and women who spent more time and taxpayer money enforcing laws and policies along the border than anyone else in the United States looked me in the eye and told me that they often did not have the slightest notion of what was going on under this transnational circus big top. If they did not know, who did?

The border in Deep South Texas meant and was many things to many different people. But maybe it could best be understood by an agent in the middle of a dark night along the banks of the Rio Grande, tracking fresh sign along a hidden trail. Agents—good or bad, strong or weak—experienced similar epiphanies when they realized that it was just them out there in the vast darkness, when they recognized that the only link with the McAllen Station was the plastic radio pinned to the shoulder of their shirt. That was when the sheer magnitude of this human conundrum could perhaps best be configured, when an image of the border could be conjured based upon empirical data interpreted within the context of real human experience including fear.

The border was at least in part this: an enormous, dark brown, hairy tarantula ten thousand times the size of Agent Humberto Taylor's specimen, a beast moving at its own pace through time and space, oblivious and amorphous, hideous yet compelling, its sweaty, infectious bite the front edge of decay and death. It waited out there along the banks of the stinking, toxic river, or in among the fields of ten-foot-tall sugar cane, or down at the bottom of the cesspool of flowing waters where the hydrilla rooted, or deep in the thick forests of prickly pear. Although not human, this border creature was a product of human society, a scumbag nightmare from the Freudian deep.

Agent Taylor, nor any of the other agents at the McAllen Station, could no more pinion this ephemeral night sweat by a polished boot heel than could a real coyote, not the human kind, amble unimpeded across the surface of the Rio Grande.

If the job of an agent of the U.S. Border Patrol was line watch, the control of goods, services, and labor in every conceivable shape and form from one country to another, then every agent who had enforced the boundary between Mexico and the United States knew from the very marrow of their bones what no one else, every nonagent, cared to admit. Real control of these lands along the Rio Grande was a pipe dream, a vacuous illusion, and a wicked pretension.

So who was the Joker and who the Thief?

After years of night sweats along the Rio Grande, even the least sentient of agents knew something else: they knew that the short fall and winter months in the Valley were a blessing and that sweet, frail spring could not mask the more lethal monster lumbering down the road. Summer in this desert was seven months of every year when people, every kind of people, suffered and died. Summer along the Rio Grande in Deep South Texas was a hell on earth.

Two

Rocking and Swaying

The Onion Girl

Summer released torrid, southern gusts clocked by the local meteorologists at up to forty-five miles per hour. Accompanied by April
temperatures nudging ninety-five degrees, the Mexican winds
turned the Valley into a blast furnace. In the northernmost suburbs
of McAllen the rich ran their underground sprinklers all night long
so that by morning their saturated St. Augustine lawns could endure another
broiling day. Everywhere else in the city, from the poor barrios south of the
tracks to the houses and apartments whose owners could not sustain monthly
water bills in the triple digits, the grass turned dead brown along with the other
plantings. The temperatures continued to climb.

The ground cracked. During the steaming afternoons red ants blazed new,
crazy trails on the all but deserted sidewalks of downtown McAllen, while the
far more dangerous fire ants, small and unimpressive to those not familiar with
their talents, lay dormant in the relative coolness of their underground nests. In
empty lots throughout Hidalgo County the hot clay shed into small flakes that
then shriveled into gritty dust soon taken by the swollen wind. Clouds of dust
blew across the parking lots at La Plaza Mall as shoppers trooped across the
tacky asphalt. At dusk, when the full force of the heat subsided, the fire ants
finally ventured out.

The air thickened as if there were a material weight to it harboring particles the lungs could not easily tolerate. The air grew visibly darker as the days passed, the southern winds transporting a residue that left a thin sheen on cars left out all night.

Not a word came from the local meteorologists or the local papers.

Normally Deep South Texas was relatively free from air pollution because of the strong winds that blew in from the northeast and across the Gulf from the southeast. McAllen's air regularly ranked it as one of the "cleanest" cities in the United States, and the city prided itself as a home to the thousands of winter tourists who spent each winter sunning under clear blue skies while most of the rest of the country endured bitter cold.[1] In mid-April, however, the experts finally broke their vows of media silence when any idiot could see and feel the gunk in the air. According to the Texas Natural Resource Conservation Commission (TNRCC), peasants in southeastern Mexico and Central America were burning their fields to make way for their seasonal plantings, sending clouds of smoke northward with the strong winds.[2] According to TNRCC, "Individuals who experience irritation as a result of the smoke should avoid outdoor activity."[3]

In the heat, burly wind, and smoky haze of early summer, Valley farmworkers, both with papers and those *sin papeles,* without documentation, harvested onions that lay like fat softballs in long, deep furrows. Stooped over and sweating, the farmworkers labored from dawn to past dusk to strip the onions from the ground, trim their green tops, then shove the 1015s into brown burlap bags. The onions, named 1015s for the month and day they were to be planted each year (October 15), were products of the biogenetic wizardry of the Texas A&M University Experiment Station in Weslaco, engineered by Aggie scientists to thrive in the Valley's tropical climate. By the first of May tens of thousands of burlap bags, each stuffed to the brim with 1015s, stood in long, lazy lines zigzagging across Valley fields. Soon the farmworkers would return to load the burlap sacks onto diesel trucks bound for the packing sheds.

Strangling spring with a raw acridity, the onion harvest filled the air in South McAllen and the strip of packing plants along Business 83, which followed the rail line. The April winds catapulted particles of onion skin far from the fields. The skins blew against the wheels of the cars at La Plaza Mall, pressed tightly against the steel by the wind, then fell to the ground between gusts and shuffled underneath the cars. As the onion trucks headed for the packing sheds, whole onions, like hobos abandoning a freight train, jumped from the truck beds and hit the pavement at a run. Whole and smashed onions collected in pools and eddies along the side of the highways and county roads and in the parking lots of HEB, Wal-Mart, and Target.

On the edge of onion fields under the shade of an expanse of the bridge linking McAllen to the Reynosa industrial park, Agents Lefty Maldonado and Speedy Allison stood watching for illegal aliens. From their spot behind a concrete bridge column the two agents could see straight south across two miles of flat onion fields to the trees that lined the banks of the Rio Grande. Before their eyes hundreds of bags of onions cooked in burlap while waiting for a ride to the packing shed. A small crew of farmworkers, all hatted against the sun, finished with their tasks after another long day, then drank from plastic water bottles before climbing into a battered pickup truck.

Lefty and Speedy (Speedy was nicknamed for his talent behind the wheel) were still recovering from their meal at Willie B's Barbecue in Alamo. Among a few remaining snowbirds who would soon pack up and return to their midwestern homes, they had consumed plates filled with steaming barbecued beef and chicken, cole slaw, ranchero beans, and tortilla chips, then had swilled down thirty-two-ounce cups of sweetened tea. All for $5.35 plus tax.

With one eye out for any undocumented workers who might choose to cross the onion fields or sneak across the bridge, they talked comfortably with each other, first about the illegals by the hundreds who had been walking nightly between the fixed positions, called X's, of agents atop the levee.

Tonight Lefty and Speedy were assigned to a "rover" position, free to pursue undocumented workers wherever they might find them. Their objective was to stem the flow between the agents in their X's. Lefty and Speedy were not optimistic about their chances. Out loud they wondered how countless aliens who chose to walk across the bridge could safely jump to the ground without breaking a leg or ankle.

"It's got to be fifteen feet at least," said Lefty.

"Maybe more," said Speedy.

Almost every night undocumented workers cut new holes or opened old ones in the chain-link fence on either side of the long four lanes leading to and from the American port of entry, then shinnied down orange ropes to the onion fields below. Each morning agents cut down the orange ropes swinging in the strong winds, then followed the sign, which frequently led to trails between the agents in their vehicles. The agents in their trucks never saw them.

Rocking and Swaying

The biggest security problem at this port of entry, one that was never discussed at the McAllen Station, was that the Rio Grande was at the far south end of the long bridge. Because the southern, Mexican, end of the bridge spanned the Rio Grande, once undocumented workers had walked past the Mexican guards who protected the south end of the bridge, they were already on American soil. Or at least above it, the onion fields fifteen feet below them. Whatever construction, architecture, and consultant firms had designed this bridge had clearly placed international security at the bottom of their list of priorities. In effect, the agents were stuck defending the border from a position two miles from the river. The onion fields created a sort of no man's land in which illegal aliens every night demonstrated their skills at avoiding capture.

Both agents now stared again at the small, irregular hole in the chain-link fence directly above them. The INS had repaired the hole cut with bolt cutters numerous times, but it was always reopened, enlarged, and improved upon within a matter of hours or days. Immigrant workers squeezed through this and other holes in the fence, then leaped to a supporting buttress a few feet below the hole before reaching a ledge ten feet from the gravel ground beneath. They used cheap orange rope purchased in Reynosa. The night before, Lefty and Speedy had hauled in three undocumented workers just as their feet landed on American soil.

"This is a gold mine," said Speedy. "It's perfect. We just sit here and catch them. They can't see us until they hit the ground, and then there's nowhere for them to run."

That was all true, but tonight's debate centered on how the illegals managed to reach the ground with leg, knee, and ankle bones intact. The two agents had stopped once in mid-sentence when Lefty shone his Mag light at two figures above them on the bridge. Outlined in the fading dusk, two young men in dark clothes turned when the light hit them to run back south until they were out of sight.

"I'd say that was deterrence at its finest," laughed Lefty, following the two figures with his NVGs. "I'm telling you, bro, we got us a gold mine here." "Deterrence" was the catch phrase of Operation Rio Grande, the logistical strategy by which the number of undocumented workers and the amount of drugs were to be controlled and diminished.[4]

The two agents measured the height of the buttress several different ways, discussed the various possibilities and techniques employed by the aliens, then detailed the degree of difficulty to reach the ground from the bridge as if they were Olympic figure skating judges. On the one hand, they were just passing time but, on the other, they were also talking shop. Such knowledge might come in handy in the future.

"I don't see how they do it," Lefty concluded. "It's got to be seven feet, maybe more, from the top of that concrete. Plus they have to edge along that thin strip while they are holding on with their hands to that piece that sticks out there." Lefty shone his Mag on the spots he was identifying.

"All I'm saying is that it's not that hard to do," Speedy maintained. "Not if you are afraid of getting caught and you got the adrenaline working for you."

"Yeah," said Lefty. "Kind of a fight or flight situation."

I could not remain silent during this discussion. I sided with Speedy. To demonstrate how easily it might be done, I scaled the buttress. Speedy's pride now forced him to prove Lefty wrong and do me one better. In spite of Willie B's recent dinner sitting like an anchor in his stomach, not to mention the twenty-five pounds of additional weight he carried in his tool belt and vest, Speedy took a running start at the concrete bridge buttress, hurled himself against the immovable object at full speed, then amid several serious grunts pulled himself up until he stood within an arm's distance of the hole in the fence.

Between deep breaths Speedy bragged, "Not that hard when you actually do it. All this gear doesn't help much." Having proved his point, at least to himself, he carefully descended the structure, finally jumping with one hand tight against his gun belt before he hit the gravel.

Lefty had to give it a try. How could he not? If his shift partner could do it, not to mention the old professor from the university, then so must he. Lefty readied himself, then charged the wall, but, like a horse afraid to clear a jump, he veered off to the left at the last possible second. Again he charged the wall, this time finding a handhold, but gravity and Willie B's won out.

Speedy had plenty of advice for Lefty's third attempt, but Lefty would hear none of it. After an unsuccessful third and fourth try, he leaned against the buttress exhausted and for the moment defeated.

"I'm going to Customs," said Speedy, sensing the time was right to give his buddy a little space. Border Patrol agents were allowed to use an employee bathroom there. Lefty nodded.

As befit a man who did not abide silences and loved to tell stories, Lefty quickly recovered his dignity and soon was deep into a tale about the "babe" at the convenience store not far from the port of entry. Lefty was happily married with two children and a brand-new mortgage payment.

"There's nothing wrong with looking. Right? That's my motto. I'm married, but I still got eyes."

Lefty was proud of his two-month-old daughter and more than agreed with his Puerto Rican relatives' pronouncement that his baby girl had his eyes and hair. But that did not mean he could not appreciate an attractive woman. So even after the quick dinner at Willie B's, Lefty had insisted that they stop at the convenience store, where he purchased one pack of gum, one Three Musketeers, and one quart of Gatorade while Speedy, as if to insult the heat, drew a cup of hot coffee from the steel canister on the back aisle.

It had been difficult not to stare directly at the gorgeous young woman behind the counter, but each man, in his own way, tried not to be too obvious. The clerk, sensing their interest, had stood up from a wooden chair as they had entered, adjusted her tight, seamless red top, then walked nonchalantly down the nearest aisle.

Outside again in the wind and the heat, Lefty had said under his breath to Speedy, "Did you see that? I joked around with her the other day for a few minutes. Nothing wrong with that. But did you see the look she gave me? Is that a babe?"

Speedy readily agreed with Lefty. Both lamented the fact that news of their babe sightings had somehow reached the station. More and more agents were coming to the convenience store to buy their candy and hot coffee, coffee that in truth was not very good even by Border Patrol standards.

"Nothing wrong with looking," said Lefty now to himself. "I'm married, but I still got eyes."

Lefty, a natural mimic, was ready to launch into his favorite impression of one of his fellow agents at the McAllen Station when he suddenly fell silent in the air laden with the smell of onions and diesel fumes. Ignoring the usual parade of eighteen-wheelers across the long bridge, each laden with manufactured goods from the loading docks of American-, Japanese-, Korean-, German-, French-, and Dutch-owned maquiladoras in Reynosa, Lefty's attention was drawn to a movement out of the corner of his eye.

Two bright red Nike tennis shoes hung from the buttress just a few feet from Lefty's head, each foot connected to a leg. First one shoe, then the other, searched blindly in the dark for a foothold in the rough concrete, seemed to hesitate, then continued the hunt. As if in a trance for a few seconds before recognizing the meaning of these disembodied parts hanging before him, Lefty shone his Mag flashlight on the bridge. Speedy returned from the bathroom.

The shoes and the legs belonged to a thin man dressed in dark jeans and a T-shirt who was frantically searching for the right place to slide down the buttress. Coming through the hole in the fence behind him was a very fat man. This second man actually appeared to be stuck in the hole.

Against the noise of the grinding diesel gears, Lefty's Mag light set in motion a memorable, pathetic charade. When the thin man realized he had been spotted, he quickly returned to the hole in the fence. But his escape route was blockaded by human flesh. Fight or flight?

In a great, silent panic the thin man began to push and shove the fat man's buttocks back through the hole in the fence. He found little success at first, his frustration growing as the seconds ticked off the clock. Lefty jumped up, grabbed one of the thin man's legs, then held on for dear life. The thin man, with Lefty tugging on one end of him, continued to shove and pushed the fat man's ass through the hole in the fence.

The struggle continued in the cooling heat, the thin man burdened by an immovable obstruction to his freedom as well as the weight of Lefty stubbornly refusing to release his grip. The fat man labored against the chain link as if his life depended on it. As the diesel trucks lumbered by on the bridge, the scene at ground level resembled less the dignified struggle of immigrant workers proudly facing the challenges and raw dangers of a new, foreign land than a trailer from a Three Stooges movie.

Lefty finally released the thin man's leg to end the stalemate. In turn the thin man immediately found the leverage and strength to propel the fat man back through the hole in the fence. The two ran back in the direction of Reynosa as quickly as they were able.

Lefty and Speedy were philosophical about this turn of events. They knew that the two men would spread the story to the other waiting undocumented workers on the Mexican side of the bridge. For at least two hours Lefty and Speedy had effectively plugged one hole in the immigration dike. Again they had deterred.

Rocking and Swaying

"I think he may have seen the red light on your radio," Speedy told Lefty.

"Could be. Have to do something about that next time." Lefty radioed the dispatcher, "We got two turnbacks on the bridge."

Before much else could be discussed, the dispatcher reported three hits on a sensor a mile west of their present position. Five minutes later Lefty and Speedy were staring at a starving cow in the moonlight. The cow, rib bones pushing against the hide of its belly, lay under a tree a few hundred yards from the sensor near the banks of the Rio Grande.

"This cow is pathetic," said Lefty in disgust. "They ought to put it out of its misery."

The cow lay in a semicoma while the two men discussed it. Its hindquarters were crooked, the results of a traffic accident. Speedy, who had seen the poor cow many times before, was convinced that the animal could not walk. The owners, added Lefty, evidently could not afford the price of hay, so they fed the animal watermelons stolen from a nearby field. The cow managed to stay alive by eating watermelons during the day under the shade of a nearby mesquite, but its fate could not be prolonged much longer.

"They ought to kill it and get it over with," said Lefty. "Somebody should call the SPCA."

"Yeah, right," said Speedy, knowing that no one would ever call and even if they did, authorities would not show up for weeks or months.

The starving cow, oblivious to the agents as they readied themselves for their surveillance of the area, remained supernaturally quiet as it waited in its private delirium for the morning light and the next load of watermelons.

After grabbing his gear and spraying himself from head to foot with repellent, Speedy hid in a line of trees by the side of yet another onion field. Lefty, with a clear, unhampered view of the area, chose a spot in a clump of prickly pear that bordered the edge of the same field. Whoever set off the sensor must cross this onion field in full view of either Speedy or Lefty before reaching a canal filled with Rio Grande water spanned by a concrete foot bridge. If the *coyote* could get his human cargo to the other side of the foot bridge, they could take several different trails to Old Military Highway.

"This is always good traffic," said Lefty as he hid himself carefully behind the prickly pear and began to scan the field every few minutes with his NVGs. Between scanning he swatted at the mosquitoes that ignored his covering of Deep Woods Off. Lefty claimed that the mosquitoes did not bother him. However, ticks made his skin crawl. Ticks too small to feel—just tiny black dots on the skin. Smaller than a freckle. Unnoticeable until a shower at the end of the shift. But then the spots become infected. The ticks collected along cattle and wild game trails, some of the same trails frequented by aliens and dope smugglers.

"The mosquitoes and the chiggers you learn to live with," Lefty stated, "but the ticks, especially the little black ones, drive me nuts."

Lefty lay flat on his stomach, wormed his way carefully to where the cactus ended and the plowed earth began, then dug himself carefully into the dirt. No one appeared. The moonlight highlighted the tops of the unpicked onions in their deep furrows, but no one tried to cross this onion field. A hundred yards west of Lefty, Speedy radioed him, "How long you want to give it?"

"Another twenty minutes."

Just as Speedy was about to show himself, Lefty whispered into the radio mike, "I got 'em. Five. Repeat five. Fifty yards out and coming directly this way. Stay where you are." Lefty could not believe his good luck. They were right there in front of him. But where had they been? They must have been walking a hundred yards, then lying flat, then walking a hundred more. That was the only explanation for how they could appear out of nowhere and suddenly be on top of them.

Five shadows picked their way delicately among the rows of onions, each figure briefly silhouetted against the partial moon. The wind muffled their footfalls, but as they got within thirty feet Lefty could hear tennis shoes crunching against the sun-parched outer earthen layer covering the fertile Valley soil. The last of the five figures, a much smaller silhouette, looked misshapen, its head bloated and oddly askew.

Lefty's plan was simple. Rather than chase after the aliens in the onion field in the middle of the night, a strategy that might result in some of them escaping, he would let them walk right up to him, then arrest them. The element of surprise would immobilize them. Lefty let two minutes pass as he waited for them to get close enough to grab, but not a single shadow reappeared. Finally rising up on one knee from his hiding place, Lefty glanced back in the direction of his truck on the other side of the brush line, heard a twig snap, then madly dashed for the canal. As he sprinted, he yelled to Speedy over the radio, "They made the road. I don't know how they did it, but they're on the road."

Rocking and Swaying

Lefty ran full speed down the trail through the brush, dodging tree limbs, thorny vines, and cactus to find himself on the shoulder of the road not far from the crippled cow. "They're on the other side of the ditch," he yelled over the radio to Speedy, still invisible.

Running along the irrigation ditch, the only sound his own heavy breathing and the jostle of his equipment belt, Lefty reached the concrete foot bridge and deftly crossed it. The bridge, constructed from crude, stacked concrete forms, was difficult to see in the half-dark. It would have been very easy in the confusion to fall from it into the canal below.

"Border Patrol!" Lefty shouted just as he reached the far side of the canal. The beam from his Mag shone on backs and necks fleeing wildly from him. Lefty overtook three of the figures before they had gone another fifty feet, yelling at them, "Get down! Hands on your head. Don't move." Three shapes, including the smallest figure, collapsed, bodies crumbling as if felled by an ax.

The mother, a woman in her early thirties, sat sobbing on the ground between attempts to catch her breath. Dressed in a short skirt spattered with mud, a baggy T-shirt, and cheap tennis shoes with no socks, she cried loudly as tears rolled down her cheeks. She pushed back her long, dark hair, then ineffectively brushed away a few of the tears with her forearm. She cried in part because she knew that if they had reached an opening in a barbed-wire fence just a hundred yards farther along the canal, she and her family would have been free. But she also cried because she did not know what would happen next. She had heard that the agents would demand a *mordida* from her, or rape and beat her and her daughters. She was not from Reynosa but from the interior of Mexico. She did not know how it worked.

On the ground next to her sat her sixteen-year-old daughter, who seemed more curious than afraid. She was exhausted, like her mother, but in control of her emotions. Next to her, sitting in an eerie, total silence, was her sister, an eleven-year-old who wore, in spite of the heat, a faux leopard skin hat atop her head.

Lefty ran down the two other aliens, both men in their thirties, then led them back, one with his wrists secured behind him by plastic restraints. The men, as if on cue, quickly declared that they were unrelated to the woman or the girls but had agreed to accompany them when they met them on the banks of the Río Bravo earlier that day. One of them was, in fact, the *coyote,* but neither he nor the others would admit it. They never did.

Speedy spent another twenty minutes searching the high grass and tall weeds by the canal before finally giving up.

"I only saw five," Lefty reminded him.

"I know," said Speedy, "but I swear I saw another one in front of them. Probably just seeing things."

The mother cried, but more quietly now, minute by minute exhaustion overcoming her along with the weight of her fear. As she cried, her teenager daughter comforting her at one point, she watched with an anxious eye as Speedy searched the two men before guiding them into the back of the truck. Maybe this was when the agents would attack them, when they were out of sight of the other Mexicanos and before the agents had radioed the station. Five minutes later Lefty was driving all five illegal aliens back to the McAllen Station for processing.

"Smell that?" he challenged as he rolled down his window. The stench from the back of the truck was undeniable, a combination of rancid river water, human sweat, and raw onions.

At two in the morning a group of young Brazilian men, with no connection to the ones who attacked the van, themselves waiting to be transferred to the detention camp near Los Fresnos, swarmed within their holding cells adjacent to the processing room to catch a glimpse of the woman with her two daughters. The voices of the Brazilian men could not be heard in the processing room outside their cells, but their intentions were clear as they pointed, gestured, and smiled at the mother and her two daughters. For a few brief minutes the Brazilians, forgetting their own troubles, appraised the women as if they were cattle going to the slaughter. Then they lost enthusiasm in the diversion and went back to sleep on the metal bunks that lined the cells. One or two of them, diehards, huddled closer to the glass to observe what would happen next to the newest detainees.

Lefty supervised the processing of the mother and her two daughters. Although she remained as quiet as her youngest daughter, who sat next to her, the mother was still very upset. The youngest slid her metal chair as close to her mother as she could get it. With unusual patience, this girl waited in her chair for whatever would come next, her large eyes set deeply into a round but gaunt face with pale, delicate skin. So preposterous in the summer heat, the faux leopard skin hat could not help but draw attention.

A fresh look at the young girl underneath the fluorescent station lights revealed that she was blind in her right eye, the iris wandering about in the orb as if it had a mind of its own.

But there was more amiss than her blind eye. Again the hat deflected and sheltered the truth of her situation. This eleven-year-old Mexican girl—the mother told Lefty they were from Monterrey—was missing her eyebrows. Absent, too, was the long, dark hair that should have been hers.

The girl slipped her cumbersome hat off for a brief second. Beneath the faux fur her scalp was shockingly bare. The glare of the overhead light bounced off a small tumor that terribly disfigured the skin on the right side of her skull. With a practiced gesture the young girl returned the absurd hat to her head.

Later Lefty said, with both shock and sadness in his usually animated voice, "Did you see that thing on her head? Looked like she's getting chemo or they shaved her head or something." He was troubled but had no answers.

The little girl continued to sit patiently beside her mother, close enough almost to be in her lap, before answering questions about her age, place of birth, and other information that Lefty required. Absently she grabbed her mother's hand at one point, held it tightly for a minute, then let it go.

Jack Spurrier appeared from the ops room with a baloney sandwich on a white paper plate. He handed the young girl the sandwich and smiled briefly at her before returning to the swivel chair in front of his computer screen. Coldly regarding the two pieces of Wonder Bread and thin meat between, the little girl did not touch the sandwich. Having come much too far in her short life to allow this trouble at the border to bother her, she was waiting to see what her mother wanted her to do. Her mother bent over her to whisper a few words that no one but the two of them could hear. The little girl handed the sandwich to her mother, and the woman placed it carefully into her mud-spattered, black plastic purse.

It took less than an hour to process paperwork on the five Mexican immigrants. A few minutes later they were seated in the back of the transport van, which dropped them off at the bridge leading to Reynosa. After notifying the Mexican authorities of the five Mexican citizens who were to be VRed, the agent behind the wheel waited for more than twenty minutes. Convinced that the Mexican authorities were yet again no-shows, the agent unlocked the entrance to the gate in the ten-foot-tall chain-link fence that bordered the bridge. He watched all five VRs walk back across the Río Bravo without the customary Mexican escort.

At the McAllen Station the two flags, the Stars and Stripes and the much smaller green Border Patrol flag trimmed in gold, were buffeted about at the top of the flagpole by the gusts that whipped through McAllen for the next six days. The hot Mexican winds blew down the streets and the narrow alleys of Reynosa, clearing the plaza of plastic wrappers, newspapers, and other trash that had accumulated during the day. The beggars, all women and children— the children asked for money but then cursed when they did not get what they wanted—were nowhere in sight, nor were the friendly, smiling pimps who offered male American tourists free directions to the "best whores in Boys' Town."

The strong winds from the interior of Mexico ripped across the waters of the Río Bravo and roared over the green tops of the onions still buried in the parched Valley fields. Before crossing the Río Bravo the same winds must have pushed hard at the backs of the mother, her teenage daughter, and the eleven-year-old girl. (The *coyote* and the other man abandoned them as soon as they reached Mexican soil.) The wind pushed against them now as they walked through the empty plaza, side streets, and alleys, found them yet again as they reached the empty stretch of paved four-lane highway heading due west through the ragged barrios and *colonias* of Reynosa.

The trio passed flimsy structures made of random bits of cardboard boxes, pieces of rotting plywood, and cinder blocks purchased ten at a time. Many of these countless houses flooded every time it rained in Reynosa; the dirt floors within turned to mud. Extension cords stretched precariously like clotheslines from one house to the next to provide the only source of electricity. The interiors of a few houses were lit, but most were dark. Interior plumbing was an unimaginable luxury. The Rio Grande valley was extremely poor by American standards, but Reynosa's desperate poverty far exceeded the extremes of the American version.

Now the three females were forced to retrace their steps where, just fourteen hours earlier, they had ridden an old bus along the highway to Monterrey. Before their *coyote* had called out to him that afternoon to stop the bus, the driver had pulled to the side of the road knowing full well what his passengers were going to do. The public bus served as a taxi to the border, each day carrying loads of undocumented workers within walking distance to the Río Bravo.

Throughout the rest of the night the winds roared past the scrawny Mexican cattle left on the riverbank to feed on whatever God provided. These same winds roughed up the brush and trees that lined the river before crossing the thin lane of water serving as the international boundary. Among the thick carrizo cane on the banks of the Río Bravo the stench of the river and the Valley onions mingled in the close, tight air as a young girl with cancer huddled with her mother and sister, the three of them waiting for dawn and another chance at a better life.

Cannibals

The banks of the Rio Grande simmered with human blood and violence. As they waited in the carrizo cane to cross the river, the onion girl and her family were the most recent newcomers to a region mired in a long history of palpable human misery.[1] In the streets and alley ways of Matamoros and the surrounding area on both sides of the river, a cult of twenty-four men and women had systematically preyed upon the population. Before they were finally arrested, the cult ritually murdered fifteen men and women; they were also suspected of an additional six murders. Early Sunday morning, March 12, 1989, cult members, just forty miles downriver from McAllen, kidnapped Mark Kilroy near Garcia's Restaurant, a popular meeting place two blocks from the bridge to Brownsville.[2] Mark Kilroy was a college student on spring break from the University of Texas at Austin. He had arrived at South Padre Island the day before, then driven with friends to Brownsville, where they had parked the car before walking across the bridge that spans the Rio Grande. On the way back to the car after a night of partying in Matamoros, a cult member lured Mark into a side street near Garcia's where others overcame him and threw him into the back of a truck. Mark Kilroy escaped from the truck as it sped through the deserted streets of Matamoros, but a car filled with cult members following the truck caught him, bound his legs and arms, and transported him to a small ranch outside of the city.

Rocking and Swaying

Mark was left overnight in a small barn. The next day Adolfo Constanzo, the leader of the pseudo-Santería and Palo Mayombe cult, ritually slaughtered him with a machete. When the Mexican police raided the ranch two months later, they found a large metal pot, a *nganga,* in the same shed where Mark Kilroy and other victims had been killed. In the pot were, "a human brain, a dead turtle, blood, burnt cigars and various spices."[3]

These modern-day cannibals were but one of the Mexican criminal organizations in the 1980s and 1990s that smuggled drugs from the state of Tamaulipas into Deep South Texas. While their crimes were horrific and the national news media paid attention to them for a week, they were fundamentally a group of petty criminals who smuggled illegal drugs across the Río Bravo. Adolfo Constanzo himself was a small-time drug racketeer who used the vestiges of exotic religious rituals to control and manipulate members of his gang. Several cult members believed in fact that Constanzo's spiritual powers made them invincible before the bullets of any law enforcers.

These crazed killers—the majority who still survive are serving time in Mexican prisons—were a piece of a much broader historical discourse on cannibals and cannibalism that was misdirection by American scholars to disguise the real blood and violence permeating the borderlands.[4] In Valley folklore, the indigenous Indians had been accused, tried, and convicted of the practice of cannibalism. The historical facts were far more benevolent. About 10,000 Karankawas, related to the larger group of Indians named the Coahuiltecans, once lived on the barrier islands and coastlines that bordered the Gulf of Mexico/Bay of Campeche including encampments along the banks of the Rio Grande. The core of the historical record charging them with cannibalism rested upon unreliable third- and fourth-hand accounts by early Spanish explorers, wayward priests, rival Indian tribes and, much later, settlers brought by Stephen F. Austin, all of whom had their own reasons for attempting to dehumanize these indigenous peoples. The best record of the Karankawas, who in retaliation against European encroachment and attacks by other Indian tribes kidnapped and killed those who invaded their land, was kept by Spanish explorer Cabeza de Vaca. Cabeza de Vaca, who lived among the Karankawas for years, recounted no incidents of cannibalism in his detailed journals.[5]

Texas naturalist Roy Bedichek and anthropologist W. W. Newcomb, Jr., both attempted to lay this myth of cannibalism aside, though few historians or social scientists took note.[6] Throughout the centuries the charges of cannibalism against the Karankawas conveniently served to draw attention from the almost total destruction of this tribe, one more tragic example of the genocide of indigenous North Americans. From 10,000 men, women, and children, the Karankawas were reduced to a feeble band of 100 last seen in Mexico in 1827.

The people to fear along the border were not the indigenous Indians who were driven from their lands, nor even the bizarre drug cult led by a petty drug dealer who acted as if he had magical powers. When the first explorers reached the Texas coastline and sailed up the Rio Grande, they found forests of palms covering the riverbanks and rich, virgin prairie lands stretching north and south from the river.[7] Alonzo de Piñeda in 1519 was among the first to appear at the mouth of Rio Grande. For the next two hundred years others came seeking gold, land, and power, but none were successful: the expeditions of Camargo, de Auz and Ramirez, Garay, and Caniedo each met with failure.[8] José de Escandón, in contrast, set out in 1748 from Querétaro with 755 soldiers and 2,515 citizens to colonize the region for Spain and ultimately quell Indian uprisings that threatened Nuevo León, Coahuila, and parts of what is now South Texas.

By the time he completed his tasks, José de Escandón had laid out fourteen towns and missions, including three on the north side of the Rio Grande. There was little real motivation at first to settle the lands on the north side of the river because the livestock, goats, sheep, and cattle thrived quite well on the virgin grasses on the south side. But in only a matter of years the colonists' animals had overgrazed the prairies on the southern side. Thus the Spanish settled Laredo in 1755 and founded Rio Grande City, the first Valley town, in 1757. Roma followed in 1767. The Spanish census of the region from Laredo south to the mouth of the river recorded twenty-four settlements and missions with a meager population, including 3,473 Indians, of 8,993.

Land grants were eventually awarded colonists on both sides of the Rio Grande by the Spanish Royal Commission. Those who had lived the longest in the region, the *primitivos,* received 9,000 acres of land for ranching and 1,200 acres for farming; a second group of colonists between 1770 and 1810 also received large tracts of land. .

Water was of extraordinary importance. Original land grants were long and narrow strips that reached to the banks of the Rio Grande, each designed to provide access to the river.[9] Farming, in consequence, was a bust. Rainfall was too sparse and unreliable, and flooding was a constant threat.[10] Colonists, lacking both the knowledge and the technology of rudimentary irrigation, relied on their herds for their economic survival. In 1757, Mier recorded 274 residents but 44,000 head of stock. Not far away in Guerrero—now called Old Guerrero—357 men, women, and children looked after 51,000 head.

These lands were geographically isolated, travel made even more difficult by the overgrazing of the colonists' herds. Mesquite and thick, impenetrable vegetation soon replaced the natural grasslands, further distancing the small communities and ranches from each other and from cities to the south. It took months for goods to arrive from Mexico City.

For more than a hundred years the colonists and their offspring suffered from the onslaught of marauding Indians displaced by settlement to the north. To protect the colonists from bands of Apaches, Comanches, Mescaleros, and Kickapoos, ranches and communities were converted into small fortresses, but even these precautions were not always sufficient. From 1812 to 1830 Indian attacks against the colonists were so ferocious in this region that many smaller ranches north of the Rio Grande were abandoned for the shelter and safety of towns.

Yet the bloody violence in Deep South Texas and northern Tamaulipas extended beyond these initial Indian conflicts. The Rio Grande was the focal point of wars of independence, the American and Mexican civil wars, and wars fanned by trade, international politics, and racism. Banditry and lawlessness plagued this frontier for more than three centuries, a record of violence and conflict second to none in American history.[11]

Brownsville, for example, was founded on the banks of the Rio Grande in 1846 by Major Jacob Brown. He built a fortress directly opposite the much older, more established community of Matamoros to taunt and inflame the Mexican citizenry.[12] During the Mexican War communities from the mouth of the river to Rio Grande City became staging areas for the invasion of Mexico. Large numbers of American troops were shipped to the region. Miserable living conditions under a steaming, tropical sun led to serious outbreaks of dysentery. Soon troops mustered from the southern states were fighting and killing Mexicans, Mexican Americans, and each other on both sides of the river. Before the U.S. Army ever initiated the invasion of Mexico, more than 500 American soldiers were murdered, executed, or died from disease. Pitched battles during this war were fought on the north side of the Rio Grande at

Resaca de la Palma and Palo Alto, but the worst destruction took place at Mier, Camargo, and Guerrero, all original Escandón settlements.

The 1848 Treaty of Guadalupe Hidalgo did not end the violence. Remnants of both American and Mexican armies plagued the region with murder and banditry as failed revolutions in Mexico fanned the flames. Epidemics of cholera and yellow fever broke out in 1843, 1858, 1866, 1867, and 1882. Hurricanes brought additional devastation to the Valley coastal populations in 1858, 1867, and 1880.

Immediately after the Mexican War opportunistic Anglos descended into Deep South Texas. Establishing a thriving but corrupt court system, Anglos took control of deeds belonging to descendants of the original Spanish colonists. While according to the Treaty of Guadalupe Hidalgo original landowners retained rights to their lands and were also granted American citizenship, in practice only a few of the most powerful were able to do so. In a matter of a few short years Anglos from outside the region owned, through legal or illegal means, the majority of the land and wealth on the north side of the Rio Grande.

Named for Scottish-born Ewen Cameron, who had led an attack on Mier during the Mexican War, Cameron County was founded in 1848.[13] Hidalgo County, named after the famous Father Miguel Hidalgo who began the Mexican Revolution, was carved out of Cameron County in 1852. The new county was named in his honor to appease the remaining Hispanics who still lived north of the river.

The often historically neglected Cortina Wars, 1859–60, were but one more example of the flavor of these times ruled by violence, spurred by overt racism, and fanned by binational conflict.[14] Juan Nepomuceno Cortina was the son of an affluent ranchowner who, against all odds, retained some of the land passed on to him from an original Spanish land grant in Cameron County. Cortina was visiting Brownsville one day when he witnessed a deputy sheriff beating one of his ranch hands. Cortina intervened and shot the deputy sheriff, then rounded up a small band of sympathizers who had tired of their racist treatment. Cortina rode back into Brownsville, took the city by force, then held the city hostage until federal troops arrived days later. For the next several years Cortina, who escaped capture by crossing the Rio Grande into Mexico, robbed from the rich and gave to the poor according to his supporters or, according to his detractors, joined the ranks of border cutthroats. The U.S. Army finally chased Cortina into Mexico where he was eventually captured.

Juan Nepomuceno Cortina soon, however, returned to prominence as the governor of the state of Tamaulipas. That a man accused of murder and hunted down by the U.S. Army could reinvent himself as the highest Mexican official of Tamaulipas highlighted the profound political and social instability of a border region premised upon conflict, racism, and senseless violence.

The business of smuggling was a fact of life in these borderlands, but after the Mexican War firmly established the Rio Grande as the international boundary between Mexico and the United States, a wide variety of goods were systematically and illegally transported from one nation to the other. Along this frontier the law of supply and demand, of abundance of one product and the scarcity of another, fueled a thriving alternative economy. While illegal immigrants, marijuana, and cocaine have been most in fashion in recent years, wood, furniture, leather, alcohol, tobacco, and guns were just a few of the various goods smuggled across the Rio Grande to supply the needs of Mexican and American populations.

In a region where jobs were always scarce and wages next to nothing, smugglers viewed their work in terms of economic survival. By extension, those who smuggled were not necessarily viewed as criminals per se but men who worked for a living just like others. In this same historical context the smuggled goods were not necessarily defined as harmful or dangerous to society. Smugglers in the small towns along the Rio Grande were profit-motivated businessmen, even respected members of the community, and the goods transported from one side of the river to the other were their inventories.[15]

Valley residents considered Los Rinches, the Texas Rangers, and later the agents of the Border Patrol, Las Patrullas Fronterizas, the real criminals. From their perspective these law enforcers not only perpetuated racial violence against Hispanics but simultaneously attempted to limit smuggling as a major source of income for an otherwise impoverished population.[16]

As in any criminal occupation, some smugglers were good at their jobs, and some were not; some made a living, and some got caught. Families in communities like Rio Grande City, families in which generation after generation smuggled every kind of product south to north and back again, were admired or disrespected by other residents less because of their chosen occupation than their skills and talents in their chosen criminal profession. Although smuggling families feuded among each other, they always sided against the law enforcers whose job it was to limit their livelihood. Smuggling—not farming, ranching, or low-wage labor work—sustained many disenfranchised Valley residents, providing dependable income.

Violence in the Valley was not a by-product of smuggling, at least not in the beginning. More typical of the causes of violence prevalent in the Valley at the turn of the twentieth century was the Plan of San Diego. Basilio Ramos was arrested in McAllen in 1915. Found on him was a copy of the Plan of San Diego, a political strategy calling for Mexican citizens and Mexican Americans throughout the Southwest to rise up against the Anglo elite.[17] Other minorities, including African Americans, Native Americans, and Japanese Americans, were called upon to join with Hispanics in kidnapping, ransoming, and assassinating Anglos. Whether the Plan of San Diego was a real political strategy or a historical hoax, it justified and legitimized a new reign of terror and brutality by Anglos. Using black lists compiled of suspected collaborators in the Plan of San Diego, gangs of Valley Anglos burned the homes of poor Hispanics, lynched their victims, or drove them back across the Rio Grande into Mexico.

Texas Rangers and local law enforcement—the Border Patrol was not yet formally established at the time—even actively directed violence against Hispanics. During a six-week period in the community of San Benito, just south of Harlingen, law enforcers killed nine Mexicans allegedly attempting to escape from the city jail. Many poor Hispanics, fearing for their lives, left their barrios to save themselves and their families by crossing the Rio Grande into Mexico.

"By the middle of September," the *San Antonio Daily Express* reported, "the finding of dead bodies of Mexicans . . . has reached the point where it creates little or no interest."[18] A decade later a Texas legislative subcommittee led by J. T. Canales, state representative from Brownsville, documented the atrocities. One result of the investigation was that the Texas Rangers were disbanded. Later, they were reconstituted within the Texas Department of Public Safety.

Political bossism, which often tacitly sanctioned or even promoted smuggling, created a variant of order and law in the Valley but at the expense of institutionalized discrimination and violence. More than one scholar referred to the resulting system of oppression of Mexican Americans by Anglos in Deep South Texas as feudalistic in nature.[19]

Judge James B. Wells was a prototypical political boss who ruled Cameron County with an iron fist from about 1880 to 1920. When, for example, yet another outbreak of lawlessness and banditry occurred in Rio Grande City— Catarino Garza was using the community as a staging area for raids into Mexico during what has been called the Garza Revolution—Wells called in the Texas Rangers. The Texas Rangers rounded up Garza's men and reestablished order in the community but made no distinctions between Mexican and American citizens of Mexican descent as they wreaked havoc on Hispanics throughout the region.

The Anglo bosses, including men like Judge James B. Wells, used the Texas Rangers as their own private army to control and constrain the majority Mexican American citizenry until the Rangers were finally disbanded.

Political patronage was part of every Valley community, a system run by bosses using the power inherent in their network of county government, municipal government, water districts, and the school system. Their power also extended to the Anglo farming and ranching operations beyond the city limits. These bosses, or *patrones,* provided jobs, favors, and influence and in return expected and received complete loyalty and obedience under a system resembling peonage.[20]

Hidalgo County, and the city of McAllen, was home to more than its share of *patrones,* including Lloyd Bentsen, Sr., one of the most powerful behind-the-scenes figures in the Valley from the early 1920s until his death some seventy years later. Othal Brand, one of Bentsen's protégés, served as mayor of McAllen for more than twenty years and in his eighties ran for the same post in 2002. But elections in 2002 did not resemble those from earlier years when poor Mexican Americans were organized by blocks and voted like chattel. Brand gained the runoff election but finally lost to a Hispanic candidate.

Since the 1970s the Anglo minority has maintained a portion of its power and political control of Valley communities numerically dominated by Mexican Americans in increasingly sophisticated and mostly legal ways. However, whether practiced by Judge Wells or the mayor of McAllen, the basis of the Valley's *patrón* system remained the same. It was a social and political force sustained by a hardcore reliance on institutionalized discrimination grounded in violence and the threat of violence.

The Pharr riot illustrated how the *patrón* system thrived in South Texas far into the second half of the twentieth century. About 300 Mexican American protestors gathered at the Pharr police station on February 6, 1971, to protest alleged police brutality against two Hispanic inmates. Chief Alfonso Ramirez, who served at the pleasure of the Anglo mayor, soon called the local fire department, which sprayed the small crowd, including small children and the elderly, with high-powered fire hoses. The crowd was stirred to action by this senseless act and retaliated by throwing bottles and bricks at the police. They and other law enforcement agents called into the area opened fire on the unarmed crowd. Alfonso Flores, age twenty, was shot and killed by Deputy Sheriff Robert Johnson while standing in front of a barber shop some distance from the disturbance in front of the police station. Although Johnson was never tried by a jury for his alleged offense, young Hispanic men, in contrast, were rounded up by the police and two, Efraim Fernandez and Alonzo Lopez, were charged with felonies. A jury composed of mostly affluent Anglos convicted the men; each received a five-year sentence.[21]

Patrones manipulated the legal system to control those who dared rock the boat. Individuals who criticized the existing system, such as Fernandez and Lopez, suffered the consequences of a racially biased court system or were intimidated, marginalized, beaten, killed, or run out of town. Community organizers who initiated credit unions, head start programs, and other services to benefit poor Hispanics in Pharr were treated similarly.[22] Required literacy standards excluded the majority of the Mexican American population from the jury system. Anglos handpicked the few Mexican Americans who served in public office. Lacking access and legal expertise, Valley Hispanics were virtually powerless before the dominant Anglo police and court systems, which over the years served not only to support the existing *patrón* system but effectively silence any critics.

Thriving well into the 1980s, traditional remnants of Valley bossism were embodied in the atrocities of the McAllen police C Shift. For more than three years McAllen officers working the graveyard or C Shift systematically terrorized low-income Hispanics arrested for minor offenses.[23] Hundreds of the beatings were recorded by an overhead camera at the booking desk of the McAllen

Police Station, and, in 1983, during one of several administrations of Mayor Othal Brand, tapes were finally leaked to the news media. A flood of litigation followed in which McAllen police officers were indicted; several were convicted and sent to prison. The entire administration of the McAllen Police Department was restructured by a court-ordered oversight panel that finally brought modern police practices and standards to the city of McAllen.

During the majority of the twentieth century this violence and mayhem extended to the vast fields and ranches of the Valley. Capital infusion into irrigation just prior to the 1920s, along with the development of the railroad and other necessary infrastructure, spawned a thriving agricultural industry made possible by Mexican and Mexican American laborers. The workers, poorly paid by the standards of the day, cleared the land of mesquite, then constructed the railroad tracks, the intricate system of irrigation channels that crisscrosses the Valley, the bridges, and the roads. The railroad first came to mid-Valley towns in 1904 when plats were laid out for McAllen, Pharr, San Juan, Alamo, Mission, Mercedes, La Feria, and Weslaco.

When the Mexican and Mexican American workforce had completed the infrastructure, these same laborers planted cotton, then irrigated and worked the fields now owned by midwestern farmers who had purchased the farmlands from developers such as Lloyd Bentsen, Sr.[24]

The farmers and the ranchers treated these men and their families—with some exceptions—like serfs, first recruiting them from the Valley or from Mexico with the promise of high wages, then locking them into the *patrón* system, which paid low wages, provided a bare, subsistence living, and frequently forced laborers into debt and servitude. Valley farmworkers repeatedly tried to organize unions to protect their best interests in the 1920s and 1930s, but growers brought more workers from Mexico to break attempts to strike and employed the local law enforcement, including Texas Rangers and, later, troopers from the Department of Public Safety, as their personal strikebreakers and goons.

The reconstituted Texas Rangers, still called Los Rinches in the Valley, were again used as strikebreakers in the 1960s. The landmark case of *Medrano* v. *Allee* documented in excruciating detail the brutality of Texas Ranger Captain Alfred Y. Allee against Valley farmworkers and organizers.[25] County law enforcement also played a significant role in subverting democracy along the Rio Grande, retrieving farmworkers who ran away from their jobs, throwing them in jail, and supporting a system of peonage that prevailed well into the second half of the century.[26]

The abuses of the local Anglo citizenry against undocumented workers, if less violent than those of Los Rinches and the Border Patrol, occasionally nagged at the general public's attention. Farmers and ranchers had begged for Mexican workers prior to the Bracero Program, initiated in 1942 when there was a severe shortage of labor within the United States; the resulting program ran well into the 1960s before it was finally abandoned. Workers for many years were actively recruited by Valley growers and their representatives from deep within Mexico then, just as in the earlier part of the century, transported to this country with the promise of high wages. After the end of the Korean War in 1954, when unemployment of American citizens once more became a political concern, the INS initiated Operation Wetback. Along the border hundreds of thousands of Mexicans and Mexican Americans, citizens of the United States, were summarily rounded up for deportation to Mexico.

The Valley received national attention in 1976 when an Anglo farmer in Hidalgo County shot and wounded several Mexican Americans who allegedly stepped on his watermelons during a strike.[27] While the local media virtually ignored the case, the national media reported the innocent verdict awarded the defendant by a jury whose majority, like that in the Lopez and Fernandez trials, was Anglo. Ten years later the defendant's son went to trial for shooting Mexican workers who trespassed on his father's farm. Running to escape the bullets, one man, José Reyes Santillán, drowned in the Rio Grande. The defendant was found guilty, but the jury magnanimously handed him a four-year sentence for his crimes.

Thus, only two viable classes in the countryside and in the towns operated in the Valley's agricultural economy throughout the majority of the twentieth century. A shackled, impoverished Hispanic majority was dominated by a town and farming Anglo elite supported by a tiny number of Mexican American families who traced their wealth back many generations. Challenged by advocates based in Catholic parishes seeking social justice, by federally funded institutions such as Texas Rural Legal Aid that were immune to pressures exerted by Valley elites, and most importantly by a generation of high school– and college-educated Mexican Americans who would no longer tolerate the system of injustice and the inequality perpetuated by violence and blood, the *patrón* system began to crumble.[28]

Rocking and Swaying

Throughout the violence in the twentieth century, poor Valley Hispanics made little distinction between Texas Rangers and agents of the U.S. Border Patrol. Both law enforcement agencies hired only Anglos, both were seen as representatives of the dominant Anglo class, both targeted undocumented farmworkers and other laborers seeking jobs in the Valley, both often failed to distinguish undocumented workers from Mexican American citizens, and both were known for their brutality. As a result, both Texas Rangers and Border Patrol agents were deeply hated.[29]

Border Patrol agents prior to the 1980s were rarely Hispanic, were rarely from the Valley, rarely held any appreciation or knowledge of Valley Hispanic culture, and rarely faced the system of checks and balances that contemporary agents of the Border Patrol endure. Brutality against Mexicans and Mexican Americans was commonplace, swift, and usually invisible to the public because it occurred on the isolated banks of the Rio Grande or far from the eyes of those who were not too afraid to complain.

A modicum of this violence against poor Mexicans and Mexican Americans was encapsulated in *corridos,* popular Hispanic folk songs that were sung and sometimes handed down from one generation to another especially in California and Texas. In place of a written account of the relationship between the Border Patrol and illegal immigrants by scholars of history there is, through the *corridos,* documentation in song.[30]

Crimes by the agents of the Border Patrol against undocumented workers were rarely brought to court by honest agents, a code of silence in place similar to the one that governed McAllen C Shift police officers. Such tacit cooperation allowed the brutality to continue. Victims who were undocumented workers were unlikely to bring charges both because they were unsure of their legal rights and because they were vulnerable to retaliation. But memories of violence did not fade. Many in Deep South Texas personally knew victims or had heard tales of abuse by the Border Patrol.

New immigrants who illegally crossed the Rio Grande had also heard stories about the Border Patrol and feared for their possessions and their lives. *Coyotes,* in their own best interests, exaggerated the stories. At the start of the new millennium many residents of Reynosa and other Mexican border communities, in contrast to those who lived in the interior, knew the truth. They recognized that they had more to fear from Mexican bandits, agents of Mexican law enforcement, and American criminals who hid in the brush along the banks than they did from agents of the U.S. Border Patrol.

In fact Grupo Beta, an amalgam of Mexican law enforcers, had already experienced some success arresting bandits and other criminals who preyed on illegal aliens on the southern side of the border first in California, then in Texas.[31] But while Grupo Beta was active in Matamoros, no Grupo Beta operated along the banks of the river opposite McAllen or farther upriver.

Statistics clearly demonstrated how dangerous the border was for illegal immigrants. In 1998 alone 260 illegal immigrants died while attempting to enter the United States. A year later 236 died in their attempt to enter the United States; at the turn of the millennium, 367 men, women, and children died.[32]

The McAllen Sector was not the most dangerous place along the Mexican border (that dubious honor went to the El Centro Sector, which accounted for 31.4 percent of all deaths over a four-year period) but more than 100 immigrants died from 1998 through the early months of 2001 in this area patrolled by the Border Patrol. Twenty-eight individuals died while trying to cross into the McAllen Sector in 1998; 23 in 1999; 40 in 2000; and 12 in the first months of 2001.

Said another way, 10 percent of all those who died illegally entering the United States from the Mexican border died in the McAllen Sector.[33]

The most common cause of death among individuals seeking work in the United States was "exposure to heat."[34] More than a third of all immigrant deaths were attributed to heat exposure in 1998, and about the same number in 2001.

"Drowning" was the next most likely cause of death, accounting in 1998 for 34.2 percent of all deaths and in 2000, 25.1 percent. The majority of these deaths occurred while trying to cross or recross the Rio Grande.[35]

"Motor Vehicle Accident" followed drowning as the next most common cause of immigrant deaths. This category included personal tragedies like the bailout in San Manuel in which the Guatemalan father was accidentally hit and killed by a passing motorist after the *coyote,* who was driving, recklessly, jumped out of the moving car on Highway 281 North. Motor vehicle accidents claimed 6 percent of all immigrant deaths in 1999 but by 2000 had risen to 13 percent.[36]

Rocking and Swaying

The number of documented human smuggling cases recorded by the Border Patrol declined in the McAllen Sector from 1997 to 2001.[37] However, some agents, especially those who had worked with the special unit designed to bust professional smugglers, knew that the statistics did not always accurately reflect problems in the field. Agents working line watch also knew, based upon their years of experience, that a local *coyote* who guided one or two immigrants across the Río Bravo differed greatly from the *coyotes* in charge of much larger groups of Brazilians and other OTMs such as the ones frequently spied upon by Agent Herman Morningside in the scope truck.

The huge money game of the *narcotraficantes,* a binational form of organized criminal activity never before witnessed in Deep South Texas, magnified the violence. It was one thing to smuggle wooden furniture into Mexico at the turn of the century along with untaxed alcohol, or to cross frozen chickens and *ropa usada* at the turn of the millennium, all products transported by those with special knowledge of the bends and twists of the Rio Grande combined with an understanding of and appreciation for the habits and customs of the Border Patrol and other law enforcement agencies. It was quite another matter, however, to float a thousand kilos of illegal cocaine across the toxic waters when one kilo had a street value of $3,200.

In the 1980s increased American pressure on Latin American criminal organizations exporting drugs into the southeast, including Florida, provided Mexican *narcotraficantes* economic motivation to develop and organize relatively sophisticated distribution systems across the Mexican border and into all parts of the United States. Driving out local Valley families who were then relegated to nickel-and-dime operations, Mexican criminal organizations monopolized a multibillion-dollar-a-year industry. The big-time *narcotraficantes* occasionally employed the expertise of local smugglers, but the big-time profits and risks were far beyond the capabilities and dreams of all but a few Valley residents regardless of their intimate knowledge of the Rio Grande. The "good old days" of family-run drug smuggling operations based in communities bordering the Rio Grande had, for the most part, disappeared. Local residents were now more likely to work for drug cartels based in the interior of Mexico.[38]

Beginning in the 1990s, Mexican drug cartels crossed illegal drugs from Mexico into Deep South Texas on a scale never before witnessed. Some indication of the tremendous amount of illegal drugs flowing into the United

States was the fact that about 50 percent of all illegal drugs seized entering the United States were in the Southwest border region: 17.6 metric tons of cocaine was confiscated in 1997; 30.4 tons in 1998; 37.3 tons in 1999; and 20.1 tons by the end of 2001.[39] The sheer volume of marijuana seized in the Southwest was staggering: 599 tons of marijuana were captured by law enforcement officers in 1997; 1,059 tons in 2001.[40]

Deep South Texas in the 1990s became a primary point of entry for cocaine shipments along the Southwest border as well as a secondary point for marijuana. In the year 2000, the McAllen Sector statistics were mind-boggling: total annual street value for both cocaine and marijuana seized was $628 million.

Month after month McAllen Station agents like Noe Escondido and Charlie Ashton deposited in the steel evidence locker kilos of cocaine and bricks of marijuana. In January 2001 the sector reported $33.9 million in illegal drugs; in February, $30.5 million. March and April figures zoomed to $51.7 million and $47.7 million, followed by a temporary "slow down" in May and June to $29.7 million and $28.7 million. But the flow of illegal drugs from Mexico never stopped night or day, fall or interminable summer.

Through diligence and hard work agents in the McAllen Sector had seized a whopping $87,921,380 worth of cocaine and marijuana in just one month, June 2000, while annual figures in 1999 and 2000 averaged more than two-thirds of a billion dollars.

The agents knew better than anyone else that an incredible volume of drugs also escaped their grasp. It happened almost every day. How much illegal product did they never interdict? Was it $10 billion worth of illegal drugs? $15 billion? $25 billion?[41]

All societies created their own special sets of myths, myths that might legitimate the status quo or explain specific acts or events, myths that went unchallenged but disguised undesirable familial, community, or institutional beliefs and values. But Adolfo Constanzo was no myth. The *padrino* of the pseudo-Santería and Palo Mayombe cult that practiced cannibalism in the twentieth century was a precursor in 1989 of the increased bloodshed and brutality that followed the booming illegal drug industry in Deep South Texas.

Sara Aldrete was unfortunately also not a myth. A young protégé groomed by Adolfo Constanzo, Sara Aldrete was born and raised in Reynosa and attended classes in anthropology at Texas Southmost College in Brownsville.

Rocking and Swaying

At the same time she was busy in the classroom, this young woman worked alongside Constanzo as he performed his crazed rituals of torture upon his unwilling victims. Boldly wearing a necklace fabricated from the bones of her victims for all her college classmates to see, Sara Aldrete was another example of how out of control the banks of both sides of the Rio Grande were fast becoming.[42]

Organized smuggling by the Mexican *narcotraficantes,* as differentiated from the activities of the long-time resident smugglers in communities such as Hidalgo, Peñitas, and Rio Grande City, ushered in new and qualitatively different waves of violence that once more wreaked havoc on the banks of the Rio Grande. The bloodshed that orbited around the maintenance and control of illegal drugs became the context for all other legal and illegal activities along the river including the transportation of undocumented workers. This same drug violence simultaneously infected the cities of McAllen and all other Valley communities.[43]

The banks of the river and the communities that flanked it were not always in constant turmoil. Those rare social critics and observers who actually took the time to visit the region often left disappointed because the Border Patrol could not produce drug busts or apprehensions of large numbers of aliens while the cameras were rolling. Most of the time, in fact, little happened along this border and frontier that was memorable, no more so than in other notoriously violent areas beset by individual, institutional, or societal rampages. The Rio Grande, and the region it defined, were in the past as in the present bucolic landscapes to the casual observer—still, quiet, and remote.[44]

Trapped in increasingly ruthless and senseless violence that inevitably brought with it graft and corruption, the agents of the McAllen Station were outgunned and overmatched at the same time they were handcuffed by agency rules and public policies manufactured in Washington. Even as they chased load after load of illegal drugs flowing through the region, thousands and thousands of illegal aliens escaped their best efforts at apprehension.

What exactly were the men and women of this federal law enforcement agency supposed to do? The executives of the U.S. Border Patrol believed that they had the answer.

X's

A lushly irrigated patch of fertile delta soil, Taylor's Farm snuggled up against a lazy bend and turn in the Rio Grande fifteen miles southeast of McAllen. *Irrigadores* struggled against the June heat as they fought with stubborn irrigation pipe and hoses while repairing sculptured earthen ditches for the next planting.

As the lazy river rolled by the southern banks, drug smugglers counted their lucky stars, because Taylor's Farm, in addition to the abundant cotton, onions, and sorghum it provided its owners, also offered the perfect spot to cross their product. Just enough vegetation provided cover from detection during most parts of the day and night and only thirty yards of shallow water divided Mexico from the United States. Add the fact that Taylor's Farm was less than one-eighth of a mile from a paved, two-lane stretch of all-season asphalt providing several routes of escape, and it was easy to see why Taylor's Farm was so popular with drug smugglers.

For many years the farming operation had been managed by a crusty old man who reportedly roared about the property on an ATV with a big black pistol stuck in the handlebars and a mean-looking German Shepherd ensconced behind him on a special rear seat. His son, Steve, was a wild card best known for his errant behavior. Although Steve had managed in recent years to stay out of prison, last winter he had climbed on top of the barn armed with a shotgun and, from this perch, threatened to shoot any agents from the McAllen Station who ventured near him. Eventually his family persuaded him to come down, but most agents believed that it was only a matter of time before Steve went completely crazy because of his affection for various illegal drugs. All agreed that when that time did come, they did not want to be anywhere near Taylor's Farm.

Agent Jesus "Chuy" Toledo took extra care as he guided his Expedition along a narrow, dusty path that bordered the Rio Grande and Taylor's Farm—on one side the sluggish river; on the other, tilled soil waiting for the seed. The last thing he wanted to do was have a run-in with crazy Steve or his father. At the same time, Taylor's Farm was continuously a drug hot spot, so any agent assigned to it had to be extra alert.

I was riding shotgun in the front seat next to Chuy, the windows sealed and the AC at full blast against the hundred-plus degrees that fried the outside landscape. All the agents told me the same thing about the heat. "You think this is hot, wait until August." The only thing on my mind as we crept along through the clouds of dust was the slow rumble in my stomach from the three greasy tacos I had gorged on at Mamacita's Restaurant off Old Military Highway. My stomach refused to accept that to save a dollar off the price of a Whataburger, fries, and a medium iced tea, I had swallowed three Mamacita's tacos.

Chuy Toledo was a ten-year veteran of the Border Patrol, a stocky man in his early forties who, like most of the other agents, looked older than his actual age because of his time under the baking sun. Chuy's experience told him that the only way he would get a drug bust in this heat was if the dumbest drug smuggler on the southern banks made an appearance. That was unlikely. Any coherent drug smuggler was downing cold beers to beat the temperatures until the evening hours. Still, Chuy had to be prepared.

As we lazily drove through Taylor's Farm, Agent Chuy Toledo waved to one of the *irrigadores* standing atop a rusted-out, red ATV pulled off to one side of the narrow lane. There was a low boy hitched to the ATV packed with irrigation tools and junk. A boy about ten years old stood at the back of the low boy.

"That's the old man's grandson," said Chuy unasked, waving at the boy as we chugged through the dust. My stomach rumbled again, but not yet danger-ously. It was going to be a long four hours until the sun set, the earth cooled, and the smugglers decided to make their moves.

We rounded a big, slow turn in the road and drove on for several hundred yards. I saw Chuy's foot hit the brakes hard just before I was thrown slightly forward against my shoulder harness.

"What do we have here?" Chuy asked aloud, some excitement in his voice. He opened the Expedition door and swung his legs onto the roadbed. Without thinking, my focus still on the tacos from Mamacita's, I mimicked Chuy and threw open my door to jump out of the vehicle before it had come to a complete stop. It was a reflex, an almost involuntary action that I had repeated since January.

I did not see the red ATV zoom past me by less than a few inches—not until it was twenty-five yards down the dusty road and the *irrigador* behind the handlebars was screaming and waving his fist at me. I stood in the road, my mouth wide open in disbelief, slowly realizing what had just occurred.

I took a step backward, the roar of the ATV's engine finally registering. I was shocked but thankful that the ATV had missed me. With the Expedition windows closed tight and the AC on full blast, I had never heard it passing us on the right side—my side—of the road. I had come close, much too close, to being hit.

I took another step back, suddenly recalling the sound of a primal crunch of metal on metal.

Chuy Toledo, forsaking the sign in the roadbed that had originally grabbed his attention, came around the back of the Expedition to ask if I was alright. I told him that I was fine, but I was already beginning to feel profoundly stupid there in the heat, increasingly out of place and a burden to this agent and to the Border Patrol. I think I was in mild shock.

The two of us eyeballed what agents at the McAllen Station, and it seemed everyone else in the free world, would henceforth refer to as "the accident." In the lower left-hand corner of the exterior door panel of the vehicle was a six-inch-long by half-inch-wide gash, the gray primer visible beneath.

We both stared dumbly at the damage, which at least to me seemed next to irrelevant. I was now thinking about the driver of the ATV who stood yelling at us from less than ten feet away. And the boy.

"I'm sorry," he hollered from where he stood. "I didn't mean to hit you. Am I going to get into trouble?" He was a darkly tanned, blond-haired man of perhaps thirty-five years of age, the *irrigador* we had passed just a few minutes before. His eyes were shaded by a crushed gimme cap. Dressed in worn, soiled jeans, an old T-shirt, and mud-spattered working boots, his words came partially garbled from between bare gums. He resembled a homeless person on the streets of Manhattan more than a Deep South Texas farmhand.

Behind him, in new Levi jeans, a brand-name, freshly laundered T-shirt with logo, and $150 basketball shoes, the grandson fidgeted nervously on the low boy.

I broke out in a sweat, not from the oppressive heat that covered Taylor's Farm like a tight glove, but from the growing awareness that this young boy could easily have been injured seriously.

"The kid okay?" I asked. Then I interrupted the farmhand who was talking again, "Are you okay?"

The boy nodded. If the *irrigador* heard me, he did not acknowledge my question.

"It's no big deal," said Chuy Toledo. "But I got to call my supe."

"Nah, it don't look like much," said the *irrigador*. Still agitated he asked again, "Am I going to get into trouble? I don't want no trouble."

By this time I did not want "no trouble" either, but it was beginning to look inevitable if the supe at the McAllen Station was already informed of "the accident." I understood that Agent Chuy Toledo was bound by policy to notify his supe, but I knew after six months of riding with the agents what was coming. It was not going to be pretty.

"They're on their way," he said. I tried not to think about crazy Steve and his old man on the ATV with the fat pistol stuck between the handlebars.

"Shit," I swore honestly. "I really didn't mean for this to happen. Shit."

"It's a scratch," said Chuy. "But you got to understand that this is federal property." He turned away.

The *irrigador* gave the door of the Expedition one more hard look, took off his hat, then sat easily on his haunches at the side of the road. Then he stood up again, checked his battered ATV and the low boy from A to Z for damage, then crouched again. Then he stood up, unhitched the trailer from the ATV, and told the boy to go tell his grandfather what had happened. The boy seemed overjoyed to be released from waiting. He jumped on the old ATV with the practiced moves of a John Wayne and roared away, his dust falling about us like a gentle snow.

Sitting on the dry clay that bordered the broad field, the *irrigador* was still visibly upset. Finally he asked Chuy, "Do I know you, sir?"

"Yeah, I've seen you around," confirmed Agent Chuy Toledo with no commitment in his voice.

"Is he with you?" he asked Toledo, pointing now at me with the fingers of his right hand.

"Yeah. He's a professor. He's writing a book." The farmhand rose and sidled toward me like a crab to get a better look at the human oddity from the university. "You really writing a book?" he asked, not believing a word of it. "You really a professor? You gonna put me in your book?" He followed it with the familiar refrain, "Am I gonna get into any trouble?"

"Don't worry about it," said Chuy Toledo.

"You writing a book?" he asked me again.

"Yes."

"What about?"

"About the Border Patrol."

"You going to put me into the book?"

"You want me to?" I was not feeling very talkative, my mind focusing upon the supe and his entourage who would be upon us soon along with, I feared, crazy Steve. Just a matter of minutes before they arrived.

"Sure," he said. "Put in it that I just got out of prison. I got sent there because I shot my wife when I found her in bed with another man. The judge sent me to prison for life. I was there for three years, but they let me out on a technicality of the law."

"You shot your wife?" asked Chuy incredulously.

"That's right. Didn't kill her, though. She had run too far away by then. Pellets got her in the back but didn't kill her. But I killed the man she was fooling with."

"And you got out of prison?" I said, also unable to avoid asking.

"My lawyer got me out. I'm working here on probation. I don't want no trouble. I seen trouble already, and I don't want nothing of it. There was a riot when I was in prison, and a guard hit me in the jaw with his stick. It broke my jaw, and I lost most of my teeth." Lending considerable credence to his story, the lower part of his skull was disfigured and scarred.

"What you writin' your book about?"

"The Border Patrol," I said again.

Rocking and Swaying

As if on cue, three green and white Border Patrol vehicles eased their way off Old Military Highway and onto the dirt path at Taylor's Farm. In another minute the convoy pulled to the side of the dirt road at the scene of "the accident."

The supe from the station—I had never met the man but knew him by name—took a close look at the damage to my door, spent twenty minutes taking photographs from every conceivable angle with a digital camera, then finally introduced himself to me and shook my hand. He asked me if I had been injured. I told him that I was fine, Agent Toledo was fine, so was the kid, and so was the convicted murderer who had recently been standing next to us but when the convoy arrived had edged back out of sight behind our Expedition. I noticed out of the corner of my eye that the boy had returned on the ATV. The murderer now grabbed the boy, whispered in his ear, then rode off at a high rate of speed on the ATV with the boy sitting behind him.

"I sure hope I'm not in trouble," he told us before he left.

Now four vehicles and seven agents crowded the dusty lane, each agent relating to the next the story. In a soft undertone the supe told me that I needed to return to the station to fill out a report. I was beginning to feel like Arlo Guthrie in "Alice's Restaurant," as if I were caught up in a gigantic misunderstanding, a bureaucratic snafu that stuck to my limbs like a giant cobweb.

Against my better judgment I climbed back in Chuy Toledo's unit, and the convoy drove to the farmhouse to tell the old man the news. I was thinking by then that I was about to revisit the gunfight at the OK Corral.

In a remarkably foul mood, crazy Steve came storming around the edge of a shed across from the main house and barn.

"We're going to sue you," was the first thing I heard him say.

"You can't sue us," said the supe, oozing patience. "Your employee ran into our vehicle. We should be suing you."

"You got to pay us $500, or this thing is going to court," countered the son, wiping dark, stringy hair out of his eyes and already sidetracked by a random thought. Steve seemed unable to focus on one topic for longer than five seconds.

Then the old man roared up on his ATV. There was, sure enough, an ominous looking German Shepherd behind him in a basket contraption attached to the ATV. I could clearly see the butt handle of a black pistol sticking out of the handlebars. To my surprise, the old man quietly listened to the supe's explanation of "the accident," nodded his head, then climbed back on his ATV and rode away. The gunfight at the OK Corral was postponed due to heat and the temporary attendance of rational judgment.

Back at the station it took two and one-half hours to complete the report and other required forms. Chuy Toledo was busy doing the same thing in another room. First I had to draw a diagram of what had happened then write a detailed narrative. I handed the paperwork to the supe. Five minutes later he reappeared to show me where I had misspelled a word and left out a comma. It had to be perfect, he told me.

I tried discussing the situation with the supe.

"It's federal property," he stated simply. "Somebody's gonna have to pay for it somewhere down the line."

"I'll give you the name of my insurance agent," I told him. "I'm really sorry about this." I really was sorry. Especially for the time it was taking Agent Toledo to complete those forms when he could have been patrolling the line. Instead he was drawing pictures and perfecting a page-long essay.

"Shit happens," Chuy Toledo told me again when I saw him two weeks later. By that time news of "the accident" had spread to everyone but the station janitors.

Agent Chuy Toledo had it only partially right. What I had peripherally encountered was not bad luck as embodied in "shit happens," but the tip of a military-styled bureaucracy that in substance had changed little over the last four decades. The Border Patrol followed rules, regulations, and policies. The agent's job in the field was supposed to be accomplished in certain ways. If it was not, someone answered for it. Someone had to account for the scratch on Chuy Toledo's Expedition.[1] Decision-making in this organization was a top-down system that mimicked the military's but was ten times more cumbersome and unwieldy.[2] Agents in the field were, of course, responsible for all their government-issued equipment. Chuy Toledo called his supe—that was what he was supposed to do. The supe, in turn, told us to fill out the forms because that was his job. It was the job of the FOS on duty to supervise the supe, and so on all the way to the top, Commissioner Doris Meissner of the INS.

But while the scratch on the Expedition was investigated with great speed and efficiency, other crucial issues were twisting in the wind. Agents at the McAllen Station all repeated the same litany: they were not doing what needed to be done on line watch. Too many aliens were easily escaping their grasp, too many loads of drugs were never apprehended. This was not a plea from a lone, disgruntled federal employee, but a chorus from experienced agents. Although the Border Patrol was ripe for change and reform, they doubted that anything was happening or was going to happen. All the agents I interviewed and observed, with several notable exceptions, desired to do their job to the best of their abilities. However, existing circumstances prevented them from accomplishing this objective.

The Immigration Reform and Control Act of 1986 promised the American public that the borders would be, once and for all, sealed. At this same time the Border Patrol also began to assume a much more active role in the interdiction of illegal drugs under the rubric of Operation Alliance.[3] From 1965 to 1986 it was estimated that about 28 million Mexicans illegally entered the United States.[4] Immediately after the U.S. Congress passed the IRCA, apprehensions by the Border Patrol from San Diego to Brownsville subsided, then once more steadily increased in the late 1980s and early 1990s.[5]

Border Patrol statistics indicated that agents were keeping illegal aliens from gainful employment in the American industrial sector as well as ruining the livelihood of drug smugglers by nabbing loads of illegal drugs. But agents remained skeptical of the Border Patrol statistics and their interpretation. The supes knew the data were suspect, the FOS knew it and so, presumably, did those who were at the top of this hierarchical, federal decision-making structure.

Although it became clear that IRCA was failing badly, managers within the Border Patrol were not about to stick out their necks to suggest reforms that might provide solutions to the problem of illegal alien entry into the United States and continuing the fight on drug interdiction as a part of President Ronald Reagan's War on Drugs. Managers within the Border Patrol, an organization choked by tradition, knew that their substantive recommendations would be criticized by not only the organizational hierarchy, but also members of the public, politicians with ideological axes to grind, and various public interest groups. Border Patrol bureaucrats were not going to put their careers and lifetime pensions at risk to fix the internal problems of an organization that had changed so little over so long a time. Not when, as everyone within the organization was aware, even the smallest, most insignificant suggestion of reform met substantial internal opposition.

Could the same agency that encouraged seven agents in four vehicles from the McAllen Station to waste time examining a minute scratch on Chuy Toledo's right front door truly advocate for substantive organizational change?

It was not just about the scratch on the Expedition. Border Patrol managers at the McAllen Station opposed anything that carried the slightest smell of reform, including technological changes adapted by other law enforcement agencies. A case in point was the outdated uniforms the agents were forced to wear on line watch.

Agents at the McAllen Station could not arouse any interest in management to consider the need for new uniforms in the year 2001. Their present uniforms were hotter than heck during the summer months, bulky, easily torn by cactus and the rough terrain, and, if that were not enough, expensive. Cumbersome and poorly designed, their uniforms were forty years behind the times.

According to station folklore, the uniforms were a gift from President George H. W. Bush.

"This is what happened," one agent told me in all sincerity. "George Bush, the former president, owns a factory that produces all our uniforms. He had the contract then, and now, because his son was elected, they have it again. It doesn't matter what we say, we are going to have to wear that there uniform because the Bush family is making big bucks selling it under special contract to the Border Patrol. Everybody knows we should have uniforms that are made of some kind of rip-stop nylon material or one of those new synthetics that is lightweight and breathable in all this heat. But we aren't going to get them until Bush is out of office and the Democrats are in again."

It was a silly, unfounded explanation, but one often heard to justify why the Border Patrol could not consider purchasing more appropriate uniforms that municipal police departments and county sheriff's departments had worn for years.[6]

The more prosaic reason agents did not receive new uniforms was the same fundamental reason Chuy Toledo and I were forced to fill out similar reports for two and one-half hours. At a certain level this bureaucracy cared far more about filing the correct reports and generating statistics than anything else. New uniforms required that someone make a decision, that someone take responsibility, and that someone take a stand in this rigid bureaucracy. Even the agents' voluntary union, the American Federation of Government Employees, seemed to have little interest in any substantive reforms involving its members.[7]

One of a number of more alarming examples of this reluctance to conform to modern law enforcement standards was the agency's reluctance to change their level one holsters. Level one holsters provided only minimum security against suspects intent on seizing agents' service weapons. Agents were constantly surrounded by undocumented workers in the field and at the McAllen Station.[8]

It was beginning to look like the McAllen Station was also fearful of new technologies including laptop computers and software programs, investigation techniques of human smuggling operations, the boat patrol, and numerous other alternative ways to accomplish agency objectives.[9]

Like most other federal bureaucracies, the Border Patrol did not tolerate whistle-blowers or employees who acted on their own volition or made recommendations that went against "common sense." Agency culture considered whistle-blowers cowardly. At the same time, the Border Patrol bureaucracy was terrified of potential lawsuits brought by the public, by illegal immigrants, or by their own employees. Clearly the Border Patrol no longer tolerated the likes of a Wayne Thornton, but behind the macho military rhetoric and style was a timid organization afraid of even the smallest changes or reforms to its bureaucratic traditions.

One individual, to his credit, did have the gumption to rock the boat, to shake the Border Patrol to its foundation. Silvestre Reyes, whose friends called him Silver, served in Vietnam before starting to work with the INS in 1969. He eventually became chief of the McAllen Sector in the 1980s.[10] Advancing through the ranks until he was assistant regional commissioner in Dallas, Silver ended up, after serving in the Valley, as a sector chief based in El Paso, an urban area in Far West Texas of approximately one million residents. In El Paso Reyes single-handedly developed the strategy that was now used throughout the entire U.S.-Mexico Border to confront undocumented workers and win the war on illegal drugs.

Reyes believed that the best way to stop the growing problem of undocumented workers in El Paso was to put all available agency resources, including agents and vehicles, in highly visible areas where new immigrants crossed the border. He explained that his strategy was based upon the idea of "deterrence." According to his theory, illegal workers would observe the Border Patrol and, realizing that units and agents were ready to rush into action to prohibit their illegal entry, turn back. Failing this, they would seek illegal entry elsewhere along the border. Thus these potential illegal immigrants would have been successfully "deterred" from their crime of illegal entry into areas that had historically witnessed high volumes of undocumented workers.

Reyes put his new strategy to work in El Paso without the enthusiastic support of his superiors at the regional or national levels; agency executives were against reforms of any kind and seriously doubted that this new strategy would be successful. Instead, like vultures, they waited for the stench of failure to waft their way.

What Chief Silver Reyes named Operation Blockade put deterrence to the test in September 1993 when the majority of agents and other agency resources were carefully placed directly on the border separating El Paso from its sister city of Ciudad Juárez. Maintaining a high degree of visibility, units were stationed in fixed positions along the Rio Grande to intimidate illegal workers from crossing into El Paso. In order to accomplish this reallocation of resources, agents were withdrawn from traditional methods of apprehension such as farm and ranch searches, sweeps of known places within the city frequented by illegal aliens, and surveillance of employers with a history of hiring undocumented workers.

To everyone's surprise in El Paso, regional headquarters in Dallas, and Washington, D.C., the numbers of apprehensions of undocumented workers dramatically declined in El Paso. Silver used statistics to demonstrate the almost immediate success of his new plan. Silver risked his career and significantly reduced illegal border crossings in the El Paso area. His supporters could argue that he had at least deterred potential illegal immigrants from entering the United States in that particular region.[11]

Chief Reyes had proved the viability of Operation Blockade, which was soon changed to the more public relations friendly Operation Hold the Line. Critics outside the Border Patrol were far more skeptical of Silver's new deterrence strategy. If new immigrants did not enter through El Paso were they truly deterred? Did they perhaps cross somewhere else? That concern at least for the moment was set aside as most pundits applauded the success of Operation Hold the Line. Statistics did not lie.

Of course, Border Patrol higher-ups were not necessarily pleased with Chief Reyes's unilateral decision and success in employing a new strategy. As

Rocking and Swaying

a good bureaucrat, he was expected to follow a top-down, established policy to avoid what others in the agency viewed as grandstanding. Sector chiefs were neither chosen to nor expected to make the kinds of choices that Silver Reyes had made. Nevertheless, given the trial success of Operation Hold the Line, the bureaucrats in Washington would seem bigger idiots if they renounced Silver.

Silver Reyes in fact presented an excellent image of the Border Patrol to the public and media, an advocate for the agency who calmly articulated the strategy and success of Operation Hold the Line.[12] Upper management threw its hat into the ring with Silver, deciding that not only was his plan laudable but that the agency would, with some modifications, adopt it lock, stock, and barrel along the border. Silver Reyes's publicity ship set sail—management wisely jumped on just as it left the dock.

For years the efficacy of the U.S. Border Patrol was measured by rates of apprehensions of undocumented workers. Representatives of the Border Patrol successfully argued in their reports to the U.S. Congress that the most legitimate measure of its effectiveness as an agency of law enforcement was the number of individuals arrested on an annual basis. The Border Patrol yearly requested funds from Congress based upon this rationale and organizational rhetoric.[13] For example, if the agency arrested more individuals one year compared to another, the increase indicated agency efficiency. The Border Patrol had consistently argued at budget appropriation hearings that the more agents and resources Congress provided, the more illegal aliens they would be able to arrest.[14]

Chief Reyes turned this logic upside down. *Declining* numbers of apprehensions now validated the newest strategy against the entry of undocumented workers. The Border Patrol recommended to Congress front-line deployment at specific localities where illegal entry was the highest. Soon Operation Gatekeeper began south of San Diego; agents initiated Operation Safeguard in Nogales, Arizona, in 1995 and expanded it in 1999 to Douglas and Naco, Arizona. Operations in El Paso were expanded as agents now staffed the line ten miles into the interior of the eastern border of New Mexico. Congress, intent on shoring up IRCA, willingly provided the necessary additional agents and other resources.

Joe E. Garza, McAllen Sector chief, commenced Operation Rio Grande in Brownsville in 1997, and four years later a similar strategy was in place at the two bridges at McAllen. Along with the deployment of agents and vehicles came the construction of new, bigger fences at the bridges, watchtowers, powerful lights, and the use of automated cameras and other gear designed to reduce the number of illegal immigrants.

Silver Reyes retired from the Border Patrol in 1995 to run for a seat in the U.S. Congress. Although he had never before been elected to public office, his popularity among those in El Paso was at an all-time high because of the success of Operation Hold the Line. Voters elected him as the U.S. congressional representative from the Sixteenth District of Texas.

Agents at the McAllen Station strongly believed that implementation of the Reyes strategy along the banks of the Rio Grande accomplished far less than was touted in statistics from Silver's new congressional office. Agents referred to the duty as "doing X's." "Are you doing X's tonight?" In June 2001 eight vehicles were regularly assigned to IBC Bridge by the McAllen Station. Station policy required each vehicle to assume a highly visible, fixed position near the two-mile-long bridge. The Expeditions parked at quarter-mile intervals. At night agents were instructed to leave their headlights on so that potential illegal immigrants could not miss seeing them. In fact people could sit comfortably in a variety of locations, including bars and restaurants in Reynosa and downriver in Matamoros, and observe various units of the Border Patrol lighting up the night.

Having assumed these front-line positions, agents were ordered to remain there for the duration of their eight- to ten-hour shift. In 1997 they were ordered not to leave their vehicles unless they observed illegal aliens with their own eyes or helped other agents in the pursuit of illegals they had seen. A rover, often a supe, drove back and forth along this line of deterrence to make sure that all agents remained in place.

In the beginning agents were told to shuffle their vehicles from one fixed position to the next adjacent position every half hour under the direct supervision of the supe. The agent who was at the end of the line nearest the Burger King was then given a brief break to tank up on coffee before rejoining the line at its beginning. Agents who needed to use the restroom or grab a cup of coffee were specifically told at muster to notify their supe before they left their X.

A few of the agents at the McAllen Station liked doing X's. They sat behind the wheel listening to Rush Limbaugh on the radio or made fun of pathetic callers to the Dr. Laura show. Big fans of the Texas Rangers or Houston Astros passed the hours listening to the games. Depending on the diligence of the supe, agents read the pages of *The Monitor* or checked out their favorite gun or motorcycle magazine. Or read novels they had been meaning to read since college. At least one agent told me that he regularly brought his personal laptop to X's. In short, agents did anything they could think of to traverse the long hours when there was absolutely nothing to do but stare out the windows of their Expeditions while drinking a cup of coffee or Jolt cola to keep awake.

Agents Fernando Rodriguez, Noe Escondido, Herman Morningside, Paco, Maria Contreras, Reynaldo "The Mole" Guerra, Steve Plovic, Rochester, Charlie Ashton, Shuman, Sandra Aldrete, Roberta Alanis, Humberto Taylor, Negrete, Gretsky, Lefty Maldonado, Speedy Allison, and Chuy Toledo, along with almost all the other agents interviewed and observed, detested doing X's. They got themselves assigned to any other duty to avoid it, including boat patrol, bike patrol, horse patrol, sensor duty, and special investigations and surveillances.[15]

These men and women liked the chase and thrived on adrenaline flow. Working on a case of hemorrhoids all night long behind the steering wheel of an Expedition, consuming large amounts of Burger King coffee—these were not reasons these agents had signed on with the Border Patrol. Some agents, like Charlie Ashton and the Mole, could not abide by the duty at all. They and others found every reason in the book to get out of their trucks, to track aliens along the river, and otherwise do what Charlie Ashton called "my real job," which Charlie pointed out was "not sitting on your frigging ass for ten hours at a stretch."[16]

The policy did not absolutely prohibit agents from apprehending illegal workers, but it was difficult, next to impossible, for agents to make arrests when they were not supposed to leave the confines of their vehicles.

Supes and higher level managers demonstrated that they were well aware that the majority of their agents detested the new strategy. Agents who transgressed informal station policies or standards were assigned to X's as a mild form of institutional punishment that did not go in their permanent file.

As the months passed under Operation Rio Grande, McAllen Station agents understood what the decision-makers in the rest of the bureaucracy were unwilling to admit. The newfound strategy may have worked in El Paso, but it was a terrible dud in Deep South Texas. Agents were on the line every shift witnessing the impact of deterrence.

"Deterrence?" said one agent. "You got to be kidding. Ain't no deterrence here. Look around you, bro. What do your eyes tell you? Check it out."

Congressman Reyes's strategy resulted in a decline in the number of total apprehensions from 1993 to 1994. In 1993 the Border Patrol apprehended a total of 1.2 million undocumented workers; just one year later, the figure was .9 million. But by 1995 the figures had risen once again to 1.3 million, then 1.5 million in 1996, and 1.4 million in 1997. The average for 1998 to 2000 was about 1.53 million.[17]

Individuals vested in deterrence theory were unwilling to consider an alternative explanation to the quick rise in statistics. Agents who were restricted in placing undocumented workers under arrest logged lower apprehension statistics in comparison to the actual flow of illegal workers. If statistics were rising even though agents were encouraged to maintain their X's, then even more undocumented workers were gaining illegal entry than the Border Patrol was willing to acknowledge or count.

Statistics at the McAllen Sector were quite sensational at face value; data certainly supported the efficacy of deterrence as incorporated in 1997 for Operation Rio Grande. In 1997 there were 246,210 total apprehensions for the entire McAllen Sector. In subsequent years those apprehended fell steadily and dramatically first to 207,005 in 1998, then in 1999 to 172,867. By 2000 the figures had dropped to 136,878, then 110,764 in 2001 and 86,117 in 2002.[18] In six short years apprehensions had dropped by a whopping 160,093. Human smuggling cases declined by roughly 50 percent during this same period, according to the sector statistics.[19] As for drugs, figures collected by the McAllen Sector did not reflect the decline that was supposed to result because of Operation Rio Grande. Drug cases and the value of the drugs confiscated actually rose from 1997 to 2002 from 1,583 cases with a total value of $234,678,887 sectorwide, to 1,659 cases valued at $492,570,628. Drug activity in the sector—if the figures were to be believed strictly—actually peaked during 1999, well after the X's were in place, at 2,140 cases with a street value of $709,699,226.[20]

By 2001 the scenario created by deterrence had become a joke at the McAllen Station, a surreal gag that stuck in the craw of agents who still believed in the integrity of their work. Evidence in the field was damning. Anyone could walk along the banks of the Rio Grande after the midnight to 10 A.M. shift ended to document what was happening. Trails broken by illegal aliens were wide and long, leading from the banks of the river at the old McAllen Bridge through a line of trees, then weaving their way between the Expeditions on their X's. At IBC it was the same story with a slight variation because of a different geography: undocumented workers frequently jumped down from the height of the bridge to circumvent the entire phalanx of vehicles affixed to X's.

These trails were not hidden. They were littered with garbage: one-gallon plastic bottles, jeans, T-shirts, candy wrappers, socks, underwear, discarded purses, and inexpensive tennis shoes. The trails led to the nearest paved roads, including Old Military Highway, where waiting cars, trucks, and vans picked up the newest illegal immigrants and drove them to safe houses. Everyone at the McAllen Station knew that thousands of illegal aliens were sneaking through or around the X's, never to appear in the station's or sector's annual statistics. Agents and managers talked about it openly and with a great deal of frustration.

Illegal aliens, those who did not creep between the vehicles visible at the two McAllen bridges, did not give up, as Silver Reyes hypothesized. Instead they walked, took the bus, a taxi, or a private car and crossed a few miles upstream or down. It was unnecessary for them to go far. After the X's were staffed the few remaining agents each had to guard several miles of twisting and turning river. The massive garbage dumps covering human landings like Cavazos Beach were surrounded by literally hundreds of smaller landings that might change from one night to the next.

On many nights Herman Morningside and other agents who were stuck in the scope truck observed the images of these men, women, and children who chose to avoid the X's at the two bridges to cross in lightly patrolled areas. If the agents were lucky, they caught a few of them. From the air, helicopter pilots saw the illegal aliens in vast numbers, sometimes in groups of fifty or more.

Agents who bothered to get out of their trucks to look for sign knew what was really going on in the field. Even as management touted Operation Rio Grande as a tremendous success, the agents knew the truth behind the numbers.

An additional source of telltale data in the battle against undocumented workers in Deep South Texas came from Sarita and Falfurrias. Checkpoints along the two major highways leading out of the region were designed as a final defense. Whether in a car or an eighteen-wheeler, drivers were required to stop for inspection by the Border Patrol at both these points. The news from Sarita and Fal, if indeed the frontal deployment strategy was at all effective, should have been that few immigrants were apprehended at or near these last barriers to illegal entry. Statistics showed otherwise. In addition, numerous trails through the desert and the brushland circumvented these checkpoints. Undocumented workers had easily walked between the deployed Expeditions on the river, then eventually, after the safe houses, had been transported by car and truck to locations south of the checkpoints. Having walked around the checkpoints, illegal immigrants were picked up by *coyotes* and driven to Houston or Dallas. The areas around Sarita and Fal were swamped with illegal aliens who, according to Silver's theory, should not have been there in the first place. Some illegal aliens were detained by Border Patrol brush patrols, but the majority escaped.

Few in management were willing to point out that the topography of El Paso was far different than that of Deep South Texas. In El Paso the concrete flat levees provided excellent observation of those attempting to cross the Rio Grande illegally. However, in the Valley and in many other locations along the Rio Grande, the twists and bends of the river prohibited a clear field of vision. A strategy that may have worked in El Paso or even San Diego was not necessarily suitable for all 2,000 miles of the border.

A second clue to the questionable deterrence of undocumented workers was that few sources in extant research literature considered deterrence or deterrence theory a legitimate theory upon which any law enforcement agency might premise, let alone construct, an effective strategy. Sure that I was in error, I kept looking.[21]

Sector chiefs were, like any good organization bureaucrats, drawn to deterrence theory in part because those who did not advocate Silver Reyes's deterrence theory were doomed to lose in the congressional stampede to pump money into a winning strategy that would curtail illegal immigration into the United States. The more undocumented workers that the Border Patrol deterred as documented in their sector statistics and subsequent interpretations of those statistics, the more their respective budgets increased. The more their budgets grew, the more the stature of these bureaucrats increased. Whether in the Border Patrol or private sector, all managers desired larger and larger budgets. For sector chiefs bigger budgets translated into greater authority, more status and prestige, and the increased possibility of promotion. Noted in the biographical statement of Congressman Silver Reyes were his monetary responsibilities before coming to Washington: "he had direct responsibility for administering a budget program exceeding $100 million for a 13-state area."[22] The bigger the budgets, the bigger the bureaucrats, and the brighter—at least in Congressman Silver Reyes's case—their future.

The Border Patrol grew in the 1990s, almost tripling in size by the start of the new millennium from about 4,000 personnel to about 12,000. As it ballooned in size and budget, according to the Border Patrol's phantasmagoric statistics and its interpretation of those statistics, the number of undocumented workers who were deterred also increased. The McAllen Station was a microcosm of this agency, the number of agents by 2001 around 300.

Census figures and other respected estimates repeatedly counted the number of illegal aliens as between 7 to 13 million undocumented workers. Certainly a portion of these illegal workers, at the very least, had not really been turned back, deterred, when they came upon the lights of Border Patrol vehicles on the banks of the Rio Grande. The INS itself estimated that 7 million illegal aliens resided in the United States and that 350,000 each year traveled to the United States between 1990 and 2000.[23]

At the McAllen Station agents were caught up in a maze of bureaucratic action and rhetoric. When they vigorously pursued and captured undocumented workers, they ultimately increased the total number of apprehensions. Increased numbers of apprehensions were not what the supes and the higher-ups desired under Operation Rio Grande. Station management badly needed declining figures upon which to claim that deterrence was working. If not, statistics had to demonstrate that deterrence was otherwise providing a stable, consistent, and controlled flow of illegal workers.[24] The harder that the men and women at the McAllen Station worked along the banks of the Rio Grande while doing their X's and when on other line watch duty, the worse they made their supervisors and other managers appear.

Anzalduas

gnoring the heat, the wind, and the rotten air, agents at the McAllen Station patrolled the line regardless of the duties and policies shackling them. What else could they do? Agents left station and public policy to the experts, but that did not mean that they did not discuss the issues among themselves and with their supes. While sitting in their Expeditions figuring out their next move, looking for sign, filling out paperwork, radioing their fellow agents for information, picking cactus needles out of their legs, smoking cigarettes, or taking coffee breaks at the Whataburger, agents frequently talked about the status of the third-world country that was just a hundred yards away and the agency policies that were in place.

Months after President Vicente Fox of Mexico replaced President Ernesto Zedillo with a fanfare of campaign promises in January 2001, agents listened with cynicism to his strident messages aimed at corruption and graft within the Mexican government.[1] One of President Fox's first acts was to appoint José Guzmán the director of customs. Guzmán, like Fox, was not shy about demanding reform from within governmental agencies and programs throughout Mexico. Guzmán announced, "We had personnel who didn't obey orders, who were wrapped up in corruption, were poorly skilled and not worried about becoming skilled. More than anything, there was a lack of supervision to make sure they did their work well."[2] Guzman summarily fired forty-three out of a total of forty-seven customs supervisors in Mexico. Customs Director José Luís Avendano Salinas of Reynosa was canned, along with his deputy director, Armando Garza Faz. They were replaced by Hector Javier Mana García, a lawyer from Mexico City, and Martín Romallone. The customs director in Matamoros, Jamie Ruiz, and his assistant were also given the boot.

All this was no news, of course, to agents at the McAllen Station, who had heard talk of reform in Mexico many times before. They knew that their counterparts across the Rio Grande were notorious for extorting *mordidas,* bribes, from both American and Mexican citizens. The miserable pittance paid to government employees drove many directly into the influence of the drug smugglers.[3] The Mexican *narcotraficantes* spawned in the 1980s had infinitely deep pockets to buy those who were for sale. Honest Mexican officials faced threats, intimidation, and murder if they refused to participate in the increasingly corrupt system or if they were brave enough to openly criticize it.[4] Mexican journalists in Reynosa and Matamoros who dared write about the impact of illegal drugs upon local citizenry were assassinated.[5] Previous attempts by Presidents José López Portillo (1976–82), Miguel de la Madrid Hurtado (1982–88), and Carlos Salinas de Gortari (1988–94) to clean up graft had met with little success. Mexican customs and transit authorities at the international bridges, the police on the street, and the jail and prison systems were riddled with crooked officials.[6]

To demonstrate the sincerity of his promise to exorcise corruption from his government, President Fox traveled to Sinaloa, the state many Mexicans considered most corrupted by the drug cartels, and to the northern border city of Tijuana, the location of some of the bloodiest violence perpetrated by the cartels.[7] In the streets of Tijuana city police and the federal police had faced off in a bloody gun battle over the spoils from the *narcotraficantes.* To its credit Tijuana had also been the site of individual acts of courage by honest Mexican officials and journalists who stood up to the drug smugglers.[8]

Soon after, John Ashcroft, U.S. attorney general, took a boat ride on the Rio Grande at Brownsville with officials from the Border Patrol. Before flying to El Paso Ashcroft told reporters, "The object of our visit is to get a close look at the needs and problems facing our border, as well as to see what is being done to prevent illegal immigration, violence and a lack of safety on the border."[9]

The agents at the McAllen Station were not impressed by Fox's visits to

Sinaloa and Tijuana, nor by his numerous public statements regarding graft and corruption. Unfairly or not, they firmly believed there was little difference between the average Mexican public official in Reynosa and the average drug smuggler. Most agents maintained that the Mexican government, including all law enforcement and the military, was corrupt to the core. Most agents interpreted the U.S. attorney general's ride-along with the boat patrol as nothing more than a photo op.

Benny *el elefantino* represented a case in point. Benny's saga appeared briefly in the national news before being smothered by coverage of President Bush's press release about his new tax cut. First sighted performing in an American circus in Houston, Benny starred several weeks later in a Mexican circus in Mexico City under the alias Dumbo. The newsworthy problem was that no record existed of a Benny *el elefantino,* or a Dumbo, legally crossing the Rio Grande into Mexico. He was an undocumented three-ton American who had magically ended up south of the Rio Grande.[10]

While American authorities struggled to find and explain Benny's paper trail, Mexican officials, sensing a publicity disaster of major proportions for the Fox administration, looked for ways to explain why the new president's promises were already being undermined by an American pachyderm. After a 7 A.M. muster at the McAllen Station, one agent said, not at all amused by the attention that Benny *el elefantino* was attracting, "Of course you can smuggle an elephant across the river. You put the thing in a truck, you drive across the bridge, and you pay off the Mexicans. How hard is that? Happens every day. You just have to know which Mexicans to bribe."

In this particular case it emerged that Mexican officials received $4,500 to look the other way while Benny was driven "across the border in a five-wheel trailer pulled by a utility truck."[11]

The American press feigned surprise and even indignation when Mexican officials temporarily placed Benny in a zoo in Mexico City. The officials said it was only temporary until the elephant's legal status was determined. Benny *el elefantino* also embarrassed federal officials on this side of the border. Most Americans, especially those not living in Deep South Texas, could claim ignorance of the scale of illegal drugs and workers coming into the country. But Benny was something else. The public might logically be driven by Benny's dilemma to ask a simple question: If a three-ton elephant can be smuggled across the Rio Grande, what cannot?[12]

Rocking and Swaying

Immediately after taking office, President Fox, a former Harvard-trained Coca-Cola executive, also advocated for immigration reform in the United States. He argued that the United States should ease its legal restrictions on the number of workers from Mexico at the same time it facilitated their safe passage from Mexico to their place of employment. During his first official American visit he spoke to an audience of recent Mexican immigrants in Los Angeles about immigrant issues, focusing on his concept of an open border. He later met with Governor Gray Davis of California and First Lady Laura Bush.[13] Fox knew that President Bush, the former governor of Texas, was particularly sympathetic to immigration issues because of his experience as an elected official of a border state.

President Bush had visited President Fox at Fox's ranch in San Cristóbal, Mexico, in February of 2001, where he made clear his foreign policy sentiments: "Geography has made us neighbors. Cooperation and respect will make us partners and the promise of the partnership was renewed and reinvigorated today." Bush continued, "Our nations are bound together by ties of history, family, values, commerce and culture."[14] There were, as a result of these talks, growing expectations in both Mexico and the United States that President Bush would support legislation that would open the border to immigrants, supplying American industries with cheap and legal labor. Negotiators for both countries were already hard at work hammering out details of the new policies by summer 2001.[15]

Agent Gester, a tall, gangly man with a boyish face, trusted President Vicente Fox about as much as he trusted President George W. Bush and Fat Man. If the new Mexican president and the new Republican U.S. president desired to change the laws about immigration, then that was up to the politicians. In the meantime, Gester and other agents at the McAllen Station would not lose any sleep over it, nor would they expect real change anytime soon. While agents at the McAllen Station acknowledged that cooperation between the two presidents was relatively unusual, they gave it only a nodding significance. Knowing that the federal government moved very slowly, if at all, they were less cynical than pragmatic.

Fat Man, on the other hand, represented a tangible reality to Gester. He had been waiting for the last two hours for Fat Man to make his move at Anzalduas Park.

Like Gester, many agents from the McAllen Station spent countless days and nights at Anzalduas Park, the popular county park that on weekends was covered from one end to the other with families relaxing while escaping the intense heat. Children and parents at Anzalduas engaged in long and glorious games of tag, Frisbee, softball, soccer, and touch football, while the banks of the river were often crowded with fishermen and boaters.

One of the other water sports at Anzalduas Park was smuggling illegal immigrants from the south side of the river, the site of a small public park and dirt boat ramp, to the concrete banks of the north side of the river. Large drug loads, on the other hand, were off-loaded south of Anzalduas Park; smaller loads were smuggled across the river during weekdays and nights when the majority of the public did not visit the popular park.

Serious birders also flocked to Anzalduas Park. They came to see the greater pewee, a flycatcher common in Mexico but rare in Texas. The black phoebe, which sometimes could be spied on the south side of the Rio Grande from the northern banks, also brought out the binoculars, as did the green kingfisher, ringed kingfisher, hook-billed kite, gray hawk, clay-colored robin, golden-fronted woodpecker, northern beardless-tyrannulet, great kiskadee, and Couch's kingbird.[16]

But the most financially profitable activity at Anzalduas Park was smuggling humans. Among the real fishermen who stood casting their lines into the sluggish waters was a handful of scouts who worked for Fat Man. Named for his ponderous beer belly, Fat Man captained a twenty-year-old piece of decrepit fiberglass that was falling apart one piece at a time.

Anzalduas Park had not always been a haven for human smuggling and illegal drugs. The park was a tiny portion of an original Spanish land grant deeded to Escandón's settlers in 1767. In 1884 French Oblates purchased the land "for the propagation of the faith among the barbarians."[17] On that land, then referred to by residents of Mission and McAllen as La Lomita, or "little hill," the Oblate fathers raised grapes and potatoes, but their attempts met with dismal failure. In 1907 they sold their extensive holdings except for three hundred acres along the Rio Grande to two developers, James W. Conway and John J. Hoit. These two men, in turn, laid out the townsite for Mission, named in honor of the Oblates. The Oblates agreed to a ninety-nine-year lease for some of the riverfront property they still owned in the 1960s that was required to access the riverfront park.

Even La Lomita Chapel, to the south of the park, originally constructed by the Oblates in the 1850s, was frequented by drug smugglers and served as a landmark for illegal workers. More than 150 years after the chapel had been erected by the Oblates, smuggling trails wove around the tiny stone building like the tendrils of a giant squid.

Anzalduas Park, through geographical and historical happenstance, was a smuggler's dream. Only two roads led into the park: one a dirt path that followed the river; the other, two lanes of winding asphalt that began at the northern entrance. If agents took the dirt road, jet skiers could spot them a mile before they reached the park. The asphalt lane had enough elevation that scouts perched with fishing poles on the concrete boat ramp could easily sound the alarm.

Powered by an antique Johnson motor as loud as an M-1 tank, Fat Man charged his customers $300 a head to transport them from one bank to the other, a distance of about seventy-five feet. He collected his cash first, then ferried his cargo across the river. Depending on the size of his passengers, his maritime cash cow held up to eight aliens for the thirty-second trip. With a full load Fat Man grossed $2,100. Figuring at least three or four trips a day, Fat Man brought in $6,000–$8,000 every time he opened his business.

Fat Man openly ridiculed the Border Patrol from the south side of the river, at times saluting agents with his ever-present beer can, because he knew he had little to fear. Fat Man knew that if the Border Patrol ever actually nabbed him, he would pay a small fine and be out of jail in no time. Drug smugglers faced harsher penalties. *Coyotes* who were first-time offenders were unlikely to spend much time in the overcrowded municipal and county jails. Human smuggling in Anzalduas Park was a low-risk operation that produced sky-high profit.

Granted, Fat Man, dressed in tattered jeans shorts and ratty T-shirt, was burdened by overhead. Part of that overhead, in addition to his fishermen scouts on the southern banks—who were not very good at acting as if they cared the slightest about catching fish—were two young men on jet skis. Roaring up and down the river on the powerful, whining machines, they watched for Border Patrol boats and vehicles whenever Fat Man was open for business. Much faster and more mobile than the agents' stodgy BayMasters, the jet skiers could easily use their two-way radios to call off an operation at the last second. Chances of the Border Patrol catching Fat Man were slim to none.

The problem was not the identity of the criminal, nor the details of his operation, but simply how to shut him down. Fat Man's strategy was low-tech and foolproof. After sipping beer for hours while he chatted up the picnickers on the southern banks, he quickly mustered his customers from behind a tree into his slapdash vessel. After loading in a matter of seconds, he motored across the international boundary to the banks of Anzalduas Park. Then Fat Man was immediately back in Mexico drinking beer.

When Fat Man was not amused by the extra units the Border Patrol assigned to the park, or if he sensed that luck was against him that day, he closed his smuggling operation. The jet skiers loaded up, Fat Man trailered his wreck of a boat back to Reynosa, and his other employees with their stage prop fishing gear departed the scene. A few days later they returned. New customers ready to immigrate illegally had come to the southern banks by bus, car, truck, and on foot.

With the prospect of grossing $30,000 or more a week, Fat Man was in no real rush. Canceling work for one or two days, compliments of the Border Patrol, was not a big deal. This smuggler knew that the Americans did not have enough boats or other units to monitor his operation constantly. If they decided to mount a major operation against him, Fat Man also knew that the rest of the river would be wide open to other smugglers. Time was always on Fat Man's side.

The McAllen Station patrolled forty-five miles of the Rio Grande with just four boats. At first they had operated only one boat before Washington officials visited and were shown Cavazos Beach and a few of the other huge landings. Most shifts it was exceptional to have two patrol boats on the same stretch of the river. Only on special occasions—for example, when dignitaries from Washington, D.C., flew down for the day—were two boats patrolling during the same shift along this segment of the border.[18]

That was exactly why Agent Gester was hiding among the cactus and scrawny mesquite trees not more than a hundred yards from Anzalduas Park. Sick to death of being bested by the brazen human smugglers, a charade in which agents roared up in the BayMaster long after the undocumented workers had disappeared down the trails that led from Anzalduas Park to Old Military Highway, Gester was determined to put Fat Man out of business and in jail where he belonged.

Gester had talked at length with some of the other Rambos who also wanted to close down the smuggling operation at Anzalduas Park. They had encouraged Gester, advising him to observe the strictest procedures and legalities in order to build a solid case against Fat Man. He could afford the best Hidalgo County lawyers money could buy and would walk on a technicality otherwise. Gester planned to catch the perp in the sketchy red boat immediately after he had unloaded the aliens on American soil. Agent Gester said that supes and other management at the McAllen Station had told him he would be following the letter of the law as long as he arrested Fat Man after he had transported the aliens to the banks of Anzalduas but before the smuggler returned to the banks of the south side of the Rio Grande. Gester knew that once Fat Man was on the southern bank of the river he was untouchable.

Gester and his fellow agents never seriously considered including the Mexican authorities in their plan. To do so would have been foolhardy. Fat Man would disappear into thin air for a few weeks, then open up for business when the coast was clear again. After researching the matter, Gester maintained that the border between the two countries was not the exact middle of the river for the purposes of this arrest and case. Therefore, Gester did not have to capture Fat Man before he crossed the theoretical middle of the Rio Grande; this was a vital point when a few seconds in time could make the difference between apprehension and a clean escape.

After Fat Man and his boat had been seized, Gester would have to obtain signed testimony from the illegal aliens. He would have to cut a deal with them to get their cooperation, but with their testimony he could build a solid case. Agent Gester was a realist, but he firmly believed that if he could put Fat Man out of business for even a few months, he would have made his point.

Agent Gester and the other agents he convinced to join him recognized that they were sticking their necks out. Management was providing them no extra resources, incentives, or consistent guidance. Even so, Gester and the other Rambos would have made a point: the U.S. Border Patrol, at least along this stretch of the border, did not tolerate smuggling. Contrary to what Fat Man and his fellow employees might believe, the Border Patrol was not a joke. Pride, integrity, and self-esteem were fueling Gester's plan.

Gester *hated* doing X's. He volunteered for the boat patrol because he initially thought it could make a difference. Some days and nights the BayMaster crew caught its share of aliens in inner tubes or ran across groups of aliens who, having been surprised on the southern banks of the river, decided to cross elsewhere or wait another day. That was real deterrence, as far as Gester was concerned. This viewpoint contradicted Congressman Silver Reyes's strategy of X's, which sapped labor resources and diluted morale. The more time Gester spent on the boat patrol, however, the more he realized the incredible successes of the human smugglers. Day after day the piles of refuse grew at landings like Cavazos Beach, evidence of the Border Patrol's failure. The *coyotes* and illegal aliens were beating them badly, much worse than the politicians or the public dared to imagine.

Besides Gester, three other agents were hiding on a back road not far from Anzalduas Park. Two of the agents were in a unit providing backup for Gester, and the third was Gester's regular boat patrol partner. After the early afternoon muster, Gester, ignoring the heat, had trucked the boat to a road that even the jet skiers could not watch. The BayMaster was both the key to the success of the plan and its major weakness. When the Mexican smuggler looked as if he was getting ready to make his move, Gester must speed to the loading ramp at Anzalduas, put his boat in the water, then nab the red boat before Fat Man could reach the south side. The timing was crucial.

Hanging onto a branch of a mesquite tree overlooking the river, one agent had a clear view of Fat Man, while upriver from the park another agent spied on the operation from behind the brush. This agent, with only a partial field of vision, could not be relied upon completely. Yet another agent in a unit on the drag stood ready to round up the aliens after they were unloaded at the park. Even seconds mattered to the seven agents, one boat, and two other units committed to the bust. If they failed, management was certain to criticize them for wasting their time. Worse still, more than a few of their own might call them glory hounds.

The plan might need a little fine tuning, but Gester believed that he could make it work. In all good conscience, he could no longer go from one day to the next patrolling the river as if he made a real difference. While Gester and other boat captains were given relatively free rein on the river to make decisions based upon their professional judgment, management was already discussing new rules and policies that might seriously limit their operations. Boat patrol apprehensions carried out by agents such as Gester, in short, were threatening to drive up the numbers and make management at the station look bad. Rumors also circulated that management feared the possibility of an international boat incident that would draw negative publicity and lawsuits.

Gester was sick to death of Fat Man. And Nature Boy. Nature Boy had been running his one-man operation for more than a year. On the face of it he was just another small-time smuggler, a minor irritant in the larger scheme of things. Yet Nature Boy, like Benny *el elefantino* or Fat Man, reminded Gester and all the other agents at the McAllen Station who still cared about their jobs of the failed system of law enforcement along the Rio Grande. Nature Boy had driven them to the Tree just as surely as had Wayne Thornton, working X's, the M&Ms, Benny *el elefantino,* and all the rest of them.

Hiding in the cane on the banks of the Río Bravo not far from the bridge to Reynosa, Nature Boy patiently waited until the patrol boat, if on duty, motored by before emerging with one illegal worker in tow. It was always just one, and Nature Boy always collected his $200 before he ever left his native soil. Entering the water silently, he dragged his human cargo across the river in a black inner tube using a combination dog paddle and breast stroke. Nature Boy was a strong swimmer and crossed the Río Bravo in less than five minutes. Picking with extreme care among a handful of convenient landings, Nature Boy always seemed to know where the sensors were placed, and he guided his undocumented worker along a series of trails that snaked their way between the agents confined to their X's. Once past them, he pointed his human cargo in a safe direction before heading back to the river for more work. Nature Boy was not any different from all other professional smugglers along the Rio Grande except for one thing: he worked totally in the nude.

One agent told other agents during a coffee break, "I thought I had him one time. I caught him out in the open and chased him back to the riverbank. He's fast. I'll give him that. He reaches the bank—it's maybe ten feet above the water—and dives right in. Head first. But get this. He never makes the water. Cuts it too short by a few feet. Lands flat in the mud a few feet from the water. Then he gets up quick, dives into the water, and is gone. Now, you know that had to hurt."

Another agent interrupted him, "That's nothing. I had him about in that same spot you are talking about and just like with you, he takes a leap off the bank. But instead of hitting the river, he hits a tree branch. Takes it right in the ribs on his left side. Then he bounced off that tree branch and knocked another alien into the water on his way down. I thought that guy was going to drown. But somehow he comes back up and swims to the other side. Nature Boy just keeps going. Doesn't say a thing to the guy he almost crushes. Like an apology or something. Nothing."

Another agent came close to catching Nature Boy. "I was lying in some grass, and he never saw me. Walks up right by me. I jump up and grab him. But he's slippery. Impossible to hold on to him. He runs back to the river and dives back in."

"Well, I'm telling you," said the first agent, "I once gave Nature Boy a run for his money. I was doing my X on the levee. Nature Boy is just taunting me the way he does. Standing there with no clothes on. So I was looking like I was ignoring him, but I got my door open a crack. When he seemed to be looking the other way, I jumped out and gave him a run for it. But he's smart. He knows exactly how much room he has. He beat me to the river and swam back."

The agent continued, still angry about the incident, "But you know what he was doing? Pissed me off. When he thought he wasn't getting my full attention, when I was making believe I was looking the other way, he stood there and shook his dick at me. Can you believe that? Just stood there shaking his dick at me."

Fed up with their stories, Agent Estrada had interceded. He had been on boat patrol for more than a year and had seen far too much of Nature Boy. "I was doing X's one day, and Nature Boy shows up. Stands there taunting me and Agent Rochester until Rochester had about enough of that so he jumps out of the vehicle and comes running at him as hard as he can. Came close to getting him, but Nature Boy dives into the river like he usually does.

"But ol' Nature Boy is pissed off at Rochester for coming so close, so he's paddling out there in the middle of the river yelling at Rochester. You know the shit, calling Rochester's mother various names and that kind of stuff. All that usual stuff. Then Nature Boy starts telling Rochester, 'Why don't you get back on your X? Get back on the levee where you belong.' Stuff like that. Like, 'What are you doing getting out of your truck? You got orders to stay on the levee, man. Get back to your fucking truck.' I'm telling you, it pissed me off."

Gester was doing something about Nature Boy and all the others. Getting Fat Man was his way of evening the score just a tad. For all the agents who were sick and tired of not being allowed to do their jobs and every day saw criminals getting rich from breaking the law. He was going to park Fat Man's boat permanently in the station lot and familiarize him with the inside of a jail cell.

Gester and the other agents waited for Fat Man to make his move. While they sweltered in the afternoon heat in their uncomfortable uniforms and bulletproof vests, Fat Man sipped his beer. Every fifteen minutes Gester's men, including the agent in a tree, reported over the radio: "He's still standing there with a beer in his hand," or "I lost him. No, there he is talking to a bunch of people."

Hours later the smuggler finally made his move.

"He's loading up," called the agent from his tree branch outpost.

As Gester jumped into the truck cab and maneuvered the boat trailer down the road, two other Expeditions sped toward Anzalduas Park.

Agent Espinoza, who had hidden his vehicle behind a line of brush about a quarter mile off Old Military Highway, was the first on the scene. For most of his shift he had been smoking cigarettes with his window down. When one of the agents finally told him to get moving, he had gunned his vehicle through and around park traffic.

Eyeballing the park crowd at the concrete banks where Fat Man would have unloaded the illegal workers, Agent Espinoza saw no one who looked as if thirty seconds earlier they had crossed an international border. "I'm here," he radioed Gester, who was barely reaching the front entrance of the park with trailer in tow. "Where are they?"

The spotter on the ground, not the one in the tree, had glimpsed the newest immigrants as they were herded onto the boat for the short ride. "Four adults and maybe three children," he reported to Espinoza. "Three adult males, one wearing a red shirt; another, a dark blue or black shirt. Two to three kids. One adult female in jeans and a white T-shirt."

Agent Espinoza respected Gester but thought his plan had little chance of success. For one thing, the logistics were all wrong. Even if they apprehended the undocumented workers, which was not going to be easy, they had to flip them to make the case. Getting them to turn on a *coyote* would be a major accomplishment in itself. Not to mention grabbing Fat Man and his boat before they reached Mexico. Without Fat Man in custody, they would have wasted everyone's time. Maybe the plan was doomed, but Espinoza would back Gester because Gester was trying to do the right thing.

As Espinoza slowly cruised by the barbecue pits and picnickers, he was keenly aware of the hostile glances thrown his way. No one shouted obscenities at him, but he knew that the men, women, and children in Anzalduas Park detested him and everyone else who wore the uniform. They would not help him, and if given the chance they might give him bad information. The newest immigrants seemed to have disappeared into thin air. When he could not find any trace of them, Espinoza searched the public restrooms.

By the time Gester finally arrived at the ramp to launch the BayMaster, Fat Man was relaxing under a tree on the south side of the river. Espinoza futilely searched two restrooms then climbed back into his truck. Then he saw them. They were sitting peacefully at a table camouflaged by the surrounding pic-nickers. Seven of them. As he parked his Expedition on the green grass nearby, Espinoza pointed out, "Did you notice they have no food? Here they are in fajita heaven, and they have no food. No beer. No games for the kids to play."

Four men, one young woman, and two children sat at an empty wooden picnic table. No one tried to run. If they had scattered in different directions, perhaps several could have escaped into the crowd. But it was much too hot in Anzalduas Park once you left the shade of the trees, the air too full and heavy to think seriously of fleeing. The new illegal workers and their children, once identified by Agent Espinoza, lost their spirit and half-heartedly surrendered themselves to the lone agent without incident. But first, to show what they were made of, they ignored Espinoza's polite entreaties, only to rise as one from the picnic table, grab their belongings from beneath it, and with all the dignity they could muster slowly walk toward the Expedition.

Gester never bothered to put the BayMaster in the river. Why give Fat Man, more than $2,000 richer for his work, the pleasure of watching the Border Patrol wasting its time? So it was back to the drawing board for Agent Gester. The geography of Anzalduas Park made logistics more difficult. Nevertheless, Gester was not giving up.

As Gester began work on his new plan to bust Fat Man's smuggling opera-tion, local and national leaders were at conference tables in McAllen, Wash-ington, and Mexico City fabricating their own plans. After more than fifteen years, a new international bridge was finally nearing completion, a bridge that would span the Rio Grande with almost three miles of concrete creating four new lanes of traffic between the United States and Mexico. The Americans would chip in $40 million for the project; the Mexicans, $20 million. By 2005 the daily vehicle count was projected to reach 9,300. The cities of McAllen, Mission, and tiny Hidalgo were on the brink of issuing $27 million in revenue bonds to help pay for the infrastructure that would attract tourist dollars to the impoverished area. Already platted for bank financing near the new bridge was

Rocking and Swaying

Sharyland Plantation, a project of Hunt Valley Development that included "residential, industrial, and retail development," while on the south side of the river Grupo Río San Juan had sixteen thousand acres ready for development.[19]

The new bridge, the Anzalduas International Crossing, was to be built immediately south of Anzalduas Park on raw land riddled with hiking trails blazed by drug smugglers, *coyotes,* and bird enthusiasts, trails constantly monitored by agents of the Border Patrol. The grand project, which proclaimed nothing less than a new economic future for this stretch of the river, was embodied in an architectural model the size of a Ping-Pong table sitting in a room at the McAllen City Hall. The built-to-scale model was replete with green agricultural fields bordering new highways bulging with tiny plastic replicas of cars and eighteen-wheelers. Tourists and NAFTA trade crossed and conquered a pristine, dark blue Rio Grande dwarfed by a mighty Anzalduas International Crossing fabricated of cardboard and plastic.

These two seemingly disparate projects, each historical and an economic outgrowth of the unique relationship between the United States and Mexico, one led by agent Gester, the other a binational effort, coexisted on exactly the same spot of the former Spanish land grant where Oblates once unsuccessfully cultivated potatoes and vineyards. The projects were as contradictory as Benny *el elefantino* and President Vicente Fox, as varied as Nature Boy and President George W. Bush. At one level public officials negotiated hundreds of millions of dollars to construct infrastructure facilitating trade in products and goods between two countries. Not far from the spot where bridge piers would be drilled deep into toxic river sediments, a real-life Border Patrol agent plotted to shut down a petty smuggler growing rich off impoverished illegal aliens.

However crazily different the intentions of these two projects, the only hurdle faced by mayors—including Leo Montalvo of McAllen, Humberto Valdéz Richaud of Reynosa, John David Franz of Hidalgo, and Norberto Salinas of Mission—was a bevy of local media asking innocuous questions. Agent Gester and other McAllen Station agents backstage at this international circus considered the stakes much higher. Their work was fast becoming a big, frustrating joke. Deterrence and X's plainly did not work. Operation Rio Grande was an embarrassment for every agent determined to put in an honest shift. Agent Gester and his group would keep perfecting their modest plan regardless of any temporary setbacks. They had to.

The Storm

The jet stream propelled the air mass from Africa across the Atlantic before it hit the coast of eastern Florida and beat its way across the breadth of the Gulf of Mexico. One night late in July, while McAllen residents slept and agents went about their work as usual, the winds shifted slightly to the east-southeast. By early morning of the next day, gusts at Miller International Airport, located across the street from Sector Headquarters, were clocked at forty-one miles per hour. This time the air covering McAllen was not fouled by smoke from Mexican and Central American peasants readying their small plots for planting. This was a sandstorm from the Sahara Desert in North Africa.

The city of McAllen prided itself on clean air. With the exception of the periodic smoke from Mexico and Central America, McAllen's air quality ranked it as one of the most pristine cities in the nation. The aromatic air that hung over McAllen most days of the year contained fewer than 50 particles per cubic meter. The average visibility in McAllen was a whopping ten miles.[1]

The Saharan sand coated the power lines, the plant leaves, and all exposed surfaces with tiny, exotic granules.[2] Visibility in McAllen decreased to three miles. The federal standard for safe air quality was 150 particles per cubic meter of air, but when TNRCC analyzed Valley samples it found 156 particles per cubic meter. TNRCC immediately announced that children and adults with respiratory problems should take special precautions.[3]

The winds from Africa did not dissipate, and the sand, lingering in the sky day after day, was replenished. At night the sand acted as a blanket of particles that kept the heat smothering McAllen and the Valley. Temperatures in the early morning hours rarely fell below eighty-five degrees and during the day skyrocketed to over a hundred degrees.

The African sand coated the blooming hydrilla strangling the waters of the Rio Grande. For months the river had failed to reach its natural destination and had become, south of Brownsville and Matamoros, a long, thin, stagnant pool of chemical and human waste. The roots of the nonindigenous plant clogged the Matamoros city water intake pipes, forming dams of plant matter that slowed other parts of the river to a standstill. Water to certain neighborhoods in Matamoros was finally cut off by Mexican officials until the hydrilla problem could be resolved. A haze covered the sun, bathing the Valley in a sea of yellow light resembling the worst smog days in Los Angeles.

In spite of the swollen heat, drug smugglers continued to transport kilos of cocaine and marijuana across the Río Bravo from Pepe's Riverside Fiesta and the Riverside Club, frequent home to German Joe's Polka Band. Even though Charlie Ashton and Jose Monteverde had busted a van filled with $1,227,200 of marijuana off-loaded in the parking lot of Pepe's Riverside Fiesta, the flow of drugs along this stretch of the Rio Grande never paused. The drug cartels considered a loss of more than $1 million in product simply the cost of doing business.

Just south of Pepe's Riverside Fiesta undocumented workers, aided by an unlimited supply of tire tubes, swam the Río Bravo to tiny landings surrounded by carrizo cane. Scores of gray, deflated rubber doughnuts, their original color faded by a torturing sun, floated lazily in the eddies near shaded banks once owned and tilled by the Oblates. Tube wranglers on the southern banks of the Río Bravo swam the river to round up the tubes as often as required, then ferried them back across in long, irregular chains formed by strands of old rope. Mexican entrepreneurs on the southern banks earned their living reselling these old tire tubes for $5 each to the next illegal immigrants who came to cross the Río Bravo.

On the north side of the river a wide and long irrigation channel fronted Pepe's Fiesta Restaurant as well as La Lomita Park, directly adjacent to it. The small park, cordoned off from the restaurant parking lot by four rusty strands of barbed-wire fence, surrounded a modest chapel constructed by the Oblates. Rough-hewn wooden doors opened onto a single main room with several rows of wooden pews arranged before a brightly hued altar.

The old wire fence surrounding the small chapel was wrenched asunder in twenty different places by illegal aliens in a big hurry to reach their waiting rides to safety. Attempts to repair the fence were futile. Each night new illegal workers forced the metal fence posts aside or cut the wire as they breached one of the last physical barriers to the United States. The strains of German Joe's Polka Band inadvertently welcomed them on more than one night as they rushed through the small park and around the chapel.

The entrance to La Lomita Park, where a few scattered picnic tables were scattered among the mesquite, was always locked at night. During the day, especially during the long six to seven months of summer, the metal gate was always left open, but only a few visitors ever ventured into the tree-shaded park or the chapel. This select group included lovers taking an hour off at noontime, carloads of teenagers bent on consuming six-packs of beer or smoking marijuana with their car windows up and their engines running to support the air-conditioner set at full blast, and birders who were often disappointed by the scarcity of specimens so close to Anzalduas Park.

Sometimes the only people at La Lomita Park were agents from the McAllen Station. They used the park as a surveillance site for drug smuggling and regularly patrolled the area looking for the vans and cars that transported undocumented workers to safe houses.

Two agents from the McAllen Station found the body of Leslie Ann Morales in the brush a few feet from the entrance to La Lomita Park on Sunday evening, July 29.[4] The little girl, who was wearing a white shirt and lavender overalls with white sandals, was twenty-one months old at the time of her death. Police said that Leslie Ann died from exposure to the sun. Strapped in a car seat, the toddler lay for hours in the soaring temperatures. The agent who accidentally discovered her was sitting in his unit when, out of the corner of his eye, he spied the car seat lying in the knee-high grass. The agent reported that at first he thought a doll was belted into the seat.

Later, as details emerged from witnesses and the police, two young brothers were accused of carjacking a father and his baby daughter on their way to a *quinceañera.* One of the brothers, Jorge Alfredo "Alfreddy" Salinas, seventeen, turned himself in to police from a pay phone five days after the baby's body was discovered. He confessed that the crime had been spontaneous and random. He and his brother, Lorenzo "Lore" Salinas, twenty-one, hid themselves in a drainage ditch bordering a rural Hidalgo County road not far Mission. When the first car drove by after they were in position, they jumped out with a shotgun, then commandeered the car with the baby asleep in the back seat.

The body of the father, Geronimo Morales, was found in an orange grove on the same day Leslie Ann was buried. Police eventually sought two other suspects in her death: Jose Luis "L. A." Dominguez and Oscar Villa Sevillo. After allegedly shooting Morales with the shotgun and dropping the baby in the brush, the four men drove the car to Reynosa. They were trying to sell Morales's car for $1,000 when a Mexican police officer noticed them and gave chase. In one of the poorest regions of the United States, $1,000 was enough compensation for committing two homicides. Police believed that the oldest Salinas brother disappeared into Mexico, but agents at the McAllen Station were betting that he would soon swim the river to see his family.

FOS Jose Monteverde had his hands full at the McAllen Station. How could he begin to discuss with agents, however hardened by their experience, the motivations behind leaving a baby to die in the desert heat? There could not have been a single agent at the McAllen Station who did not consider the suffering the little girl must have endured before she finally succumbed. In spite of his sixteen years of experience in the Border Patrol, Jose Monteverde could do little for the agents under his supervision who were disturbed by the senseless murder of the small child. Agents requiring professional counseling could call a special hotline, but few at the McAllen Station ever did regardless of the seriousness of their problems. In the macho culture of the Border Patrol, agents did not complain about their problems even though they might be job related. The Tree was their only sanctuary.

It was getting *loco*. Two days before the double homicide, agents had stopped a lone driver at the Falfurrias checkpoint. Examining his papers, agents determined they were fake and arrested the driver. Although handcuffed by Border Patrol agents, the suspect managed to jump back in his car and start the engine. One agent tried to pull him from the car, but instead his arm became jammed in the driver's window. The driver dragged the agent more than one hundred yards before intentionally smashing the car into a tree. The agent was finally able to reach his holster with his free hand and shoot the driver through the windshield. Shot in the chest, the suspect was recovering at a local hospital. The agent had narrowly escaped serious injury.[5]

Two days after the double homicides agents discovered nearly $1 million in cocaine hidden in a van near Pepe's Riverside Fiesta. Two weeks later thirteen illegal immigrants were found near death in the brushlands not far from Roma, fifty miles west of the McAllen Station. A *coyote* had abandoned them in the desert heat with no water or directions to safety, According to one of the illegal workers, they believed *"se iban a morir,"* they were going to die.[6] Smuggling cases, which had declined in the late 1990s, now appeared to be increasing at a significant rate in spite of Operation Rio Grande.[7]

Amid the yellow haze and the craziness, Sector Chief Joe Garza held a press conference at the Holiday Inn on Highway 83 in McAllen to announce the expansion of Border Patrol facilities in Hidalgo County at an estimated cost of around $55 million. Along with invited representatives from seven different Valley towns who planned to submit offers to the Border Patrol for two major construction projects, the local media were in attendance. Mayors and their entourages lunched from the all-you-can-eat buffet table beneath the three-story glass arboretum at the Holiday Inn as they were serenaded by mariachis, then patiently listened to a twenty-minute presentation on the vital construction needs of the Border Patrol in Deep South Texas.

A well-rehearsed Bill Valdez, assistant chief of the McAllen Station, explained that Silver Reyes's Operation Rio Grande required more agents, more staff, and more administrators to support the logistical effort. Sector Headquarters, the 28,345-square-foot home to the Border Patrol since 1934, was no longer big enough. Neither, in fact, was the McAllen Station on Old Military Highway. It was built in the early 1970s to accommodate seventy-five agents, but almost three hundred agents now were based at the facility.[8]

The stakes were high for representatives of the Valley communities invited to the presentation. In a local economy with double-digit unemployment, the contracts and jobs that went along with this new construction attracted considerable attention. There was, in addition, the total economic impact from the two facilities, which including salaries estimated at $75 million a year, heady figures for a region mired in poverty.[9]

Highlighting the reasons why municipalities should join in the competitive bidding process for the new facilities, Assistant Chief Valdez walked the audience through his PowerPoint demonstration. If a mayor could persuade the Border Patrol that his city was the best location for the new buildings, the municipality would reap significant short- and long-term benefits, and the savvy politician could garner the political benefits come the next election.[10]

A consultant from Washington, D.C., specializing in environmental issues sat next to the assistant chief. Next to him sat another consultant from the Border Patrol's regional office in Dallas. He was seated, in turn, next to Alberto Davila, chair of the Economics Department at the University of Texas–Pan American and a coauthor of the study on the impact of the new construction on local communities. I sat to the right of Professor Davila in the darkened room while we watched Valdez's presentation. As if afraid to miss a vital piece of information that might make or break their forthcoming proposals, the mayors and their staffs remained totally silent throughout the talk. There were few questions from the politicians after the presentation, although Alberto Davila and I had drilled Assistant Chief Valdez on possible responses. Just minutes after the presentation Bill Valdez pulled me aside.

"There's something I want to tell you before you hear it from the guys at the station," he said, his voice unmistakably serious. I had just shaken his big hand after congratulating him on his speech. I knew that he had been anxious about standing up in front of a room full of mayors and the Valley media even though he was prepared.

"Okay," I answered.

"You know Jose Monteverde?" Bill went on, not enjoying what he had to tell me. "The FOS?"

"Sure," I said.

"Well, we arrested him last night. It appears that he was taking money."

I did not know how to respond. Chief Garza, head of the McAllen Sector, had given me the name of FOS Jose Monteverde when I had first begun the research project. FOS Monteverde had cheerfully introduced me to most of the management at the McAllen Station, had patiently described the responsibilities required of agents and their supervisors, had so righteously testified at the trial of Wayne Thornton, and each year had taught agents the required workshop on ethics in the Border Patrol. FOS Monteverde, in short, was a respected, trusted, and experienced member of the management team at the McAllen Station.

They arrested him in the parking lot at Wal-Mart. Another agent was with him at the time but was not under suspicion. The two were just stepping out of Jose's car when they were surrounded by armed law enforcement personnel.

"Scared the crap out of me," the agent later admitted.

After FOS Monteverde was released, he briefly stopped by the McAllen Station to turn in his service weapon and other equipment. He told shocked agents, "We got a big problem."

No one at the McAllen Station could believe the charges against him.

FOS Monteverde was privy to all the scheduling of agents and supervisors at the McAllen Station. He knew which agents were assigned to specific areas along the river, how long they were going to be in place, and where agents would be positioned the next day. He knew where the most capable agents were posted at any one particular time, the locations of working sensors and those that needed to be repaired, and what areas, if any, were lightly patrolled because of scheduling problems. With this and other critical information, a professional smuggler could cross a herd of Bennys into Mexico, unimpeded.

Jose Monteverde had been in the Border Patrol for more than sixteen years. At the time of his arrest he was earning more than $85,000 a year as a GS-13. He was the last individual a rational person might expect to be on the take. A few years down the line he was looking at a comfortable retirement with a lifetime federal pension. It did not make any sense. With what must have been a very strange expression, I looked back at Assistant Chief Valdez, speechless. Why would Jose Monteverde take a bribe? If there had been one bribe, there had likely been others. But why would he betray the trust of his coworkers and put their lives in jeopardy?

Assistant Chief Bill Valdez said only, "I thought you'd want to hear it from me."

I smiled and shook hands with several other people in the conference room at the Holiday Inn, then found myself roasting in the parking lot as I searched for my car. It was close to two o'clock in the afternoon, and the sun was turning the asphalt into a thick soup. I ran into Alberto Davila, who was headed back to campus, and shook his hand, but I have no idea what I said to him. Still in shock, I finally found my car and drove home.

Maybe Jose Monteverde had fallen into debt. I thought that he had kids in college, but I was not sure. Or maybe he had become embittered at his approaching retirement. Maybe it was blatant materialism that got to him in the end, the price of a new swimming pool or a bigger house or travel to

Rocking and Swaying

Europe. There were a hundred possibilities, but all of them seemed wrong and did not fit the character of the man I knew. One thing was certain in this absurd arrest of a respected administrator. If the Mexican drug organizations could bribe FOS Jose Monteverde of the U.S. Border Patrol, they could get to anyone in the agency.

All the way home, and long into that night, I thought about the infernal summer that was far from ended, about FOS Jose Monteverde, the dead baby, the desert sand from Africa, the dying immigrants rescued by agents in the nick of time, the bricks of cocaine, the ruthlessness of the drug cartels, and all the other composite parts of this ferocious stew of human misery and loss along the Rio Grande. Few outside the Border Patrol and a handful of groups supporting immigrant rights appeared seriously concerned.[11]

In Deep South Texas it seemed there was no moral, rational core or order. More to the point, it was only getting worse.

The Tree

Gester was a new school Border Patrol agent; Noe Escondido, old school. Gester knew the policies, but he was going to drive Fat Man out of business personally even if he had to bend the rules. Although at times the rules made Noe's job next to impossible, he always followed station policies. After his shift, Noe went home to his family. Gester went to the Tree. The Tree was his shelter from the craziness.

On yet another torrid day in August, Noe Escondido made himself comfortable at the agents' table at McAllen's Shoney's off State Highway 83. Shoney's cheap buffet and coffee attracted old school agents like Noe. Four other agents were seated at the back of the restaurant ordering food and waiting patiently for Noe to tell them how they were going to spend their next ten hours. While their Expeditions steamed in the parking lot just a few feet from the busy six lanes of traffic, a young waitress in a pressed uniform hovered over Noe's shoulder taking orders.

When it was Noe's turn, he turned on his considerable charm as he winked at Humberto Balderama across the table. Humberto was a large man with a ready smile and quick laugh. Noe always kept him laughing.

As the waitress retreated, Noe nodded in her direction. "A snack," he told his audience of four.

Rocking and Swaying

Summing up the situation, Humberto Balderama said, "He doesn't even leave us the crumbs."

By all rights Humberto and Noe should have been sworn enemies, because after the first day of last January, Noe had replaced Humberto on sensor duty. It had taken Noe and his fellow agents six months of digging holes to update the fractured sensor system, one of the mainstays of their defense against the drug smugglers and the *coyotes*. They had fixed the malfunctioning sensors, hunted down missing units that had not even been catalogued and, finally, transferred working sensors from Rio Grande landings abandoned by smugglers and *coyotes* to locations that bore heavy traffic. Although Noe had inherited a mess from Humberto, the two men held no ill will toward each other.

Now, for reasons known only to station management, Humberto was once again on sensor duty, and Noe was back patrolling the line. Noe was philosophical: if management wanted it that way, Noe could accept it. If Humberto screwed up again, Noe would do his best to clean up the sensor system a second time if management asked him.

"You know the 231?" Humberto asked, picking up where they had left off before the "snack" had distracted Noe. "Well, it was so bad that I had to separate the chip from the repeater by two or three feet. For some reason they wouldn't work together in the same box, so I separated them with talkie wire and buried them a few feet apart."

Eyes sparkling from beneath the brim of his cowboy hat, Noe looked across the table at his friend. "Listen to him. What did you call that equipment? A 'talkie wire.'" Noe chuckled, then sat back in his wooden armchair. "You mean the main communications wire between the two units?"

"Whatever," said Humberto, long since used to Noe's ribbing. He and Noe went way back. Because Humberto knew he could count on Noe he could tolerate any teasing. "You know what I mean. Why make it more complicated than it is? I always try to keep it simple."

"Remember what you used to call that one part?" Noe went on, unwilling to let it drop. "What was it? Mac, what is that part really called?" Noe was addressing Mac Zavaleta now. A frail man with a tired visage but a keen mind, Mac was smoking furiously while he sipped his hot coffee. It did not matter to Mac Zavaleta if it was 105 degrees in the shade, he was going to drink his coffee and smoke his Winston cigarettes. Only then was he ready to start his shift. Mac, who had eleven years in the Border Patrol and who next to Noe was the senior agent at the table, had been counting for the last five years the days before he could retire with his pension.

He scrunched his lined face as he searched his long-term memory bank, then proudly announced the result after only a ten-second silence: "The enunciator."

"Shit," said Humberto.

"Okay," said Noe, now going for the kill, "What did you call it, Humberto? I know you remember what you called that thing."

Noe was not flaunting a college education in Humberto's face like the know-it-all Rambos did. Noe, Humberto, and Mac were proud of their high school diplomas and their years in the army. Their education, they would be glad to tell you, did not come from the inside of books. With good nature in his smile, Humberto answered, "The speaker. But why call it something complicated when what it really is is a damn speaker? 'Enunciator.' What kind of person would use a word like that?"

The table erupted in deep laughter all around.

"Lay off me, Noe," Humberto said, pretending to be upset. Then, as if Noe's insults had pushed him too far, he dramatically grabbed a knife from the table and pretended to cut his left wrist. The other agents, including Noe, roared.

After a few more jokes and some juicy station gossip, Noe decided it was time to get down to business. Purposely ignoring the other two agents at the table—both younger men who had worked less than two years at the McAllen Station and whose opinions, in the viewpoint of Noe, Mac, and Humberto, counted for squat—Noe looked directly at the senior agents and asked, "What are we doing tonight, bros?" Noe did not expect the "new" agents to utter a word, not if they knew their place. The two men kept silent.

Before Humberto or Mac offered an opinion, Noe informed them of the most recent intel regarding Anzalduas Park. Noe was keenly aware of Gester's operation to shut down Fat Man. One of the supes had updated him just before the 2 P.M. muster. Noe identified Gester as a brash upstart who had yet to earn his respect, did not follow orders, and was a glory hound to boot. Nevertheless, Noe could appreciate Gester's sentiments, and most of all he admired Gester's dogged determination. Every agent at the station would like to see Fat Man inside a cell.

With the temperature surging over a hundred degrees, all the agents at the

Rocking and Swaying

table at Shoney's, including the less experienced men, knew that nothing was going to happen along the river until after sunset, when the earth began cooling down.

Noe planned to cut sign until about 9 P.M., when he would take up a position with a clear view of Anzalduas Park. Humberto and Mac Zavaleta and their partners for the shift would serve as backup. When Noe gave them the go-ahead on the radio, they would charge into the park to bust whoever had fallen into Noe's sights. Noe was hoping it would be someone with a load of cocaine. The other agents nodded in turn to show that they agreed with this plan—formulated by the best agent at the McAllen Station.

By the third week in August the African sandstorm had finally subsided, but had been replaced by a stiff wind from Mexico, which, along with the scorching sun, buffeted the people and the land on both sides of the Rio Grande. Thirty minutes after Mac Zavaleta finished his last cigarette at Shoney's, Noe rounded the drag in his Expedition. The truck stirred up a thick cloud of dust that the Mexican wind then took and blew north.

On the other side of the dirty windshield stretched a twenty-acre onion field awaiting new planting. The harvest long since over, segments of rotting onions peeked from beneath the tops of new furrows.

Reflecting on his years as a migrant farmworker, Noe lowered his window to scan the dusty onion field as stale, burned air rushed into the front of the truck cab. "This year I hear they're making seventy cents a sack," he said. "I'm almost forty-three years old. Twenty-five years ago when I was picking onions with my family they were paying us the exact same thing. Can you believe it?"

"You know, I took that supe test two months back and scored a sixty-nine. One point short. You got to pass that test with a seventy to make supe. That'd be a GS-12 for me. You're talking $75,000 a year counting the overtime. All I got to do is pass that test. With my fourteen years of experience and annual evaluations, I'm automatically a supe. I know they'll give it to me."

Noe was not bragging, just stating the facts. For a former migrant farmworker from the Valley to be considering a guaranteed $75,000 annual salary was nothing short of a miracle.

"The supe is always the field advisor for the regular agents. He should be out there with them all the time. Most of the supes really don't get away from the station much except for Jack Spurrier. I'd be like him if I were a supe. But more so. I like getting out there rain or shine and cutting sign. I'm good at it.

The supes keep me off the X's and airport duty because they know they'd be wasting me. Some of the other agents get a little jealous about it, but they know I'm good. If I was a supe, I could be out doing what I like and getting paid the big bucks at the same time.

"I had seventeen dope busts last year I was involved in. Not always the primary, but I was a part of them in some way. There aren't many agents bringing in as many aliens as I do. I track them down the old-fashioned way."

The history of the Border Patrol in Deep South Texas did not bother Noe. Many McAllen Mexican Americans, including some of his neighbors, hated the Border Patrol with a passion. What mattered to Noe was that he did not have to worry about farmers' trying to cheat him by offering seventy cents for a bushel of onions. His children were not the children of Valley migrants, neither were they looked down upon in school by Anglos and other Mexican Americans when they arrived late for classes every fall after working up north or, every spring, ridiculed when they left classes early to begin working the fields. His wife, moreover, was not the spouse of a migrant farmworker who each year had to pinch and save to keep food on the table. Noe and his family lived in the suburbs in a house they owned. They had two cars, including Noe's truck, their kids wore brand-name clothes, and the family took a vacation at least once a year.

After his shifts Noe always headed home to his wife and kids. Not Charlie Ashton, or Maria Contreras, or Rochester, Rodriguez, Plovic, or many of the younger agents, including Gester. They headed for the Tree. Almost every law enforcement agency in the United States had a place like the Tree, although it might take a different form.[1] It was a cop bar in a big city or, in a smaller town, a table at the back of a restaurant that remained open around the clock. It was a place where they could unwind after work and not worry about offending anyone because they had been through the same thing. It was a place to go when going straight home was the last thing in the world they wanted to do. Not because they did not love those closest to them, but because they needed time to cool down, time to socialize with others who knew exactly what they had been through.

The place was around the corner from the McAllen Station, then south two long blocks. Assembly plants, warehouses, and wholesale *ropa usada* sheds filled to the rafters with bales of used clothes surrounded the McAllen Station on three sides. But the industrial park and free enterprise zone thinned out a few blocks to the south, where large agricultural fields abutted the walls of the enormous metal buildings. Between a wholesale welding supplier and an empty lot stood a scraggly elm tree less than fifteen feet in height: the Tree.

A chunk of cast-off concrete sat on one side of the ragged lot, and broken glass and stuffed garbage bags circled the base of the wannabe tree, but late at night under the glare of the powerful security lights of the McAllen Station, it was still possible to imagine this bleak stretch of ground was a lush city park with thick grass, bushes, trees, and even a fountain.

Agents routinely washed their vehicles in the parking lot behind the station, filled out their final shift paperwork, then climbed into their civilian cars and trucks to drive two blocks to the Tree. Still drenched in sweat from their work, they parked off to the side of the wide, empty street. Someone at the Tree always had a big cooler filled with iced beer. The agents kept count of the beers like gold bars: who owed what to whom and when it should be repaid. Standing in small groups of two or three, the off-duty agents drank their cold beers in the waning heat. But the Tree was not really about drinking.

Charlie Ashton pulled up in his late-model sport truck with a big blue cooler full of beer in the back. As the minutes passed in the early morning hours, he described his upcoming trip to Big Bend National Park.

"I'm going there to check the place out. They got a station out there with eight agents. You're on your own. No supe looking over your shoulder, bro. And no X's. There's miles and miles of nothing. Sounds good to me."

Rodriguez was dubious. "I'd get bored," he said.

"Nah, not me. I'm thinking I could move out there and learn the place real well. I've heard that certain times of the year there are tourists with big RVs, but most of the time it's just you and the desert. I'm taking a week of vacation time to see the place. I tell you, bros, I'm stoked about this place. Soon as I see it with my own eyes, I'm putting in for a transfer."[2]

Charlie Ashton was considered one of the best of the new agents, a Rambo who had quickly learned that doing X's was not for him. A former university parking cop, he had signed up to work in the outdoors, not to sit ten hours a day staring out the windshield of an Expedition. The more he learned how the system worked at the McAllen Station, the more cynical Charlie Ashton became. The supes tried to rein in his enthusiasm by giving him more than his fair share of X's.

Agent Maria Contreras drove up in her powerful, gut-churning Camaro, parked, then stepped onto the pavement dressed in her standard-issue pants, white T-shirt, and black work boots. On Maria the uniform, although stained with sweat and covered with dirt, was more than enough reason for every male agent still breathing to strain his neck in her direction. Agent Maria Contreras, even after ten hours on the job, was an eyeful. Agent Plovic, still pining over their recent break-up, turned his back to avoid seeing her.

Someone offered Maria a beer. "Just a Coke," she said. "You know I'm not a drinker, and I'm not going to get popped by the locals for DUI." Another truck drove up, then another. Ten vehicles now lined the empty, quiet street at 2:30 in the morning. In the distance a mourning dove began its four-note song.

"I'm going to go out there for four days, look the place over, then make my decision," repeated Charlie Ashton, still dreaming about Big Bend. "What do I have to lose? One thing I know is I sure as hell am not staying here the rest of my life."

In some ways the Anglo agents from the north, like Charlie Ashton, had the hardest time adjusting to Deep South Texas. Not only did they have to learn the job, but they had to adjust to a different culture. Shuman and the other agents originally from the East Coast were used to big city life. For fish out of water like Shuman, Charlie, and the other Anglos, especially the single men, McAllen was as foreign to them in the beginning as Humphrey Bogart's Casablanca.

Wives or girlfriends who relocated with these men faced an even more daunting task. Not only were they also likely to be unfamiliar with border culture, but they frequently arrived in McAllen without a job and with no support system of family and friends. Of course, jobs were difficult to find in a region with double-digit unemployment. And the available jobs seldom paid the salaries customary in less impoverished regions. At the same time the new culture provided few immediate friends who might serve as a buffer to the difficult transition. Separation and divorce were a common consequence of the adjustment to the Texas border.

The agents at the Tree, whether Anglo or Mexican American, drank beer cold as ice, grilled fajitas, talked, bitched, and argued among themselves for a few minutes or for hours. Here race mattered little. The single men talked about women, motorcycles, handguns, the best bars in McAllen, and the best gyms at the cheapest rates. The married men talked about the houses they were buying or had just purchased, their kids, where they were taking their vaca-

Rocking and Swaying

tions, and the football, baseball, and soccer teams they coached. Female agents rarely came to the Tree and, when they did, did not stay long.

After a long shift it was not easy going home to an empty apartment— even one with a big-screen color television. If married, going to the Tree might be better than returning home to a wife already snoring in the bed. It was not that married agents did not love their families. In fact, it was mostly because they cared about them that they went to the Tree first, then drove home. Their wives and children kept normal hours. Employed spouses worked nine to five and the kids rose at seven every weekday morning to get ready for school. From hard experience many married men knew not to mess with their family's schedule.[3]

Keeping mentally healthy from one week to the next, from one year to the next, depended on leaving behind at the Tree what they witnessed as agents. It could be the onion girl, or the sight of the dead baby, or whatever else was on the truckload of human misery the agents daily confronted during line watch. The Tree also provided the place and the time to recover from the adrenaline rush garnered after a high-speed chase or a night along the Rio Grande dark as the inside of a cave.

There was, too, idle chitchat at the Tree, rumors flying back and forth like gossip at a high school dance. Which agent was reading while doing X's, which supe was on a rampage, and who was squarely looking at a reprimand for his or her permanent file.

They could talk about almost anything at the Tree and not worry about it coming back to them. Except no one ever talked about Wayne Thornton, who was still awaiting sentencing for his jury conviction of assaulting an illegal alien with his flashlight.

Or the arrest and prosecution of FOS Jose Monteverde. Overnight FOS Monteverde had become a living ghost at the McAllen Station. When I asked agents about him they shrugged their shoulders in my direction and looked uncomfortable. No one honestly seemed to know what was happening in the case against the administrator other than that he was no longer at the station. It was rumored that he was on paid leave pending the findings of the investigation.

Trying not to be too obvious about it, Plovic walked over to Maria Contreras. Maria smiled up at him, then continued listening to another agent describing the new house he was buying in Northeast McAllen. He was going through the house room by room as he detailed every little feature from the style of woodwork to the color of the carpet. Maria must have been bored, but there was no way she was going to give Plovic the time of day in front of the other agents. After another ten minutes, she said her good-byes, climbed into her Camaro, and roared off through the empty streets. Plovic, not blinking an eye, reached for another beer from Charlie Ashton's big cooler.

The single guys were usually the last to leave. By 4 A.M. the wide street in front of the Tree was once again empty. The agents always policed the beer cans and the other trash that ended up on the rock-hard ground. The ratty lot was as spotless as they could possibly make it. A truck driver turning into one of the plants off Old Military Highway used his Jake Brake, the downshift a disruption to the silence pervading the empty lot with the lone tree.

Noe Escondido never went to the Tree. The idea of going to the Tree was no more an option for Noe Escondido than enrolling in night classes in criminal justice at UTPA. He adjusted his straw cowboy hat on his head after cutting sign for two hours, turned his boyish face toward the Rio Grande, and stomped on the brakes before he described one more time his plan for the night for Anzalduas Park. But then the plan had to wait. A sensor by the river took eight straight hits. Noe had never seen dope landed near that sensor; however, he knew the landing was a solid prospect for illegal aliens.

"What we do is we drive down close to the river, then cut sign to get behind them. Then we're between them and the river and if they decide to head south when they see our guys in front of them, they got to come through us. I'll get my guys in position. Whether they come out on the road or the irrigation ditch, we'll grab them."

Avoiding the deep ruts and the washouts along the drag that followed this stretch of the Rio Grande, Noe turned the tuner until he found one of his favorite country tunes before speeding in the direction of the hot sensor. Noe was a big fan of Reba, and he hummed contentedly along with her song on the radio. Once more adjusting his straw cowboy hat as he opened the truck door, he searched for sign in the pale dust along a narrow trail leading into thick brush.

"We got three, maybe four sets of tracks here. See this one? Sort of a combat boot. Easy to follow. That's our perp." His eyes always on the ground before him, he took off at a brisk pace down the trail that soon gave way to concrete top soil that did not take a print except to the eye of an expert. Noe stopped, backtracked, stopped again, then checked two trails that led in opposite directions before he once again found the sign. In his element, Noe was a human bloodhound.

After another half mile in the heat, the trail ran into dense vegetation before coming into an open, parched field filled with tree stumps. Then the sign headed back into woods, following a deep creek bed that forged gullies into the fragile bottomland. Every few minutes Noe held up his hand for me to halt, checked intersecting trails that led to nowhere, then motioned me forward again. He soon came to a bend in the trail where, mixed among scant human tracks, was the fresh sign of a bobcat.

It was quiet along these trails in the desolate brushlands, just the sluggish song of a few unseen birds among the yucca and the sound of our own breathing grown louder as the chase progressed. There were resting places along the way, natural indentations in the clay from erosion and flash flood where hundreds, if not thousands, of the newest immigrants stopped to drink from their plastic water bottles or spend the night. Wedged underneath prickly pear, stuck in the limbs of the mesquite, or scattered in piles in the dry creek beds, plastic gallon water bottles littered the rugged landscape. Never breaking stride, Noe stepped over a pair of men's gray cotton briefs lying in the middle of the trail, the underwear unrecognizable except for the discernible brand lettering on the spandex waistband.

Noe lost the sign several more times, but each time he backtracked, circled, then deciphered the slightest of marks that set him off again on the right trail. The ground again hardened and the sign all but disappeared as we distanced ourselves, one long mile at a time, from the banks of the river. Noe would point out the sign to me, but I could not see it. Although he told me to look again, I honestly could not discern even a trace of human imprint.

"This guy is smart," Noe finally admitted, stopping to wipe his forehead with his sleeve. "See where they walk in the middle of the grass there? He has them keeping off places in the softer gravel that would carry sign. This man definitely knows what he is doing. Right here he heads northeast, but he has the others following him swing far out over there so it looks like their tracks disappear. Then further up the trail they come back together. This guy is experienced. I really want to get him."

Noe kept his backup constantly informed of his location. Mac Zavaleta and his partner covered the road heading east while Humberto Balderama and his partner were responsible for the north side of the irrigation ditch. Noe also had called Jerry Ambrose to watch the west side of the expanse of brushland, but Jerry had not responded.

"I don't know. I've been calling Jerry since after muster and I haven't heard from him. Where's he at?" This was not the first time that Jerry had all but disappeared.

After more than an hour and a half cutting sign, sweat saturating his uniform, Noe emerged from the brush about a hundred yards south of an empty stretch of Old Military Highway. Agent Gutierrez, Mac Zavaleta's partner, came out from his hiding place behind a fence post. First thing Gutierrez said, excitement in his voice, was, "Never saw them."

"I can't figure it," said Noe, wiping his brow. "We were right behind them all the way. At most they maybe had a thirty-minute head start on us. *Chingalo,* bro. Usually we get them when they stop for water. But they never stopped and then just disappeared. I never did get Jerry. They could have headed west, and Jerry wasn't there to stop them. If they did that, they're halfway to Houston by now. Shit."

While Noe reluctantly radioed the dispatcher to record the four illegals as gotaways, Gutierrez had something else on his mind.

"When Mac and I parked, maybe thirty minutes ago, I figured they might be already out of the brush and laying in over there on the other side of the ditch. I saw a flash of clothing or something. It looked white from where I was hiding, so I go over there and put my face down to get a good look. Shit, bros. It was a rattlesnake! All coiled up and looking straight at me. I'm not this far from it." Gutierrez gestured that his nose had been less than two feet from the mouth of the poisonous snake.

Agent Gutierrez opened the tailgate of his Expedition. Lying in a lifeless heap on a carpet remnant was a four-foot-long diamondback rattlesnake.

"I was freaked, bro. I grabbed a stick and beat the shit out of it. I'm telling you, I was totally freaked."

Noe eyeballed the rattlesnake. "That's the fourth one I've seen since January. Last year I didn't see one rattlesnake the whole year."

"Seen any coral snakes?" asked Gutierrez. "Those are the ones they told us at the academy to watch out for."

"Not this year," said Noe dismissing the fact as if one of the world's most dangerous snakes were a common toad.

Rocking and Swaying

"When I get back to the station I'm going to take a picture of it. Man, I was too close to that thing for comfort."

Undistracted by the sight of the rattler, Noe radioed Jerry one more time. If Jerry had been in place, an agent would be hauling four undocumented workers back to the station along with the rattlesnake.

Even Noe needed a break from the early evening's heat, still well over the century mark, so he stopped at a convenience store in Los Ebanos. While the woman behind the counter cooked his hamburger on a small, greasy grill, Noe stood cooling himself in front of a wall unit chiseled directly into the cinder block. He drank the coldest can of Coke he could find in the store freezer and flirted with the woman. Noe would flirt with any woman.

Little Debbie products completely filled one aisle of the tiny mom-and-pop store: Little Debbie cupcakes, Little Debbie pecan pies, Little Debbie powdered donuts, and the rest of the line of Little Debbie pastries. The next shelf displayed boxes of pork rinds and small cellophane packages filled with jalapeño-flavored dried shrimp.

Drenched in a permanent summer sweat, Noe ate his modest dinner in the front seat of the Expedition with the motor running and the AC on full blast. He was still fuming at Jerry Ambrose as he made quick work of the burger and fries. "If he'd been where he should have been, we'd have caught those illegals. I wasted two hours of my time for nothing." His anger diminished, however, as he set his mind on sign cutting for the next hour and a half. All of it was old sign from the day before or prints left by agents on the early morning shift. He was heading back toward Anzalduas Park when the dispatcher called out a nearby sensor.

Perking up from a frustrating shift, he said, "This one is good for illegals." He parked his truck after a short ride and once again headed into thick brush. Easing himself between the strands of a barbed-wire fence, Noe brushed his leg against a six-foot-tall prickly pear.

"Got my knee," he said simply. Later he spent twenty minutes pulling out the thorns, but now he followed a narrow trail that led lazily toward the river. Halting several times, he listened with his right ear for any sounds while, with his left, he monitored the dispatcher on his radio. As the shadows of night around us darkened I wished that I had brought my Mag light.

"The sensor went off again," he said as he pulled up short without warning then backed slowly into the brush for cover. "Wait here," he whispered, "and they should come right by us."

Ten minutes passed but no one came our way.

"It took another hit," Noe said. "I don't get it. They should have been here by now. Let's take a look at the sensor. Something is screwy."

Noe never rushed a sensor. He lived by what he preached to new recruits: wait for the illegals to come to you, then arrest them. If illegals were still near the sensor, rushing it would only scatter them. Easing toward the sensor, which Noe knew lay buried fifty yards from our hiding place, we heard a loud, unmistakable animal sound in the brush. Noe moved forward a few feet, then shone his Mag light on the forest of prickly pear surrounding us. Two big, dumb eyes stared back at us.

"A damn cow," said Noe, backing slowing away as he kept the cow in sight. As the dark brown cow on spindly legs grazed on the buds of the prickly pear, the animal set off the buried sensor, which was incapable of discerning new immigrants from domestic animals. The cow, in turn, watched us retreat with little interest before returning to its meal.

Noe had run into bulls before. "They never charged me or anything. But you got to be careful out here."

"Maybe tonight is just one of those nights," Noe concluded as he climbed back into the truck. "Everybody has them. There's just not much going on."

Noe did not give up. He radioed the agent in the scope truck, which was set up for the night near Miller's Farm. Unfortunately the agent had nothing to report because he could not get the video screen to work properly. Noe offered some technical advice, then hung up. He spent the next forty-five minutes scanning the area with his NVGs. The agent in the scope truck radioed Noe back fifteen minutes later to tell him he had fixed the problem and was observing a clear picture of the area.

"What you got?"

"A dog and a jackrabbit. So far the two haven't run into each other yet, but it's going to happen sooner or later." The way things were going, the inevitable intersection of the two animals might be the highlight of Noe's shift.

An even stiffer wind from the southeast came up along the floodway a quarter of a mile from where Noe scanned the darkness. The wind forced Noe either to dump his hat or risk losing it. Hatless for the rest of the night, Noe continued to scan the tree line to the south. Noe knew that any illegal immigrants in the area would be hiding there. The illegals could either wait there until daybreak or traverse an open area of knee-high, parched grass that lay between their hiding place and Old Military Highway. Impatience finally getting the better of him, Noe kicked the dry dust with his boot.

He radioed the scope truck once more, only to learn that the dog had caught the rabbit's scent and was now frantically circling it.

"It's all I got to give you," the agent said apologetically.

Noe could not stand still another minute. He immediately jumped in his truck and drove at a high rate of speed toward the tree line he had been eyeballing. Finding the trail he knew was there, he followed it for a hundred yards in the pitch black before he stopped, pulled out his Mag light, and shone its powerful beam where men, women, and children might be hiding. Wordless, he walked ten feet farther up the trail, backtracked slowly, then dove into the brush again. I could hear him thrashing about and see his flashlight as it fabricated dismembered shadows against the trunks of trees and thick yuccas.

"See it there?" Noe asked me when he returned. "You got to look hard to see it," he said again. Then he got down on his knees and shone his flashlight horizontally across the dirt to make his point. "Looks different now, don't it?"

I saw before me a very faint imprint of half of the heel of a tennis shoe headed in a northerly direction.

"There were two of them. They both jumped the dirt here, and one of them didn't completely clear it. This is all that's left. It's brand new. They're the ones who set off the sensor an hour ago. I found a set of their full tracks about fifty feet north of here in the brush."

I stared at the faintest of prints. Just a trace of previous action, motion, and intent, the barest of mistakes by individuals who surely were not illegal immigrants.

"They started going north, then turned back. That's what's weird. They jumped the trail again over there, then turned back for no reason I can tell."

Why did two men risk swimming the Rio Grande at eleven at night, hide their tracks as well as any professional spooks, then swim the river yet again? They could have been scouts for a drug load or men on some kind of other surveillance. But what kind of surveillance? Noe did not know, could not know, and would never know unless events in the future provided the answer.

One shift at a time Noe and the other agents at the McAllen Station faced an uncomfortable truth that challenged the legitimacy and credibility of the new strategies based upon "deterrence" and "prevention through deterrence."

Noe did not know that the validity of deterrence theory had been disputed long before becoming the linchpin of the Border Patrol's frontal deployment of resources.[4] First advocated in 1764 by Italian Cesare Beccaria in his classic treaty *On Crimes and Punishment,* deterrence believed that human behavior, assumed to be consistent across all cultures and times, was the rational product of free will based upon the avoidance of pain and the attraction of pleasure.[5] According to Beccaria, and later the English utilitarian Jeremy Bentham, potential criminals, after thoughtful consideration of their best options, made rational decisions that governed their behavior.[6] Free will was a fundamental requirement of deterrence theory; individuals could act in regard to the law in any way they chose.

More specifically, the three major tenets of deterrence held that: "as the perceived certainty of punishment increases, the probability of norm violations declines"; "as the punishment response becomes swifter, the probability of norm violation declines"; and last, "the severity of punishment was accorded less importance than certainty and celerity."[7] The first tenet, jargon aside, argued that laws must be clearly stated and consistently enforced. The second tenet suggested that swift punishment decreased the likelihood of violations. The third principle of deterrence maintained that quickly enforcing the law was more important than the severity of the punishment.

These concepts, radical when advocated in eighteenth-century Europe, still made good sense at the end of the twentieth century. Nevertheless, criminologists who have tested deterrence in the real criminal world have encountered mixed results. Although researchers have found that cases such as battering offenses of females, drunk driving, and white-collar crimes provide limited support for the efficacy of deterrence theory, researchers who have examined criminals and the effects of capital punishment have consistently found deterrence theory to have little real impact.[8] One criminologist with years of experience in law enforcement stated succinctly, "The only people really deterred by capital punishment are those we execute."[9] At the very least, deterrence theory bordered on an overly simplistic evaluation of human behavior and the legal system that failed to account for the complexity and diversity in perpetrators, victims, and the structure of modern societies.[10]

To be generous, deterrence theory assumed much and allowed little for human variation, thereby creating a model in which the enforcement of laws became problematic at best. When the Border Patrol applied deterrence to illegal immigrants from around the globe, its consequences were unpredictable. Could the same strategies used by the Border Patrol to deter Mexicans, for example, be reasonably expected to deter Brazilians, Bosnians, Afghans, and Chinese? Indeed, why did Mexican illegal immigrants not act in a rational way, as advocates of deterrence theory would have predicted, by returning to their homes in Mexico when they saw the visible show of force exhibited by the agents at the border? Not to mention the illegal immigrants from other cultures who were demolishing the strategy. At the same time, deterrence theory seemed to have had little effect on drug traffic, which had not abated since the plan was launched in El Paso.

Deterrence theory as practiced by the Border Patrol in Deep South Texas was a one-size-fits-all strategy that hard-nosed agents like Noe Escondido recognized as a grand failure. Regardless of the bad fit of Silver Reyes's strategy, management at the McAllen Station and the other stations along the Rio Grande acted as if deterrence theory was a godsend even as their most experienced agents continuously met frustration and failure. Tonight Agent Noe Escondido, the best damn tracker and sign cutter at the McAllen Station, had struck out. After a ten-hour shift he had nothing to show for his labor but three puncture wounds on his right knee cap, four gotaways, and one cow.

Jerry Ambrose finally radioed Noe. He said the supe had told him to cover the far east side of the line, so he had never been available as backup. Noe was not buying it, and Jerry was not apologizing.

Noe went through the usual motions of hosing off his truck, filling out the paperwork, and checking his M16 back into the armory along with the NVGs. He even cracked a few jokes with the supes in the control room as he finished a cup of station coffee. There for the first time he learned—although not to his surprise—that Gester and several agents were in hot water with management. They had gone after Fat Man one more time and instead of corralling suspects and hard evidence to make their case had created an international incident.

Old school Noe had done everything in the book to earn his pay this shift, but he had nothing, absolutely nothing, to show for it. There were no illegals to process. No dope for which to account. No real intel. No nothing.

Noe Escondido, feeling every one of his forty-three years, climbed into his truck and headed home.

Shifts

Although the Border Patrol swam in the same political sea as the Federal Bureau of Investigation, the Drug Enforcement Agency, and other federal law enforcement agencies that were common household names, it was an entirely different creature.[1] Far from the beltways of Washington, farther still from the public's interest, the Border Patrol was recognized by few citizens who did not reside in border states.[2] In nonborder states the public frequently ignored immigrants and the policies that regulated them. For years the only publicity the Border Patrol received was generated by elements of the Far Right periodically patrolling the borders with their own armed vigilantes and at the other end of the spectrum by those who represented the rights of immigrants. Although concerned with agents of the Border Patrol who abused their powers, groups on the Far Left cared less about the daily problems encountered on line watch than about protecting both illegal and legal aliens from exploitation during their stay in the United States.[3]

Typically public interest waxed when immigrants drowned while crossing the Rio Grande, died from exposure in the desert, or suffocated in a train car. But all too soon these horror stories disappeared from the headlines along with the political will to create new policies addressing the problems. Immigration and immigration policy have been political, economic, and social issues that have inadequately dovetailed with media sound bites.[4] Throughout history legal and illegal immigrants to the United States were granted little attention until a severe economic downturn, the outbreak of war, or some other event drew attention to their presence within our national boundaries. At these times quick and easy solutions were offered to complex issues involving immigrants along with American citizens who might be mistaken for them. New laws, for example, were passed to control Chinese immigrants in the nineteenth century because of a fear of the "yellow peril"; the federal government constructed internment camps for Japanese American citizens during World War II; and the Bracero Program, after a labor shortage of indigenous Americans developed, invited hundreds of thousands of Mexican laborers to harvest American crops.[5]

While most Americans knew next to nothing about the Border Patrol, older residents of the Valley still remembered 1954 when more than 50,000 Hispanics throughout South Texas, including Mexican American citizens residing in McAllen and surrounding Valley communities, were summarily deported against their will after the economy soured. The Border Patrol rounded up anyone who resembled a Mexican laborer and with the aid of local law enforcement herded them onto a special freighter docked at Port Brownsville. With little regard for civil liberties, illegal immigrants and others whom law enforcement officers believed resembled illegal immigrants were shipped to remote regions of Mexico. In at least one instance Border Patrol agents also erroneously deported an Anglo Valley citizen.[6]

Perambulating into August 2001, the Border Patrol managed to accomplish what other federal agencies could only dream. Despite numerous warning signs that would have placed other federal agencies squarely in the limelight of reform and reorganization, this agency successfully resisted serious attempts to transform and modernize management policies guiding its operation. Piecemeal reform from outside the agency went nowhere unless there was a lawsuit attached, while individual reform from within was a waste of time because of the pervasive top-down military mentality that trivialized the suggestions and observations of agents in the field. Managers at the McAllen Station identified the best agents as those who, like soldiers, unfailingly followed orders from their commanding officers. From this perspective, honorable agents never blew the whistle on ineffectual policies and procedures. Those who did were by definition troublemakers and political enemies of the Border Patrol.

Over the years other federal agencies raised their standards of recruitment to meet new challenges in a changing world. In stark contrast the Border Patrol welcomed anyone in August 2001 who had pocketed a high school diploma. The Border Patrol mimicked the U.S. Army, Navy, Marines, and Air Force in bearing and structure, but in fact these military branches had outdistanced the Border Patrol by nurturing their recruits in college and graduate school programs that furthered their general expertise and management skills. Other federal agencies encouraged their employees to continue professional development as measured against private sector standards. In contrast, the small group of agents who held college, graduate, and professional degrees at the McAllen Station encountered suspicion and distrust along with management's daily mantra that "military and police experience are the only things that really count." Not surprisingly, most Border Patrol managers at the McAllen Station had few, if any, years of education beyond high school.

Specific lawsuits may have spurred minimal reforms at specific Border Patrol stations, but for years key labor issues affecting agents in the field had rarely reached the negotiating table.[7] For example, an agent at the McAllen Station was forced in the mid-1990s to file a union grievance against management when it refused to provide health benefits or back pay after the agent was stricken seriously with tuberculosis. At the time management declared that agents must prove beyond a doubt they had contacted TB while on the job. Agents in 2001, as a result of the eventual settlement of this dispute, were regularly tested for this disease and other communicable diseases commonly carried by immigrants from third-world countries. While this change in management practice was certainly a step in the right direction, it only occurred because of a filed grievance.

Many agents at the McAllen Station viewed the union as a waste of their time. "They take too much from you every paycheck, and there's no way I'm going to join," said one agent when asked. Even agents who did not object specifically to the dues said that they had little use for a union. Whatever financial resources and expertise that did reach the Border Patrol had to run the gauntlet of INS bureaucrats keenly intent on protecting their best interests. Although the two organizations were joined at the hip, the INS constantly treated the Border Patrol as a poor stepchild.

Managers at the McAllen Station appeared fearful of all management tools, practices, and programs defined as new and innovative, a mentality engendered by leadership with little formal education or experience outside the military. Geopolitics passed by the Border Patrol even as the employees union quixotically attacked micro-level issues and management clung tightly to the unproven policy of deterrence. The structure and culture of the Border Patrol as evidenced at the McAllen Station had changed in remarkably limited ways since the initial 1924 congressional mandate for the Border Patrol.

The summer heat in Deep South Texas grew yet more intense. For fifteen straight days in August the temperature averaged one hundred degrees or higher, ranking McAllen as the hottest city in the United States. Hotter than Laredo, El Paso, Del Rio, Eagle Pass, and, at least for a few days out of that fifteen-day run, hotter than Death Valley.[8]

Even by local standards the weather was intolerable. The ground in McAllen cracked in long zigzags and fissures. The heat burned the hardy St. Augustine grass on many suburban lawns as the city was forced to instigate water restrictions. At Falcon Dam the supply of water dipped below 25 percent of capacity, a record even in the middle of a five-year drought. Wild buffalo grass withered to fragile straw fractured by the roaring wind, and the tougher-than-concrete prickly pear turned a deathly brown. To avoid starvation ranchers hauled hay to their lanky cattle that normally fed on the wild grasses and the prickly pear. Life during the daylight hours slowed to the sluggish pace of a turtle on Prozac as both humans and their domestic animals sought shelter from the unbearable heat.

In spite of the appalling heat that raged throughout the month of August, Agent Roberta Alanis did not complain during her daylight shifts. Roberta was born and raised in the Valley, and she knew how to negotiate the day with ice water, shade, air-conditioning, and foods that cooled the heart. It was not the heat that she despised, but the organizational baggage that had become her beast of burden. From the moment she entered the academy Agent Alanis faced three rebukes: first, she was a woman; second, she was a Mexican American; and third, she was college educated.

Selected to represent the Border Patrol to the public because of the exact characteristics that found so little resonance within the Border Patrol bureaucracy, Agent Alanis frequently traveled throughout the United States to recruit new agents. In one of my classes at the University of Texas–Pan American the student audience hurled hostile questions at her. She was accustomed to the grilling wherever she went—Kansas, New York, Detroit.

"My uncle was stopped last week at the checkpoint in Falfurrias. He's been a citizen for more than thirty years. Isn't profiling against the law?"

"You said the Border Patrol only has about 5 percent of its agents who are female. How come?"

"If the Border Patrol is doing such a great job, why are there so many illegal aliens in the United States?"

Chin out, back stiff, dark eyes regarding the audience before her, Agent Roberta Alanis, dressed in full uniform, including service weapon, held her ground before this verbal onslaught. A former high school English teacher, Agent Alanis was Texas stubborn, unwilling to give up on the sons and daughters of migrant farmworkers mired in long-term poverty. She knew the potential power of education and had only left the classroom when she decided to follow in her father's footsteps.

Roberta's father, a thin, slight man with a penetrating stare, set the family standard. Her father was one of the first Hispanic FBI agents in Deep South Texas, an unsung pioneer who broke the FBI's color line but also paid the price. Without any hesitation Roberta entered the Border Patrol with the intention of transferring to the FBI after she had gained experience in federal law enforcement. However she had found that the Border Patrol and the FBI were not alike. A seven-year veteran of the Border Patrol at thirty-four years of age, Agent Alanis was also a wife and the mother of two young children. She had hoped as the years passed by that it would get easier for her. It had not.

Agent Roberta Alanis was having serious second thoughts about her career in the Border Patrol. In spite of her experience and expertise, the chances of advancement at the McAllen Station appeared bleak. In August 2001 there were no female supes at the McAllen Station and not one field operation supervisor. In the long history of the Border Patrol in Deep South Texas there had never been a female sector chief.[9]

Agent Alanis shelved her personal doubts about the Border Patrol as she honestly handled the questions from college students. Her sincerity found a wide reception. "Did the Border Patrol profile?" In South Texas most illegal workers were from Mexico. "So," she asked her audience of thirty-five university students, "do you waste your time questioning all the Anglos you see? What would you do under these circumstances?"

It was true that in the Border Patrol only about 5 percent of the agents were women. "But the Border Patrol wants more female agents, and that's why I'm talking to you today," she said, again looking them squarely in the eye. "It's also true that there are many illegals in this country. But I don't make the policies. That's for the politicians in Washington. I just follow orders and do my job the best I can."

After her presentation, Roberta was surrounded by five students majoring in criminal justice. Two of the five were women. All five wanted more information along with application forms for the Border Patrol. They were attracted by the starting pay, but also by the image that Agent Roberta Alanis presented of a competent, experienced federal law officer.

Racism, class snobbery, and antifeminist attitudes were impossible to ignore, but what really bothered Roberta and many other married agents with families were the work shifts. Each of the four units into which agents were divided worked four separate shifts in monthly rotation throughout the year. At the McAllen Station these shifts included the same three shifts scheduled at other stations plus an additional shift that was unique. The "day" shift ran from 6 A.M. to 4 P.M.; the "evening" shift, from 2 P.M. to midnight; and the "midnight" shift, from midnight to 10 A.M. Every shift was eight hours long, plus an extra two hours of overtime pay. Agents regularly worked the overtime and, if it were available, additional overtime because they desired the extra income. At least on paper, that translated to a fifty-hour minimum workweek plus any additional overtime. Many times, however, just as the shift was ending agents apprehended undocumented workers who they then processed through the system. An eleven- or twelve-hour workday was not uncommon.[10]

After two supes marketed the advantages of a fourth shift to management, the assistant chief installed the extra shift with negligible input from patrol agents. From the beginning some agents disliked the shift simply because it symbolized another imposition on them from above. The intent of the controversial shift was to place more agents in the field at times when they were needed. In theory agents during the new shift covered the early evening and late-night hours when traffic was peaking along the Rio Grande. Station intel had determined that both illegal aliens and drug traffickers recognized the vulnerability of the Border Patrol between the two shifts and were taking advantage of it. The extra shift, from 5 P.M. to 3 A.M., also made it more difficult, management believed, for aliens or smugglers to cross the river between the day shift, which ended at 4 P.M. and the evening shift, which might not—after muster and coffee—reach the banks of the river until late in the afternoon or early evening.

The timing of these four shifts at the McAllen Station, while intended to wreak havoc on drug smugglers and new immigrants, simultaneously had unintended consequences for patrol agents and their families. Married agents with children desired the day shift because, though they did not get to see their children off to school, they were at home for after-school activities, dinner at the dining room table, homework, television time, and getting the kids ready for bed. Agents on the day shift also could spend time with their spouses or significant others, since many partners worked during the day while the kids were at school.

But "days" only came one month out of every four—three months every year. The other three shifts, 75 percent of the year, carried serious disadvantages for those with partners and/or families. The evening shift, from 2 P.M. to midnight, permitted agents to awake with their children to see them off to school. However, the early morning was really the only time of day, five days out of seven, that agents were likely to see their children when their eyes were open. When agents returned home after midnight, the children, along with working spouses, were long since in bed. Because an agent might return at 1 or 2 A.M., it was difficult to rise after five or fewer hours of sleep to see the kids off to school and the wife or husband to work. After a normal seven hours of rest, most agents rose to an empty house. Friends who were not in the Border Patrol were also unlikely to be available.

Agents who worked mids, from midnight until 10 A.M., did not see their families until the afternoon. This shift advantageously permitted "normal" evenings. Parents could coach a son's or daughter's soccer team, take the family to dinner or a movie, and spend some time with a spouse.

Patrol agents had little good to say about the extra shift because it made evenings with families impossible. The extra shift also resulted in agents' spending little time with their children because, after returning home at 4 A.M., few awoke two or three hours later when the kids did.

Agents could not spend time in a high-speed pursuit of a van loaded with $1 million worth of drugs, then immediately return home after the shift ended, drink a glass of warm milk, and go to bed. Blood chemistry would not allow it. The shift structure, including the extra fourth shift, in some ways made the Tree an even more significant alternative in the life of patrol agents.

Rocking and Swaying

Most police departments and other law enforcement agencies realized years ago that their officers performed best when allowed to accustom themselves to the demands of working odd hours of the day or night.[11] In 2001 few police departments required their employees to change shifts every month. The rotation of shifts varied, but most were six months to a year in length to allow officers to acclimate themselves to the physical and psychological demands of the odd hours. The shift structure at the McAllen Station, in contrast to that at many other law enforcement agencies throughout the nation, served to isolate agents not only from their own families and friends but also from community social networks.

Even more problematical for agents were double-backs. At the end of each month agents rotated back to the previous shift and thus worked two ten-hour shifts—technically on two sequential days—in just one twenty-four-hour span of time. If lucky they might catch two to three hours of sleep between ending their old shift and beginning their new shift cycle. Management refused to discuss agents' abilities to perform efficiently during double-backs. Time and again I observed patrol agents in various stages of sleep deprivation during a double-back or the days following. No amount of coffee or other forms of caffeine adequately compensated for the fatigue created by monthly double-backs.

Agents worked five days on followed by two days off. Their days off, however, did not necessarily coincide with the weekends when their families, relatives, and close friends were more likely to be available. Days and nights off during weekends were assigned to those in management and agents with seniority. Unfortunately these days off might further complicate the sleeping schedules of agents. Should one keep on the same schedule as the monthly shift demanded or adjust to the "normal" routines of family and friends? Either was a bad choice. Agents choosing the latter might face the shock of serious fatigue when they returned to monthly work hours; the former choice afforded agents little time with family and close friends.

Overtime shift work at the McAllen Station translated into unsafe and unhealthy conditions of work. Single agents minded the hours less, but they were also unwilling victims of stress and fatigue caused by rotating monthly shifts. For example, just when agents might get used to staying up all night during mids, they were forced to change shifts at the end of the month. So it went every year, with agents frequently not acclimated to the demands of their work hours until perhaps the last few days before the next shift change. Agents could not avoid two constants: sleep deprivation and fatigue.

Biological pitfalls aside, the social aspects of shift work were just as detrimental to any agent—single, divorced, or married—who desired to lead a healthy and rewarding life. Spouses and partners were forced by the nature of agents' work hours to arrange their personal routines to complement their spouses' priorities. Female agents seldom had children because the shift schedules and rotations left little time for parenting. In households in which male agents were fathers, wives almost always bore the majority of child-rearing responsibilities. One parent had to get the kids off to school, arrange for transportation and activities after school, and be at home for the children in the evenings. In short, one parent had to be the caregiver upon whom the children could depend. Working spouses were forced to accommodate the demands of agents' ever-changing work routines and simultaneously provide the emotional stability and support upon which children and agents thrived. Family support systems including relatives, close friends, and neighbors only went so far.[12] Working women married to agents not only worked double shifts—one shift at work and another at home, as did wives of men in many other occupations—but were required to do much more while their husbands were absent from the household.

Because of the system of work schedules and rotating shifts wives of agents spent little time with their husbands.[13] Many wives and partners taught in public schools or worked nine-to-five, white-collar jobs only to return home to shoulder the same responsibilities as a single parent. Agents' wives shopped, cooked, cleaned, chauffeured, paid the bills, and completed other required chores, including monitoring their children's progress in school. Although they often consulted their husbands by cell phone as their husbands worked line watch, wives made vital household and family decisions to the best of their abilities. Husbands steered their vehicles along the dusty drag road as they discussed with their wives the grocery list, their daughter's chance of scoring in the next soccer match, the color tile that looked best in their new house under construction, and why their wife's boss was being unreasonable. Decisions were made, postponed, and reconsidered in these scattered conversations. Wives defended and explained their decisions, negotiated household plans, and comforted their spouses when they complained of fatigue, illness, or having to work in bad weather. Wives were expected to handle any household crisis. The lives of Border Patrol agents in many ways resembled those of long-distance truck drivers, offshore oil workers, commercial fishermen, and workers in other occupations requiring husbands to be away from the household for significant periods of time.[14]

The emotional cost to women who regularly compensated for the absence of their husbands could, therefore, be considerable, especially if they were uncomfortable or unwilling to assume permanently the roles, tasks, and expectations that automatically resulted from marrying a patrol agent. Women who worked this kind of double shift were squeezed, whether willing or not, into extremely circumscribed roles. Pressure to conform to these consistent restraints within the marriage relationship could strain even the strongest of marriages. While some wives adapted, others at times were overwhelmed by the regular absence of their partners.[15]

Single and divorced agents faced a different set of conflicting social arrangements brought on by their work schedules and rotating shifts. Starting a new relationship or maintaining an old one was hazardous when they had to tell partners that three months out of the year during the fourth shift they would not see them until 4 A.M., that three months out of the year when they worked the 2 P.M. to midnight shift they would not see them until I A.M., and that three months out of the year during mids they had to leave them at midnight not to return until the late morning hours. Only during the day shift, from 6 A.M. to 4 P.M.—three months out of the year—did normalcy prevail.

It was easy to understand, given their shift schedules, why single agents at the McAllen Station found it difficult to meet partners interested in long-term relationships. In fact few agents survived the initial innocent question, "What do you do?" Although agents earned annual salaries two to three times higher than the median family income in McAllen, many Mexican American females would never seriously date an agent, either Anglo or Mexican American, because of the Border Patrol's reputation for brutality against Hispanics. Agents constantly complained about the dating scene in McAllen, with many gripes tied to the nature of their work patrolling the line.

Social activities with friends besides other agents were also impractical. Because all four units were scrambled every year, agents in the same unit knew that friendships with other agents were difficult to sustain. An agent could spend a year being the best bro of another agent in the unit only to see that person rarely the following year because he or she was assigned to a different unit.

Given these kinds of restrictions created by their job, agents at the McAllen Station were left to be with their families when schedules permitted and to hang out with other agents on an irregular basis. Some spouses of agents were able to initiate and form supportive networks. Agents held parties to celebrate shift changes or other events during the year, but attendance was uneven. In general agents who were born and raised in the Valley fared far better than those who were not, because they could count on their families and networks of old friends. Outsiders to Deep South Texas, both Anglos and Mexican Americans, found it challenging to lead a normal life.

Single female agents like Maria Contreras faced greater barriers than male agents. Not only were the demands of shift work a sure way to obliterate a budding relationship, but some Hispanic males, along with Anglo males, felt threatened by a woman who did not seem likely to assume the traditional role of wife and mother as fostered within Valley Mexican American culture. Agents such as Contreras more often dated other agents who could be sympathetic to the demands of the job. Workplace relationships, as suggested, also generated their own set of problems.

Cops frequently hung with other cops for a variety of reasons, but agents at the McAllen Station were even more prone to this behavior because of the limitations imposed by the shift times, the rotating shifts, the status of their jobs in the community, and the other constraints discussed. At the very least agents had to be sure that new friends and acquaintances were not part of the local drug culture or did not employ illegal aliens. One agent said, "I found out my neighbor has an illegal working for him as a maid. What am I supposed to do? How can I go over to his house? I'm telling you, you got to be very careful who you make friends with in this town."

Dating was not an issue for Agent Roberta Alanis, but like other female agents she continually confronted male managers oblivious to family-related issues and needs. Roberta had two young children at home but like agent fathers saw them only a small part of each day. She did her best to be a wife to her husband and a mother to her kids, expecting no special treatment at work. "I try to do my job by the book," she told me repeatedly, because she knew from experience that she was scrutinized more than male agents.

On this day Agent Roberta Alanis headed for Los Ebanos, a tiny settlement upriver from the McAllen Station, close to the western boundary of the sector. A sensor buried beneath the riverbank had recorded seven hits, so Agent Ala-

Rocking and Swaying

nis was not surprised to find two men when she arrived, one of them standing almost directly on top of the sensor. It was just past five in the afternoon; the temperature was holding at 103 degrees.

The privately owned Los Ebanos Ferry had already closed, and no one was around except two customs agents inside the Butler building's modest facilities. After pointing out to Agent Alanis the illegal aliens spied with an ancient pair of binoculars, they scurried back to their dinner. One of the customs agents was starved for conversation, but Agent Alanis waved him off until her work was completed.

As the steel barge ferry tugged slowly at its lines near the sand ramp on the north side of the Rio Grande, the two men had dog-paddled their way to a point about twenty-five yards south of the landing. Drying themselves the best they could, they had never known they were standing atop a sensor that had, by way of the dispatcher, brought Agent Roberta Alanis directly to them.

Too far away to grab either of the men and afraid to spook them if she edged any closer, the agent stood on the riverbank trying to persuade them to make the right decision.

Agent Alanis soon recognized the younger of the two men as the other slipped his old tennis shoes from his feet to wade back into the waters of the Rio Grande. Without looking over his shoulder he began swimming toward the Mexican bank. Roberta shouted, *"Es muy peligroso!"* it's very dangerous. She kept shouting in Spanish to him, but he ignored her as he concentrated on his painfully slow strokes. He was not a strong or experienced swimmer, but soon he was twenty feet from the southern bank.

"I know you," she told the other man in Spanish. "You're Mr. Peña. I stopped you a couple of days ago."

"I needed the job," said Israel Peña, answering the question before it was asked. Israel was in his early thirties, stocky with a prominent paunch, short dark hair, and bloodshot eyes. His quiet voice was difficult to hear above the squabble of birds chattering in the branches of the gnarled ebony that gave the community and the ferry its name.

"Tell your friend to come back. The river is very dangerous here."

"I can try," Israel said, "but he won't listen." He called to his friend, but the man continued to his journey.

"You already know my speech about the river, Mr. Peña." Agent Alanis said, one eye on the swimmer. If he started to go under, she knew she had to make a quick decision. Did she jump in after him? Did she run to her truck for the rope and float? "It's not worth risking your life to swim the river. There are currents and hydrilla. It isn't worth losing your life to swim back."

Israel Peña stood on the muddy bank while the hot sun dried the river water from his back. Was it best to join his friend on the other side of the river, perhaps waiting until the coast was clear to cross once more, or go again with the agent? He knew that she could not reach him if he chose to jump back into the murky water, and even if she could get to his side he outweighed her by at least a hundred pounds.

At this time of day no one was going to help Agent Alanis detain an undocumented worker. Los Ebanos was a bend in the Rio Grande that was ideally suited for the small ferry but, after the ferry stopped running at 4:30 every day of the week, few ventured to the remote Mexican village of Ordáz. Unless it became a life-threatening situation, capturing aliens was not on the job description of the two customs agents eating their early dinner in the prefabricated building.

The southern and northern banks of the river bent toward each other at Los Ebanos as if in an international *abrazo*. An old man with hands of leather, along with three young helpers, earned a bare subsistence wage by pulling and tugging a thick rope that spanned the water from one country to the other. Slowly and in complete silence, the ferry almost imperceptibly crept across the brief expanse as it was pulled by human will and labor. The trip lasted less than ten minutes. Then the rusting steel barge rested on the Mexican side while a handful of passengers and a perhaps a car disembarked and, at the same time, a few other disparate passengers boarded the ferry for the return trip. There was no other crossing for twenty miles.

During the day the hand-drawn ferry, the last in the state of Texas, was part of a peaceful, bucolic picture, the machine age stood on its head. But the same characteristics that made this bend in the Rio Grande an ideal setting for the hand-drawn ferry also offered a haven for undocumented workers and drug smugglers "deterred" by the Border Patrol at the two bridges downstream at McAllen. Those who believed it was too risky to cross where the Border Patrol agents guarded the river simply traveled upriver to more isolated lands where the Border Patrol ventured irregularly. Only after dark did Los Ebanos really come alive. Desperate men, women, and children and poorly paid mules with heavy burlap sacks filled with marijuana and cocaine blazed trails through the gnarled stands of ebony and brush.

Agent Roberta Alanis asked illegal immigrant Israel Peña if his wife and kids would miss their husband and father when he drowned in the river. The smart thing, she repeated, was to come with her. She would put him in her air-conditioned truck, take him back to the station where he could get a drink of cold water on this hot day, then see that he was safely driven to the Reynosa Bridge. Sure it was a hassle, but it was the best thing to do.

The more she talked to Israel, the more hesitant he became about recrossing the Río Bravo. Finally he gestured with both hands that he had heard enough. He buttoned his soaked shirt as he approached her. Agent Alanis, in turn, motioned him to follow her toward her truck. When they reached the Expedition, she asked him if he was carrying any weapons, searched him, then unlocked the door to the cage. Israel Peña climbed into the back of the truck with a degree of resignation seen only among those who have few real choices in their lives.

"You made the right decision, Mr. Peña," she reassured him as she slammed the door.

Transport picked up Israel Peña and soon carried him back to the McAllen Station before VRing him to the Reynosa Bridge. As transport was driving away Agent Alanis looked down at her left rear tire.

"Oh, shit," she said as she saw it was flat. She knew that the tire might have been at least partially deflated when she had left the station parking lot after muster, but she had been in a hurry to get to the river. She had run through her vehicle inspection without her usual care. Maybe it would not have mattered one way or the other. Shit happens. When she opened the tailgate and fished in the back of the truck for the jack and the lug wrench, I could tell that she would have given a week's paycheck not to have to deal with the flat tire. She hated to look incompetent in front of others, so she pushed herself to the extreme to avoid any kind of predicament where her effectiveness as an agent might be questioned.

"You ever change one of these?" I asked her.

"No," she admitted defensively.

One of the customs agents, a young, overweight man with his shirttail hanging out of his pants, came lumbering out of the building. Out of sheer boredom he had probably been watching us all along. When Agent Alanis shot him a withering look, he turned in his tracks and retreated to the portable building.

"These units are different," she commented, standing squarely under the last brutal heat of the day. She was reading the driver's manual, recovered from the glove compartment. "Somehow you crank down the tire, which is located under the truck, and swing it out." But she did not know how to do it, and it was killing her to have to rely on someone else, me, even if just to change a lousy flat tire.

The two of us staggered through the directions in the manual as I lowered the tire on its wobbly steel cable. I had to get down on my knees in the gravel to wrestle the spare and swing it free from the chassis.

"You don't have to do this, Professor," Agent Alanis told me. I sure as hell did not want to have to play Mr. Macho in front of a patrol agent who was a hundred times more competent than I. But what else were we going to do? For a brief moment she stared at me coldly.

I grunted with effort as I tried to remove the five lug nuts that had been torqued so tightly that, even with the full weight of my body behind the handle, the wrench barely moved. Then I felt the handle of the wrench begin to bend between the force of my leverage and the immovable nuts. The young customs agent suddenly appeared again, carrying a big wrench in his right hand. He also brought with him another customs agent who insisted on helping us. I stood back and, with some effort, they finally removed all the lug nuts with their wrench. After they fired up the portable generator that powered an air pump and filled the spare to the proper pressure, I balanced the tire against my knees, hung it, and retightened the nuts. Agent Alanis watched in silence, her arms folded across her chest.

"Thanks, Professor," she said sullenly as we climbed back into the truck. Then she asked me if I had heard about the lion. When I nodded—other agents had told me about it—she offered to show me where it had been kept.

We headed upriver along a path that led to a small, junky clearing and a rusting steel cage. The lion's dingy, pitiful prison had been a small trailer reinforced with rebar. In the summer heat the cage must have become an oven.

"The lion didn't even have room to pace," I observed, examining the trailer on its dead tires.

"It used to make terrible noises," Agent Alanis said. "The story I heard was that the lion was in a circus and somehow this man who lived in a nearby house bought it for a pet. You could hear it roar from miles away. The owner lived over by the ferry. I'll show you his house."

"What happened to the lion?"

"I don't know for sure. Some agents told me that someone took pity on it and poisoned it."

Some of the senior agents used to play a joke on the newest agents at the station. They would bring them to the Los Ebanos Ferry in the dead of night and tell them to search for aliens over by the lion's cage. The new agents then got the surprise of their lives.

As we walked slowly back to Agent Alanis's truck I decided that it was the right time to ask her about Wayne Thornton. She had been his partner the night that, according to the jury's verdict, he went ballistic and beat a one-armed, old man with his giant black flashlight.

"I didn't see a thing," she told me as we were driving back across Old Military Highway to trade out vehicles while a mechanic checked the other tires. "I had to stay on the radio back at the truck because the batteries on our mobile radio had failed. I stayed behind to maintain radio contact. By the time I got to the scene, the man was on the ground and bleeding around his head area."

A pair of defective batteries had saved her the agony of testifying against a fellow agent. Of course if she had actually witnessed the attack, she would have testified against her partner and never blinked an eye during cross-examination. It mattered little to other agents at the McAllen Station that Agent Alanis held herself to the highest standards. Surprisingly few seemed to trust or respect her, even though they might rely on her for advice on how to write a report or respond by memo to an outraged supe. The former English teacher turned their toadish narratives into princely paragraphs that safely traversed the paper trail. But this particular skill did not earn her any favors or minor acclaim. She would never be a supe.

I asked male agents a crucial question: "Could you count on Agent Alanis, or any female agent at the McAllen Station, in a high-risk situation?" Most male agents answered in the negative. "Look at her," said one older male agent nodding in Agent Alanis's direction after a muster. "Do you think she can carry her weight when it comes to a fight? What does she go? Maybe 110 pounds?"

Both Anglo and Mexican American agents were more than willing to sidestep the race card in favor of gender issues when it came to Agent Alanis. "Don't get me wrong," one Anglo agent stated as we eased along the drag road in the middle of the night. "I'm all for equality and equal rights for men and women. But who do you want to have as a partner if you get in a tight situation? Noe Escondido or Roberta Alanis?"

It was an unfair comparison. Few agents, male or female, stacked up against Noe Escondido. But nevertheless male agents continually discussed the question, one that fouled the professional relationship between Agent Alanis and her male counterparts as surely as it did for Maria Contreras and the handful of other female agents at the McAllen Station. Female agents were not accepted as equals.

Agent Roberta Alanis was trapped. Her special talents, including her bachelor of arts in English, were trivialized. At the same time the shift schedule and monthly rotation at the McAllen Station placed marriages and families in jeopardy. Everyone called each other "bro," but everyone was not each other's bro. "I don't see myself here in five years," said Agent Alanis on a night in late August. "I'm exploring my options. I have some other opportunities that may be coming my way. I've got a college education, seven years' experience as a federal law enforcement officer, and I have a good record here. When the time comes, I'll weigh my options."

On the morning of September 11, 2001, barely two weeks after the flat tire at Los Ebanos Ferry, the work of international terrorists reduced the World Trade Center towers to a vast, hopeless pile of toxic dust, bent steel, and human body fragments. In a matter of hours the federal government began scrutinizing the American border with Canada and Mexico even as a stunned public continued to be mesmerized by the slow-motion media images of the two jets crashing into the Twin Towers and the information coming in about the attack on the Pentagon and the plane crash in rural Pennsylvania. Because it was the enforcement branch of the INS, the U.S. Border Patrol was suddenly yanked from virtual obscurity into a public spotlight as a thousand questions were asked about the security and safety of our nation's borders.

Three

The Substance
of Chaos

Fighting Back

Armed to the teeth and ready for war, agents of the U.S. Border Patrol blockaded the parking lots surrounding the McAllen Station with Expeditions and old Tahoes. After they constructed a wall of steel, chrome, and safety glass, access to their headquarters could only be gained after close scrutiny by agents on duty around the clock. Agents assumed strategic defensive posts and, like every other American, grimly awaited whatever came next.

Disbelief mixed with a heightened sense of professional duty and service. At musters agents were both anxious and excited. While there was talk of revenge and retaliation, agents at the McAllen Station were as stunned by the terrorist attacks in New York, Washington, and Pennsylvania as were other Americans.

Extra overtime beyond the normal fifty hours a week became the standard. No one complained about the work load while potential targets of terrorists were identified and defenses along the border fortified. Most agents were reassigned from line watch to reinforcing the ports of entry and the two bridges in the McAllen Sector that spanned the Rio Grande. Also closely guarded against possible terrorist attack were the U.S. Customs facilities at the Los Ebanos Ferry across from Ciudad Ordáz.

In the first weeks after September 11 long lines of traffic formed at both of

The Substance of Chaos

the major bridges as all vehicles were checked and rechecked for arms, bombs, and terrorists. Delays for drivers and passengers lasted up to several hours as vehicular traffic slowed to a standstill on both sides of the border. In spite of the delays, few drivers complained about the increased inspections.

At Miller International Airport, where the public had been free to park as close as twenty feet from the main terminal, security was tightened as never before. By September 21 a fleet of McAllen tow trucks transported all remaining vehicles to an alternate parking lot south of the terminal. Only necessary vehicles such as those of the city police and the Border Patrol were allowed to park in the no man's land that now separated the terminal from the free public parking. Cement forms intended to stifle the impact of a car bomb buffered the zone.

The sensors along the river were silent. Few illegal immigrants attempted to cross the Río Bravo immediately after September 11. They feared that it might prove impossible to return to Mexico. Illegal workers were also afraid they might be mistaken for terrorists or persecuted in a country that suddenly distrusted anyone who was not a native citizen. *En el otro lado* undocumented workers waited, like the agents of the McAllen Sector, to see what happened next.

Even the *narcotraficantes* shut down their operations along the Rio Grande in Deep South Texas. No scouts. No vans. No encrypted messages on scanners in the middle of the night. No lightning-quick landings by high-powered boats. Like everyone else, the *narcotraficantes* waited.

Rumors flew at the McAllen Station. The first wave of half-truths insisted that the U.S. Army was being assigned to the border. There were also rumors about call-ups of units of the National Guard and about the possibility of agents' being transferred to the Canadian border where several of the terrorists had allegedly entered the United States. The public, during the imposing media coverage that followed the tragedy, learned that fewer than a thousand agents of the U.S. Border Patrol guarded the enormous northern border. Along the border with Canada solitary agents patrolled vast expanses of forests, lakes, and grassland. After the initial call for federally employed and regulated security guards to replace the private sector rent-a-cops at airports came talk of ramping up the Air Marshals. Like foul balls at the playoff games of the Edinburg Road Runners, a Valley semi-pro team playing its first season of baseball, rumors flew hither and yon.

On the morning of September 15, 2002, the second shoe dropped. The children of McAllen awoke to discover that their Saturday morning cartoon fare had been preempted by live local media coverage from Port Isabel. A span of the Laguna Madre Causeway linking the mainland to South Padre Island had been destroyed, a stretch of barren space extending more than a hundred yards between two of the highest spans of the four-lane bridge. Many residents of McAllen and the Valley considered it the second act of terrorism everyone had been awaiting.

Visibly shaken, local reporters first at the scene in Port Isabel were unable to piece together the puzzle as they aired fragmented, confusing stories. First-person accounts by fishermen on a private dock adjacent to the causeway provided details, but no one could pinpoint the cause of the disaster. One fisherman stated that around 2 A.M. Saturday, drivers had futilely slammed on their brakes before catapulting from the bridge pavement and diving into the dark waters of the Laguna Madre. He saw clearly, he said, the vehicles as they sank into the bay, their rear brake lights finally fading beneath the waters. Reported among the missing was the Port Isabel fire chief, who had responded to a call that something was wrong on the bridge.[1]

Before the first authoritative reports began to filter in, most residents of McAllen and the surrounding communities would have sworn that the two-mile bridge spanning the Laguna Madre had been bombed by international terrorists. Finally news reports announced that an intercoastal barge had accidentally rammed the underpinnings of the bridge. Eight people, including the fire chief, were killed and a number of others were seriously injured. Bodies were soon found, but it took weeks for large cranes perched on barges to locate and remove the vehicles from the wreckage of the bridge.

Time slowed to a standstill after the bridge collapse at Port Isabel. As the dust finally began to settle, agents were confronted with the same issues, policies, and routines dominating their work lives prior to the terrorist attacks. The hours, days, and weeks spent protecting border assets or sitting in the front of their truck cabs idling their engines in the rigid X formations provided plenty of time for agents to reflect upon the limitations of Operation Rio Grande and the frontal deployment of resources. Many agents remembered "the good times" when they had been allowed to perform their jobs as trained. Guard duty was tedious and the same old X's even more tedious. Agents were chomping at the bit to be tracking down the bad guys, not wasting time in their truck cabs as their shift ticked by one minute at a time.

Even before the events of September 11 a handful of the more embittered agents, symptomatic of the general malaise experienced by many others, had developed their own resolution to the dilemma posed by X's. If agents really wanted to rid themselves of the dreaded X's, they reasoned, the way to do it was to stop catching illegal aliens. All illegal aliens. If agents stopped catching all illegals, then management might declare Operation Rio Grande a success. A return to this normalcy might then trigger a sane and rational policy from management regarding line watch. Guided by this misplaced hope, a few agents argued that it was counterproductive to apprehend aliens until management proclaimed Operation Rio Grande a glorious victory.

The majority of agents at the McAllen Station still believed in the logic and dignity of their jobs prior to September 11, and they ignored both the instigations of management and alienated agents sickened by the status quo. This numerical majority had never bought into the logic of X's in Operation Rio Grande and now avoided its antilogic.

Although the response to X's after September 11 was diverse, there was one commonality: many agents at the McAllen Station became increasingly demoralized.

The problem of illegal aliens—who were theoretically supposed to exist only in minute numbers because of the effectiveness of Operation Rio Grande—was pervasive in McAllen and neighboring Valley communities. Local police departments picked up immigrant workers as they walked along city streets, hid in the brush near retail businesses and suburban homes, congregated in the parking lot at Wal-Mart and Target, waited for rides to Houston at the HEB grocery stores, and bought tickets at the McAllen bus station. Then the police, the sheriff's department, or the DPS troopers were forced to call the Border Patrol to pick up the illegal immigrants who did not exist. Illegal aliens were also arrested in large numbers at the checkpoints at Falfurrias and Sarita as well as apprehended by the hundreds and thousands in the brushlands that surrounded these two checkpoints. In the late spring and summer months of 2001 management took reluctant action. In the days before September 11 the decision-makers at the McAllen Station quietly instituted the "soft" X.

The "hard" X, as defined in hindsight in this lexicon of rhetorical strategies, was an agent who was required to stay the course of the shift in his or her

unit. Agents who had been assigned the two bridges to Reynosa and other terrorist targets after September 11, for example, were now unofficially described
by management as working hard X's.

While never admitting that the hard X had been less than successful, management in the weeks preceding the terrorist attacks talked freely about the
new "soft" X's. Although this dialogue was nowhere to be found in agency
documents, policies, job descriptions, or other agency papers, soft X's were a
central topic of conversation as agents began to understand the implications of
the newest strategy about which they had, yet again, never been consulted.

Under the precepts of soft X's agents were assigned and responsible for
certain prescribed areas along the Rio Grande just as in the hard X, but they
now were encouraged to leave their vehicles to patrol, track, and apprehend
illegal aliens. After the immediate terrorist threat failed to materialize, the two
bridges, ports of entry, and several other designated facilities were still designated hard X's. Managers explained that they were not rejecting deterrence,
only tweaking and refining it so that agents could rely more on their professional judgment. The soft X, management assumed, would resolve the obvious
problems with the hard X and bring with it a restoration of morale.

At muster, behind closed office doors, and over coffee the benefits and
drawbacks of hard and soft X's were argued by agents and supes. Agents
believed that soft X's were imperfect but a significant improvement over hard
X's. Soft X's allowed agents, who most often were partnered with another
agent for the duration of the shift just as before Operation Rio Grande, to
respond to sensors in their assigned areas, cut sign, and function in a more
consistent and traditional role for which they had been trained at the academy.
Soft X's, in sum, made better sense to agents, allowing them to be more proactive. To a limited degree agents felt empowered by this new policy.

Because of their dissatisfaction with the hard X, many agents, including
the Rambos, had been operating according to soft X strategies. To some
degree, management was sanctioning something already in place. When
agents were assigned the remaining hard X's at muster, those who were lucky
enough to draw soft X's sometimes laughed out loud or mouthed sarcasm at
their less fortunate brethren. This was meant, and usually taken, in good fun
but signified the agents' continuing frustration about the futility of Operation
Rio Grande and hard X's. No one wanted the duty except those who intended

to catch up on their reading or their sleep. Agents sighed unconsciously out of personal relief when they were informed that their ten-hour shift would be on soft X's and not be spent staring at the inside of a windshield.

Not everyone, of course, was happy with soft X's; it was virtually impossible to placate every agent. The older agents were most likely to be the least satisfied, because they compared the soft X not with the hard X but with line watch before the advent of Operation Rio Grande. In contrast the newest recruits who recently graduated from the academy seemed much more content with the unofficial policy because their only frame of reference was the hard X.

Agent Gester and a number of the younger agents who were gung ho Rambos pushed the definition of the soft X to the limit. Time and again Gester retrofitted his plan to nab Fat Man at Anzalduas Park only to come up empty handed. Fat Man grew richer and richer off his $300 price tag per alien as he motored hundreds of aliens across the slender stretch of Rio Grande bordering the popular park. In turn Gester continued to research the law on international boundaries in hopes of finding ways to legally slam the door on Fat Man and his friends. More than once he attempted to arrest Fat Man and his crew.

Because Fat Man committed his crime in thirty seconds or less, arresting him in the act was, as always, a matter of exact timing. With two scouts on jet skis providing him intel, and an unknown number of scouts on the Mexican side of the river watching for signs of the Border Patrol, Fat Man loaded up his human cargo between beers, dashed to the north side of the river in his sketchy power boat, and was back again on his side of the river before he had to burp.

Agent Gester finally made his big move in July 2001. Depending on who told the story, the exact sequence of events and facts of the chase and attempted arrest of Fat Man and his crew varied widely. Gester's version of the events held that, after hiding the BayMaster around the bend of the river, he zoomed in at exactly the right second to catch Fat Man after he off-loaded a group of undocumented workers at the foot of the docks at Anzalduas Park.

The anonymous complaint lodged with the Mexican Consulate described a far different story. Fat Man, according to this version, had reached the southern bank when Agent Gester took control of the smuggler's boat after employing excessive force. A struggle ensued and when it ended—and here details diverged yet again—the smuggler's boat was beached upon the southern bank with its hull and engine badly damaged. According to the version lobbied by the Mexican Consulate, in the process of this attempted arrest Gester and his fellow agents endangered the lives of Mexican picnickers who witnessed this international incident.

Whatever the disputed facts, the Mexican Consulate vigorously complained to the McAllen Station about this injustice to Mexican citizens. In turn management summarily required an exacting report from Gester and the other participants.[2] To the surprise of many agents at the McAllen Station, management placed Gester and the other agents on the defensive with off-the-record accusations and assumptions based upon the complaint. Why had the agents broken station policy and international law by endangering the lives of Mexican citizens? Why had they taken such great risks with the limited resources of the Border Patrol? It seemed as if management was more willing to believe a complaint from a Mexican official than its own agents. The agents had expected to be commended for their initiative and expertise in taking down a known criminal and his major smuggling operation. Instead, management was poised to punish them.

Other agents took notice of the "incident" and immediately defended their own. "They should give Gester and the others commendations," said one agent. "Instead the word is they're going to give them reprimands. Maybe worse. It'll be in their permanent record."

Management sent a clear message to the Rambos and their sympathizers that the major purpose of the boat patrol was to deter. Nothing more or less. From management's perspective Gester and the bros who helped him had gone far beyond the boundaries prescribed by deterrence. The boat patrol was on the Rio Grande to present a visible presence that would discourage immigrants and smugglers from crossing. Regardless of how successful the criminal operation, the boat patrol, they let it be known, was never intended to pursue smugglers.

When the first boat patrol was organized in 2001 then nurtured to the present tiny fleet of four boats, agents volunteered for the duty because it promised to be a novel, productive way to apprehend illegal aliens and drug smugglers. Agents including Rochester and Reynaldo Guerra, and even those without any previous boating skills, had signed up to patrol the line in potentially new and effective ways. Management's policies about the boat patrol were ambiguous. In this antiquated decision-making structure agents were not told what to do; they were told what they could not do after they had done it. Gester was a

The Substance of Chaos

Rambo who truly believed he could put Fat Man in prison for a long time. Without clear guidelines, he felt free to follow the dictates of his job as did the other agents who aided him.

As word was leaked that Gester and his crew faced serious consequences, Agent Rochester quit the boat patrol in anger. So did the majority of agents who had originally volunteered for the duty. Rochester remained diplomatic about his reasons for quitting. "Look, let's just say I disagree with the new policies." He was still obviously frustrated by management's attempt to turn Gester and the others into scapegoats but was unwilling to say more.

Management was not contrite. Even under soft X's deterrence remained the dominant policy. Although managers might be unsure of exactly what they wanted the boat patrol to do during its shift on the water, they were very sure of what they did not want it to do. Management hated and feared complaints, especially complaints that might blossom into legal suits or publicity disasters. Complaints of any kind from the Mexican Consulate were particularly odious. Any agent who generated complaints from the Mexican Consulate was naturally in hot water.

At about this same time, perhaps to clarify its ambiguous policy of deterrence, management abandoned the horse patrol. After a year's trial there had been numerous problems, chief among them a number of serious accidents. One horse slipped and fell on wet ground, and his rider required months of therapy and recuperation before he could return to work.

Agents who were first attracted to the new duty initially prided themselves on their horsemanship and the opportunity to apprehend undocumented workers and perhaps even drug smugglers. However, management inexplicably accepted not only those with proven skills but those with virtually no experience. Training for those with limited skills was sporadic and of limited practical utility. Again a clear vision from leadership seemed lacking as agents from the McAllen Station began patrolling the line from atop their mounts. Also in short supply were foresight and an investment of resources in the reconstituted horse patrol. Animals were leased from a local businessman with ties to the Border Patrol, but the horses were largely untrained for tasks demanded of them. Tack was substandard. The once proud traditions of the horse patrol of the U.S. Border Patrol, dating back to the turn of the century, were jettisoned after only twelve months.

The boat patrol was in many ways a variation of the horse patrol. The four

BayMasters were not built to law enforcement standards or with prior consideration of their function and utility. The vessels were constructed in nearby Harlingen; only a few special features, including a reinforced hull, were added to the standard BayMaster model. The 150-horsepower Johnson motor made them identical to the boat recreational sports fishermen could purchase at the corner marina. Ditto the electronics. In an apparent attempt to save federal dollars, management limited the effectiveness of boats deployed on the river.

Perhaps the most outlandish feature of these patrol boats based at the McAllen Station was that they were audible on the Rio Grande at least five minutes before they arrived. They carried absolutely no possible element of surprise. The echoes of the Johnson engines, which were known among recreational fishermen as "temperamental," broadcast the position of the Border Patrol far more effectively than any drug scouts. Management might argue after the fact that the blast of the engines was part of an effective deterrence strategy, but these boats were so loud that they were largely ineffective. Other security and patrol options were available for purchase, including engines that operated faster and far quieter and could turn the boats into the equivalent of stealth bombers. The Border Patrol never purchased these engines, which cost only a few thousand dollars more than the Johnsons.

The boat patrol was also hampered by BayMasters' limited range. The boats could carry only ten more gallons of gasoline than a typical fisherman setting out for a day on the Laguna Madre. While on patrol it was not unusual for agents to run out of gas. Management policy required agents to trailer the boat, haul it to the station, then refill it at the station's pump. In the meantime, of course, the Rio Grande became wide open to undocumented workers and smugglers.

Regardless of Gester's botched arrest of Fat Man, the underfunded boat patrol was doomed from its inception. So, too, was the once proud horse patrol. Operations that lacked leadership, resources, and expertise had little chance of success.

After September 11 agents at the McAllen Station maintained high hopes that the newest version of deterrence—an amalgam of guard duty, hard X's, and soft X's—would be scrapped and new policy would emerge to address concerns with international terrorism. But instead of new leadership and policy, the Border Patrol at the McAllen Station hunkered down and continued to wait to be attacked by unknown assailants. It was "a war," as one supe told the agents during muster. If so, the enemy never attacked or even showed itself. Agents grew impatient and sympathized increasingly with the action Gester had taken against Fat Man. These same agents openly criticized management's talk of punishment.

After weeks and months, agents found it exceedingly difficult to sustain their high level of preparedness and enthusiasm guarding the ports of entry, Miller International Airport, or other potential targets. One agent succinctly placed the role of the Border Patrol and the no-show terrorists in perspective when he observed, "The last thing they [the terrorists] are going to blow up is the people who gave them their visas."

A case in point was the U.S. Customs shed that served as the port of entry across from the Los Ebanos Ferry. Although the ferry closed every afternoon, two customs agents along with four to six Border Patrol agents were assigned there after September 11. At times management ordered double the number of agents to protect and defend this possible terrorist target.

Agents from the McAllen Station had nothing to do at Los Ebanos. Traffic in illegal immigrants slowly began to return, but the real issue faced by agents became a grinding boredom—no distractions except a small village several blocks away and an occasional curious resident who wandered by to chat. At Los Ebanos there was not even a retail establishment selling coffee. Agents talked among themselves, but there was only so much to be said. Boredom was their constant, numbing companion.

The three times I was at Los Ebanos after the early weeks of September, agents were going stir crazy. Feeling as if they had been reduced to the role of rent-a-cops in the middle of nowhere, their mission was to stand guard over a ramshackle facility that all agreed would never be on any terrorist's list. A rusting prefab building in the middle of a desert? The agents did their job as the hours crept by, but sometimes they read magazines, or slept, or talked about what they were going to barbecue.

The *narcotraficantes* were the first to jump-start their old business operations along the banks of the Río Bravo and Rio Grande. The market demand never subsided because of the events in early September. Rain or shine, terrorism or no terrorism, American drug users demanded product; the *narcotraficantes* were more than pleased to supply it. Concluding long before the management at the McAllen Station that there would be no second shoe, or at the very least deciding they could no longer warehouse their time-sensitive product, drug smugglers restarted their smuggling operations with renewed vigor.

Nothing suited them more than the new defensive strategy imposed by the border patrol. Instead of patrolling miles of riverbanks, after September 11 the majority of agents congregated around potential terrorist targets while a minority who were not assigned to hard X's worked soft X's. Such a strategy, given an increasing shortage of agents, left vast stretches of the Rio Grande wide open to drug smugglers. By the time available agents could reach the crowing sensors, the marijuana and cocaine were long gone.

Undocumented workers waited somewhat longer than the *narcotraficantes* before they returned to the banks of the Rio Grande, but they came, although in smaller numbers compared to figures for previous years, for the same reasons they always had: they desired the jobs and the dollars generated by their labor. As the recession deepened in the United States, hardships worsened on the other side of the border; Mexico's economy had for some time closely mirrored its northern neighbor's. The maquiladoras in Reynosa and other nearby Mexican cities began laying off workers as the American economy faltered. With far fewer agents in place along the river, even though agents at the station were working extra overtime, chances of avoiding the Border Patrol rarely had been better.

Some of the rumors first heard after September 11 became reality. Volunteers were needed from the McAllen Station to protect the northern border with Canada from terrorists. Several McAllen agents eagerly accepted duty in places such as North Dakota and upstate New York. Babysitting a concrete bridge was far less meaningful to these agents than traveling to far-off places in a time of national emergency. After looking at the figures, agents determined that they could also earn more money in Fargo than working X's in South Texas. Both single and married agents signed up for the special duty, packed their bags with winter clothes, and left their bros to deal with the numbing boredom.

The National Guard eventually arrived to help the INS at the two ports of entry and to provide additional security at Miller International Airport. Security procedures at the airport check-in were formalized as uniformed reservists with M16s hanging from their shoulders patrolled the terminal and its four gates.

At the two bridges, as was the case up and down the southern border, the professional truckers, residents, and tourists had lost patience with the long delays caused by the increased security. The INS weighed calls for speeding up inspection against the need for security against terrorists. Small retail businesses in Reynosa suffered visibly by the downturn in cross-border traffic as tourists shied away from the slowdowns at the bridges, but the owners of the corporate maquiladoras also voiced loud complaints against the delays.

Another rumor that in the end proved accurate involved the hiring frenzy for Air Marshals. Border Patrol agents represented ideal recruits, because they already had much of the training required by the Air Marshals, including the necessary background checks and clearances. Agents signed up without hesitation for what promised to be exciting work serving their country. On the face of it working for the Air Marshals was everything that patrolling the line was not. Recruits could directly serve the country in a time of need in a job that was anything but boring, flying at 30,000 feet with a New York, Los Angeles, or Paris destination.

For agents who were stuck in the foreseeable future at the rank of GS-9, the Air Marshals offered a substantial annual raise. Benefits were transferable from one federal agency to another. Instead of being based in an isolated community like McAllen, the Air Marshals would fly out of Dallas, Miami, and other exciting cities. No serious recruiting was necessary. Agents were ready to leave the Border Patrol before September 11, even more ready after. Every day agents flew off to be interviewed in Dallas, Miami, or Detroit before review panels, then they returned to McAllen to await the final call notifying them of their acceptance.

Gester was one of the first agents at the McAllen Station to join the Air Marshals. For months management failed to inform him of their decision on his actions against Fat Man at Los Ebanos. While the rumors and the gossip ran heavy, no manager ever stepped forward to praise this agent for his initiative and hard work. All that came from management was a series of rumors, each of which suggested that Gester and his fellow agents would be punished for their actions. Gester must have known that they were going to make an example of him, that hereafter management would point to Gester as an agent who placed himself above the rules and policies of the station. Agents did not make the rules. Just like soldiers, agents were expected to follow orders and never question their commands. Gester signed with the Air Marshals before station management ever handed down the final decision that would have to become a part of his permanent record.

Agent Maria Contreras joined the Air Marshals too, as did Agents Shuman, Plovic, Paco, and at least forty more. By spring, the majority of the Rambos at the McAllen Station had departed, along with other agents who were dissatisfied with their jobs patrolling the line. Many believed such a rare opportunity would never come along again. Those who left for the Air Marshals—eventually they numbered almost one out of every six agents at the McAllen Station—were more likely to be the younger, single agents, including those who were not from the region. But some married agents who were born and raised in Deep South Texas also chose to leave the Border Patrol for greener pastures.

One of those who stayed remarked, "It's not all bad. Some of the guys who left weren't really dedicated to the Border Patrol." But bled dry of the majority of ambitious and younger agents with experience, the law enforcement capabilities of the McAllen Station remained an open question.

Public criticism of the INS swelled in the meantime as the media documented examples of its bureaucratic ineptitude. Perhaps the lowlight was the INS's mailing visas to two of the dead terrorists. President Bush and other elected officials found considerable political support when they called for a total reorganization of all security services and programs into one mega-agency. In the past various critics had urged the INS to separate from the Border Patrol, but this new and radical call for reform clearly resonated with a public fearful of additional terrorist attacks.

Every day it seemed as if new recruits fresh from graduation at the academy replaced agents who had shipped out either for temporary duty on the northern border or for the Air Marshals. Oldtimers who had no interest in volunteering for the Canadian border, including agents like Morningside, who was approaching his sixteenth year of service, grew more annoyed at answers they received from their informal inquisitions and musters.

"What did you do before you joined?" Morningside gruffly addressed three new faces standing at the back of the room. One had been a cop; another, a clerk at Wal-Mart; and the third had been in "the food service industry."

"We know what that means," said another experienced agent from across the room. "It means, 'Do you want fries with that?'" The supe silenced the guffaws by reading new intel, but it was evident that the academy was accepting recruits who could not have met Border Patrol standards in prior years.

The best intentions of management notwithstanding, events of September 11 dealt a crippling blow to the agency designated to protect the southern border of the United States. The terrorist attacks by Muslim fanatics inspired agents as never before to defend the banks of the Rio Grande; however, the strategy developed and amended by management at the McAllen Station led to a numbing routine that few endured well. As September, October, and November passed, agents were infected by the mundane; cynicism trumped exuberance, and pride succumbed to disappointment in the uniform and the vision of the agency. Some of the best agents were replaced by new recruits who lacked experience, commitment, and motivation. High alert status in Deep South Texas became no alert as weary agents spent their ten-hour shifts and extra overtime shuffling their feet in the dust and praying for something, anything at all, to happen.

Drowning

A number of unsung heroes worked at the McAllen Station, agents like Butch Lopez, who single-handedly rescued an undocumented worker drowning in the Rio Grande. Some months later Agent Lopez saved another new immigrant who was crossing the river. Most often these demonstrations of exceptional courage went unrecognized by the public, at best acknowledged in a brief ceremony at the end of muster during which the agent was presented a $15 plaque and a handshake from the supe. In the middle of November, Agent Montoya helped extinguish a fire that, fanned by high winds, had jumped from the Reynosa city dump across the Río Bravo to the parched northern banks. Because of his training, Agent Montoya was able to prevent any loss of life or property. His brave acts never received the slightest public attention.

When the Border Patrol made news it was much more likely to be an embarrassment to the federal agency than an account of the courage of agents who risked their lives during the course of line watch. But in all law enforcement, corruption traditionally stole the headlines. The Border Patrol also suffered lack of credibility borne by a history of mistreatment of immigrants.[1]

For most Americans saving a life was a decisive action in which personal bravery superseded all other adversity. In part this belief was sustained by media that portrayed the act of rescue as almost an everyday occurrence. If someone were drowning, the hero jumped into the water, swam to the victim, then gracefully pulled the victim to safety by means of his or her training, strength, and moral right. Such incidents were regularly depicted in action-based television and screen melodramas to the point that their outcomes were both highly predictable and unexceptional.[2]

The reality of saving the life of an undocumented worker drowning in the waters of the Rio Grande was, however, far more complex. Rescuers were forced to contend with practical, moral, and legal constraints. The McAllen Station seemed incapable of coherently packaging and presenting these and other acts of heroism to the media and to the public. This failure was part of its inability to influence the media news machine favorably and help shape public opinion. One result of this failure was an inevitable tide of negative publicity, some of which was undeserved. The Border Patrol could be its own worst enemy.[3]

At the McAllen Station many agents simply did not know how to swim. Why should they? As children most agents played football or basketball in the streets rather than anchoring the relay for the swim team. The majority of Valley high schools, regardless of the subtropical climate, could not afford practice pools or swim teams. Mexican American agents from the Valley and Anglo agents from other regions of the United States did not know how to swim for the same reason that blacks from South Central Los Angeles did not play professional ice hockey and whites from South Boston rarely excelled in the ranks of the PGA. Candidates at the academy easily passed a swimming test, but the test did not measure their basic swimming skills. Moreover, swimming at the academy was not a significant part of physical training, and water rescue skills were never taught.

Even agents who were strong swimmers—and there were some—confronted a variety of issues before jumping into the unknown waters of the Rio Grande. Agents carried a minimum of ten to fifteen pounds of equipment around their waists, not including their work boots and their bulletproof vests, which added at least another twenty pounds. In a crisis situation the first thing to do was to strip off this excess poundage or risk, regardless of swimming skills, sinking to the bottom. Throwing off a tool belt, work boots, and bulletproof vest was essentially a minor decision, but it might absorb crucial seconds during which the swimmer was swept farther downstream. And what if when agents returned to the spot where they had left their gear, they found it missing? They risked losing $2,000 or more of personal equipment, including their service weapon, which might never be recovered.[4]

Reaching the water to save a drowning immigrant could be problematical. There were few spots where banks were completely cleared along the forty-odd miles of the Rio Grande patrolled by McAllen Station agents. Most banks were covered with carrizo cane, thick brush, or cactus, and there was usually a drop-off into the waters below; twenty-foot bluffs were not exceptional. The river bottom was uneven along these same banks, while in other places it gradually declined to a thirty-foot bottom. Currents were always unpredictable depending on the season and the release of water from the upriver dams. As Nature Boy had demonstrated repeatedly at the Reynosa Bridge, diving from the banks was risky.

Hydrilla made rescue far more dangerous for agents. Thick as a carpet in some sections of the river, much of the hydrilla floated in random patches alongside both banks. Lily pads on the surface of the water were attached by strong root systems to the river bottom. The hydrilla not only was a potential contributor to immigrant drownings, but rescuers were intimidated by its presence.

By the time the mighty Rio Grande reached McAllen, it was a receptacle for human excrement, agricultural pesticides, and effluents from American factories and towns.[5] It was the sewer of choice for Mexican municipalities and maquiladoras from Juárez to Matamoros. Mexican municipalities dumped their raw, untreated sewage directly into the river even as waste from pigs and other domestic animals regularly fouled its banks and waters. Outhouses covered the banks of the south side of the river as they once had on the north side. Just ten miles from the McAllen Station a sixteen-inch Mexican sewer pipe churned the gray metallic waters of the Rio Grande a deep brownish purple. From the ever-present stench, boat patrol agents easily located the sewer pipe that was yet another source of contamination to the river.

Because the river was a cesspool, agents took long and frequent showers to rid themselves of possible bacterial contaminants and chemicals they may have contacted when sprayed by river water or when forced to enter the waters of this toxic sewer. Agents readily acknowledged that even a brief swim to rescue a drowning immigrant might mean personal exposure to serious waterborne diseases.

What about tossing a flotation device or safety ring to a swimmer in trouble? Sitting at home in front of the television it seemed simple enough, but agents were provided no flotation devices, no safety disks, and, even if they had such aides, throwing them through, over, or around carrizo cane and other thick vegetation was not feasible. The only safety tool that agents possessed was a rope. If they had a rope they could tie it to a nearby tree or bumper of a truck, then heave the line into the water if they could find an opening in the vegetation. Maybe they would get lucky.

If an immigrant were drowning, radioing one of the patrol boats for help seemed a reasonable solution. But by the time the call could be made and received and the boat captain arrived on the scene, the swimmer might have already drowned. The fleet of four boats was stretched very thinly in its patrols. Also illegal crossings often were in difficult-to-reach sections of the river, and some portions of the river were not navigable by the Border Patrol BayMasters. The fleet of four boats was inadequately equipped, as suggested, and their marine mechanics were hard pressed to keep the boats fully operational. Seldom were all four boats in running order at the same time.

The rescue of a drowning immigrant from the waters of the Rio Grande, discounting all these real constraints, was simultaneously problematic and dangerous. When confronted with a rescue, lifeguards at pools and beaches were trained to toss a safety line, offer a long pole, launch a small boat, or, if absolutely necessary, offer their own arm or leg when anchored to an immovable object. These options were chosen to avoid being yanked to the bottom by the swimmer, or accidentally struck or choked by a victim literally fighting for his or her life. Water safety experts agreed that the last choice was to enter the water to save the swimmer.

One agent stated bluntly: "I have a wife and kids. What happens to them if I drown saving an illegal? Do you think the Border Patrol is going to take care of my family?" Another agent said, "I do my job every day. But they don't pay me enough to throw my life away on some guy who, if I save him, is maybe going to go back the next day and try it again."

Agents therefore went out of their way to avoid situations that might involve a potential drowning. For example, agents tracking immigrants who had crossed the river always tried to get behind them, between them and the riverbank, so that the immigrants would not attempt to recross the river and risk drowning. If agents chased immigrants back to the northern banks or caught them as they were landing on the northern banks, they always tried to negotiate the immigrants' safety. While not always successful, an agent such as Roberta Alanis would do everything in her power to keep immigrants from swimming back to the southern bank. Some agents, when seeing that immigrants were running back toward the river, simply gave up the chase.

"I don't want the guy to die because of me," said one agent. "I'll get him the next time he crosses."

Strategies to protect new immigrants were not foolproof and certainly were subject to human error. When caught off guard, the natural human reaction was not calm thought but panic; at night in an unfamiliar place immigrants did not always consider their wisest options. The most experienced agents created situations in which the best option was immediate and peaceful surrender. Nevertheless, some immigrants ran from agents, at least in part because of the stories they had heard about the Border Patrol or their own previous experiences with agents. Immigrants did not recognize the U.S. Border Patrol as their ally.

One confounding variable in this equation was the treatment that illegal immigrants received from Mexican law enforcement. Immigrants frequently complained that they had been harassed, threatened, beaten, sexually assaulted, or robbed by Mexican officials either before they crossed the Río Bravo or after they had been caught on the northern banks of the river and VRed to Mexico. Grupo Beta, the Mexican federal agency designated to protect all immigrants, was active in Matamoros but did not function in and around Reynosa.[6]

In practice agents usually attempted to negotiate with illegal border crossers as the situation demanded. This might mean an outcome in which the immigrant was not apprehended, a resolution logged in the "gotaway" category. Yet most agents would have settled for another gotaway than a possible drowning. Some agents negotiated more than others depending on a number of factors, not the least of which were patience and good will. Both could be in short supply at the end of a ten-hour midnight shift or after hours of chasing undocumented workers through cactus forests under a hundred-degree sun. Undocumented workers during weekend shifts, for instance, were much more likely to be drunk and verbally abusive. In all these situations and others agents were less likely to accommodate immigrant needs.

Although agents' personal values and attitudes determined their actions based upon a number of situational factors, agents especially looked after children, women, and the elderly, as well as illegal immigrants who were noticeably ill. The attention given the onion girl was not unusual. At the same time, agents could provide little lasting care.

That said, some agents grew angry in specific situations or brought that same emotion to their shift. For example, it was not unusual for agents to rush a sensor only to find that they were the victims of a mean-spirited prank. On more than one occasion I observed young Mexican males intentionally taunting agents. These men swam the river, jumped on the sensor that they knew was buried in the bank, then waited until the agents arrived. Hurling elaborate insults from the safety of the middle of the river, they hooted and howled at agents who watched them on the northern bank. Agents might return the insults, believing that the exchange was just another part of wearing the uniform. Agents who were physically exhausted from a long shift or otherwise stressed might respond differently to the same incident. More than one agent alluded to a sling shot he carried to retaliate against obnoxious tormentors who wasted agents' time.

Known drug smugglers were treated very differently than the average illegal immigrant. Agents treated cocaine smugglers with zero tolerance. *Coyotes* like Fat Man who made their living from smuggling illegal immigrants were also at the bottom of this human heap. Alongside Fat Man in this highly stratified scale were those who had previous records for drug smuggling or human smuggling but were out on bond. Agents presumed, often with good reason, that these suspects continued their criminal activities to pay off their bond and legal fees. Those who were sympathetic to drug smugglers, such as known scouts who made their living watching the Border Patrol, were also likely to be treated harshly by agents.

A number of others whom agents at the McAllen Station knew personally, often those with police records, were also never given the benefit of the doubt. These individuals were never negotiated with and always were viewed with great skepticism regardless of their public behavior. Agents knew these individuals from personal contact as well as by their reputations in the communities. Agents regardless of race referred to convicted smugglers, smugglers out on bail, friends and associates of smugglers, scouts, and others in the community with bad reps as "local scum."

The Border Patrol could be self-defeating because of its inability to present its most positive attributes and contributions to the public. On the one hand, real heroes often went unnoticed, while, on the other, the Border Patrol frequently failed to represent or explain its actions and interests to a skeptical public. It did not employ a professional public information director (known as a PID) and, as a result, suffered predictable consequences. Instead of a professional PID, the public heard and viewed several different agents who were assigned the task on an irregular basis. The public spokesperson for the McAllen Station rarely possessed any professional training and was inept at responding to questions from reporters on camera. At best media responses were filled with unfamiliar law enforcement jargon that viewers and readers found incomprehensible. At worst the spokespersons for the Border Patrol seemed insensitive to—even combative about—issues. Agents voiced in private their hesitancy about serving as spokespersons but for various reasons did not believe that they could refuse the assignment.

Although the major local papers were highly sympathetic to the Border Patrol, the agency never contested newspaper accounts of events in which the Border Patrol played an active role.[7] Rarely did the Border Patrol, for example, use the op-ed section to voice institutional sentiments, to explain policy, or to respond to issues raised by the media or the public. The lone, consistent supporters of the Border Patrol in McAllen were Anglo winter tourists who could be particularly tactless and whose comments sometimes were racist in nature.

Without a PID representing its best interests, the Border Patrol squandered opportunities to present its side of the story, to influence public opinion, and to enhance its standing in the community.[8]

Reporters' stories about the McAllen Station were formulaic and appeared in the crime section in *The Monitor* alongside homicides, armed robberies, sexual assaults, and traffic accidents.[9] The first paragraph of a story usually described Border Patrol agents' confiscation of illegal drugs and named the type of drug, the location of the interdiction, and the street value of the drugs. If there were a second paragraph, it vaguely described in a couple of sentences the way in which the drugs were confiscated.

Depending on the amount of news for a particular day, if agents confiscated marijuana in excess of approximately 1,000 pounds, or 200 pounds of cocaine, a story was likely to find a place on the second page of the first, second, or third sections of the newspaper. Only exceptionally large amounts of illegal drugs, those valued at more than $2 million, secured a place on the front pages.[10] In most other regions of the United States the incredible amounts of drugs confiscated by the Border Patrol would have demanded regular head-lines, but in the Valley reporters, editors, and the public had long since lost perspective. In many ways residents of McAllen, in part because of the treatment of the stories by news professionals, had become anesthetized to the magnitude of the amounts of drugs smuggled across the Rio Grande.

The apprehension of immigrants went similarly under-reported, and the role of the Border Patrol was trivialized. Only if an unusually large number of illegal aliens were detained did *The Monitor* place the story on the front page.[11] The death of an illegal immigrant was also unlikely to be deemed newsworthy. When the Guatemalan man, for example, bailed out of the *coyote's* car near San Manuel, his death was never published in a Valley newspaper.[12] A story was published in spring 2001 about the body of an illegal alien found floating in the Rio Grande, but the story was only "newsworthy" because the drowning victim was at first alleged to have been found with a knapsack containing illegal drugs.[13]

In sharp contrast to individual deaths of illegal aliens, media stories involving multiple deaths were much more likely to see print in Valley newspapers or to reach the air.[14] The greater the number of immigrants who died crossing the Rio Grande or were found in the brush at the Sarita or Falfurrias checkpoints, the bigger the story. This same pattern occurred for new immigrants who died or were murdered outside of the region.

However, stories about illegal drugs, again depending on the amount confiscated, were much more likely to be published than stories about the apprehension, drowning, shooting, or traffic deaths of illegal immigrants.[15]

The single public relations effort of the McAllen Station was the Citizens' Academy. Offered each year in the fall and spring to residents of McAllen and surrounding communities, this training purposed to "keep the community we serve abreast of what we do. We give them [the students] the opportunity to experience it firsthand."[16] The Citizens' Academy I attended, eight successive weeks in early fall 2001, was typical. Purporting to represent diverse segments from the community, the eighteen to twenty "students" were employed by area public and private institutions, including the McAllen Chamber of Commerce, the Economic Development Council, the mayor's office, and the largest commercial banks. Although low-wage workers composed the majority of the labor market in McAllen, none were invited to this Citizens' Academy.

The curriculum of the Citizens' Academy, which was covered in three- to four-hour sessions each Thursday night, addressed the mission and purpose of the Border Patrol, immigration law, the apprehension and processing of immigrants, firearms training, and the boat patrol. Presentations by Border Patrol supervisors, senior agents, and employees of the INS were followed by field trips to the firing range, a brief ride on a flotilla of boats along the Rio Grande, a tour of the Border Patrol facilities at Miller International Airport in McAllen, a demonstration by the canine patrol in the parking lot of Sector Headquarters, and an informal barbecue.

At the end of the eight weeks, students of the Citizens' Academy were presented individual certificates and plaques at a special morning ceremony at the McAllen Station presided over by the chief of the sector. At the ceremony I attended, a federal district judge talked briefly about the enforcement of immigration laws. Students also received black ceramic beer steins with the insignia of the Border Patrol emblazoned in gold.

My fellow students seemed to enjoy the Citizens' Academy and to learn much from the lectures and field trips. They came with little knowledge of the role and function of the Border Patrol, including its focus upon problems associated with undocumented workers and illegal drugs. For example, after the sniffer dog successfully retrieved a big bag of marijuana from where its handler had hidden it under a truck in the Sector Headquarters parking lot, two female students in my class asked if they could smell the marijuana. The handler complied with their request by cutting for them a portion from one of the bricks of marijuana. Then, after the sniffer dog located a brick of cocaine in the same parking lot, the same two women again requested to smell it. Apparently the students had no idea that taking a quick snort of this pure form of cocaine was neither advisable nor appropriate.

Adult students in my Citizens' Academy classes gasped at the efficiency of the boat patrol when several new immigrants were deterred on the south side of the river just before they entered the water. Equally impressive was the display of technical gear and weapons available to agents. Each student was allowed to handle and shoot a shotgun firing beanbags at a concrete block building on the target range outside Edinburg. Later that same evening students were encouraged to assume the role of hostages. After a flash-bang was exploded to divert the attention of the hostage takers, the hostages were rescued from the interior rooms of a mock-up house by the Border Patrol SWAT team dressed in black and sporting some of the same gear and gadgetry previously displayed. Students also were intrigued by the Border Patrol helicopters at Miller International Airport. Pilots demonstrated their capacity to fly with night vision goggles and other specialized equipment. Everyone also seemed to have fun at the barbecue that followed one of the last Citizens' Academy sessions.

Students asked numerous questions of the presenters during these sessions about issues including profiling, brutality against immigrants, and the impact of the Border Patrol upon the local community. Although it was evident that several participants harbored hostile or skeptical attitudes toward the Border Patrol prior to the Citizens' Academy, no one maintained these viewpoints by the end of the sessions. Agents, most with years of experience, seemed genuinely willing to communicate the purpose of the Border Patrol, its problems, and the legal and moral rightness of its vision. Trust and respect for agents increased each week.

The Citizens' Academy I observed effectively informed participants of the Border Patrol's mission, operations, and perspective. From a pragmatic public relations standpoint, however, the effort was a dismal failure because it reached so few citizens. My class enrolled eighteen students, which was about average; another Citizens' Academy convened in the spring. Through this effort, then, approximately thirty-six citizens in a region with a population of more than one-half million were annually exposed to the Border Patrol's mission and contributions.

Lacking a professional PID also caused the McAllen Station to miss opportunities to promote its interests in several other ways. In May 2001, for example, the assistant chief of the McAllen Station asked me to write a report on the economic impact of the Border Patrol upon Hidalgo County. In turn I contacted Dr. Alberto Davila, the chair of the Economics Department at the University of Texas–Pan American, who had closely studied immigration and labor issues along the U.S.-Mexico border.[17] Under Davila's guidance we met on several occasions throughout May and June with various representatives of the McAllen Station and Sector Headquarters who provided data for the study.[18]

Not unexpectedly the research found that the McAllen Station and Sector Headquarters injected a fiscal bonanza into the local economy. The annual operating budget alone for both entities exceeded $8.6 million, not counting an additional $3.8 million in payroll and overhead expenditures of $1.5 million.

When a proposed $22 million construction project was added to the figures, the economic impact was estimated at $65 million in 2003. Over a thirty-year period, the numbers were a staggering $3.533 billion in one of the poorest regions in the United States.

Other direct benefits to the City of McAllen and Hidalgo County, while difficult to quantify in dollars, were also revealing. Agents frequently were the only law enforcement in parts of rural Hidalgo County, where officers from an understaffed Hidalgo County Sheriff's Department might take an hour or more to respond to a felony in progress. In fact, the greatest loss of life suffered by the Border Patrol in the Valley occurred in 1998 when two agents responded to a homicide near Harlingen. First officers on the scene, the two agents were shot and killed by a suspect hiding in a corn field.[19] The Border Patrol also provided backup to local law enforcement agencies in traffic stops and other violations. Their roles were limited by law, but the agents of the Border Patrol undoubtedly had a significant impact upon the safety of their fellow law enforcers and upon the crime rate.

During natural disasters such as the hurricanes that periodically decimated the area, the McAllen Station contributed a law enforcement presence of three hundred trained officers who provided emergency support and rescue. In short supply during an emergency, their four-wheel-drive vehicles, boats, generators, and other equipment represented an invaluable contribution. It was also difficult to calculate a dollar value of the contribution of agents and their spouses to community activities including the Cub Scouts, Little League Baseball and other youth sports, the United Way, the Muscular Dystrophy Association, food banks, and blood banks. In a poor region with limited resources these services to the community helped keep social services for the poor from becoming even more overburdened.

Management planned a press conference in July 2001 to announce the findings of the report on the economic and social significance of the Border Patrol to residents of McAllen.[20] The press conference was in part a direct response to the frigid reception the agency had received when management had approached public officials in McAllen about a possible site for new construction of both the McAllen Station and Sector Headquarters. City officials had argued that because the Border Patrol paid no local taxes as a federal agency, it made no significant contribution to the local economy. After the press conference, the Border Patrol was courted by a variety of municipal officials from McAllen and surrounding communities, all of whom were anxious for the Border Patrol to locate new facilities in their respective communities.[21]

I worked directly with Border Patrol personnel to prepare them for this press conference. It was obvious that, while eager to learn, they lacked both the professional experience in presenting their views to those outside their own agency and the expertise to seize opportune times to publicize their best efforts. Agents assigned to the press conference, for example, had no professional training in public speaking or public relations. As a result agents found it difficult to analyze and present their own agency data in a positive and coherent fashion.[22]

News stories in the print media often failed to delineate the purpose or importance of public events sponsored by the Border Patrol. A fashion show held in Harlingen to raise money for the family of a Border Patrol agent killed in the line of duty, for example, was advertised in a misleading way that did little to promote the agency's interests or image. The newspaper story began: "If you can't resist a man in uniform, you need to attend 'Men in Green,' a benefit style show featuring U.S. Border Patrol Agents."[23]

When tragedies involving the Border Patrol occurred, it was not at all surprising, therefore, that the public automatically assumed the worst. McAllen residents lived in a media-driven culture in which saving a swimmer from drowning in the Rio Grande was considered a no-brainer. If attractive women in bikinis could rescue those in trouble in the ocean, then surely trained, adult men in a federal law enforcement agency could accomplish the same feat in the Rio Grande.

In a political climate in which few residents clearly understood the mission, function, and benefits of the Border Patrol in their own community, many believed that agents were capable of brutality along with a litany of other offenses. Recent cases such as Wayne Thornton's lent added veracity to skeptics who believed that a purposive, racist pattern of behavior within the Border Patrol condoned brutality and neglected the humane treatment of undocumented workers.

Within this broader context of the public's inability to understand the harsh realities involved in the rescue of a new immigrant from the waters of the Rio Grande—a context and history that the Border Patrol did little to clarify or explain—an enraged public responded to the senseless drowning of two Mexican immigrants.[24] Given the brutal, racist history of the Border Patrol, the accusations from the media and public officials on both sides of the Rio Grande initially seemed both justified and convincing. The actual event, like that of the notorious beating of Rodney King in Los Angeles, was caught on video and broadcast repeatedly on both local American and Mexican television channels.

Pictures did not lie. Or could they? Not far from the bridge that links downtown Brownsville to the main streets of Matamoros, two Mexican males attempted to cross the river illegally but were swept helplessly into a strong current. As shocked bystanders watched from various points on the bridge and both banks, one of the victims called out for help. He yelled that he was drowning, then disappeared beneath the water. A few moments later, as Border Patrol agents on the north side appeared to do absolutely nothing but watch, unidentified men on the south side threw a line into the waters. The line fell nowhere near the second Mexican man, who, in obvious desperation, flailed wildly in the water before he too disappeared from sight. Several days later American officials recovered the bodies of the two men and returned them to Mexico.

The media maelstrom in northern Mexico and Deep South Texas lasted for weeks. The Border Patrol was directly accused of refusing to aide the two Mexican men and, therefore, of being directly responsible for their deaths. One popular television reporter asked, "How could they do this?"[25] Citizens believed that the two agents were guilty of discrimination based upon nation of origin. The incident was one more example of the brutal treatment that new immigrants, especially Mexicans, received when they chose to work in the United States.

Several months later I viewed a copy of the complete, unedited video. I had already watched clips countless times on television and had been sickened, like many others, by what I saw. But the entire video—rarely, if ever, broadcast to the public—portrayed quite a different set of events than the highly edited television version. The first frames, shot by a Mexican cameraman who, for unknown reasons, was present to film the crossing of these two new immigrants, showed the first immigrant entering the river from the Mexican side. Several other unidentified adult males besides these two men were present. The first immigrant obviously misjudged the rapid current as he entered the water and was quickly swept along the river close to the Mexican bank. It sounded as if he yelled for help several times, but the audio was badly garbled.

The Substance of Chaos

An agent in uniform appeared on the northern bank, observed the man in trouble, then tried to follow him as the current swept him downriver. The agent was moving slowly over the irregular terrain, it can be assumed because he did not want to spook a second immigrant, who appeared to consider whether to enter the water to help the first immigrant. Another agent was then visible cautiously approaching the Rio Grande through knee-high grass. The two agents moved along the bank as best they could as they followed the plight of the first immigrant who had been swept up by the current. Neither agent possessed any rescue devices—lifejackets, safety disks, or ropes.

The second Mexican waded carefully to a small sandbar that was ankle deep and perhaps five feet from the southern bank. He presumably had some knowledge of this part of the river to place himself in this advantageous position. Perched on the sandbar, the second Mexican reached with his right arm to save the drowning man as he was swept by. The drowning man, panicked from his battle against the current, grabbed the arm extended to him, then unintentionally yanked his rescuer into the river. The second immigrant, who was obviously unprepared for the force generated by this act of desperation, was flung into the river face first, went under, then bobbed back to the surface.

Shouts from both sides of the river could be heard. An unidentified Mexican male appeared with a rope, which he futilely threw into the river time and again. This same man, or perhaps one who closely resembled him, then appeared in the video in a lifejacket. At no time, however, did this individual wearing the lifejacket enter the water. Instead, he followed the two drowning men as they continued downriver. The southern bank was relatively flat at this place along the river, more a beach than a bank, while the slope of the northern bank was pronounced and difficult for the Americans to traverse.

Although the agents appeared agitated and concerned as they watched these events, they never threw a line to the drowning men or entered the water to save them. The final frames, most commonly broadcast, showed the two immigrants drowning as several Mexican men continued to cast their rope into the water. Within a matter of seconds the first man drowned. Then the second man went under. The agents did nothing during this time but follow the victims as they were dragged along by the current. The unedited video lasted about ninety seconds.

I reviewed the video a second time, this time taking notes of the sequence of events, the participants, and their actions. Viewers who only witnessed the edited frames could easily conclude that agents did next to nothing to save the lives of the two Mexican immigrants. But if members of the enraged public on both sides of the border had had an opportunity to view the unedited video in its entirety, especially in the context of the constraints placed upon agents, they might have reached quite a different conclusion. By showing the two Mexicans already in the water, the broadcast version of the video ignored the fact that one immigrant had inadvertently caused the other to drown. Responsibility and blame instead fell upon uncaring agents on the north side while those on the south side, even though their efforts were futile, seemed heroic.

But what exactly should the two agents on the north side have done? They had no rope, safety disk, nor lifejacket at hand to attempt a rescue of either man. In the time it would have taken to retrieve a rope from their vehicle—if indeed they had a rope there—the two victims would have been swept far downstream or drowned. Before entering the water, they would have had to remove their Kevlar vests, boots, and equipment belts, or risked drowning themselves. Valuable seconds would have been lost. Neither safety disks nor lifejackets were issued as standard equipment to agents. Did the agents even know how to swim?

If one of the agents had been a strong swimmer, then he conceivably might have entered the water, traversed almost the full breadth of the river and then, perhaps, reached one of the Mexican workers before he drowned. The victims were unfortunately on the far side, the Mexican side, of the river, making their rescue from the northern bank much more improbable. The video showed that it was difficult enough for the agents even to keep pace with the drowning men because of the contours of the northern bank. Hindsight suggested that one of the agents could have dashed ahead of the victims, swum the river, then, with more great luck, intersected the path of one of the victims. But even given this kind of exceptional scenario, the agent was then faced with an almost impossible task of rescuing a panicked victim from the river current without a lifejacket, rope, or safety disk. It was also important to remember that the panicked first swimmer had already pulled a potential rescuer into the river. If indeed either agent was a swimmer, neither had prior training in river rescue at the academy nor while stationed in Deep South Texas.

A point never investigated was the failure of the unidentified Mexican male wearing the lifejacket to enter the water. Only after the immigrants had both drowned did he wade into the river. On this particular day anyone in these same circumstances who entered the waters of the Rio Grande would have placed his or her own life in jeopardy with little chance of saving either of the victims. Once set in motion, these events unfolded so quickly that there was virtually nothing that anyone, including the agents on the north side of the river, could reasonably have been expected to do.

Rumors among the agents at the McAllen Station after the double drowning hinted at conspiracy. Several agents believed that the two men who drowned were actually part of a staged media event gone awry. "Why was a guy with a camera there?" one agent asked defensively. "And that guy with the lifejacket on. Who was he? Why didn't he save them?"

The Border Patrol and its agents felt heat from the public, yet the agency's media response to the tragedy was, as usual, tepid. Spokespersons for the Border Patrol assumed that the public knew far more than it did about the agency's ability to save a drowning immigrant in the Rio Grande. But instead of a rational explanation of the agents' behavior on the northern banks, the public was offered a discourse burdened by law enforcement jargon. The Border Patrol could have clearly and concisely constructed a strong case against the inflammatory charges, but it did not. As a result citizens' attacks grew more vehement.

Months after the furor had finally died down, one angry agent at the McAllen Station demanded, "What do they [the public] want from us?"

Most agents and the citizens of Deep South Texas were unwilling or incapable of discussing the larger public policy issues involved in this drowning tragedy. Certainly Americans in nonborder states were uninformed and even more disinterested. In contrast, the Mexican public was quite familiar with immigration issues, including years of charges of discrimination against the Border Patrol. Remittances from Mexican workers—legal and illegal—in the United States to family and relatives in Mexico totaled $7 billion and were an integral part of the Mexican economy.[26] More than 1,600 new illegal immigrants, a majority of whom were Mexican, died in their attempts to cross illegally into the United States from Mexico 1993–97.[27] Most recently it was estimated that 350–400 immigrants died each year illegally entering the United States from Mexico. Even these grim statistics were conservative.

After the double drowning, agents at the McAllen Station and elsewhere along the Texas border continued to bear the public's outrage. Such public sentiments hurled their way were not novel. Whenever the bodies of new illegal immigrants were found floating in the Rio Grande, decomposing in the desert and brush country north of McAllen, or rotting in the backs of tractor-trailers, many citizens ultimately blamed the agents. Few citizens of McAllen were willing to consider that agents in the McAllen Station did not formulate immigration policy.

"It goes with the job," one agent explained, referring to the abuse hurled at him after the double drowning. "After a while, you get used to it."

Twelve months after the double drowning, agents at the McAllen Station finally received safety disks and ropes for their Expeditions. Agents were required to attend an all-day workshop at a community pool where they were taught basic water safety techniques by a certified instructor. They were also taught how to use the new safety disk. Most agents agreed that, given the situational constraints that day at the river, a safety disk could not have saved the two victims. One agent told me, "It's better than nothing. But in many places along the river it's totally useless."

The instructor told agents during their training session that saving a life by entering the waters of the Rio Grande was a personal decision that they would have to consider when and if the time ever arrived. This message was reiterated at subsequent musters.

At the training session those agents who did not swim, estimated at more than half of all agents at the McAllen Station, practiced rescue procedures in the shallow end of the swimming pool.

Bubbles

Race mattered at the McAllen Station just as it did in most American institutions enforcing public laws and policies.[1] Along the U.S.-Mexico border, race had been a historical catalyst of violence and bloodshed. Deep South Texas had endured the War of Texas Independence, the Mexican War, the Civil War, the Mexican Revolution, and the Plan of San Diego, to name but a few of the significant struggles founded on racism.[2]

Critics on the left were prone to assume agents of the Border Patrol were little more than Nazis in green uniforms; those on the right were equally certain that these same agents coddled undocumented workers and drug smugglers. Most recently ranchers and farmers in western states, including Texas, patrolled the borderlands ostensibly to protect American citizens from undocumented workers. Several shootings had resulted along with a spate of lawsuits.[3] Racism was also detectable among those who posited more moderate viewpoints.[4]

Although a number of prosaic issues also greatly influenced agents, at certain times and in certain situations a brand of racism found a cozy home at the McAllen Station. Male and female agents who entered the Border Patrol could bring with them the same racist attitudes that permeated American culture and society in spite of the Civil Rights movement, Affirmative Action, and all the past and present laws and policies aimed at eradicating racism.[5] Never in the admittance process to the Border Patrol or during the five months at the training academy were recruits administered any psychological tests that may have identified those with racist attitudes unsuited to a career in federal law enforcement.

Once within the confines of this tightly knit agency, once joining others in the field who had spent their careers chasing men, women, and children from Mexico, Central America, South America, and from all over the globe, the work experience could reinforce a racist mentality. New illegal immigrants who were desperate to cross the Rio Grande might do almost anything to keep from being returned to the other side. The drug smugglers, of course, were much worse. A partial repertoire included driving cars and vans into the Rio Grande, bailing out in the middle of busy traffic on a four-lane highway; and other ruthless behavior endangering the lives of both the public and agents. Agents lumped drug smugglers, their families, and friends into a homogeneous pile, as suggested earlier, ignominiously labeled "local scum." The vast majority of these individuals were Mexican Americans and Mexicans.

Agents, no differently than many other Americans, generalized from their own specific and personal experiences. In so doing they reached ethnocentric conclusions based on skimpy social facts. For example, it was true that the majority of the criminals involved in drug smuggling in Deep South Texas were Hispanic. But it was also true that the majority of citizens on the north and south side of the Rio Grande were also Hispanic, which meant that not all Hispanics were involved in drug smuggling or bore the negative characteristics of those whom agents continually confronted along the river. But some agents, both Anglos and Mexican Americans holding a preexisting set of attitudes, nevertheless concluded from their work on the line that Hispanics were an inferior race to Anglos.

Class differences aggravated many of the daily antagonisms between agents and illegal aliens.[6] Agents annually earning $50,000 chased after impoverished, unemployed immigrant workers from third-world countries. Though many of the agents, especially Mexican Americans born and raised along the border, came themselves from the same backgrounds as those apprehended, they did not necessarily empathize with workers from Mexico, Central America, and other cultures.

At the McAllen Station insensitivity to class differences offered a rampant breeding ground for racism. For example, agents in the processing room at the McAllen Station and in the front seats of their Expeditions commented that illegal aliens smelled bad. In addition, their clothes were inferior, they spoke Spanish poorly, and they lacked civility. If social and historical context were totally disregarded, there was no denying some of these charges. Absent among many agents was an emotional and intellectual comprehension of these newest American immigrants in search of work.

At the same time, those with little experience along the banks of the Rio Grande might romanticize new illegal workers. I observed some new illegal immigrants who were so drunk that they could barely stand. It was not uncommon to see undocumented workers who appeared stoned or high on drugs. I also saw new immigrants who were abusive when apprehended, eager to take out their frustration on other immigrants or agents. Among those apprehended was also a small percentage of hardened criminals with prison records in Mexico and/or the United States. Those who, in defense of illegal immigrants, deny such observations risk not only blindly romanticizing these new illegal workers but also robbing them of their diversity and humanity.[7]

According to their detailed accounts, agents had been propositioned by female illegal aliens after they were apprehended. These women were willing to trade sexual favors for their freedom. For example, before Operation Rio Grande there were numerous bars on Old Military Highway where professional prostitutes from Reynosa plied their trade on a regular basis. When agents busted the illegal workers who gathered at these bars, they also encountered the Mexican prostitutes. Some agents generalized from these experiences and others involving the apprehension of non-prostitutes who offered sex that many immigrant women were immoral. Though encounters with women who offered sexual favors were rare, they reinforced agents' beliefs about all undocumented immigrant women. A recent case in Brownsville involving an agent and a female illegal immigrant suggested that it was in fact agents who were at fault. In this particular case an agent was accused of soliciting sexual favors from a female illegal immigrant in exchange for releasing her.

The vast majority of new illegal immigrants appeared physically exhausted and emotionally defeated after they had been apprehended by agents, too tired to resist, negotiate, or even complain. When confronted by agents, many followed the command to stop, sit down on the ground, and wait for further orders. Because of the toxic waters they had traversed, because they had sometimes slept in the same clothes for days, because they had previously eluded capture by running through the brush and cactus, the illegal workers did in fact smell of sweat, fear, and filth. They were also frequently hungry and fatigued. Because most faced an immediate voluntary return, they could be angry as well as scared. Those who had paid *coyotes* had wasted their money. A few, by the time of their capture, had completely lost hope. But these newest job seekers were rarely violent.

Far from the knowing eyes of the public, agents daily performed their jobs as best they could in demanding terrain requiring personal risk. Members of the general public seldom photographed or witnessed chases and arrests. There were many opportunities for abuse of undocumented workers, but the subculture of agents in combination with structural factors mitigated against crimes directed toward undocumented workers. First, agents were partnered for much of their shift or, if not partnered, in frequent contact with other agents in the general area. To commit an offense required a partner's acquiescence or compliance. Partners, if they had not personally observed the offense, would soon know or find out what had occurred. The possibility of partners working together to protect each other from an undocumented worker's charge of brutality was unlikely. An offense, or an attempt to help cover up an offense, carried with it shame and embarrassment within the agent subculture, possible loss of a high-paying job, and a possible federal prison sentence. For those agents with families, committing an offense also threatened the welfare of the agent's spouse and their children. ·

Every shift at the McAllen Station randomly partnered one agent with another, and every year the entire unit was reorganized. The same station policy that could alienate agents from each other also made it more difficult to commit a crime against new immigrants or drug smugglers in isolated areas along the Rio Grande. If an assault or other crime against those apprehended did take place, it would inevitably surface in the spate of gossip passed between agents on their ten-hour shifts. The so-called code of silence prevalent in many law enforcement agents was largely absent in the Border Patrol by 2002 both because of the nature of the agency and situational factors which constrained it. Within sixty minutes of Wayne Thornton's striking an undocumented worker, for example, his field operation supervisor was investigating the scene of the alleged crime. Prosecutors from Washington gave the case a high priority, evidence was collected in a professional matter, and the jury wasted little time in reaching a guilty verdict after hearing the considerable evidence.

Solitary agents in Expeditions had a greater opportunity to abuse undocumented workers, but even then the risks of discovery were great. An illegal worker might complain to other workers in the transport, behavior easily overheard and acted upon by the agent behind the wheel. Agents played few favorites when aiding in concealing a crime was itself a crime. When immigrants walked through the back door at the McAllen Station en route to the processing room, they confronted a large poster in Spanish that listed their rights along with a phone number to call. Within the station there were additional opportunities to complain or, if injured, to be aided by other agents and the supes in charge. Wary of lawsuits, supes and the field operation supervisor were always on the lookout for those who required medical attention. Once the medical problem had been addressed, the specific cause of the injury would be ascertained.

Solitary agents on line watch also remained in close contact with other agents in the general area. It was to their advantage, because it minimized their exposure to risk. Agents who were alone in their vehicles commonly checked in with their supe using their unit's radio or their personal cell phone, communicated with other agents on the shift, discussed issues with families, and arranged social events and schedules with friends. The supes at the station monitored all conversations on the radio, and they also randomly took to the field to check on their agents. Any unusual behavior or action could be noticed and documented. Agents were not professional criminals. If they assaulted an alien or committed some other kind of crime, they would carry that burden with them just like anyone else. Agents, after personal communication with Wayne Thornton, for example, subsequently joined several of his college classmates as witnesses for the prosecution at his trial.

In sharp contrast, some station policies and rules, even the special vocabulary utilized, could facilitate abuse by dehumanizing undocumented workers. "Wetbacks" and other racist terms had long since fallen from the vocabulary of agents, but undocumented workers were often referred to as "bodies." "Do I VR the body to the Reynosa Bridge or transport it back to the station?" Such language, for example, desensitized agents from the grim realities of their work but also contributed to the dehumanization of new workers by reducing them to the level of freight carried from one place to another.

United by similar work goals and objectives, Mexican American and Anglo agents worked together in the field. Along the banks of the Rio Grande there were agents of the Border Patrol, those who wore the green uniform, and there were civilians. Facing a hostile work environment that could be life threatening, agents depended on their partners and other agents for their personal survival. In this "them" versus "us" mentality, even those who were not citizens of the United States maintained certain rights that had to be honored and preserved. Only occasionally did agents act as if they were free to supersede the rights of undocumented workers.

At the same time, racism existed among agents. It was always difficult to quantify racist discrimination and subsequent inequalities. Most agents, regardless of race or ethnicity, seemed to get along with each other at musters, in the field, and at social gatherings. Spanish and English were spoken freely between and among groups, handshakes were de rigueur, and the word heard most frequently in a conversation between two agents was "bro." Agents shared coffee, food, cigarettes, and confidences, kibitzed at the Tree, and partied to celebrate shift changes, transfers, retirements, and holidays. They donated money and time to the same causes, lent expensive equipment, offered free advice, and stood united before the wrath of the supes. They traded shifts with bros who wanted to expand their vacation time, donated blood to fellow agents after chipping in for flowers, and attended funerals of family members of agents at the McAllen Station and throughout the entire sector. In many ways they were extremely generous with their emotional support, their time, and their money.

Some Mexican Americans at the McAllen Station nevertheless believed that they were the victims of racist attitudes and opportunists even as Anglo agents contended that they were discriminated against because of the color of their skin. Both races pointed to the ways in which groups of agents formed, accurately noting that frequently Anglos socialized with Anglos, Hispanics with Hispanics. Anglos believed that proportionally fewer Anglos were promoted to supervisor and management—a case of reverse discrimination. "Look at Joe. He's got less time in than me, but he's already set up for supe." They explained this perceived pattern of discrimination by observing that promotions came from the top down. Because the sector chief and the assistant chief of the McAllen Station were both Mexican Americans, some Anglos argued that Hispanics favored their own. According to this line of reasoning, Hispanic agents received special treatment, including better assignments at muster, when compared to Anglo agents, or Hispanics got choice assignments to the Anti-Smuggling Unit (ASU), or Hispanics were more likely to get salary increases, or the Hispanic supe was more likely to cut Hispanics some slack, or even though a certain Mexican American was less educated and less experienced, he was selected over a more qualified Anglo.

In turn some Mexican American agents were just as likely to feel that they were discriminated against in many of the same ways and for many of the same reasons as Anglos. In addition, they also thought that Anglo agents did not genuinely appreciate Hispanic culture in McAllen or Hidalgo County, that although the Anglo agents might speak passable Spanish, they did not respect Hispanic customs, traditions, values, and standards. Particularly suspect were Anglos from the Northeast. In contrast, Anglos from the western states, including California, were identified as more sympathetic.

The ultimate demonstration of racist beliefs was in friendships. Few Anglo agents socialized with Mexican American agents outside the confines of the McAllen Station, and few Mexican American agents did the same with Anglos. In McAllen real friendships were defined and determined by whom you invited over to watch the college football game, or a special cable movie, or boxing match. Real friendships involved knowing the names of agents' spouses and children and being invited into the home for family dinners, celebrations, and other special times. The status of relationships corresponded to the level of sharing or exclusion from other agents' family life.

Although some agents alluded to racial discrimination at the McAllen Station, and in particular complained about special treatment including promotions, agents got along remarkably well at the station, in the field, and in other social settings related to work. Compared to other segments of the Valley population, agents were much less concerned about the color of their partner's skin than whether he or she, regardless of race or ethnicity, could "carry the weight." Agents told me repeatedly that in a crisis what mattered most was whether they could count on the person sitting next to them in the truck. Could that agent cover their backs or would they place them in a compromising situation? Were they Energizer rabbits or slugs who rarely ventured far from the front seat of their Expedition? Neither Hispanics nor Anglos maintained a monopoly on trust. It was the same at the management level. Agents at times distrusted certain managers not because they were Anglo or Mexican American but simply because they were part of management. An exception to these observations was a small group of older Anglos who had been a part of the Border Patrol, or influenced by agents who had been part of the Border Patrol, when *only* race mattered. These men, close to retirement, fostered beliefs and attitudes no longer widely tolerated among the vast majority of agents.

Racism in the Valley was complicated. Everyone knew that Anglos in McAllen and the rest of Deep South Texas did not always get along with people of Mexican heritage. Nor, unfortunately, did many Mexican Americans always tolerate Anglos. Many Mexican nationals, in turn, disliked both Mexican Americans and Anglos. Racism's long and illustrious history within Mexico was, for example, embodied in individual and institutionalized discrimination against indigenous peoples.[8]

Students in my classes at the University of Texas–Pan American, 95 percent of whom were Mexican American, frequently shared personal stories about discrimination hurled their way by Mexicans.[9] They selected research topics about racism and discrimination, then wrote about their perceived discrimination, documenting the exact ways in which Mexicans mistreated them. These papers revealed in great detail the discrimination these Mexican American students felt they had endured at the hands of Mexican nationals. Much of the time the discrimination emanated from wealthy Mexican women who shopped in McAllen. In retail stores where my college students worked to put themselves through the university, these wealthy women ordered them about as if they were their maids or gardeners. My students complained that when they visited Reynosa, Mexican merchants also treated them badly. Their Spanish was ridiculed and the service they received in restaurants and stores was inferior to that extended to Anglos. Finally, these same students distanced themselves from new immigrant families from Mexico who crossed the Rio Grande *sin papeles* by frequently failing to recognize any similarities between their own family's entry into this country and the problems that new legal and illegal immigrants such as Mexican nationals might face.

Since Texas won its independence, generations of Valley Anglos, although numbering less than 15 percent of the total population, have supported and participated in a two-tiered system denying equal rights to Mexican Americans in education, health, jobs, housing, and the political arena.[10] In the early 1970s the balance of power finally shifted from the hands of the dominant Anglo minority to the Hispanic majority. While the old, affluent Anglo families still possessed a disproportionate amount of wealth and power, they increasingly contended with new generations of affluent and well-educated Mexican Americans and were subsequently forced to position themselves in a predominantly Hispanic society.

Racism at the McAllen Station could perhaps best be compared to racism in the American military. While racism in the Border Patrol had once exerted maximum control over human behavior, it was now one among many factors that might influence behavior. This racism was tempered by the subculture of agents, the power of law, the values of the community, and other structural factors that diminished it.

I ran into Noe Escondido at the McAllen airport on the night of January 2, 2002. Because I had been on vacation and before that had been busy with finals at the university, it had been more than five weeks since I had gone on patrol with the agents at the McAllen Station. Noe looked pleased to see me in the holiday crowd, as if he could not wait to share news. As he talked he and his partner, a new recruit, eyed those around us like hawks a covey of quail.

He told me, "You're not going to believe what's happening at the station. It's getting crazy."

"What do you mean?" I asked, puzzled.

Noe looked around, then pulled closer to me so that only I could hear what he said. "It's getting really crazy. They've got us so that it's wide open out there." Then he looked at me in a funny way. I thought about his look, previously unfamiliar to me, for several days but was only later able to interpret its meaning. Noe Escondido, the best agent at the McAllen Station, was disgusted with the organization to which he had devoted his life.

A week later, hoping to find a familiar face, I stared at the agents at the McAllen Station's two o'clock muster. There were so many new recruits that at first I felt as if all the men and women at whose side I had been working for the last eighteen months had been replaced by a roomful of imposters. Finally I recognized Roberta Alanis, leaning against the back wall, then Herman Morningside, talking with another agent at the second row of tables. As I continued to scan the room a few other friendly faces nodded in my direction. At the front of the room the new field operation supervisor, the replacement for Jose Monteverde, ran the muster.

One of the supes read the shift assignments. When I totaled the assignments I was astonished that 75 percent or less of the banks of the Rio Grande would be covered by agents. A significant proportion of them were assigned to fixed positions, X's, at the ports of entry and sleepy little Los Ebanos Ferry. I looked around the room a second time, counted the agents on the shift, then looked at the assignment sheet lying on the table in front of me. With only thirty-nine agents at muster they could not possibly cover forty-five miles of river, especially when a third of the force was tied to hard X's. Hard X's had required agents to stay virtually inside their vehicles in a fixed position while soft X's had allowed them greater freedom to investigate and to pursue.

Noe was right. Any *coyote* now had his pick of landings for his human cargo. Miles and miles of riverbanks were no longer regularly patrolled by agents. Drug smugglers could easily cross their loads at a hundred different spots. Given the supe's assignments, a long stretch of river on the far west side lay wide open to *coyotes* and *narcotraficantes,* because by the time agents could reach the sensors in these spots, new illegal immigrants or bricks of cocaine and marijuana would already be headed north.

While management at the McAllen Station was intentionally vague about the exact turnover rate in agents since September 11, so many McAllen agents had departed for the Air Marshals and other federal agencies that there were not enough men and women to patrol the line adequately. Even if management assigned all the available agents in the field to soft X's, they could not cover the miles and miles of twisting river.

And so with little fanfare the "Bubble," son of the soft X, grandson of the X, was born.

Bubbles, along with the demise of the widely despised fourth shift, were bureaucratic quick fixes to the high turnover of agents that was not, at least officially, occurring. Regardless of the official discourse, daily operations had changed dramatically. Were Bubbles the result of a new management vision? Was the force of reason overwhelming the decision-makers as agents like Noe Escondido, recently promoted to supe, voiced their concerns?

Managers were typically tight-lipped, pretending that nothing unusual had transpired. Agents only knew that they were being asked to patrol the border between Hidalgo County, Texas, and the Mexican state of Tamaulipas in a brand-new way called Bubbles. An outsider studying the McAllen Station would have had little reason to suspect any notable changes. However, I had been studying this group of agents for more than a year; the changes within this context were both obvious and enormous.

The Substance of Chaos

If management was silent about Bubbles, it had to be in part because of profoundly embarrassing events that could not be easily explained under the existing policies and guidelines of Operation Rio Grande, X's, and soft X's. Agents in the field knew that illegal workers were crossing the Rio Grande in numbers at least as great as those prior to September 11 even though these statistics never made it into the reports. Drug traffic, in a similar fashion, had also substantially increased. The material evidence of increases in human and drug traffic at landings all along the river could not be denied. Take Sector 306 for example. The piles of garbage at this popular landing did not disappear in the winter and spring of 2002 in spite of Border Patrol statistics suggesting otherwise. Only now, with the patrol at 75 percent, more illegal aliens than usual were able to avoid apprehension as they made their way northward.

Agents were confiscating more drugs than in the past, but even these statistics masked a harsher truth. More drugs were being crossed, but even greater quantities were reaching drug users throughout the United States. The good news was that because of tips, surveillance, and intel tons of marijuana and cocaine were stopped at the border. The bad news, which only agents in the field seemed willing to admit, was that huge amounts of drugs were being transported across the border and getting past the Border Patrol and other law enforcers. The men and women in the field saw the evidence: the flattened grass where the drugs had been off-loaded from boats and rafts, the pungent smell of marijuana, the footprints, and the tire tracks leading to Old Military Highway. The *narcotraficantes* were beating the Border Patrol badly in the winter months of 2002.

One arrest that escaped the public's attention was symptomatic of the deteriorating situation along the Rio Grande in Deep South Texas. Border Patrol checkpoints at Sarita and Falfurrias in Deep South Texas were the last defense against both illegal aliens and illegal drugs. In the early morning hours of February 17, 2002, the Border Patrol pulled over a vehicle traveling north of the checkpoint at Falfurrias. The vehicle, which had already cleared the checkpoint, slowed for a bailout. Luckily no one was hurt when the driver and passengers jumped from the car before it came to a complete stop along the highway.

"We pulled the vehicle over to the side of the road, and everybody ran. Six people were apprehended, and it is unknown if anybody else escaped."[11] Two of the young men captured were Mexicans. Two of the others, however, were from Afghanistan, and a third was a Pakistani.

"Agents said they do not know if any of the detainees have terrorist connections, but they suspect they do not."[12]

Questions never posed were more disquieting: How did two Afghans and one Pakistani illegally cross the Rio Grande and circumvent the Falfurrias checkpoint just six months after the most lethal terrorist attack against the United States? At a time when the U.S. military was on the brink of war against Al-Qaeda and the Taliban in Kabul, what were these citizens from Afghanistan and Pakistan doing in a car headed toward the interior of Texas? How many other Afghans and Pakistanis had already escaped detection? Were these undocumented workers looking for higher-paying jobs, or were they connected to terrorists?

Though these arrests clearly suggested that our Mexican border was no more secure from potential terrorists than our Canadian border, neither the Border Patrol nor the public responded with alarm. A defensive strategy based upon deterrence theory, Bubbles as concocted by the Border Patrol was intended to seal our borders from terrorists, immigrants in search of low-wage work, and drug smugglers.

How did Bubbles really work? The forty-five miles of the Rio Grande were covered during the daylight hours by single agents assigned to fixed, specific positions. There were fewer holes in the line, at least in theory, because agents were assigned larger areas to cover than when doing soft X's. However, in order to cover the banks of the Rio Grande with fewer men and women, something had to give. The fifteen to twenty miles in the far western part of Hidalgo County was left virtually unpatrolled, a lack of foresight that enraged senior agents. "Rovers" covered these gaps between Bubbles, but the rovers could not reach the sensors fast enough to stem the tide of immigrants, drugs, or citizens of Afghanistan and Pakistan.

Before September 11, during the era of hard and soft X's, agents of the McAllen Station patrolled approximately twenty-three specifically named areas. These assignments did not include transport/identification, airport duty, bike patrol, horse patrol, and boat patrol. After the new assignments, approximately twenty-seven areas were patrolled.[13] Agents were initially enthusiastic about Bubbles in part because at the same time that Bubbles were unveiled, the fourth shift was quietly eliminated. The controversial shift, from 5 P.M. to 3 A.M., freed one entire unit, 25 percent of all agents at the McAllen Station, to cover the Rio Grande. No written explanation was provided for the elimination of the extra fourth shift. Mourned by few agents, the fourth shift disappeared with nary a whimper.

A new strategy that sounded meritorious around a table staffed by management sipping their morning station coffee, Bubbles did not necessarily make rational sense in the field. As agents worked their Bubbles, problems quickly emerged. The biggest potential problem was that agents were now left to themselves during the daylight hours to patrol the line. When hearing that a sensor had been hit or upon observing aliens or discovering sign, in practice agents were forced to investigate by themselves. Normal procedure for a two-agent unit responding to a sensor was to place one agent behind the new immigrants; the other, in front. This minimized the chances of the aliens' escaping or being forced back to the banks of the Rio Grande, where they might come to some harm.

"Look at it this way," said one agent. "What exactly am I supposed to do if I see a group of twenty illegals coming at me? You know a bunch of them are going to run when they see me. Who's going to back me up if there's trouble?"

Agents also were less likely to leave the safety of their vehicles even though they were now encouraged by management to do so. New recruits never experienced patrolling the line in the traditional manner prior to Operation Rio Grande. Now as they worked Bubbles by themselves they were even less motivated to tackle a group of illegal workers. Agents working Bubbles were far from backup and medical aide should it be required.

"Be real," said one agent. "You're going to take fewer risks."

The logistical and social dimensions of Bubbles were problematic. Agents of the McAllen Station, especially those from other regions of the United States who were without their families, were already socially isolated from the larger community outside the walls of the station. Spending ten hours alone in an Expedition patrolling the line did not contribute to solidarity among or between agents. For agents who already tended to become disengaged from the usual routines of the rest of the working public and the community, the social isolation at work was an additional aggravation.

Having another agent upon which to depend, confide, and rely was a humanizing experience at the McAllen Station. Partners at the same time could potentially provide another barrier to antisocial or violent behavior. Partners watched other partners, observed, commented, controlled through a variety of reinforcing techniques that could set boundaries and limits for unacceptable behavior ranging from the trivial to the unacceptable. It was one thing, for example, for a partner to look the other way when a new recruit on probation needed a few hours' sleep during mids because he or she faced a tough exam on immigration law the next morning. But partners could also, especially if they were bros and good friends, offer advice, listen to family problems, and serve as a sounding board for any normal resentment an agent might feel toward their employer, undocumented workers, or drug traffickers. If an unsympathetic bro rode shotgun, then perhaps the next shift would bring a different agent more willing to listen and be supportive. Partners served as the representatives of the professional values and standards of the Border Patrol. Opportunities to do the wrong thing at the wrong time geometrically increased when the professional judgment and behavior of one agent under stress and great personal risk was not buffered by another.

Hard X's, soft X's, and Bubbles, all based upon the problematic foundation of the deterrence of human behavior, were equally inadequate against the tide of illegal drugs that flowed through South Texas to major markets throughout the United States.[14] Bubbles were ineffective against illegal drugs because, like the previous strategies employed by the Border Patrol, the policy failed to understand or respond to the methods and attitudes of organized traffickers highly motivated by profit. The Border Patrol strategy remained immersed in a questionable paradigm that was perhaps most effective in catching criminal operators with limited resources. *Narcotraficantes* such as the notorious Gulf Cartel, in contrast, ran billion-dollar-a-year businesses that were cost effective, opportunistic and, unlike the Border Patrol, highly responsive to change.

The typical smuggler who supervised the transportation of drugs across the waters of the Rio Grande was a small part of a very large operation.[15] The typical smuggler, or *pasador,* was an expendable cog in a relatively sophisticated organization structure. If he were caught, injured, or killed, the smuggling cartel rolled on without him. It did not matter, regardless of the publicity, if specific smugglers or families of smugglers were apprehended by the Border Patrol or the DEA because the supply of potential *pasadores* was unlimited. For many small border communities on the south side of the Rio Grande, as on the north side, smuggling had been a prime occupation for more than a century. Many, many young men were willing to work as either *pasadores* or mules, referred to by smugglers themselves as *morraleros* or *burreros.*

Drugs transported to the border in Deep South Texas were dispensed and distributed from Monterrey, one of the largest cities in Mexico. They were shipped to Reynosa on the backs of trucks hidden among the produce, or in tankers carrying gasoline or, much less often, asphalt. Although these commercial trucks had to pass at least one Mexican government checkpoint between Monterrey and Reynosa, they were not searched, because the Mexican military was bribed to look the other way. According to one informant, sometimes these shipments were not even disguised by smugglers, another measure of the control that the *narcotraficantes* exerted over the military and the other branches of the Mexican police. In fact Mexican *federales* were even known to escort these trucks to the northern border of Mexico.

Symptomatic of the political power of the Mexican drug cartels, particularly the Gulf Cartel, was the fact that Mexican officials rarely confiscated illegal drug shipments either when the drugs were imported from outside Mexico or when they were being stored in Mexican warehouses before being transported to the American border. Mexican trucks, which might carry from five to ten tons of marijuana in one haul, regularly lumbered with impunity along the toll road from Monterrey to Reynosa. Shipments of up to one ton or more of cocaine were common. Off-loaded at warehouses in Reynosa, the drugs were then quickly separated into smaller shipments and transported from the central warehouse to "security houses."[16] Mexican police frequently guarded the central warehouse against bandits and drug competitors while the drugs were *enfriadas,* cooled down, before being moved again. At the security houses the drugs were weighed again, and the numbered bricks were placed in numbered *morrales,* sacks. The sacks of drugs weighed from sixty to one hundred pounds or more.

Only paid if the illegal drugs reached the safe houses on the north side of the river, the *morraleros* or *burreros* commonly received $400 to $500 for their efforts. If because of their actions the drugs disappeared into the waters of the Río Bravo, or into the arms of the Border Patrol or the DEA, or the drugs were hidden but lost in the dense brush, these men received nothing for their efforts and labor. These men were motivated to complete their work regardless of potential dangers awaiting them. They were never going to be deterred. They would simply try again another time with another load; a $400 payoff was huge when workers in Reynosa frequently earned less than $7 a day.

In a similar fashion the *pasador* would rarely be deterred from completing his work. If by bad luck the drug load was confiscated by the Border Patrol, he received nothing, but if successful he earned $45 to $50 per pound of marijuana crossed to the safe house.

It was the job of the *pasador* to direct the *morraleros* to the exact crossing point, *el punto rojo,* the red point. The *pasador* determined *el punto rojo* after he had negotiated an agreement with the farmer who owned the land fronting the Río Bravo. The *pasador* approached the landowner, sometimes referred to as the "mediator," with a bribe of $1,000 to $2,000 to use his land as *el punto rojo.* The mediator owned and worked his land, so he naturally knew the best places to access and cross the river. In fact, he and his family may have smuggled drugs or other goods across the Río Bravo in the past. The mediator identified *el punto rojo,* gave the *pasador* specific directions to the location, then left the fence gates to his land unlocked so that the smugglers could pass through easily with their load.

The mediator also bribed the Mexican soldiers, commonly offering the soldiers 40,000 pesos, equivalent to $400. The mediator rarely bribed the army officers because they were much more honest than their conscripts. Instead, he would target a sergeant who was in direct command of a platoon. Mexican soldiers, drafted from various regions of Mexico, were young, often less than eighteen years of age, poor, inexperienced, and uneducated. After providing them perfunctory military training with minimal equipment, officers unceremoniously dropped them by the banks of the Río Bravo with orders to patrol the area for months at a time.

In turn the ill-trained soldiers received meager weekly rations of water, eggs, and tortillas while they patrolled the Río Bravo. Much of the time the sergeant left them to their own diversions. Far from their real homes, isolated from even the small villages and towns that dotted the area, these men possessed little ambition, motivation, or expertise. Most counted the days and nights until their lieutenant picked them up in the Humvee. However, they did not know when this day or week would come. When the heat became oppressive, they bathed in the Río Bravo. Out of boredom they occasionally talked with the local people who lived and worked along the river. One day they were bivouacked by the river; the next, they were gone and replacements just like them were on patrol.

The Substance of Chaos

All these soldiers possessed were rifles, basic camping gear, and the uniforms on their backs. They were not even given field radios to communicate with each other while on patrol. Only their sergeant had a radio. Sometimes these young Mexican soldiers fell into trouble. For example, one time a platoon got drunk on beer they had bought from a farmer. They then hitched a ride to Ordáz, where they chased the local women around the small plaza until confronted by the town police. A fist fight broke out between the soldiers and the police.

As they patrolled the banks of the Río Bravo, the sergeants and their soldiers met the farmers working their fields. Sometimes when they took a few hours off to fish along the banks of the Río Bravo they also saw the farmers at work. The soldiers also saw new workers waiting to cross, commercial fishermen, and other entrepreneurs who made their living, some legally and some not, along the banks of the Río Bravo.

To replace their tasteless rations the soldiers bought from the farmers food, along with beer and far less often drugs. When approached by the mediator, whom they might have come to know quite well during their days and nights along the river, they did not refuse "work." More rarely an ambitious sergeant would approach a farmer and ask for "work."

The sergeant and his soldiers were expendable. If caught by Mexican authorities, they would soon be replaced by others who would find themselves in identical circumstances. Like everyone else, the soldiers were paid only if the drugs successfully reached a safe house on the north side of the river. Like other new immigrants to the United States who sent hard-earned money back to their family and relatives in the form of remittances, the soldiers frequently had the mediator wire their money to relatives in their hometowns. In this way the soldiers, when ordered by their commanding officer to strip and to empty their pockets before returning to their base, were never found hiding wads of pesos earned from their drug work. Officers beat soldiers found with pesos. The officers knew that if their soldiers had money, it had to have come from the *narcotraficantes.*

At a time of the *pasador's* choosing, when the soldiers had either left the area around *el punto rojo* or stood guard to make sure the drugs were not intercepted by border bandits or other Mexican law enforcers, the scouts, called *campañas,* or bells, were positioned. These men, frequently trusted cousins or other relatives of the *pasador,* were paid at the same rate as the *morraleros.*

The *campañas* hid amidst the terrain or waited in cars alongside Old Military Highway to warn of any unwanted intervention on either side of the river. They were also just as likely to take a seat in the front yard of the many small houses that bordered Old Military Highway and offered a view of the agents as they motored by. At the hour of reckoning *campañas* closely observed agents who were assigned the area covering *el punto rojo* from the time they left the McAllen Station to when they arrived to patrol the bank of the river. The drug smugglers referred to the agents as *perreras,* female dogs, or *vaquitas lechera,* dairy cows, or *limones,* lemons.[17] *Campañas* also covered the highway from Ciudad Miguel Alemán to Reynosa along which soldiers might come who had not been bribed by the cartel.

The *pasador* waited for the time, "*Cuando se duerma el gallo, ahí mero,*" loosely translated as "when the rooster sleeps, then go for it." The *pasador* was always someone capable of waiting for the exact time when the *limones* were not patrolling the landing where the drugs would be crossed. When the Border Patrol targeted certain landings along the Rio Grande with teams of special operatives for days or weeks at a time, the drug smugglers shut down their operations in these areas until the agents left. The Border Patrol always, at some point, packed up and went home. A *pasador* had to be patient.

As the mules hid in the tree line or the grasses on the south side of the Rio Grande, and the *campañas* radioed in code the exact location of the agents, the *pasador,* monitoring his radio, waited to give the orders to cross. According to one informant, former agents of the Border Patrol sometimes aided *el pasador* by monitoring communication between agents as they patrolled the line. This same informant recounted that it was not difficult to purchase maps that identified the specific sites of the Border Patrol sensors.[18]

The smuggler's biggest problem was *la mosca,* the fly, the Border Patrol helicopter. *La mosca* could suddenly appear and be on top of the smugglers before their scouts spotted it. The smugglers feared *la mosca* and did everything within their control to avoid it. The slightest indication that *la mosca* was in the air could put the operation on hold for hours until the *campañas* reported that the aircraft was back in its hangar or refueling. The *pasador* knew that the Border Patrol frequently flew only one helicopter at a time; when that helicopter was grounded for refueling, no other helicopters were on patrol in that area. The smugglers waited as long as was necessary for *el punto rojo* to be clear of any Border Patrol agents and *la mosca.*[19]

The Substance of Chaos

The drug smugglers gave code names to all the landings along the Río Bravo. The landing adjacent to the Los Ebanos Ferry was named La Chalupa. When the landing was finally determined to be clear of *la mosca* and agents, the smugglers carried two ropes tied to an immovable object on the banks of the Río Bravo and tied them to trees on the northern banks of the Rio Grande. After filling inflatable boats with air from metal tanks transported to the banks of the Río Bravo by the *morraleros,* they placed the sacks of drugs into the boats. Then they used the two ropes to pull and guide the inflatable boats across the river. As one boat was being pulled across the Río Bravo, the smugglers unloaded another and sent it on its way back across the river. In a matter of thirty minutes or less a load of drugs possibly exceeding one ton was transported to the banks of the Rio Grande, where the *morraleros* shouldered the loads and then carried them to waiting pickups or vans. If at this point agents were spotted, the loads might be hidden in the brush to be picked up later. A powerful motor boat was sometimes used in place of the inflatable rafts.

If their *campañas* warned that *la mosca* or agents were nearby, the *pasador* likely halted the entire operation and cut the ropes across the river. The smugglers hid in the cane and the brush until it was safe to continue. Once they had loaded the drug vehicles, the smugglers sped to safe houses in the small communities and towns that lined the northern banks of the Rio Grande. Here again the drugs were cooled down, *enfriadas,* for a few days before being transported to Edinburg or other Valley cities after they were counted and weighed yet again. The majority of the drugs were placed in hidden compartments on eighteen-wheelers that, more times than not, passed easily through the final Border Patrol checkpoints at Falfurrias and Sarita.

One informant claimed that the drug smugglers owned sniffer dogs that had undergone the same training as those of the Border Patrol. If one of these dogs smelled the drugs hidden aboard a tractor-trailer rig, the contraband was removed, repacked, and hidden again until the sniffer dog could no longer detect it. Estimations of the amounts of drugs transported on a weekly basis from the south side of the Río Bravo to the north side of the Rio Grande varied greatly; however, most agreed that ten tons of illegal drugs was not an unreasonable figure along this section of the river.[20]

Agents at the McAllen Station devoted much of their time and effort to drug interdiction. Agents who interdicted loads were highly praised by other agents and by management, who gave those agents higher annual evaluations.

But in many ways this effort was both impractical and a consummate waste of time. Although this section of the Rio Grande in Deep South Texas was particularly infested with drug smugglers, who crossed their product at hundreds of different landings, drugs illegally transported across the Rio Grande, according to the DEA's own estimates, accounted for just 15 percent of all illegal drugs entering the United States from the south. The majority of illegal drugs entered the southern border through the ports of entry in commercial trucks and other vehicles.[21]

These drugs were hidden in tractor-trailers among legitimate products manufactured in Mexico or points south that were allowed legal entry under the terms of NAFTA. Given the large number of trucks entering the United States along the Mexican border as well as the limited resources of U.S. Customs, it was extremely difficult to screen even a small percentage of the thousands of trucks that daily crossed the bridges spanning the Rio Grande.[22]

Drug smugglers became anxious if their product began to rot in warehouses or safe houses. When that happened, they lost money. Smugglers intent on crossing their loads between the bridges knew that eventually the Americans always ended their surveillance. *La mosca* was a hindrance but not an impossible impediment. Professional smuggling organizations were not fearful of or deterred by the Border Patrol's Operation Rio Grande. Not only were these criminal groups highly successful at crossing illegal drugs between the bridges across the Rio Grande, they were even more successful crossing drugs at the American ports of entry. The smugglers expressed their indifference toward the Border Patrol and other federal agencies even in the words they chose to describe the agents as well as their green patrol vehicles. The *narcotraficantes* referred to the green trucks of the agents of the U.S. Border Patrol as *pericos*. *Pericos* was Spanish for parakeets.

Operation Rio Grande was, at the same time, a bonanza for the small-time smugglers of illegal aliens as well as professional criminal organizations. The price to guide an undocumented worker across the Río Bravo had exploded to $300 per head since the Border Patrol placed most of its resources in plain sight along the river to deter aliens. The Border Patrol was a wonderful form of advertisement for small-timers like Nature Boy at the Reynosa Bridge and Fat Man at Anzalduas Park. If potential customers balked at the price, a *coyote* could just point across the river to the parked *pericos*. Who could haggle about price when they saw the Border Patrol units lit up like Christmas trees?

The Substance of Chaos

Stories of drownings, robberies, and rapes detailed how much more dangerous it was to cross the Río Bravo since the initiation of Operation Rio Grande. Others died attempting to circumvent the checkpoints at Falfurrias and Sarita without benefit of a guide.[23] Only fools crossed without a *coyote* who knew when and how to avoid the border guards and, after passing the interior checkpoints, could safely lead illegal immigrants to their final destination.

The *coyotes* often found their customers at the bus station in Reynosa, the city plaza, or on the banks of the Río Bravo. Climbing down the steps of the sleek Mexican buses—more than ten Mexican bus lines terminated at the Reynosa bus station—first-time workers could arrive bewildered in an unknown border city. An experienced *coyote* spotted these would-be immigrants in a second, then approached as he seasoned his sales pitch with stories of the perils of crossing without someone who knew the intricacies of the Río Bravo.

If newcomers still hesitated at the price, the *coyote* might throw in gruesome tales of the U.S. Border Patrol, tales already supported by stories in Mexican newspapers and scenarios documented in Mexican movies and songs. Injecting a scare into the undocumented workers ensured not only loyalty—new immigrants never revealed the names of their guides when apprehended by agents—but faith and trust. Unfortunately an unfailing belief in a *coyote* could directly lead to personal tragedy and death.[24]

The *coyotes* knew when the waters were high and the currents dangerous in the Río Bravo, when the dam at Falcon had released waters and when the flow was steady, the location of sandbars that could provide a delicate path into the river, and where sensors were buried on the northern banks. Although exceptional because he worked in the nude, Nature Boy was typical of the *coyotes* because he knew the crossings, worked as often as he desired, and was virtually unstoppable.

Even when identified by agents with the help of the scope truck or NVGs, the *coyote* rarely was charged if apprehended. I frequently observed *coyotes* guiding groups of aliens across the border. When agents confronted the groups, the *coyote* ran for the Rio Grande. Abandoning illegal workers to flail wildly in the brush and cactus showed that *coyotes* cared only about their personal welfare. If by chance he was captured, none of his clients would testify against him even if offered a temporary visa as an inducement. Rarely prosecuted, at the worst a Mexican *coyote* was VRed with the rest of the aliens to the Reynosa Bridge.

Coyotes of course knew the law. Being caught smuggling five or more undocumented workers across the river was a felony charge. A felony translated into real jail time and a record on the computer. Second-time offenders might face a stiffer sentence if convicted. So the smart *coyotes* always transported four or fewer illegal aliens. If caught, they would only be charged with a misdemeanor, carrying with it a modest fine. At $300 a customer, paying a small fine was simply part of the overhead of doing business on the river. And if by dumb luck a *coyote* ended up in the county jail, hundreds of other *coyotes* would soon steal his business. Along the banks of the Rio Grande there was never a shortage of *coyotes.*

The fact was, especially now that the big cartels had cornered most of the drug business, people could make a ton of money smuggling humans with one-hundredth the personal risk. Why should people work as *muleros* hauling eighty-pound bags of marijuana on their backs in the dead of night when the life of *coyotes* was so much easier, safer, and rewarding? One proof of the advantages of smuggling humans over illegal drugs was that *muleros* often drank or smoked to provide themselves the *cojones,* balls, to carry out their mission. *Coyotes* were much more likely to work sober. They waived the extra confidence provided by a bottle or a joint.[25]

Small-time smugglers transported their human cargo across the Río Bravo in inner tubes or a small boat, then guided them to safe houses. Located in the same small towns harboring illegal drugs, the safe houses boarded new workers for a day or more before a car or van transported them north. Exhausted from their journeys, the illegal workers slept and talked while waiting for rides.

At the HEB grocery stores in McAllen *coyotes* who lived on the north side of the Rio Grande filled their carts with large quantities of plastic water bottles along with big cans of frijoles and packages of corn tortillas. Sometimes they also bought their customers beer. The *coyotes* did not try to disguise their purchases at HEB, although many shoppers and grocery clerks recognized what they were doing. The neighbors of *coyotes* often knew too but kept quiet. In one of the poorest areas of the nation, smuggling aliens was a good-paying job.

After a day or two in a safe house, illegal aliens were dropped off several miles south of the checkpoints at Sarita or Falfurrias, given directions along with maps, supplies, and cell phones, then picked up several miles north of the checkpoints at a specific spot and time. It was simple enough to circumvent the checkpoints where the agents of the U.S. Border Patrol stopped traffic to check for illegal aliens and drugs. It was only necessary to follow one of the many trails heading north. It might take a few hours or more to hike the trails, but with water and food it was easy enough to dive into the brush on the south side of Sarita and emerge on the north side of the checkpoint far from the sight of the Border Patrol. Along the way the newest of immigrants passed evidence of the thousands who had preceded them: discarded water bottles, plastic bags bearing various logos of Valley-made tortillas, old clothes, green garbage bags that once carried a change of clothes, and beer cans. Some illegal aliens did not receive adequate guidance, took a wrong turn on the trail, became lost and confused in the heat, or chose to go it alone without directions. Occasionally their remains were discovered by hunters or agents near Falfurrias or Sarita.[26]

Professional smuggling operations were at a level of organization and expertise as far removed from Nature Boy and Fat Man as the heads of the drug cartels were from the rank amateurs who smuggled one or two bricks of marijuana. To catch these professional smugglers the Border Patrol in Deep South Texas operated the Anti-Smuggling Unit. The ASU was specially designed to identify, investigate, and prosecute big-time, transnational smugglers. These crime organizations rapidly sprouted when Operation Rio Grande was initiated in the late 1990s. There was little reason for organized crime to bother with smuggling humans when any idiot like Nature Boy could turn a decent profit from guiding small groups across the Río Bravo for $50 to $75 a head. But when deterrence was initiated along the border, human smuggling became much more attractive to criminal venture capitalists capable of organizing complex, multinational organizations. If Nature Boy or Fat Man could charge $300 a pop on the open market, then the price for transporting an illegal immigrant from El Salvador to Houston was no longer chump change.[27]

One busy international smuggling organization identified and recruited illegal workers in Brazil, brought the Brazilians to the U.S.-Mexican border, crossed them, then transported them to destinations throughout the United States. For this service they charged the illegal Brazilian workers $16,000 per head. The smugglers guaranteed the trip. Aliens arrested by the Border Patrol in the United States were immediately bonded out by a bonding company that guaranteed full payment to the INS should their clients fail to appear at their hearings. None of the aliens smuggled in by this criminal organization ever appeared at their immigration hearings; they had found work and did not want to risk deportation by appearing before an INS judge.

The INS periodically demanded the bonding company to pay for legally defaulting on the bonds when their clients skipped court. The bonding company in turn informed the INS through its attorney that it did not have the full price of the bonds because it was on the verge of bankruptcy from so many defaults. Instead the company offered the INS a few cents on the dollar for each defaulted bond. The INS repeatedly accepted this pittance from the bonding company. The criminal organization, which included the bonding company, earned tremendous profits from charging $16,000 per head, profits by no means offset by overhead, including partial repayment of the defaulted bonds.

The new Brazilian immigrants rarely could afford the $16,000 required up front by this crime organization. The illegal Brazilians paid the balance of the money they owed to the smugglers by making weekly payments from their new jobs in the United States. If they failed to pay, the bonding company threatened to contact the Border Patrol.

While this transnational criminal operation may sound rather crude, one informant reported at least seven others just like it were currently working in the United States. This same informant believed that both the Border Patrol and the INS were aware of these organizations, but technicalities in immigration law along with internecine wars between federal agencies allowed these criminal groups to operate with impunity.

The ASU had its own problems. Staffed by experienced, older agents selected especially for this duty by their supes, these senior law officers were provided additional resources about which agents like Gester could only dream. But the ASU was no crack team of highly motivated investigators; rather, it was populated by over-the-hill agents lacking training and motivation to take advantage of the extra resources with which they had been provided. In effect the ASU served as prize duty for agents approaching the end of their careers in the Border Patrol, men who were rewarded by management for currying favors rather than demonstrating ability and motivation to bust professional smuggling organizations. As a rule it was not the Rambos at the McAllen Station who ended up at ASU; it was the brown-nosers looking at a few more years until they retired with a pension.

The Substance of Chaos

One informant stated bluntly: "They come in late to work, spend time with their girlfriends, drink coffee, check out a few cases, then go home." The rare Rambo who made it into the ASU was cautioned to tone down his enthusiasm and was viewed as a rate buster. With little direct supervision or leadership, limited special skills, and no motivation, the ASU was a good idea run amok in a stilted system of rewards and punishments.

The ASU did make busts. In spring 2002, for example, Operation Dark Shadow led to the sentencing of 10 smugglers convicted of transporting illegal aliens for two years from Brazil to California, Florida, and New York by way of Deep South Texas.[28] "The group is believed to have smuggled up to 100 Brazilians a week."[29] But these smugglers were not part of the management structure and would soon be easily replaced. This criminal organization was not destroyed by Operation Dark Shadow; its crimes and profits were just temporarily disrupted.

From the desks of the managers at the U.S. Border Patrol McAllen Station on Old Military Highway the work of patrol agents was an amalgam of complex forms, memos, policies, weekly and monthly reports, and more forms situated within the context of fragmented radio communications from the field. The supes knew much about their seasoned agents but found it increasingly difficult to keep up with new agents who were transferring to the McAllen Station. Few managers, all of whom had risen through the ranks, still remembered the day-to-day problems they had faced patrolling the line. Fewer still had significant experience on line watch since Operation Rio Grande was initiated or since the events of September 11.

While management argued in public that Operation Rio Grande was a sound and sane policy, some in private voiced serious doubts about the sanctity and credibility of deterrence. New recruits direct from training at the academy soon discovered the wicked truth: the strategy of hard X's, soft X's, and Bubbles, buttressed by the logistics of Operation Rio Grande and the conceptual paradigm of deterrence, did not function well in Deep South Texas.

Only a few miles from the McAllen Station, the banks of the Rio Grande were a different world than the one envisioned by those who initiated Operation Rio Grande with the intent of stemming the flow of illegal immigration and drugs. Confronted by this human conundrum, their bureaucratic rhetoric, order, logistics, and objectives made little sense. Bubbles were doomed to failure even as other adjustments to deterrence theory had failed. None of these strategies accounted for, accommodated, or recognized the hierarchal organizational structure embedded in the criminal drug culture and human smuggling, including the transnational individual and institutional motivations that fueled these same activities.

The Border Patrol, and to some degree other federal law enforcement agencies in Deep South Texas, for the most part focused on arresting individuals who stood at the bottom of the criminal cartels and were of no importance to the maintenance and future of the organizations. Thousands of replacements on both sides of the Rio Grande stood ready to accept an offer of $400 to transport illegal drugs or to pocket $300 a head to direct a new immigrant to the promised land. The Border Patrol's ASU, adrift in its own sea of dysfunctions, was not successful in attacking the head of human smuggling organizations. Even the arrest of drug kingpins did nothing but generate power vacuums among the drug cartels. Subsequent turf battles were a danger to the public. Relative peace between cartels signified that the river of illegal drugs had resumed its flow.

Managers at the McAllen Station acted as if the War on Drugs and an undeclared War on Human Smugglers were winnable wars. Yet they lacked a comprehensive understanding of the rudimentary operations of organized drug and alien smuggling, were committed to an ineffective strategy that demoralized agents, and were somewhat burdened by convoluted manipulations of their own in-house statistics. Agents in the field realized that both wars were over, and the Border Patrol had lost.

At ground zero the banks of the Rio Grande in Deep South Texas were an elusive carnival of humanity. A partial list included bailouts, fresh tube, Benny *el elefantino,* armed, bored, and bribed M&Ms, Nature Boy, gotaways and turnbacks, cannibals, weary immigrants intent on wiring back remittances to their families, Waylon and Willie, and many, many more.

The banks were populated, each in their season, by those who bartered avocados from the back of their ancient bikes, professional prostitutes, and unattended livestock. Smugglers of frozen chickens by the ton found their way to these same riverbanks, along with gun smugglers and those who traded in tractor-trailer loads of *ropa usada,* leather boots, electrical products, and anything else that American, Mexican, and Central American consumers might demand.

The Substance of Chaos

Regulation and control of this sideshow was ephemeral. If there were any ringmasters, they were the kingpins of the drug cartels, not agents of the U.S. Border Patrol or any other law enforcement agency.

The criminal carnival certainly did not resemble the international border envisioned by NAFTA policy makers entrusted by the American public in 1994 to fashion and hone international laws governing the trade of goods. This was a world along the U.S.-Mexico border that few observed from political junkets; reporters with exacting deadlines rarely spent more than a few hours on the line. Goods and services under NAFTA were transported across the Mexican border in Deep South Texas in remarkable order and sense after being manufactured, assembled, priced, packaged, and weighed.[30] But NAFTA did little to curtail the number of illegal aliens who hired *coyotes* to help them cross the Río Bravo.[31] And the increase in the number of trucks from Mexico into Deep South Texas served to facilitate the flow of illegal drugs.

Agents were forced to practice their law enforcement craft of patrolling the line within, and bound by, this substance of chaos.

Charged with enforcing drug and immigration laws virtually impossible to enforce, agents' own human flaws further hindered their performance in the field. Racism was not unknown, nor discrimination based upon gender and class, nor small acts of senseless violence, nor the lure of easy money from the drug lords. Working ten-hour shifts day after day, night after night, taking home their paychecks at the end of each two-week pay period, these men and women lived out their lives in communities that disdained them.

There was, then, not just the problem of the "bad apples" unfortunately found in every facet of law enforcement. The bureaucracy of the Border Patrol was rigid, inflexible, and prone to penalizing those who demonstrated initiative and motivation. Organizational values and attitudes embodied in management practices burdened the agents with additional restraints. Microstructural and cultural factors situated within the McAllen Station and its environs, in combination with macrostructural and cultural variables from without, all served to constrain agents severely in their job performance.

It was equally fair to say that the performance of these men and women, when considered over a two-year period of time, was in many ways exemplary. These agents frequently faced outlandish and sometimes highly dangerous predicaments and generally maintained their personal integrity and upheld their federal oath as enforcers of public law. Even as some agents lost, at least temporarily, their moral path or foundered in their close human relationships, others managed to retain a sense of sanity, even humor, about their work as they patrolled the line from one shift to the next.

The events of September 11 drew the INS, along with the U.S. Border Patrol, into the national spotlight, where, under intense scrutiny, some of the immediate problems in the INS and the Border Patrol became all too evident. The public's understanding of the depth of INS's vast inadequacies heightened after the INS mailed visas to two of the dead terrorists responsible for the disaster. Subsequent failings of the INS emerged under a critical public eye.

And what of international terrorism? If every year drug smugglers could transport hundreds of tons of illegal drugs across the Rio Grande, if every year thousands and thousands of new workers made this same journey, if a three-ton elephant named Benny could work in Houston one day and Mexico City soon after, it was reasonable to conclude that motivated international terrorists might easily make their way to Mexico and into Deep South Texas with relative impunity.

In spite of all this, these men and women of the U.S. Border Patrol rose every day from their beds, dressed in their pressed green uniforms, and drove to work at the McAllen Station on Old Military Highway. They spent the next ten hours of their lives patrolling chaos.

Power

This analysis found that McAllen Station agents worked in a profoundly disorganized environment in which they were highly constrained by institutional policies, rules, goals, and objectives. Some of these constraints were a product of the management at the McAllen Station; others, the consequences of varied and much larger social, institutional, national, and global forces. To date many of the issues raised by experienced law enforcement officers have been systematically ignored. Based upon their knowledge of patrolling the line, the voices of these agents, along with the subsequent issues raised by a serious study of these voices, should be not only heard but also closely examined and questioned. This is not to argue that the viewpoints of agents should automatically be endorsed or accepted. The insights and expertise of dedicated employees within an organizational setting must be carefully weighed against their own self-interest and the bias inherent in their perspective. In completing this research and considering pragmatic recommendations I did not accept opinions and statements of agents as credible until I compared and tested them against my own first-hand observations, available research literature, and my other border research experience.

In a democracy public institutions and organizations can be changed by the will of the public predicated upon accurate information and data. Many issues at the McAllen Station were not impossible to resolve. The findings from the participant-observation suggested ways in which disorder along the Rio Grande can be reduced, managed, and regulated beyond public policies that were frequently little but symbolic attempts to portray order and the maintenance of public laws. Ports of entry and the highly visible units of the Border Patrol assigned under the auspices of Operation Rio Grande were, in reality, a grand pretense, because the majority of illegal immigration and opportunities for international terrorists existed far from the public eye. At the same time, while drug interdictions by the Border Patrol and other federal agencies along the line frequently stole media attention, the majority of the most serious drug smuggling occurred at these same ports of entry in spite of the barbed wire, trained canines, sophisticated technology, and other security measures.

While it is admittedly hazardous to develop any public policy and institutional reform from a case study, this exploration of the U.S. Border Patrol in Deep South Texas suggested a number of alternatives that naturally evolved out of and are predicated upon the data collected and the inductive analysis of those data.[1] Given the dearth of ethnographic information about the U.S. Border Patrol and its status along our Mexican border, I believe it crucial to include a brief discussion of institutional reform and public policy. In this discussion I will limit my comments to issues rooted directly in the data and its analysis.[2] Some readers will undoubtedly argue that I have gone too far in suggesting changes, while others will assert that I have not gone far enough. My overriding concern is that certain issues, many for the first time, be publicly discussed by a variety of constituencies.

Reform and Change

History has already demonstrated that the U.S. Border Patrol, like many other governmental agencies, is incapable of reform from within. Under the U.S. Department of Homeland Security the U.S. Border Patrol is now closely aligned with the newly named U.S. Bureau of Customs and Border Protection. The Border Patrol's merger with more than twenty other federal agencies into the U.S. Department of Homeland Security on March 1, 2003, does not guarantee substantive reforms at the McAllen Station or any other station.

Any reform under Homeland Security, a bureaucracy of more than 170,000 federal employees, may not resemble the following suggestions. If reform is solely developed from within the confines of the law enforcement community and federal hierarchy driven by the political ideology of the current adminis-tration, it will undoubtedly include a range of cosmetic attempts to appease its pundits along with its strongest political critics. Substantive reforms are unlikely if limited to those offered by the federal bureaucracy and, whether Republican or Democrat, the dominant political party.

The McAllen Station was examined from the perspective of more than 300 agents. Their viewpoint, admittedly one-sided and biased, was frequently in opposition to that of their managers, undocumented workers who were processed at the facility on Old Military Highway, employers of undocu-mented workers who depended on their labor for the source of their profits, and additional stakeholders, all of whom had vested interests in creating a Border Patrol that suited their own purposes. Consultants hired and paid by the Border Patrol to "reform" the organization will also view it in a fundamentally different way than will agents who spent twenty years or more of their careers patrolling the line.[3] It is unfortunately unlikely that whistle-blowers will step forward. It remains far easier for them to walk away from their Border Patrol jobs, pension intact, than to face possible institutional retribution and—worse to most agents—ostracism by the bros.[4]

Given these considerations grounded in real world politics, I call for the creation of a bipartisan, binational task force to study the U.S. Border Patrol. The task force would then recommend a viable legislative agenda providing new guidance, direction, and vision. Such a task force would listen closely to the federal law enforcement hierarchy and the usual Beltway consultants and experts, but it would also include immigrant rights groups, farmers and ranch-ers whose land illegal immigrants traverse, illegal immigrants, local and county law enforcement directly involved with disputes between ranchers and illegal immigrants, citizens of border communities and, along with manage-ment, experienced agents of the Border Patrol. The Mexican government must be at this large table, along with Mexican law enforcement agencies, including Grupo Beta, whose agents work closely with undocumented immigrants.

Against what standards or models should the Border Patrol be compared? I advocate that the task force focus its efforts on commonly accepted best prac-tices and standards of human resource management; recruitment, orientation, and professional development of all employees; motivational rewards and compensation based upon job performance; maintenance of a positive work environment that is safe and sustains good health practices among employees; labor-management relations; active institutional strategic planning; and career planning for employees facing retirement.[5]

Based upon the data from this study, I have outlined reform measures that might serve as talking points for a task force whose major objective is to transform the Border Patrol into a modern, efficient, rational, responsible, and responsive agency within Homeland Security. The following are minimum topics that fall within this purview: organizational structure and culture; job requirements; recruitment, training and professional development; working conditions; salaries, job tenure and promotion; risk management; gender and racial equity; adoption of technology; labor-management relations; community relations; and media relations. Where pertinent, public policy also should be discussed.

Corporate Culture and Management Styles

The management style that created and maintained the decision-making structure and sustained organizational culture of the Border Patrol requires serious evaluation. Since its formal inception in 1924 the Border Patrol has held to a paramilitary model with a highly centralized, rigid management hierarchy. This tradition-bound, often inflexible institutional structure employed citizens but treated them as soldiers paid to follow orders. Employees achieved rank through a rather subjective system of promotion based primarily on seniority, favoritism, and male superiority, all of which was—from the agents' perspective—tinged by racism.

This decision-making structure maintained a Border Patrol culture that was androcentric and motivated by the firm belief that males were superior to females. Females were considered a burden brought on by gender equity laws. In short, males at the McAllen Station were "the normative standard against which women should be judged."[6]

The Border Patrol is certainly not the only federal, state, or local law enforcement agency burdened by an androcentric culture. Women in fact remained a significant minority in other branches of law enforcement, suffering overt discrimination in the form of lower wages, sexual harassment in the work place, and a variety of other inequities.[7]

Professional employees expect managers to value their opinions. They

289

thrive and are most productive in a corporate culture that provides and constantly re-creates a work place that is supportive, fair, and responsive to their personal needs. These needs might include, for example, family-friendly services including in-house day care or counseling and referral for drug abuse.

The faux military hierarchy of the Border Patrol is outdated in the twenty-first century and engenders an employee culture that is an anathema to modern professional law enforcement principles, techniques, and skills predicated upon professional training and development. Management was sorely burdened by a lack of professional training and development except for time served in the military. Even the military experience of these managers was of doubtful utility to a clear vision of leadership and resource management; the majority held no rank higher than the equivalent of sergeant.

Management practices at the McAllen Station excluded most modern precepts of successful business organizations and institutions, including those of the twenty-first-century American military. At the McAllen Sector I never encountered a manager who had seen the inside of a business school. Few managers remembered relevant personal lessons from their own years patrolling the line. Ephemeral leadership at the very top of the institution was filled by a political appointee replaced by each new administration. Promotions to management positions were attained in part by passing a standardized written test of questionable utility.

Education, Recruitment, and Training

The job of patrolling the Mexican border requires a workforce of trained, professional, and proud law enforcement agents with a special knowledge of, and sensitivity to, the borderlands. While big city police departments have long realized the efficacy of a college education and degree as the foundation upon which competent officers are trained, and even many small-town departments require at least some college education of their new recruits, the U.S. Border Patrol currently accepts those with a high school diploma. At the McAllen Station agents with college credits or a college degree were penalized for their educational achievements by those who never attended a college or university. Those with graduate degrees were suspect.

College degrees should be a requirement for all new agents. Those with college degrees, when determined deserving, should be given preference to management positions rather than stigmatized by their academic achievements. Agents without a college education should be encouraged as well as financially supported by the Border Patrol, as is the case in the military and many private sector businesses, to gain this minimum credential. Wage incentives, time off to attend courses, and flexibility in shift assignments are just a few of the ways in which the Border Patrol can encourage agents to work on their college degrees as well as appropriate graduate degrees to further the special objectives of this agency.

Critics may argue that a college degree requirement will make the Border Patrol less competitive compared to other federal agencies. Any labor pool ultimately responds to the marketplace. Entry-level salaries of agents should match or exceed those of competing agencies. As it is, the ranks of the Border Patrol have already been raided by several different federal agencies including the Air Marshals.

The recruiting process will only be able to attract more female agents—currently 6 percent of all agents—when the Border Patrol replaces its outdated culture of testosterone with a professional law enforcement environment based upon principles of gender equity. Almost half of the recruitment pool is automatically eliminated because of the androcentric culture that permeates the agency and discourages women from full and equal participation.

Appropriate psychological testing prior to acceptance into the training academies, and throughout the training, is necessary. Such tests are far from perfect, but they may help to identify recruits with antisocial attitudes and racist beliefs. Testing at the point of entry could eliminate those who are for whatever reasons emotionally unsuitable for a career in the Border Patrol.

The core educational curriculum at the training academies, bound by the strictest of traditions, emphasizes competency in immigration law, fluency in Spanish, and physical fitness. Though these areas of education are certainly central to becoming a trained professional agent, other skills are also critically important in the field. For example, agents should be good trackers, yet the academy provides no significant training in this art. Also, agents receive little formal training in the validation of papers of those suspected to be illegal. Comparing the identification papers of one man who is detained to those of another is a frequent, commonsense, but inefficient method of establishing immigrant status.

Agents should be trained in basic computer literacy courses. Some agents at the McAllen Station, for instance, were fearful of the machines and took two to three times longer to process forms than did other agents with basic computer skills.

Also absent at the training academies is exposure to cultures of immigrants' countries. Such exposure would serve to sensitize agents to the needs of immigrants, especially those who may have suffered life-threatening experiences that demand immediate attention and concern. Few agents at the McAllen Station knew, understood, or could identify cross-cultural signs of severe stress, malnourishment, maltreatment, including physical and sexual assault, or other symptoms that might suggest psychological disorders or disease. New immigrants cannot receive humane treatment by agents who are not trained to be culturally sensitive to their needs. Exposure to and appreciation of the rich cultures of the countries of origen is grounded in pragmatic law enforcement practices. Cultural information can provide agents with a foundation for intelligence gathering and the basis for sound decisions in the field. Such knowledge can facilitate the interrogation of undocumented workers, hasten the determination of OTMs, and speed up processing of illegal workers.

Spanish-language training is essential to agents; however, teaching them Castilian Spanish at the academies is highly questionable. The vast majority of illegal immigrants who cross the southern border are Mexican, have the equivalent of a sixth grade education, and do not share the same vocabulary, pronunciation, or syntax with a college-educated, Castilian-speaking Spaniard. Academy training in spoken, regional Spanish would be of far greater benefit to agents who are currently forced to learn the local dialect on their own. Some agents are not as successful as others in this process of language acquisition and thus arc excluded from full communication with illegal aliens. This inability to communicate can put the safety of the agent and the new immigrant at greater risk. As one agent put it, "The Spanish I learned at the academy doesn't help me much in the field."

Agents are rarely fluent in other useful languages besides Spanish, including, for example, Portuguese as spoken by Brazilians. An appreciation for and exposure to languages other than Spanish could begin at the academy among those who are already competent in Spanish. These agents could be encouraged to continue to develop their language skills throughout their careers. As patterns of migration change over time, agents who are capable of learning new and relevant languages can contribute much. These agents can be rewarded instead of being stigmatized for their special talents.

At the training academies agents are required to meet certain fitness standards. Agents in the field should be in excellent physical condition for their own safety, health, and ability to perform their jobs and to aid illegal immigrants in distress. Once finished with training, however, agents no longer have to meet any physical fitness standards. Consequently, many agents are significantly overweight at the McAllen Station, several to the point of obesity as defined by exceeding 25 percent of their ideal weight. These same agents had difficulty entering and exiting their vehicles and were not physically capable of doing their jobs in the field.

Two issues lie at the heart of the need for physical fitness standards for agents. The first is the safety of agents, including their personal health and well-being. At the training academies no curriculums inform the agents, for example, of basic principles of nutrition, cardiovascular health, treatment of minor on-the-job injuries that can become chronic, or coping with physical stressors including sleep deprivation. The necessity of swimming and life-saving skills for those who patrol a river border was discussed previously. Although agents with no swimming skills may not be able to learn these skills within the limited training period at the academy, certainly in subsequent years they can be expected to learn how to swim and to save a life. Is it unreasonable to suggest that those who cannot learn these life-saving skills be reassigned to regions that do not border a river?

The second reason to require physical fitness standards for agents throughout their careers is to protect the safety of the public. Agents who cannot exit their trucks or track sign because they are in poor condition or are obese are far less able to protect members of the public from physical harm if a situation arises. Agents must be able not only to out-think undocumented workers, but outrun them as well.

A curriculum that directly addresses the psychological stressors agents commonly encounter is absent. Agents can benefit from professional training that would empower them to cope with their own psychological problems as well as those of other agents or family members. Strategies to resolve substance abuse problems should also be incorporated in the academy training. Techniques of anger management are certainly of importance in this demanding career, as are knowledge of and remedies to marital problems created by the job and therapies to help those undergoing divorce. At the present agents can call an anonymous hot line for alcohol or family counseling, but few at the McAllen Station chose to do so in a male-oriented culture that characterizes such efforts as personal weaknesses or failures.

The Border Patrol does not attempt to ease the transition of families to border locations and cultures with which they may be completely unfamiliar. Spouses and families from New England and the Midwest found themselves entrenched in a South Texas culture foreign to them. Here, the military model is particularly appealing and could serve as a template. For many years military programs and networks of and for military families have provided emotional support, advice, and information.

Agents in the Border Patrol are inundated throughout their careers by information on weaponry, specific advancements in first aid, and financial investments that will provide them more ample retirements, and other specialized knowledge. Ongoing professional education that builds upon training that agents receive in the academies and does not neglect challenges throughout the life course is absent. Such opportunities as those suggested would ultimately increase the efficiency of the organization by stimulating individual job performance and satisfaction and, at the same time, reducing personal risk to agents, illegal immigrants, and the general public.

Mentoring

The mentoring of agents represents a low-cost and efficient reform that can address many work-related problems. New agents at the McAllen Station were partnered with more experienced agents during their probationary period, but little serious thought was given to matching mentors with new recruits. After new agents passed their probationary tests, the mentoring ended.

A system of mentoring that matched a qualified and experienced agent with an agent new to the McAllen Station could create and foster pride in the job. At the same time mentoring could ease the difficult transition that agents and their families face when they move from a nonborder to a border culture. Mentoring, in short, provides positive role models for young and inexperienced agents to emulate. Mentors can also benefit directly from the experience.

For example, the arrest of the McAllen Station field operation supervisor could have been followed by discussions to alleviate the anxiety and fears of younger agents as a result of a respected leader and role model's quite sudden removal from his job. Instead, the arrest and subsequent investigation were clouded in mystery and seldom discussed; management pretended that the respected FOS had never existed.[8] If a strong mentoring program had been in place, mentors could have minimized the effects on morale among agents and emphasized the real dangers of the alleged drug smuggling relationship upon the FOS and his family as well as the jeopardy in which the offender's actions placed all other agents.

Of equal importance, mentoring can foster friendships along with other social networks in the community absent in the lives of some agents. These essential relationships provide emotional support and well-being to agents facing normal family problems and are indispensable in the handling of work-related stress.

Conditions in the Work Place: Scheduling and Resources

Conditions in any work place directly affect the performance, efficiency, and morale of workers. At the McAllen Station one of the most damaging of conditions in the work place was a schedule dictated by four rotating shifts. This four-shift rotation influenced the safety of the work place, the efficiency of the work accomplished, and morale and directly affected the family and friends of agents. Although management eventually eliminated the fourth shift, the remaining shift structure is hazardous to the work that agents do and to the agents themselves because it exacerbates job alienation, self-destructive behaviors, and antisocial behaviors.

The existing shift structure is particularly damaging to female agents because it makes it extremely difficult for them to have children and to raise them under positive family conditions. Female agents without a supportive spouse or significant other find it virtually impossible to work as an agent in the Border Patrol and have and raise children. Female agents are thus unfairly forced to choose between their career and having children.

Male agents who have children are, under this same system of shifts, also placed in a difficult situation in which their spouse must shoulder tremendous responsibilities that place undue burdens upon both the marriage and the family. The shift schedule makes it impossible for a single male parent to raise his children in a positive family environment unless he is fortunate enough to have a strong network of former spouse, family, and extended family support.[9]

Other viable alternatives can greatly reduce the kinds of family problems aggravated by the shift structure at the McAllen Station. Truly family-friendly institutions take into account the psychological and physical welfare of their workers, create work-related policies that strengthen family bonds, and facilitate the engagement of workers in the community. These alternatives should be explored using other agencies of law enforcement as models.

Although many work-related problems could benefit from reform, this discussion will focus on the status of equipment, facilities, and resources at the McAllen Station. In general the equipment appeared to be of substandard quality, often requiring continual repair. Rarely was it state-of-the-art, more often appearing to be cast-off, second- or third-generation military supplies. Scope trucks and patrol boats provide two examples. The scope trucks were fragile and poorly designed and more often than not required expensive and constant repair. The design and configurations of the patrol boats, including the quality of the materials used, were unreasonably cheap. What the McAllen Station lacked in forethought, quality, and design was not compensated for by quantity. Agents there could employ a minimum of ten more scope trucks and an equal number of patrol boats.

The buildings that housed the McAllen Station were constructed and designed in the early 1970s for approximately 70 agents. By 2003 the facilities housed about 325 agents and other personnel. New facilities were constructed in recent years in Harlingen, but the planned construction of new McAllen Station facilities was indefinitely delayed.

The processing room at the McAllen Station was especially inadequate and placed agents and illegal aliens at risk. With their service weapons holstered, agents routinely passed among, between, and in front of illegal aliens standing in groups against a cinder-block wall waiting to be processed. Armed agents also regularly opened and entered holding cells for undocumented workers.

The holsters of agents, as discussed, are at security level one. A motivated undocumented worker would have clear and repeated opportunities to seize and quickly bypass the rudimentary safety devices on a level one holster.[10] Undocumented workers had open and free access to agents who were regularly outnumbered in the processing room. Certainly the vast majority of illegal workers were peaceful, but it should be remembered that a significant few had long criminal records in Mexico and in the United States and were poor safety risks.[11] Agents in the field were also put at risk because of their apprehension techniques while using these same level one holsters.

The radio communications system at the McAllen Station was grossly inadequate. Agents often were forced to stand on the front bumpers of their vehicles as they attempted to establish better contact with the radio dispatcher. Even these extreme tactics could fail along many banks of the Rio Grande in Deep South Texas, leaving agents without contact with their dispatcher or other units. At the same time, overworked dispatchers did not always relay potentially important information on sensors to units in the field in a timely manner. Because of this delay agents could not be certain when a sensor had been hit and thus how far along the trails and paths the illegal workers or drug smugglers may have advanced. A functional and reliable communication system is a fundamental requirement of any effective law enforcement agency.

Along these same lines, vehicles were fitted with panic buttons. However, if agents activated them during an emergency it might take hours before they could be located.[12] Location devices embedded in the structure of Border Patrol vehicles could remedy this potentially life-threatening situation.

The computer system appeared third-rate along with, as discussed, the computer literacy of the average agent.[13] Compounding this situation, other federal agencies prior to September 11 were reluctant to share their criminal data and files with the Border Patrol. In spring 2002 these barriers finally began to fall when agents at the Border Patrol were given access to CLERIS, the Criminal Law Enforcement Reporting and Information System. This first step in shared data between agencies clearly enhanced the agents' ability to perform their duties.

Finally, in good conscience I must mention that many agents did not regularly wear their body armor. Some wore their protective vests throughout their shifts; others used them as seat cushions. Regardless of attempts to rationalize not wearing this life-saving equipment while patrolling the line, agents must be required to wear their vests at all times to protect themselves and those they protect. A zero-tolerance policy by management will quickly rectify this situation.

The Substance of Chaos

Management-Labor Relations

Prior to the merger of the Border Patrol into Homeland Security, a variety of management-labor problems existed at the McAllen Station. The government employees union found mixed, uneven support among agents because it tended to mount its largest battles against relatively insignificant employment issues while ignoring problems that agents faced on a daily basis. On the other hand, given the pseudo-military culture and decision-making structure of the Border Patrol, agents had little other recourse than the union in a rigid system that frequently rewarded complacency above all else.

The Bush administration and the Republican-led Congress have strongly advocated eradicating the employees union from the U.S. Department of Homeland Security.[14] Union sentiment and membership at the national level is indeed dwindling.[15] At the McAllen Station the union seemed to oppose a reform agenda. For example, it rallied against annual physical fitness tests for agents although fitness tests would increase and reward physical fitness among agents, reduce obesity and weight-related health problems, and in general lay the foundation for fewer and less serious accidents in the line of duty. That said, without any union representation whatsoever there would be even less room for feedback from agents on job-related issues, expression of individual opinion free from management reprisals, or reform based upon the contributions of those who know from the inside which policies are successes and which failures. A flawed union was better than no union in this regard.[16]

After the events of September 11, entry-level wages of Border Patrol agents were finally raised. But wage raises came several months after the pool of agents had been seriously diminished by transfers to the Air Marshals and other federal agencies.[17] Automatically raising G-9s to G-11s pleased those who were G-9s but demoralized some G-11s at the McAllen Station who had worked and waited years for promotion to that grade. If the Border Patrol desires to avoid additional raids on its force of agents, it must reevaluate its entry-level salaries and promotional policies.

Detailed, annual work evaluations continue to neglect those Rambos who are assertive and motivated and outperform others who are notable for their compliance with existing decisions and policies. An evaluation system to reward and promote the most capable employees is still not in place.

Management Strategies: Media Relations and Public Information

Modern leadership, consensus building, and professional development seemed almost totally absent in this organization. Promotion to middle and upper management, for example, was determined in part by a system of promotional testing. There was little evidence, however, to suggest that these exams, from supervisor on up, had any direct relevance to leadership capabilities, talents, or skills.

Good managers, as defined by the institutional culture, were individuals who blindly followed station policies, kept their professional opinions to themselves, and continually reaffirmed and praised the performance of their bosses. This kind of management hierarchy left little room for real dialogue, the discussion of innovative procedures, or new management practices. As evidenced by the creation and burial of the fourth shift, decisions were strictly top-down processes with little or no input from agents.

Management at the station assumed a defensive, litigious stance against the employee's union, the public, other law enforcement agencies, the Mexican Consulate, and the Mexican and American media. Management's bunker mentality of them versus us divorced it from meaningful engagement with its constituents and natural audiences.

Investment in and commitment to a system of professional public information directors would go a long way toward resolving some of these issues. A professionally trained PID could stimulate and maintain a positive working relationship between the working media and the Border Patrol in Deep South Texas. A PID would consistently place before the public the objectives, mission, and goals of the Border Patrol, explain procedures of agents in the field when necessary, and minimize misunderstandings and rumors that naturally arise. A professional PID also would be a strong voice for the Border Patrol to clarify policy, functions, and the positive impact of the Border Patrol on the local economy. A professional PID would begin to build a relationship of trust between the Border Patrol and the communities it serves.

The gulf between the McAllen Station and the citizens it served was indeed wide and deep. Agents rarely stopped to chat with residents of neighborhoods and towns they patrolled. Their spatial isolation from those whose interests they represented was embodied to some degree in the language they invented and employed; this language was part of the shared agent culture from which civilians were excluded. For example, there was one household in a community by the Rio Grande that was located near a dirt road used by both illegal workers and drug smugglers. In the backyard of this modest house lived two to four dogs. Firmly attached to posts by thick chains, the dogs rotated around the posts incessantly as they ferociously barked at anyone who approached the vicinity of the house on foot or in a car. Agents referred to this house and place as "the house with the dogs that go in circles." While the description was apt, it precluded any knowledge of the names of the residents who had lived there for many years. In other words, agents understood the residents less than the dogs.

A few agents always talked to residents of McAllen and other communities in Hidalgo County during line watch. Noe Escondido was one; Herman Morningside, another. But most residents experienced the Border Patrol as an Expedition speeding down their streets and highways, tinted windows rolled up, AC at full blast, followed by a whirlwind of dust. Some agents as they sped down the roads did not bother to acknowledge residents by even a wave of the hand or a nod of the head. In contrast, agents who were approached by citizens while drinking coffee or grabbing a Whataburger were very personable and patient. But then these same agents climbed into their fortresslike Expeditions and once again seemed to lose real awareness of the citizens they were sworn to protect.

Many citizens expressed their hatred and distrust of agents by taunting agents, yelling at them, cursing them, and making obscene gestures for no other reason than that the agents wore the green uniform of the Border Patrol. It was more than natural for many agents to try to avoid this kind of confrontation, and it was easy for them to generalize their response to all of the public. But by ignoring their constituency they discredited themselves and, more importantly, reaffirmed the community stereotypes about the Border Patrol.

Community Policing

Principles and practices of community policing might offer new ways to conceptualize strategies of policing the border.[18] Community policing is defined here as "a preventive approach through an empowered problem-solving partnership of police and community to control crime, reduce the fear of crime and enhance lifestyle experiences of all community constituents."[19] Community policing requires the active participation of community members in the decision-making process that includes partnerships with private- and public-sector agencies in the community. Implicit in community policing is a decentralization of authority, including empowering front-line law enforcers with limited decision-making capabilities. Community policing emphasizes a problem-solving approach to daily tasks, an approach that emphasizes the professional capabilities of law enforcers at the same time it requires community investment into the benefits of law enforcement.[20]

Community policing strategies could benefit agents in several ways. First, the public becomes better informed about the daily tasks of the Border Patrol and the benefits of these tasks to the community. An educated public by definition is less likely to be led astray by sensationalist media or accusations by interest groups with an ideological agenda. This public is also the same pool from which juries are drawn to serve on cases directly involving the interests of the Border Patrol. Second, intelligence data are a direct by-product of community policing techniques that can increase arrests of drug smugglers and illegal aliens and reduce risk to the public and to agents. Last, strong community support of the Border Patrol would lift morale among agents and provide additional incentive to remain with the agency. Through community policing and other reforms the Border Patrol could slowly overcome its bitter historical legacy in Deep South Texas.

New Strategies for Enforcement and the Scientific Method in the Social Sciences

These and other possible reforms form the basis for a reconsideration of strategies to patrol the line. Whatever the origins of new concepts and ideas, it is foolish to apply new strategies without first testing them in the field for reasonable periods of time.[21] Operation Rio Grande in Deep South Texas and Operation Gatekeeper clearly demonstrated that a one-size-fits-all strategy may not be suitable for a border that stretches for more than two thousand miles.

Measures besides apprehension rates should be considered when the Border Patrol tests new programs. Apprehension data and annual comparative rates of apprehension, as discussed throughout these pages, can be very misleading. Apprehension rates employed as the only test of the reliability and validity of a specific strategy can be particularly misleading.

Credentialed professional social scientists have been excluded by the Bor-

The Substance of Chaos

der Patrol although other local, state, and federal law enforcement agencies, including the FBI and the CIA, have benefited from their expertise. Social scientists, including anthropologists, criminologists, economists, psychologists, and sociologists, bring with them a set of quantitative and qualitative skills otherwise foreign to management in this agency.[22] The objectives and the goals of the Border Patrol can clearly be advanced by employing social scientists.

Proactive Reforms

The Border Patrol is not proactive. For example, BORSTAR, the agency's search, trauma, and rescue team, was an excellent idea but took much too long to initiate. Initiated in October 2001 along the Texas border, the program was designed to provide medical aide and care to aliens who became lost or were placed in harm's way as they illegally crossed the Rio Grande into remote regions.[23] Though this objective was admirable, it was begun only after hundreds of illegal aliens had already died.

A proactive Border Patrol would not be tragedy-driven. For example, demands for reform were loud and long after the shocking discovery of eleven bodies in a Union Pacific railcar near Denison, Iowa. The car began its tragic journey in Deep South Texas.[24] No significant procedural changes were put into effect as a result of these deaths. Later, no policies or procedures changed after nineteen of seventy immigrants locked in the back of a tractor-trailer in Deep South Texas suffocated to death. The dead included a small child and a man in his eighties.[25] To the credit of law enforcement the suspects of this international smuggling operation were indicted, but no reforms, including special allocations of resources, were initiated to prevent similar incidents.

Border Patrol special smuggling units should be critically evaluated and if having crucial problems like the one at the McAllen Station should be reorganized, given additional resources, and provided a clear vision of their objectives and goals.

Labor Management Programs

This study once more raises the question of the wisdom of our current national policy toward illegal workers. We will always require a Border Patrol to protect the security of our border, but a labor management program that considers not only the needs of employers but also the needs and vulnerabilities of foreign workers would go a long way toward removing a majority of criminal activity from the banks of the Rio Grande. Several different kinds of programs have been suggested.[26] In the absence of large numbers of desperate undocumented workers, life along the banks of the river would be substantially less chaotic. Fat Man and Nature Boy would be put out of business; thousands of illegal immigrants would no longer have to place their lives in the hands of *coyotes*. A minority would still seek for whatever reason illegal entry, but their numbers would be much more manageable. Agents might then better focus their efforts on criminal activities that pose a serious threat to the public.

In early 2004, President Bush introduced a guest worker program, the specific details of which, by summer, remained vague.[27] Employers who traditionally hire low-wage workers, including undocumented workers, appear satisfied with the proposed program. Issues of amnesty, citizenship, and other considerations with regard to the needs of foreign workers have not been detailed. What pragmatic implications this politically expedient plan might have for the policing of the border have received little attention.

Illegal Drugs

Management at the McAllen Station in annual evaluations rewarded agents who consistently caught loads of marijuana and cocaine smuggled across the Rio Grande. But it is legitimate to question whether the agency should focus on its drug interdiction efforts to the detriment of its apprehension of undocumented workers. Agents who stumble onto drug loads should obviously be rewarded for their efforts, but long and labor-intensive surveillance by agents seems counter-productive and wasteful of limited resources. The role, duties, and eventual evaluations of field agents need to be defined vis-à-vis drug interdiction.

Illegal drugs are an imminent social issue ignored by most politicians and the public except during elections.[28] As long as Americans continue to demand drugs, cartels will thrive as they creatively invent new ways and methods to transport their product to market. Those implications aside, agents utilized a number of strategies to annoy, delay, and frustrate drug smugglers. These included patrol boats on the Rio Grande and flyovers by helicopters.

The Substance of Chaos

Cooperation between the Border Patrol and local law enforcement, itself suspect, can be improved through training and professional development of municipal police and county sheriff's departments in border counties. Because the vast majority of illegal drugs were crossed at the ports of entry, new technologies to scan the trucks and other vehicles must be refined, developed, and deployed.

Graft and corruption in the Border Patrol is unacknowledged and highly stigmatized within the agency. Suspected employees are removed from their jobs; little information but unsubstantiated rumor follows. As long as the agency hides the accused individual and denies the corruption, little progress will be forthcoming.

If the Border Patrol cannot handle its own corruption problems, it is unlikely that it will effectively work with Mexican law enforcers who are also burdened by this same problem. There remains, for instance, a high degree of bureaucratic denial about the criminal role of the Mexican military and other Mexican law enforcement. The troubling role of the Mexican military in drug smuggling requires serious and systematic investigation.

International Terrorism

As one of the first barriers to terrorists seeking illegal entry into the United States, the Border Patrol can play a vital role in controlling international terrorism. This role must begin with the acknowledgment that the southern border with Mexico is porous, that if Benny *el elefantino* can illegally cross from one country to the next a motivated terrorist can certainly do the same.

The underlying strength of the Border Patrol in combating international terrorism along the border is that it is a trained force of federal officers. New tasks and roles for agents to reduce the terrorist threat can be creatively developed and tested.

Terrorism experts must be encouraged to think imaginatively about the Border Patrol. How can 10,000 federal agents be employed in the war against terrorism? What kinds of training do these officers require? One partial solution is to give these federal officers full law enforcement powers. In Deep South Texas understaffed city and county law enforcement agencies could greatly benefit from the assistance of professionally trained Border Patrol agents.

While new technologies are vital in combating terrorism, ultimately it is human decisions and actions that are essential. The Border Patrol can serve as a vital component in counter-terrorism if professionally trained, equipped, and motivated.

Disorganization prevails in Deep South Texas. By surrendering "to drift, to accident, to fate," we evade real problems and issues and provide for similar dilemmas in the future. There is power in organization driven by political will, power inherent in openly addressing the issues, debating the problems, and fostering wise decisions that may involve the denial of traditional but misleading myths and rhetoric. The American public has the power to decide what kind of international borders it wants, what kind of immigration policies are fair, what products are allowed entry into the country, and what types of men and women patrol and guard the borders. Organization becomes power. The reorganization and reform of the Border Patrol is a crucial step toward the creation, invention, and nurturing of human order from chaos along the banks of the Rio Grande in Deep South Texas.

Epilogue: Drift

The three Mexican men began digging in the sand early Monday morning, October 7, 2002. Eight months before, in February 2001, the Rio Grande had ceased flowing to the sea. The small wooden homes these men had built along the banks of the Río Bravo filled with three feet of toxic, stagnant water from a river that, no longer able to reach the sea, backed up along its flood plain.

For nearly eight months these men and their families waited patiently for the American or the Mexican government to take action. Floods were a part of the natural cycle along the banks of the Río Bravo, but in their entire lives these men and their neighbors had never experienced permanent flooding.

The mighty waters of the Rio Grande that form the international border between the United States and the Republic of Mexico begin as an infinitesimal stream in the San Juan Mountains of southern Colorado just a few miles from the Continental Divide. For eons of time, in fact precisely until the month of February 2001, the currents of Colorado water, mixed with a hundred other New Mexican, Mexican, and Texan streams and tributaries, completed another complex cycle of nature by flowing into the Gulf of Mexico.

The men's plan was simple enough: to free the waters of the Río Bravo they would dig a 400-foot trench that would once more link the river with the gulf.

Connected by the modest trench, the backlogged waters would recede, and the men and their families could resume living along the former banks of the river. While the three Mexican men worked under a hot October sun, agents of the U.S. Border Patrol eyed them from afar. The area was under constant surveillance now that undocumented workers and drug smugglers could *walk or drive* across the Rio Grande with impunity. Representatives from the International Boundary and Water Commission, along with assorted Mexican officials, also watched as the men worked.

From sunup to sundown it took them two days of hard work before they set their rusty old shovels aside and admired what they had achieved.

A supe from the McAllen Sector was impressed by the efforts of the three Mexicans. "To do it by hand, that's a pretty laborious job."[1]

As the sun began to set on the evening of October 8, a thin trickle of putrid water from the Rio Grande flowed 400 feet through the new, shallow ditch to mingle with the salty waters of the Gulf of Mexico. Even before the three Mexicans had trudged back to their flooded houses, the sand walls of the thin, fragile channel began to cave in. The blockages of sand could easily have been scooped up with the bare hand or a plastic bucket not unlike the ones used to build sand castles on the beaches of nearby South Padre Island. But there were no bare hands available and no one to maintain the tenuous channel.

Said the same Border Patrol supe: "It almost takes an act of Congress to do something like that."[2]

The IBWC had dredged the river bottom to free the river soon after the waters in February 2001 failed to reach the Gulf of Mexico. But four months after dredging, the mouth of the Rio Grande again filled with enough silt to stop the current's flow. The fundamental problem was that after Mexico and the United States had siphoned off their share of river water for cities, farms, and industry, there was not enough water left to reach the sea. Because only the homes of poor Mexicans were inundated, there was no organized public outcry from either nation.[3]

The IBWC moved at a snail's pace. "Sandia National Lab and University of Texas at El Paso contractors are working with us to determine the velocity, or volume, of water required to keep the mouth of the river open, based on a geological analysis of the characteristics of the sand in the area," said a spokesperson for the IBWC.[4]

Epilogue

A few days after the three Mexicans completed the trench linking the Río Bravo to the sea, the river once again ceased to flow. And two weeks after the men had sweated under the sun to finish a task in which no governmental agency seemed to take much interest, not a sign of their work remained in the shifting bottom sands.

Thirty miles upriver from where these three poor Mexicans took international law into their own hands, Agent Raphael Rivera was about to see more than he had counted on when he signed up with the Border Patrol. At thirty-two years of age, Agent Rivera was not much older than the three Mexicans with the shovels. A graduate of Porter High School in Brownsville, Agent Rivera spent four years in the U.S. Marines before joining the Harlingen PD. Although he still believed that the Harlingen Police Department was the most professional department in the Valley, and the least corrupted by the *narco-traficantes,* he could not support his growing family on $27,000 a year. He signed up with the U.S. Border Patrol.

Agent Rivera, having already served in the Gulf War, was not averse to danger or violence. Aboard the USS *Saratoga* during Desert Storm, he witnessed the sinking of a ferry that killed twenty-two navy men. But that experience and others in the military did not adequately prepare him for what he was about to see in the waters of the Rio Grande not far from the hand-drawn ferry at Los Ebanos.

Beneath a boiling sun, there was just Agent Rivera and the floater. Along with the M&Ms on the other side of the river.

When he arrived at the banks of the Rio Grande, it seemed that the M&Ms were all over the southern banks, trotting in and out of the vegetation as they struggled to keep up with the sluggish current pushing the body. They would stop, look over at Rivera, then point at the floater in the water as if Rivera did not see it. The river moved very slowly that day, parading the body of the man for all to see.

So near the M&Ms, Rivera felt too exposed and vulnerable. There were at least fifteen of them, only one of him. If they decided to shoot him, it would be an hour before backup could arrive.

Because at first the floater hugged the northern bank of the river, the M&Ms were enthusiastic as they gave chase. Through complicated and rare binational communications, Agent Rivera had been notified that there might be a floater on the northern banks. When he arrived on the scene, he immediately identified a more important question: who would take responsibility for the body?

As the floater edged to the middle of the Rio Grande, the M&Ms noticeably slackened their pace. Their enthusiasm waxed only to wane quickly as the body headed back toward the southern bank. As the floater made its way atop the putrid waters they commenced, must have commenced, silent prayers. *Oh, God, please take this body to the north side of the Río Bravo.* The M&Ms certainly did not want the body. Better that the Americans should have it. If identified as a Mexican citizen, then it would soon enough be sent back to Mexico in a McAllen ambulance. On a day that was this hot, the only thing to do was rest up for the night patrol.

Experienced in enforcing the law, Agent Rivera took his job as seriously as any other agent. He was not insensitive, but he was honestly hoping that the floater would find its own way back to the south side of the Rio Grande. Otherwise he was going to spend the rest of his shift calling the proper authorities, filling out endless forms, and all the rest of it.

Was the floater an immigrant who had failed to heed the directions of his *coyote* as he stumbled blindly into the river? Was he a mule who, overburdened by his load of drugs, became entangled in the roots of the hydrilla? Or perhaps he had been dead long before his body touched the river waters, another victim in the turf battles between the *narcotraficantes.* Circumstances did not matter much; tomorrow's edition of McAllen's paper would not record the death.

The floater rounded a sharp bend in the river as Agent Rivera struggled through the dense vegetation to keep apace. For several moments it was completely out of sight. As he made his way through the carrizo cane, he looked across at a sandbar that stretched out into the river from the southern banks. The floater snagged on the sandbar, the current inch by inch working to free the body. When finally released, the passive resistance of human flesh against the slow current generated enough momentum to push the body onto the shallow southern bank. There the floater finally came to rest.

The M&Ms, their words easily crossing the isolated expanse of river, cursed their fate. At the same moment Agent Rivera let out a sigh of relief. He had, after all, followed the rules and handled a tricky situation. Checking in

Epilogue

with his supe to report that the body was safely in the hands of the M&Ms, he was given clearance to be on his way. First he waited a few more minutes at the scene to make sure that the M&Ms secured the body. Then Agent Rivera climbed back into the cab of his truck, popped the brake, and, dead straight toward whatever awaited him along the banks of the Rio Grande, drove on down the line.

Notes

The Agent and the River

1. The majority of illegal workers who cross the Rio Grande in Deep South Texas are low-wage workers from Mexico. See, for an overview, Alejandro Portes and Ruben G. Rumbaut, *Immigrant America.*

2. "Illegal alien" is used here and throughout these pages because it is the term used by agents. I also use "undocumented worker" and "new immigrant" in its place. I first criticized the usage of this term in 1986. See Robert Lee Maril, *Cannibals and Condos: Texas and Texans along the Gulf Coast,* 62–68.

3. On several different occasions I have followed the Rio Grande from Colorado to where it feeds into the Gulf of Mexico. *La Frontera: The United States Border with Mexico,* by Alan Weisman and Jay Dusard, is a good place to develop an overview of the border with Mexico. Also see *Views across the Border,* edited by Stanley R. Ross. For a historical overview of life along the Rio Grande, see Paul Horgan, *Great River.* For an understanding of the rich cultural history of the Rio Grande view the traveling exhibit of the Smithsonian Institution *El Rio* (Washington, D.C.: Center for Folklore and Cultural Heritage, Smithsonian Institution, 2003).

4. Since the list of top ten most toxic national rivers was first initiated in 1986, the Rio Grande has frequently been cited as one of the most polluted rivers in the United States. In 2003, the Rio Grande was ranked the fifth most polluted river. See J. Joel Espinoza, "A River in Trouble," *The Monitor,* Apr. 12, 2003, 1A.

5. The prehistory of the Valley is described in the work of Thomas R. Hester. See, for example Thomas R. Hester, "Late Prehistoric Cultural Patterns Along the Rio Grande of Texas," *Bulletin of the Texas Archaeological Society* 46 (1975): 106–25; *Hunters and*

Notes

Gatherers of the Rio Grande Plain and the Lower Coast of Texas; "The Archaeology of the Lower Rio Grande Valley of Texas," in *Proceedings, An Exploration of a Common Legacy: Conference on Border Architecture,* 66–74. For an overview of European contact in the Valley to the present, see Robert Lee Maril, *Poorest of Americans,* 19–54. See also David Montejano, *Anglos and Mexicans in the Making of Texas, 1836–1986;* and Emilio Zamora, *The World of the Mexican Worker in Texas.* Very little has been written about the history of the lower Rio Grande valley. See Carlos E. Castaneda, *Our Catholic Heritage in Texas, 1519–1936;* Oakah L. Jones, Jr., *Los Paisanos: Spanish Settlers on the Northern Frontier of New Spain;* J. Lee Stambaugh and Lillian J. Stambaugh, *The Lower Rio Grande Valley of Texas;* and Brian Robertson, *Wild Horse Desert.* See the volume *Studies in Brownsville History,* edited by Milo Kearney. Unfortunately there are few similar sources for McAllen, Texas. A sociological perspective is offered in Maril, *Poorest of Americans;* Thomas A. Lyson and William W. Faulk, eds., *Forgotten Places: Uneven Development and the Loss of Opportunity in Rural America,* 102–24; Rogelio Saenz and Marie Ballejos, "Industrial Development and Persistent Poverty in the Lower Rio Grande Valley," in *Forgotten Places,* ed. by Lyson and Faulk; and Chad Richardson, *Batos, Bolillos, Pochos, and Pelados: Class and Culture on the South Texas Border.* For culturally sensitive fictional accounts, there are none better than Rolando Hinojosa Smith's *Klail City Death Trip* series, especially, *The Valley.* See also the equally stimulating work of Genaro Gonzalez, *The Quixote Cult.* Américo Paredes also has few equals in his descriptions of life along the border. See, for example, *With a Pistol in His Hand* and *George Washington Gómez.* The region has served as a background to various fiction including a detective series by R. D. Brown, *Villa Head.* More serious fiction includes Earl Thompson, *Caldo Largo.* Most recently, see the first novel of Oscar Casares, *Brownsville.* Part of this newest generation of Valley writers includes Jose Skinner, *Flight and Other Stories;* David Rice, *Crazy Loco;* and Rene Saldana, Jr., *The Jumping Tree.*

6. The cleanup was not completed until 1997. See Sarah Ovaska, "TCEQ's $1.3M Lien on Munoz Home Dropped," *The Monitor,* Apr. 17, 2002, 1A.

7. See "Mission Historical Museum Gala," *The Monitor,* Mar. 8, 2003, 3D. Groundwater beneath the chemical plant at Sixth Street and Nicholson Avenue is contaminated with Lindane, a pesticide. Lindane has been linked "to non-Hodgkin's lymphoma and leukemia, as well as neuroblastomas and aplastic anemia, both of which are precursors to leukemia." "The city's drinking water is located less than half a mile away, but city and state environmental officials said Tuesday there is no chance the water supply is contaminated" (Sarah Ovaska, "Groundwater Contaminated," *The Monitor,* May 7, 2003, 1A).

8. The lower Rio Grande valley of Texas is one of the poorest regions in the United States. See, for example, Maril, *Poorest of Americans.* For the numbers of individuals in poverty, see U.S. Census Bureau, *County Estimates for People of All Ages in Poverty for Texas: 1998.* For median household income, see the United States Census Bureau, *County Estimates for Median Household Income for Texas: 1998.* Most recently, seven

out of the top ten poorest communities in the United States were identified by the U.S. Census as located in the Valley. These Valley towns include: Cameron Park, the poorest community in the United States as measured by per capita income at $4,102, followed by Mila Doce, Río Bravo, Progreso, La Homa, Alton North, and Hidalgo. Average American household income is $40,816. See "Poorest Places in the U.S.," *The Pan American,* Mar. 27, 2003, 12. In 2000, according to the U.S. Census, the residents of McAllen-Edinburg-Mission had a per capita income of $14,053, ranking them as the poorest metropolitan area in the United States. Brownsville-Harlingen-San Benito, directly adjacent in Cameron County, closely followed at $14,691, which made it the second poorest metro area in the country. See "McAllen's Per-Capita Income Lowest of More Than 200 Cities," *The Monitor,* Sept. 3, 2000, 1A. The Mexico-U.S. border region has a very low per capita income, but residents of the Valley are poorer by this measure than others along the border. The forty-three Texas border counties, for example, had a per capita income of $18,390 in 2001 compared to the much lower rates for Valley counties, which included Hidalgo and Cameron. See Carole Keeton Rylander, *The Border: Where We Stand.*

9. See Maril, *Poorest of Americans.*

10. As measured by increases in the number of jobs, McAllen has the fifth fastest growing economy in all of the United States. It is also the third fastest growing metro area in the nation with a population of 534,907, ranking just behind Las Vegas, Nevada, and Naples, Florida. There was a 28 percent increase in job growth in 2002 over the previous year. See "Best Places," *Forbes,* May 27, 2002, available at www.forbes.com/forbes/2002/0527/bestplaces2.html as of March 19, 2003.

11. R. Daniel Cavazos labeled McAllen a "hot zone of growth" ("The Two Sides of Brownsville's Growth," *Brownsville Herald,* Mar. 19, 2003).

12. The vast majority of American citizens of Hispanic descent who reside in the lower Rio Grande valley identify themselves as Mexican American or Hispanics. This includes the younger segments of the population as well as those who are more traditional. The majority of this population in the Valley is uncomfortable being labeled Chicano or Latino. Native Caucasians refer to themselves as Anglos and are identified by the Hispanic population in the same way. I have, therefore, used these same terms throughout these pages. Other researchers who are unfamiliar with this specific population have at times insisted upon different nomenclature for this population.

13. Laurence Arnold, "Bush's EPA Nominee Also Hired Immigrants," *The Monitor,* Jan. 9, 2001, 1A.

14. "The inspector general reported in February, 2003, that for aliens ordered deported by the immigration court system, 97 percent of all asylum-seekers who were released from immigration custody disappeared and were never deported; 94 percent of aliens from terror-supporting countries who were released from immigration detention walked out of custody and out of sight, never to be deported; and 87 percent of all aliens released from immigration custody were never caught again, and were never

Notes

deported" (Michelle Malkin, "Chicken Littles Slam Ashcroft for Illegal Immigrant Policy," *The Monitor,* May 1, 2003, 6C).

15. Wild and free under a tropical sun, these birds were once domestic pets whose McAllen owners released them out the back door when they realized the insanely loud caws were not suitable for their kitchen, sunroom, or anywhere else in the house. Solitary Mexican parrots from *el otro lado,* the other side of the Rio Grande, hear the cacophony and join their numbers as they swarm over the barrios and gated communities of the city. My thanks to Ralph Fielding for his knowledge of birds in South Texas.

16. The immigrant experience is complex, based not only upon the economy of the sending and receiving countries but also social networks, immigration experience and strategies, public policy, and many other factors. A neoclassical economic push-pull model of immigration is simplistic and, worse still, can lead to public policy that creates more problems than it resolves. See, for example, Douglas Massey's *Beyond Smoke and Mirrors: Mexican Immigration in an Era of Economic Integration* for an overview of the Mexican immigrant experience and American public policy. Several other theoretical understandings of immigration to the United States exist, all of which suggest the complexity of the immigrant experience. Among these theories are: world systems theory, the new economics of migration, social capital theory, relative deprivation, cumulative causation, and transnationalism. For an overview see, for example, Immanuel Wallerstein, *The Modern World System;* O. Stark, *The Migration of Labor;* Douglas S. Massey, *Worlds in Motion: Understanding International Migration;* Douglas S. Massey, Rafael Alarcón, Jorge Durand, and Humberto González, *Return to Aztlan: The Social Process of International Migration from Western Mexico;* Charles Hirschman, Josh Dewind, and Philip Kasinitz, eds., *The Handbook of International Migration: The American Experience;* and P. Levitt, *The Transnational Villagers.* Also, Saskia Sassen, "Immigration and Local Labor Markets," 87–127, in *The Economic Sociology of Immigration,* ed. by Alejandro Portes. I am indebted to conversations with Molly Sheridan about the theoretical underpinnings of immigration, especially transnationalism, and for her detailed understanding of the impact of remittances on sending and receiving countries.

17. See "INS Releases Updated Estimate of U.S. Undocumented Resident Population" (U.S. Department of Justice, Immigration and Naturalization Service, Washington, D.C., Jan. 31, 2003). These numbers are ballpark figures because some estimates run as high as 13 million illegal aliens residing in the United States. See "Feds Undercount Illegal Aliens," NewsMax.com, Mar. 16, 2001.

18. See, for example, Massey, *Beyond Smoke and Mirrors,* 7–23.

19. See for example, Adalberto Aguirre, Jr., and Jonathan Turner, *American Ethnicity: The Dynamics and Consequences of Discrimination,* 3rd ed.

20. See Peter Andreas, *Border Games: Policing the U.S.-Mexico Divide;* see also "Drug Intelligence Brief: Mexico" (Drug Enforcement Administration, July 2002), available at http://www.usdoj.gov/dea/pubs/intel/02035/02035.html.

21. U.S. Drug Enforcement Administration, http://www.usdoj.gov/dea/pubs/states/

texas.html; also see "Drug Intelligence Brief: Mexico" and "Drug Intelligence Brief: Texas" and J. Noel Espinoza, "Cocaine Seizures in McAllen Sector of Border Patrol Most in Nation," *The Monitor,* Sept. 22, 2002, 1A.

22. Officials confiscated 84 pounds of cocaine in the first seizure, followed by 13.6 pounds of cocaine in the second, and 3,347 pounds of marijuana in the third. See Travis M. Whitehead, "Border Patrol Seizes $5.8 Million in Drugs," *The Monitor,* Mar. 12, 2003, 9C.

23. Deep South Texas is geographically isolated from a major urban media center such as New York or Los Angeles. Coverage of news, including drug violence, is sparse. In contrast, see Sebastian Rotella's detailed description of drug violence in Tijuana and San Diego in *Twilight on the Line.*

24. See, for example, Douglas A. Harper's *Good Company* in which he discusses the value of experience and knowledge gained from years of work and the resulting "deep knowledge."

25. See, for example, Josiah Heyman, "United States Surveillance over Mexican Lives at the Border: Snapshots of an Emerging Regime," *Human Organization* 58, no. 4 (1999): 429–37; Josiah Heyman, "State Effects on Labor Exploitation: The INS and the Undocumented Immigrants at the Mexico–United States Border," *Critique of Anthropology* 18, no. 2 (1998): 157–80; and Josiah Heyman, "Putting Power into the Anthropology of Bureaucracy: The Immigration and Naturalization Service at the Mexico–United States Border," *Current Anthropology* 36, no. 2 (1995): 261–87.

26. Readers are encouraged to examine the work of others who have written about the border from various perspectives including, among others, Luis Alberto Urrea, *Across the Wire;* Sebastian Rotella, *Twilight on the Line;* Ruben Martinez, *The Other Side;* Andreas, *Border Games;* Maria Herrera-Sobek, *Northward Bound: The Mexican Immigrant Experience in Ballad and Song.* Also see my own research, which specifically focuses upon the Texas counties of Cameron and Hidalgo. See Maril, *Poorest of Americans* and Robert Lee Maril, *Living on the Edge of America.*

27. Participant-observation was ideally suited to this research topic. See, for example, the discussion by Norman K. Denzin in *The Research Act: A Theoretical Introduction to Sociological Methods,* xxvi. See also, more recently, Norman K. Denzin and Yvonna S. Lincoln, eds., *The Landscape of Qualitative Research.* In contrast, note the interpretation of ethnographic research and participant-observation advocated by Jeffrey C. Johnson in "Research Design and Research Strategies in Cultural Anthropology," in *The Handbook of Method in Cultural Anthropology,* ed. by R. Bernard, 131–71.

28. The other stations were located in Brownsville, Harlingen, Port Isabel, Mercedes, Rio Grande City, Falfurrias, Kingsville, and Corpus Christi. The entire sector covered seventy-three miles of the Rio Grande. There was no specific agreement on the exact number of river miles the McAllen Station patrolled although the most common answer from agents was forty to forty-five miles.

29. From 1976 to 1989 I was a teacher and researcher in the Department of

Notes

Behavioral Sciences Texas Southmost College in Brownsville, Texas. Prior to that I was an instructor at Texas State Technical Institute in Harlingen, where I taught in the migrant reading program. I was chair and professor of the Sociology Department at the University of Texas–Pan American in Edinburg from 1999 to 2003. I have engaged throughout these years in a wide variety of research projects that focus upon the border region and authored three books specifically based upon this research. See Robert Lee Maril, *Texas Shrimpers;* Maril, *Poorest of Americans;* and Maril, *Living on the Edge of America.* As well as working in and formally studying this region, I have directly participated in a number of community organizations in Cameron and Hidalgo Counties, consulted for not-for-profit programs representing the interests of the low-income Mexican American population, and presented public testimony based upon my research.

Targets

1. Kate Hunger, "Trial to Begin for Dad of Escapee," *San Antonio Express-News,* June 12, 2003, 2B.

2. Almost one million people (978,369) lived in the four-county region. The Valley Hispanic population, including Hidalgo, Cameron, Starr, and Willacy Counties, accounted for approximately 85 percent of the total population with Anglos at 15 percent. Less than one percent of the total population was either African American, Asian American, or Native American. Data were derived from Census 2000 Summary File 3, U.S. Census, available at http://factfinder.census.gov/servlet/DatasetTableListServlet?_ds_name=DEC_20000_SF3_U&_lang=en.

Gumbys

1. Sprint was the cell phone of choice because the company's coverage of the banks of the Rio Grande was superior to that of any competitors. New recruits were immediately conspicuous with their non-Sprint cell phones.

2. See Arthur J. Rubel, *Across the Tracks.*

3. For a more complete description of NAFTA see, for example, Massey, *Beyond Smoke and Mirrors,* 48.

4. The Border Industrialization Program (BIP), originally initiated in 1967, created the legal framework for American corporations to invest in or relocate American plants to a system of twin plants, maquiladoras, along the U.S.-Mexico border. A variety of products were manufactured from Matamoros to Tijuana which then were shipped across the Rio Grande tax free to be assembled in an American plant. Workers are most frequently young women, while management is Anglo males who frequently live on the American side of the river in cities like McAllen. See Maril, *Poorest of Americans,* 50–51.

5. This discussion borrows heavily from ibid., 35–54.

6. Average family size in the Valley was declining in 2000 relative to previous decades, but Valley Hispanics still had roughly twice the number of children as the national average for Anglo families. The result of this demographic trend was a population pyramid highly skewed towards the young. Valley public schools were always overcrowded even before new buildings were completed. Ibid., 4–18. Only two other counties in Texas had higher birth to death rates than Hidalgo County, 19.1 per 1,000: Cameron County, 16.3, and Starr County at 21.9. Willacy had an 11.6 ratio. This data is derived from the table "Rate of Texas Estimated Components of County Population Change: July 1, 2001, to July 1, 2002," available at http://tables/CO-EST2002/Co-eire.census.gov/popest/data/countiesEST2002-08-48php.

7. See Maril, *Poorest of Americans,* 37–42. And also John R. Peavey, *Echoes from the Rio Grande.* See also Douglas E. Foley, Clarice Mota, Donald E. Fost, and Ignacio Lozano, "From Peones to Politicos: Ethnic Relations in a South Texas Town, 1900 to 1977"; and Herman S. Taylor, *Mexican Labor in the U.S.: Dimmitt County, Winter Garden District, South Texas;* Leroy P. Graf, "The Economic History of the Lower Rio Grande Valley, 1820–1875" (Ph.D. diss., Harvard University, 1942).

8. For details of the treatment of these workers and their daily wages, see Maril, *Poorest of Americans,* 38–39.

9. See, for example, David J. Weber, ed., *New Spain's Far Northern Frontier: Essays on Spain in the American West, 1540–1821;* Robert S. Weddle, *Spanish Sea: The Gulf of Mexico in North American Discovery, 1500–1685;* and Florence Johnson Scott, *Historical Heritage of the Lower Rio Grande.*

10. Gene J. Paull, "Climatic Variations in the Lower Rio Grande Valley," *South Texas Journal of Research and the Humanities* 1 (1977): 6–28.

11. Tom Lea, *The King Ranch.*

12. Evan Anders described this system in great detail in *Boss Rule in South Texas.*

Cavazos Beach

1. At this writing there is an ongoing legal debate over the use of the Rio Grande in deep South Texas as a barrier to immigration or as a wildlife corridor. In essence, the Border Patrol would like to clear-cut the area so that it can perform its duties more efficiently, while the environmental side has little sympathy for the problems dense vegetation and hostile wildlife present and would, in fact, seek to protect the existing flora and fauna further.

2. These and the following descriptions are based upon participant-observation, two interviews with this agent, and correspondence with the agent.

3. Unemployment rates for Valley residents have historically been among the highest in the nation. Since the 1970s Valley unemployment rates have been between two and three times higher than the state and national averages. Even during the booming

Notes

economy of the 1990s, the Valley saw double-digit rates of unemployment. Unemployment in the winter of 2003 for the McAllen-Edinburg-Mission area was 15.4 percent compared to 6.8 percent for the state of Texas. See Maril, *Poorest of Americans,* 13. See also the table "Civilian Labor Force Estimates for Texas Metropolitan Statistical Areas," *Texas Labor Market Review* (Texas Workforce Commission, Austin, Feb. 2003), 5.

4. X's are fixed positions that agents were first assigned under Operation Rio Grande in August 1997. This topic will be discussed in much greater detail.

5. Long-time residents of the Valley still have fond memories of time spent along the banks of the Rio Grande. See Sean Marciniak, "Essence of Rio Grande Tarnished by Drug Problems," *The Monitor,* Mar. 11, 2001, B1. I want to thank Juanita Garza, Department of History at the University of Texas–Pan American, for her elaboration of this theme.

Noe Escondido

1. The Bracero Program began in 1942 and ended in 1964. During the war years alone an estimated 168,000 Mexican workers were recruited to the United States. See Massey, *Beyond Smoke and Mirrors,* 34–41.

2. This abuse is documented in subsequent chapters.

3. There are a number of excellent ethnographies of migrants and the experience of the Bracero Program. See, for example, Ernesto Galarza, *Merchants of Labor: The Mexican Bracero Story,* and Ernesto Galarza, *Spiders in the House and Workers in the Field.*

4. The C Shift and its impact upon McAllen are discussed in greater detail in a later chapter. I am grateful to Professor Dan Dearth for detailed information about this topic and its long-term implications for Valley law enforcement.

5. Noe Escondido possessed a deeper understanding and knowledge of his job than other agents and management. This understanding was not based upon his formal education but upon his experience and his powers of observation, analysis, and judgment. See, for example, the work of Douglas A. Harper, *Working Knowledge: Skill and Community in a Small Shop.*

6. These monetary values of illegal drugs are from the Border Patrol. Estimates from informants are lower depending on their distance from the border and whether the drugs have been transported past the checkpoints at Falfurrias or Sarita. This topic is discussed further in the following pages.

7. This has been a constant problem in many border counties including Hidalgo and Cameron Counties. See, for example, Megan K. Stack, "Border D.A.s Still Unpaid for Trying Federal Cases," *The Monitor,* Sept. 20, 2000, 1C, 12C.

The Mole

1. Anecdotal evidence indicates that the mouth of the Rio Grande closed in the 1950s. There is also some inconclusive evidence that a mud bar at the mouth obstructed General Zachary Taylor from supplying his troops in 1846. See R. J. Brandes Company, "Study of the Mouth of the Rio Grande and Potential Impacts of the Proposed Brownsville Weir and Reservoir Project," July 2002, Austin. I want to thank Sally Spener, International Border Water Commission, for her information about this topic.

2. See Lynn Brezosky, "Sprouting Weeds Cut Water Supply for Matamoros," *The Monitor,* May 31, 2001, 7C.

3. Mel Huff, "Hydrilla Halt," *The Monitor,* Jan. 14, 2002, 1C, 8C.

4. Elizabeth Pierson, "Under the Seaweed," *The Monitor,* June 19, 2002, 1A, 12A; and Ibid.

5. See Rod Davis, "Rio Grande No Mas," *Texas Parks and Wildlife,* July 2002, 92–101.

6. About 60,000 Valley acres were planted in sugar cane.

7. At Channel 23 in Brownsville, the NBC affiliate, management did not field a weather team.

8. See Angeles Negrete Lares, "Retaliation Suspected in Murder of Editor," *The Monitor,* Mar. 28, 2001, 1C.

9. See especially Rotella, *Twilight on the Line.*

10. The total number of apprehensions in January of 2000, the year preceding this study, was 15,844 compared to January 2001, the first year of the study, when agents at the McAllen Station arrested 10,309. See "United States Border Patrol McAllen Sector: Blue Sheet Report" (McAllen, Tex., 2002). Apprehension statistics are further discussed in detail in "X's."

11. For further examples, see Sean Marciniak, "Smugglers Attempting to Transport Larger Groups across Border," *The Monitor,* Mar. 7, 2001, 7A; and Sean Marciniak, "Agents Discover 25 Immigrants Amid Truckload of Watermelons," *The Monitor,* Mar. 14, 2001, 8C.

Spring

1. At this writing there are few, if any, measures in the language tests that actually address speaking ability. In addition, agents are taught how to speak Castilian Spanish, not Spanish frequently heard along the U.S.-Mexican border.

2. See Maril, *Living on the Edge of America,* 145–52.

3. See the chapter entitled "Cannibals" for a detailed description of this set of events.

4. See Maril, *Poorest of Americans,* 19–34.

Notes

The Onion Girl

1. Although air was relatively clean, maquiladoras in Reynosa and Matamoros caused major pollution in those communities, the Rio Grande, and the Valley. One indication of the severity of this pollution was the fact that neural tube defects in newborn babies were three times the national average. Since the early 1990s, researchers had been tracking down the sources of Valley pollution and its impact on public health. See, for example, Megan K. Stack, "Scientists Seek Pollution Link in Border Birth Defects," *The Monitor,* Jan. 21, 2001, 1B.

2. See Daniel Garcia Ordáz, "Smoke Returns to South Texas," *The Pan American,* Apr. 10, 2001, 1. The last record of this phenomenon was in 1998, when the smoke reached as far as Chicago.

3. Ibid.

4. This strategy will be discussed more specifically in the following pages.

Cannibals

1. For an excellent description of the lives of the Mexican poor in the borderlands, see Urrea, *Across the Wire.* For a comprehensive view of race and class in Texas, see for example, Montejano, *Anglos and Mexicans in the Making of Texas,* and Mario Barrera, *Race and Class in the Southwest: A Theory of Racial Inequality.* See also, for a specific historical case of law enforcement and lawbreakers, Americo Paredes, *With His Pistol in His Hand.* Emilio Zamora documents the history of Mexican workers in Texas in his *The World of the Mexican Worker in Texas.* Also, see Milo Kearney, ed., *Studies in Brownsville History.* Mary Kidder Rak presents a highly romanticized view of the Border Patrol in Arizona in the 1920s and 1930s in *Border Patrol.* See also Jonathan Treat, "Charges of Human Rights Violations Continue to Dog INS, Border Patrol," *Borderlines* 9, no. 3 (Mar. 2001): 76. South Texas was not the only place along the border with a history of violence. See Debbie Nathan, *Women and Other Aliens.*

2. Gary Provost, *Across the Border: The True Story of the Satanic Cult Killings in Matamoros, Mexico.*

3. Ibid., 129.

4. For a more detailed discussion of this topic, see Maril, *Cannibals and Condos,* 48–52. For an academic overview of Indians in Texas, see W. W. Newcomb, Jr., *The Indians of Texas.* See especially Kelly F. Himmel, *The Conquest of the Karankawas and the Tonkawas, 1821–1859.*

5. See Maril, *Cannibals and Condos,* 49.

6. Newcomb, *Indians of Texas,* and Roy Bedichek, *Karankaway Country.*

7. This discussion closely follows a more detailed presentation found in Maril, *Poorest of Americans,* 19–54.

8. Ibid., 21.

9. Grantees some distance from the banks of the river received more traditional looking blocks of land for their growing herds.

10. Gene J. Paull, "Climatic Variations in the Lower Rio Grande Valley," *South Texas Journal of Research and the Humanities* 1, no. 1 (1977): 6–28.

11. See, for example, T. R. Fehrenbach, *Lone Star,* 507–21.

12. Ibid., 270–71.

13. Ibid., 291.

14. Ibid., 512–14. There are several excellent books on this topic.

15. This discussion relies on interviews with two long time residents of Rio Grande City and also finds strong support in the work of Graf. See Leroy P. Graf, "The Economic History of the Lower Rio Grande Valley, 1820–1875" (Ph.D. diss., Harvard University, 1942). Also, see Martinez, *The Other Side.*

16. The U.S. Border Patrol was established by the U.S. Congress in 1924. It began with a force of less than 500 men along the entire length of the Mexican border. There were guards on horseback who patrolled the border as early as the 1880s apprehending illegal Chinese immigrants. After the restrictive immigration policies of the 1920s, there was a need for a more organized force. See Mary Kidder Rak, *Border Patrol.* Also see *Immigrant America* by Portes and Rumbaut.

17. See Maril, *Poorest of Americans,* 44.

18. Evan Anders, *Boss Rule in South Texas,* 225.

19. Ibid. Also, see T. R. Fehrenbach, *Lone Star,* 677–701.

20. See, for example, the cases of peonage described in Maril, *Poorest of Americans,* 45–46. The *patrón* system invaded and infected the public school system. When the public school system was finally confronted, violence was not always avoided. See Roy Venecia, "The 1968 Edcouch-Elsa Walkout" (unpublished paper, Department of Sociology, University of Texas–Pan American, 1999). See also Maril, *Poorest of Americans,* 114–36. Other Texas Hispanics faced similar kinds of problems. See Michael V. Miller and James D. Preston, "Vertical Ties and the Redistribution of Power in Crystal City," *Social Science Quarterly* 53 (1973): 772–84; and Michael V. Miller, "Chicano Community Control in South Texas," *Journal of Ethnic Studies* 3 (1975): 70–89. For a discussion of low-income housing and *colonias,* see Peter M. Ward, *Colonias and Public Policy in Texas and Mexico.* Also, *Children of the Colonias Project: Through Our Own Lenses.* This same kind of region is aptly described by John Gaventa in *Power and Powerlessness: Quiescence and Rebellion in an Appalachian Valley;* and, in a broader perspective, in Janet Fitchen, *Endangered Spaces, Enduring Places: Changes, Identity, and Survival in Rural America.*

21. The five-year sentences, the first offenses of each defendant, were later thrown out by the presiding judge. The defendants instead received five years of probation. Lopez, it appeared, was not even at the scene of the riot. See the documentary "Strangers in Their Own Land," written and directed by Hope Ryder, produced by ABC News, narrated by Frank Reynolds (1974). Also, Roberto Garza, "The Pharr Riot of

1971 Thirty Years Later" (unpublished paper, Department of Sociology, University of Texas–Pan American, 2001).

22. See "Strangers in Their Own Lands," directed by Ryder. I have documented this same pattern in Maril, *Poorest of Americans.*

23. While this topic remains ripe for analysis by criminologists and others who study law enforcement agencies, there has been, to date, a curious silence in the academic world to this horrendous set of events. I would like to thank Professor Dan Dearth, chair of the Criminal Justice Department at the University of Texas–Pan American, for sharing with me his knowledge of the McAllen C Shift.

24. For an overview of King Cotton, see Neil Foley, *White Scourge: Mexicans, Blacks, and Poor Whites in Texas Cotton Culture.*

25. Maril, *Poorest of Americans,* 100–102.

26. Ibid., 24.

27. Throughout most of the twentieth century the Freedom Newspaper Chain, owners of the *Brownsville Herald, The Valley Morning Star,* and *The Monitor,* have represented the vested interests of the *patrones.* Stories that discredited the Anglo power structure were not published. See Maril, *Poorest of Americans,* 95–97. See also, Arnold De Leon, *They Called Them Greasers.*

28. Maril, *Poorest of Americans,* 47–54.

29. I would like to thank Rudolfo Rocha, dean of Arts and Humanities at the University of Texas–Pan American, for his insights on this topic.

30. See, for example, "El Corrido del Ilegal," "The Ballad of the Illegal Immigrant," which describes the plight of immigrants when confronted by the Border Patrol. Maria Herrera-Sobeck, *Northward Bound: The Mexican Immigrant Experience in Ballad and Song,* 187–88.

31. Unfortunately the quality of law enforcement in Grupo Beta, including its policing powers, varies from one Mexican state to another. See Rotella, *Twilight on the Line,* 90–102.

32. Figures derived from "Migrant Deaths by Sector: Fiscal Year '98–'01 Comparison" (Border Safety Initiative, U.S. Border Patrol, 2001). Immigrant drowning is specially addressed in a later chapter.

33. Ibid. It should be noted that these figures are, in my professional judgment and experience, undercounts of the actual numbers of individuals who died. The figures do not include those whose bodies were never discovered along with those who died but were, for a variety of bureaucratic reasons, not counted.

34. These names of categories are from "Migrant Deaths by Type: Fiscal Year Totals, FY03 through October 2, 2002" (Border Safety Initiative, U.S. Border Patrol, 2002).

35. By 2001, "Unknown Causes" had, at a rate of 24.1 percent, overtaken drowning as the second greatest cause of immigrant deaths while crossing the border.

36. "Migrant Deaths by Type."

37. From 1997 to 2001 the number of human smuggling cases declined from 2,287

to 1,254, as had the number of immigrants smuggled, from 21,383 to 7,454. Data from "United States Border Patrol, McAllen Sector Intelligence Section Blue Sheet Report" (U.S. Border Patrol, 2002).

38. These comments are based upon interviews with informants. This topic is specifically addressed in a forthcoming chapter.

39. "Drug Intelligence Brief," U.S. Drug Enforcement Administration, July 2002, http://www.usdoj.gov/dea/pubs/intel/02035/02035.html, 7.

40. Ibid., 7.

41. All statistics derived directly from "United States Border Patrol McAllen Sector Intelligence Section Blue Sheet Report, McAllen Sector" (U.S. Border Patrol, Aug. 2002).

42. Journalist Bill Buford understands some of the ways in which violence can exponentially increase in the hands of those with a purpose. See Bill Buford, *Among the Thugs*. If deep South Texas were adjacent to a major media market, the amount of drugs exported across the Rio Grande, and the violence which accompanied it, would have been national news.

43. Rotella writes of a similar kind of violence in Tijuana in *Twilight on the Line.*

44. Neither am I suggesting Hispanic culture along the river was in and of itself violent in nature. See, for example, the rich Hispanic cultural tradition documented in the traveling Smithsonian exhibition "El Rio" curated by Dr. Juanita Garza and Olivia Cadaval.

X's

1. I am not arguing here that it was an unwise decision by the supervisor to bring several vehicles and agents to the scene of "the accident," especially given the history of the farm. I am rather suggesting that this is but one example, out of a great many, of the Border Patrol's fascination with minute, unimportant events while ignoring significant structural and cultural problems within the agency.

2. Structural and cultural organizational reforms will be discussed in the last chapter.

3. See Timothy J. Dunn, *The Militarization of the U.S.-Mexico Border, 1978–1992,* 52–54. Also see "The National Border Patrol Strategy," 1–2, at http://www.ins.usdoj. gov/graphics/lawenfor/bpatrol/strategy.htm.

4. See Massey, *Beyond Smoke and Mirrors,* 43–46. While approximately 28.0 million Mexican undocumented workers entered the United States during this time period, 23.4 million also departed. I have benefited from conversations with Alberto Davila and Jose Pagan about these and related migration issues. See Campbell J. Gibson and Emily Lennon, "Historical Census Statistics on the Foreign-born Population of the United States: 1850–1990" (Population Division working paper no. 29, Population Division, U.S. Bureau of the Census, Washington, D.C., 1999).

5. See, for example, Figure 3.4 in "Mexican Emigration to the United States,

Notes

1965–1998," derived from U.S. Immigration and Naturalization Service data in ibid., 44.

6. Border Patrol agents were not the first or only ones to complain about the inadequacies of their uniforms in the field and other equipment. Soldiers in the U.S. Army, as well as other military branches, have long complained about their equipment. See John Diamond, "Buying Own Gear is Common for Troops," *USA Today,* June 26, 2003, 6A.

7. This topic will be discussed in detail in later chapters.

8. These and other necessary reforms are discussed in detail later in the book.

9. These and other related issues will be discussed in detail in the following chapters.

10. Biographical data about Silvestre Reyes is from his website: http://www.house. gov/reyes/biography.asp.

11. See Andreas, *Border Games,* 85–114. Also, for a historical perspective of the entire border, see Dunn, *Militarization of the U.S.-Mexico Border.*

12. I first heard Silvestre Reyes speak at UTPA in 2001. He was an effective public speaker who appeared knowledgeable, reasonable, and well-informed about border issues.

13. See, for example, "The President's Fiscal 2001 Immigration Budget" (available at http://uscis.gov/graphics/publicaffairs/factsheets/services.pdf), where this same logic is still to be found although the rhetoric of community quality of life was a relatively new addition to the discourse. "A total of 430 Border Patrol Agents and $52 million will strengthen INS multi-year border enforcement efforts. On the frontline of INS efforts to deter illegal immigration, these Border Patrol Agents will be critical to continue restoring integrity and safety to the borders, thereby improving the quality of life in border communities."

14. The logic of these reports and presentations to various branches of government and to the public is at once obvious. See, for example, "Testimony of Commissioner Doris Meissner Immigration and Naturalization Service (INS)" before the Committee on Appropriations Subcommittee on Commerce, Justice, State, and the Judiciary United States House Concerning the President's FY 2001 Budget Request, Mar. 22, 2000, Washington, D.C. The increase in the FY 2001 budget request, for example, by the Border Patrol, "includes $164.2 million and 699 new positions to enhance INS' border management strategy, facilitating the flow of legal immigration while preventing the illegal entry of people and contraband." "Fact Sheet," President's Fiscal 2001 Immigration Budget, prepared by the Office of Public Affairs, INS, Feb. 7, 2000.

15. The horse patrol at the McAllen Station was disbanded in 2001 because of a variety of problems including lack of fiscal resources, an unreasonable number of accidents, and poor organization. Management did not appear to be committed to the horse patrol or believe that it was a viable method of patrolling the line.

16. In the late 1990s a significant number of agents at the McAllen Station took duty at Port Isabel, South Padre Island, and the Port of Brownsville to avoid doing X's. They aggressively chased after and apprehended undocumented workers in all three

areas. All agents reported being severely criticized for their job performance and strongly encouraged to remain within their vehicles.

17. See, for example, the discussion of the rise in figures in Pauline Arrillaga, "Officials at Odds on How to Create Safe, Orderly Border," *The Monitor,* June 18, 2001, 1A.

18. "United States Border Patrol McAllen Sector Intelligence Section Blue Sheet Report, McAllen Sector," McAllen, Tex., 2003.

19. From 2,287 in 1997 to 1,254 in 2002. A later chapter discusses an alternative explanation of these figures.

20. Ibid.

21. Deterrence theory is discussed in detail in "The Tree." See, for example, Massey, *Beyond Smoke and Mirrors;* Andreas, *Border Games;* and Dunn, *Militarization of the U.S.-Mexico Border.*

22. Biographical data about Silvestre Reyes is from his website: http://www.house. gov/reyes/biography.asp.

23. "INS Releases Updated Estimate of U.S. Undocumented Resident Population," US. Department of Justice, Immigration and Naturalization Service, Washington, D.C., Jan. 31, 2003. See also, "Feds Undercount Illegal Aliens," *NewsMax.com* Wires, Mar. 16, 2001.

24. The same of course was true all along the entire Mexico-U.S. Border. Managers needed fewer apprehensions in their annual numbers.

Anzalduas

1. For example, many months after President Vicente Fox had taken office, six Mexican immigration inspectors at the Reynosa airport were accused by a Brazilian immigrant of forcing him upon landing at the airport to pay a smuggling operation to take him across the border to McAllen. See Sean Marciniak and Leonardo Andrade, "Reynosa Officials Target of Inquiry," *The Monitor,* Oct. 27, 2001, 1A.

2. From Valley television newscasts on or about January 15, 2001. Six months later *The Washington Post* reported that Victor Manuel Romero was describing in great detail corruption in Veracruz. Mexican customs officials earning $400 a month sported Versace designer clothes and drove expensive SUVs. See "Informer Blows Lid off Illegal Immigration," *The Washington Post,* July 11, 2001, A16.

3. Lest some Americans be tempted to seize the high moral ground regarding corruption in business and government, it was about this same time that the news of corporate scandals began to crowd the headlines. Still more corporate giants, including Enron, were hiding in the shadows. See, for example, the editorial "As Business Scandals Mount, Both Parties Share Blame," *USA Today,* July 8, 2002, 11A.

4. Rotella documents the intimidation of Mexican journalists and law enforcers in Tijuana in *Twilight on the Line.*

5. This topic is discussed in further detail in the chapter titled "The Storm." See, for example, Angeles Negrete Lares, "Retaliation Suspected in Murder of Editor," *The*

Monitor, Mar. 28, 2001, 1A; and Angeles Negrete Lares, "Twelve Questioned in Journalist's Death," *The Monitor,* Mar. 29, 2001, 8A.

6. Two Mexican transit police at the Reynosa Bridge, including Commander Carlos Gabriel Grajales Hernandez, were under investigation after being caught on videotape beating three American tourists. See Latie Burford and Leonardo Andreade, "Police Caught on Tape Sent on Leave," *The Monitor,* Oct. 6, 2000, 1A. The Reynosa jail was notoriously corrupt. One recent incident involved a prisoner who was able to switch identities with his cousin and walked out of the Mexican jail a free man. See Sean Marciniak and Melissa Sattley, "Man Who Switched with Cousin in Reynosa Jail Apprehended in U.S.," *The Monitor,* Mar. 22, 2001, 1A.

7. Rotella, *Twilight on the Line,* 217–56.

8. Ibid.

9. Angeles Negrete Lares, "Ashcroft Kicks off Initial Leg of Border Tour in Brownsville," *The Monitor,* May 5, 2001, 1A.

10. See "He's Mexico's Biggest Illegal Alien," *San Antonio Express-News,* Feb. 3, 2001; and Associated Press, "Benny the Elephant Busted After Crossing into Mexico Illegally," *North County* [California] *Times,* Feb. 3, 2001, The Back Page.

11. "He's Mexico's Biggest Illegal Alien."

12. The Benny scandal was soon followed by media frenzy surrounding $443 towels and $1,060 sheets purchased for the president's residence. See Traci Carl, "Fox Promises to Fire Those Responsible for Buying $400 Towels," *The Monitor,* June 24, 2001, 8A.

13. President Fox was immediately forthcoming about his foreign policy priorities. See Angeles Negrete, "President Fox's Priorities Include Immigration," *The Monitor,* Jan. 2, 2001, 1A; and Traci Carl, "In First U.S. Visit, Fox Looking for Investors," *The Monitor,* Mar. 21, 2004, 6A.

14. Sonya Ross, "Presidents Talk Trade, Immigration," *The Monitor,* Feb. 17, 2001, 1A.

15. President Bush faced tough going in Congress with his new immigration policies. See Ruben Navarette, Jr., "Mexico Has What the U.S. Wants: Immigrant Laborers," *The Monitor,* July 5, 2001.

16. Based upon written correspondence with Ralph W. Fielding, March 19, 2003.

17. See Robert E. Wright, "La Lomita Mission," *The Handbook of Texas Online,* http:www.tsha.utexas.edu/handbook/online/articles/view/LL/uql7.html.

18. Frequently when there were VIPs the Border Patrol would put two boats on the river in tandem and, with the cameras rolling, pass by a certain known landing with the first boat. Smugglers, seeing the first boat pass by, would then emerge from the brush on the southern side to lead small numbers of illegal workers across the river. The second boat, a few hundred yards behind the first, would then, to the delight of the VIPs, capture the aliens in the water or "deter" them back to Mexico. But the Border Patrol rarely used this strategy on a daily basis, because it required two boats operating during

the same shift. One grand dog and pony show was put on by the boat patrol for Mexican officials. See Sean Marciniak, "Officials Experience Difficulties First Hand," *The Monitor,* Sept. 23, 2001, 1.

19. Stephen W. Spivey, "International Link," *The Monitor,* Feb. 15, 2001, 1, 8.

The Storm

1. The long-time use and abuse of pesticides and herbicides by the farmers and growers were virtually ignored by elected officials, as were quality of life issues pertaining to the twin plants. Polluting industries were historically welcomed to this region for the jobs they offered to an impoverished population. About one quarter of the Hidalgo County population lived in *colonias,* which frequently lacked basic services including access to potable water. Inadequate septic systems often contributed to the spread of communicable diseases in these same *colonias* when seasonal flooding occurred. See Jane E. Larson, "Free Markets Deep in the Heart of Texas," *The Georgetown Law Journal* 84, no. 2 (1995): 179–260. Locally elected officials rarely discussed the polluted Rio Grande. See Maril, *Poorest of Americans,* 16–17; and Robert Lee Maril, "Contracts for Deeds" (unpublished paper, Texas Rural Legal Aid, Weslaco, 1995), for specific discussions of these topics. For a broader view of *colonias* and environmental issues on both sides of the border, see Peter M. Ward, *Colonias and Public Policy in Texas and Mexico.*

2. Jose Ozuna and Susan Martinez, "Saharan Dust Blows Thru Valley," *The Monitor,* July 28, 2001, 1A.

3. Ibid. According to TNRCC, the air quality "exceeds the safety range."

4. Because of legal issues I did not directly interview the two agents. Information about the case is from interviews with other agents and from newspaper accounts, including Sean Marciniak, "Authorities Seek Brother in Double Murder," *The Monitor,* Aug. 3, 2001, 1A; Jose Ozuna, "Suspect in Double Murder Confesses," *The Monitor,* Aug. 4, 2001, 1A; Sean Marciniak, "Police Find Body of Slain Girl's Father," *The Monitor,* Aug. 2, 2001, 1A.

5. These details are from interviews with agents and from Associated Press, "One Wounded at Checkpoint," July 27, 2001. According to statistics released by the McAllen Sector, the number of smuggling cases had increased, compared to the previous year, by a colossal 145 percent. Agents had filed 1,114 alien smuggling cases since the start of the year involving 1,171 smugglers and 6,310 aliens. See Anthony Caskey, "Border Smuggling Down, But Arrests Up," *The Monitor,* Aug. 6, 2001, 1C.

6. Adrian Altamirano, "Otro Rescate de Migrantes, Abandonados por El Coyote," *El Mañana,* Aug. 17, 2001, 1.

7. Agents, according to Border Patrol figures, filed 1,114 alien smuggling cases since the start of 2001, involving 1,171 smugglers and 6,310 aliens. Smuggling in this sector, according to one reporter who did not have annual figures by which to compare

2001 statistics, had declined while arrests had increased. This explanation was typical of the deterrence paradigm, which the media accepted without question. See Caskey, "Border Smuggling Down, But Arrests Up."

8. See Alberto Davila and Robert Lee Maril, "The Socio-Economic Impact of the McAllen Sector Border Patrol" (unpublished paper, Department of Economics, University of Texas–Pan American: Edinburg, 2001). Also, Stephen W. Spivey, "McAllen Office Cannot Accommodate Agency's Growth," *The Monitor,* July 16, 2001.

9. Davila and Maril, "The Socio-Economic Impact of the McAllen Sector Border Patrol."

10. In return, the Border Patrol wisely expected to receive from the municipalities incentives that reduce the costs to the agency and to taxpayers.

11. In March and April of 2001 I gave presentations of my ongoing research at Tulane University and at the annual meetings of the Society for Applied Anthropology in Atlanta. On both occasions I was struck by the gulf between my research and the audience's commonly accepted notions of the problems of illegal drugs and illegal immigration along the border.

The Tree

1. Other professions also have third places. See Roy Oldenburg, *The Great Good Place.*

2. Big Bend is a unique frontier. See, for example, Ronnie C. Tyler, "The Big Bend" (Washington, D.C.: National Park Service, U.S. Department of the Interior, 1975).

3. This topic is discussed in detail in "Shifts."

4. See, for example, F. E. Zimring and G. J. Hawkins, *Deterrence: The Legal Threat in Crime Control.*

5. For an overview of the contribution of Cesare Beccaria, see Stephen E. Brown, Finn-Aage Esbensen, and Gilbert Geis, *Criminology,* 4th ed., 182–87.

6. Jeremy Bentham, *Political Thought.* For an overview, see Larry J. Siegel, *Criminology,* 8th ed., 108–11.

7. Brown, et al., *Criminology,* 4th ed., 186–87.

8. Ibid., 228. See H. L. Ross, *Deterring the Drinking Driver: Legal Policy and Social Control;* and H. L. Ross, *Confronting Drunk Driving: Social Policy for Saving Lives.*

9. Mark Dantzker, associate professor of criminal justice, University of Texas–Pan American, interview by author, Edinburg, Mar. 6, 2003.

10. Rational choice theory, in all fairness, does expand upon deterrence theory by offering a more comprehensive understanding of behavior under certain circumstances. See Marcus Felson, *Crime and Everyday Life: Insights and Implications for Society;* Lawrence Cohen and Marcus Felson, "Social Change and Crime Rates: A Routine Activities Approach," *American Sociological Review* 44 (1979): 214–41; and Derek

Cornish and Ronald Clarke, "Understanding Crime Displacement: An Application of Rational Choice Theory," *Criminology* 25 (1987): 933–47.

Shifts

1. It was remarkable how well the description of the U.S. Border Patrol in the 1920s and 1930s resembled the McAllen Station in 2000. See Mary Kidder Rak, *The Border Patrol.*

2. The exception was towns, cities, and areas where new immigrants had resettled. For example, midwestern towns with meat-packing facilities attracted significant numbers of Hispanic low-wage workers. On the eastern seaboard Hispanics were increasingly attracted to a variety of different kinds of low-wage industries. See for example Peggy Levitt, *The Transnational Villagers.*

3. Ranchers in counties bordering Hidalgo began to arm themselves against illegal immigrants in 2001. In Arizona armed vigilantes patrolling the border had become commonplace. Columnists on the right increasingly called for President Bush to seal our borders. Typical of this perspective, see Michelle Malkin, "Bush Needs to Put More Focus on Our Borders," *The Monitor,* Jan. 26, 2003, 7D. At the other end of the political spectrum, *Projecto Libertad* was very active in the defense of the rights of illegal immigrants in Harlingen, Texas. Academics remained uninterested in the study of the U.S. Border Patrol with the notable exception of Josiah Heyman. See, among others, Josiah Heyman, "Finding a Moral Heart for U.S. Immigration Policy: An Anthropological Perspective," *American Ethnological Society* (Monographs in Human Policy Issues, Washington, D.C., 1998); "United States Surveillance over Mexican Lives at the Border: Snapshots of an Emerging Regime," *Human Organization* 58, no. 4 (1999): 429–37; "State Effects on Labor Exploitation: The INS and Undocumented Immigrants at the Mexico-United States Border," *Critique of Anthropology* 18, no. 2 (1998): 157–80.

4. Many Americans cling to the melting pot theory which asserts that most new immigrants quickly assimilate into mainstream American culture. If they do not assimilate, they have no one to blame but themselves. Such a theoretical perspective carefully circumscribes racism, class antagonisms, and nationalism in favor of an idealistic view of American life and history. For a different perspective, see, for example, Portes and Rumbaut, *Immigrant America.*

5. See, for example, Montejano, *Anglos and Mexicans in the Making of Texas;* Carey McWilliams, *North from Mexico;* and Emilio Zamora, *The World of the Mexican Worker in Texas.*

6. I would like to thank Rudolfo Rocha, dean of the College of Arts and Humanities at the University of Texas–Pan American, for his interpretation of Valley history. I am also grateful to an anonymous agent for the telling of the same story from his perspective. More than one Valley citizen was deported to Veracruz, Mexico, including a young man from Harlingen who was only able to contact his parents after the INS ship landed.

Notes

7. See, for example, the problems associated with the presence of the Mexican military along the Rio Grande as discussed in "Bubbles." Also note the problems faced by female agents as discussed in the present chapter.

8. From August 13 through August 23 the daily highs in McAllen, Texas, were 102 degrees, 101, 102, 100, 100, 100, 102, 99, 101, 101, and 100. The temperatures I experienced along the banks of the Rio Grande were 105 degrees or higher during this same period of time. A very strong wind from Mexico frequently blasted through the region during the day, then tapered off after sunset.

9. In June 2002 a female supervisor was hired at the McAllen Station.

10. Commuting was relatively short because most agents lived in close proximity to the McAllen Station. In the past several agents had resided in Brownsville, which lengthened their one way commutes to ninety minutes or worked at the inspection station in Falfurrias, ninety miles to the north of McAllen. These agents eventually moved closer to their jobs.

11. See, for example, Bryan Villa, "Tired Cops," *Law Enforcement Bulletin,* Sept. 2001, 25–32, and Bryan Villa, "Reducing Stress," *Law Enforcement Bulletin,* Jan. 2000, 5–12.

12. Some of these same issues are discussed in Robert Lee Maril, *The Bay Shrimpers of Texas: Rural Workers in a Global Economy,* 183–200. See, more specifically, Perry Jenkins, Brenda Seery, and Ann C. Crouter, "Linkages between Women's Provider-Role Attitudes, Psychological Well-Being, and Family Relationships," *Psychology of Women Quarterly* 16 (1992): 311–29.

13. See Christa Reiser, *Reflections on Anger: Women and Men in a Changing Society.* See also Nancy C. Gunther and B. G. Gunther, "Domestic Division of Labor among Working Couples: Does Androgyny Make a Difference?" *Psychology of Women Quarterly* 14 (1990): 355–70, along with Dorinne E. Kondo, *Crafting Selves: Power, Gender, and Discourse of Identity in a Japanese Workplace.* Also see Susan Faludi, *Backlash: The Undeclared War Against American Women;* Sandra Bem, *The Lenses of Gender: Transforming the Debate on Sexual Inequality;* Jessie Bernard, *The Female World;* and Rea Lesser Blumberg, "A General Theory of Gender Stratification," in *Sociological Theory,* ed. by Randall Collins, 104–34.

14. See, for example, Robert Gramling, *Oil on the Edge: Offshore Development, Conflict, and Gridlock.*

15. Further research would explore the divorce rate among agents compared to others in law enforcement along with comparable rates of substance abuse, child abuse, spousal abuse, and other possible measures suggesting the costs of the double shift.

Fighting Back

1. From multiple broadcasts on the local NBC and ABC affiliates.

2. Interestingly enough, no local American or Mexican paper ever reported the incident.

Drowning

1. This history is outlined in the chapter "Cannibals."

2. In television's *Baywatch* and its spin-offs briefly attired men and women regularly saved victims from the surf after furiously swimming up to them, throwing a toned, tanned arm around their chests, then lugging them to safety through the waves and around dangerous rocks.

3. The Border Patrol was inept both at presenting the facts of an incident, including its interpretation of those facts, as well as responding to media information that was misinformed, heavily biased, or simply incorrect. For example, see Yolanda Chavez Leyva, "Message Sent: INS Officers Indicted in Immigrant Death," *The Monitor,* Oct. 20, 2002, 4D, which outlines what purports to be a brief history of Border Patrol abuses against illegal immigrants. Representatives of the Border Patrol never responded to this or other charges against it, leaving the reading public to assume them true.

4. Handguns used by agents sold with a discount for $500 to $700. An inexpensive vest cost $700.

5. The quality of water in the Rio Grande has been previously discussed. In 2003 the Rio Grande was ranked among the top ten most polluted rivers in the United States.

6. Grupo Beta will be discussed further in a later chapter.

7. The Freedom Newspaper chain, owners of "28 dailies, 32 weeklies, 8 television stations, and 6 regional web portals," practiced a unique brand of libertarianism in all of its local newspapers. The chain owned the major Hidalgo and Cameron County newspapers, including McAllen's *The Monitor,* Harlingen's *Valley Morning Star,* and Brownsville's *The Brownsville Herald* along with Spanish editions. "Freedom Communications Inc. was founded by R. C. Hoiles after his 1935 acquisition of the *Santa Ana Register* in California. His political philosophy of libertarianism was based on the readings of Baruch Spinoza, John Locke, Rose Wilder Lane, Ludwig von Mises, Frank Chodorov, Henry David Thoreau, Ralph Waldo Emerson, Frederic Bgastiat and Ayn Rand." Taken verbatim from Stephen W. Spivey, "Monitor Parent Company Up for Sale," *The Monitor,* Mar. 7, 2003, 1A.

8. The role and importance of a PID in the international arena is detailed in Barbara DeSanto and Danny Moss, eds., *Public Relations Cases: International Perspectives.*

9. See, for example, Juan Ozuna, "Half a Ton of Pot Seized After Agents Spot Vehicles," *The Monitor,* July 12, 2000, 3C.

10. For example, see Britney Booth, "Agents Seize Drug Caches Worth 7.5 Million," *The Monitor,* Jan. 9, 2001, 1C.

11. See, for example, "Human Cargo," *The Monitor,* Oct. 1, 2000, 7B.

12. The details of this story were described in "The Mole."

13. See Sean Marciniak, "Unidentified Body Found on Banks of Rio Grande River," *The Monitor,* Mar. 9, 2001, 2C.

14. See April Castro, "Two Dead, 14 Hospitalized in Truck Carrying Immigrants," *The Monitor,* July 29, 2002, 6C.

15. The media in Hidalgo and Cameron Counties function as a virtual news monopoly. See Robert Lee Maril, "Towards a Media Theory of the Lower Rio Grande Valley," *Borderlands Journal* 1, no. 1 (1977). One or two publications such as *The Mesquite Review* offered an alternative political perspective but focused primarily on the arts. Substantive political issues in mainstream commercial media are largely ignored or trivialized on a regular basis.

16. See Anthony Caskey, "Eighteen Graduate from Latest Citizen's Academy," *The Brownsville Herald,* Oct. 19, 2001, 8C.

17. See, for example, Alberto Davila et al., "Immigration Reform, the INS, and the Distribution of Interior and Border Enforcement Resources," *Public Choice,* June 1999; and Alberto Davila and Marie T. Mora, "English Skills, Earnings, and the Occupational Sorting of Mexican Americans along the U.S.-Mexican Border," *International Migration Review* 23 (winter, 2000).

18. Calculations were accomplished using the most conservative economic assumptions. See Alberto Davila and Robert Lee Maril, "The Economic and Social Impact of the United States Border Patrol upon Hidalgo County" (unpublished report prepared for the U.S. Border Patrol McAllen Station, Department of Economics, College of Business, University of Texas–Pan American, Edinburg, 2001).

19. See Fernando Del Valle, "Family Loses Ground in Civil Suit," *The Monitor,* June 22, 2001, 1A; Fernando Del Valle, "City Wants Second Case in 1998 Deaths Dropped," *The Monitor,* June 29, 2001, 1A.

20. This press conference was briefly described earlier in "The Storm."

21. Six months later the City of Edinburg was chosen as the site for the new facilities but groundbreaking for construction did not occur until March 2003.

22. For example, the majority of agents working on this project were not familiar with PowerPoint.

23. "Special to the Monitor," *The Monitor,* Sept. 1, 2000.

24. Though the drownings occurred June 8, 2000, the debate ranged for many months into the new year. For several additional years it was consistently referred to in the media and remained a serious concern on the south side of the river. See Angeles Negrete Lares, "President Fox's Priorities Include Immigration," *Brownsville Herald,* Oct. 1, 2001, 1C; and Anthony Caskey, "Eighteen Graduate from Latest Citizen's Academy," *Brownsville Herald,* Oct. 9, 2001, 8C.

25. Reporters, editors, and panels of experts on a number of Mexican newscasts and specials voiced their opinion that the agents who allegedly had stood watching the two drownings were part of a general conspiracy by the agency to bring direct harm to Mexican nationals working in the United States.

26. See the work of Douglas Massey and Kristin E. Espinosa, "What's Driving Mexico-US Migration?: A Theoretical, Empirical and Policy Analysis," *American Journal of Sociology* 102 (1997): 939–99; Douglas Massey, "Social Structure, Household Strategies, and the Cumulative Causation of Migration," *Population Index* 56 (1990): 3–26; Joan B. Anderson and Martin de la Rosa, "Economic Survival Strategies

of Poor Families on the Mexican Border," *Journal of Borderlands Studies* 6, no. 1 (1991): 51–68; Elizabeth Fussell, "The Effect of Tijuana's Bi-National Economy on Migration to the United States" (unpublished paper, Department of Sociology, Tulane University, 2002); Elizabeth Fussell, "Making Labor Flexible: The Recomposition of Tijuana's Female Maquiladora Labor Force," *Feminist Economics* 6 (2000): 59–79; and Molly Sheridan, *The Importance of Remittances on the Honduran Economy* (master's thesis, Tulane University, 2004).

27. *International Migration Review* 33 (1999): 430–54, as cited by the Center for Immigration Research, University of Houston (http://www.uh.edu/cir/death.htm).

Bubbles

1. See, for example Cornel West, "Race and Social Theory," *The Cornel West Reader,* 251–65; William Julius Wilson, *The Declining Significance of Race;* William Julius Wilson, *The Truly Disadvantaged;* Melvin L. Oliver and Thomas M. Shapiro, *Black Wealth/White Wealth;* Juan Williams, *Thurgood Marshall: American Revolutionary;* Josiah Heyman, "U.S. Immigration Officers of Mexican Ancestry as Mexican Americans, Citizens, and Immigration Police," *Current Anthropology,* June 2002; and Josiah Heyman, "Respect for Outsiders? Respect for the Law? The Moral Evaluation of High-Scale Issues by US Immigration Officers," *Journal of the Royal Anthropology Institute* 6, no. 4 (2000): 635–52.

2. See, for a brief description of this violence, the previous chapter, "Cannibals."

3. See John MacCormack, "Border Shooting Trial Starts Today," *The Monitor,* May 7, 2002, B1.

4. For the more liberal perspective, see the research of the Center for Immigration Research, University of Houston. For example, Karl Eschbach, J. M. Hagan, N. P. Rodriguez, R. Hernández-León, and S. Bailey, "Death at the Border," *International Migration Review* 33 (1999): 430–54; and Nestor Rodriguez, "The Social Construction of the U.S.-Mexico Border," in *Immigrants Out! The New Nativism in the Late Twentieth Century,* ed. Juan Parea, 223–43. Also see the work of the Refugio del Rio Grande, a "45 acre refuge located outside Harlingen, Texas, USA, . . . to offer a place of rescue in the United States for political refugees from Central America" (http://members.tripod.com/RefugiodelRioGrande/).

5. For an overview, see for example Adalberto Aguirre, Jr., and Jonathan H. Turner, *American Ethnicity: The Dynamics and Consequences of Discrimination,* 3rd ed.; along with Cornel West, *The Cornel West Reader,* 495–535.

6. Although it is always difficult, except within the dense pages of sociology tomes, to separate racial inequities from those embedded in social class, class differences clearly confounded the relationship between agents and those they apprehended. Again, see Aguirre and Turner, *American Ethnicity,* especially 21–42.

7. There was diversity among illegal immigrants I observed that further research should continue to explore. Portes and Rumbaut in *Immigrant America* have already

distinguished in detail between legal and illegal immigrants as part of their theoretical typology of new immigrants.

8. For an overview of this topic see, for example, Alan Riding, *Distant Neighbors: A Portrait of the Mexicans.*

9. From 1999 to 2003 I taught lower division, upper division, and graduate courses in the Department of Sociology at the University of Texas–Pan American. I found this same dislike among my Mexican American students at Texas Southmost College in Brownsville where I taught classes, from 1976 to 1987.

10. This social, political, and economic system is detailed in Maril, *Poorest of Americans.*

11. Jo Napolitanno, "Afghans Among the Border Patrol Detainees," *The Monitor,* Feb. 18, 2002, 1A.

12. Ibid.

13. Closing down the horse patrol freed up only a handful of agents.

14. See the earlier discussion of deterrence theory. Also, see Silvia M. Mendes and Michael D. McDonald, "Putting the Severity of Punishment Back in the Deterrence Package," *Policy Studies Journal* 29, no. 4 (2001): 588–610. Also, see James M. Galliher and John F. Galliher, "A 'Commonsense' Theory of Deterrence and the 'Ideology' of Science: The New York State Death Penalty Debate," *The Journal of Criminal Law and Criminology* 92, no. 2 (2002): 307–33.

15. These comments are based upon informants who wished to remain anonymous. I have attempted to verify their information by cross-checking particular points among all informants as well as other agents in law enforcement.

16. At this stage, before the drugs were transported to safer and small security houses, the drug operation was particularly vulnerable to disruption by law enforcement.

17. They were called *vaquitas lecheras,* dairy cows, because American law enforcers traditionally had driven black and white vehicles.

18. During my research at least two agents at musters had discussed how they discovered maps in the vehicles of drug smugglers which located the exact placements of the hidden sensors.

19. Informants also reported that drug smugglers feared and respected the National Guard, who they considered part of the American military.

20. The value that informants placed upon illegal drugs substantially differed from the prices set by agents and reported to Valley newspapers and other government agencies. A kilo of cocaine cost $9,000 to $11,000, not $30,000, while a pound of marijuana was valued at $250, not five times that amount.

21. "In 1995 the DEA estimated that 85 percent of illegal drugs entered the country through regular ports of entry in commercial trucks and passenger vehicles." From Massey, *Beyond Smoke and Mirrors,* 99. The authors cite the work of Dunn, *Militarization of the U.S.-Mexico Border;* and Andreas, *Border Games.*

22. One example would be two tractor trailers stopped at the El Paso bridge that

were hauling shipments of ceramic floor tile. Agents found more than three tons of marijuana, valued at $6.4 million, between the stacks of tiles. See Associated Press, "More than Three Tons of Marijuana Found during Border Inspection," *The Monitor,* Apr. 5, 2003, 2C.

23. Three undocumented Mexican workers died of exposure not far from the Falfurrias checkpoint on February 26, 2003. The evening news on Channel Five, the ABC affiliate, aired the discovery of their bodies after four other stories about local news events had been reported. The lead story during this broadcast was a report of a local schoolteacher accused of molesting a thirteen-year-old student.

24. Outside of Raymondville, a small town north of Harlingen, the bodies of six Mexican and Guatemalan undocumented workers were discovered in a sugar cane field that had been burned to ready the cane for harvest. See Vanessa Salinas, "Six People Burned in Cane Field," *The Monitor,* Mar. 25, 2003, 1C.

25. Fat Man drank beer under the hot sun, but he was not drunk.

26. See, as one of many examples, Travis M. Whitehead, "Heat Exhaustion May Be to Blame in Death," *The Monitor,* June 7, 2002, 8C.

27. See Chris Roberts, "Officials: Smuggling on the Rise," *The Monitor,* Nov. 2, 2001, A1.

28. See Juan Ozuna, "Immigrant Smugglers Plead Guilty in Federal Court," *The Monitor,* Apr. 4, 2002, 4C.

29. Ibid.

30. See, for example, Dunn, *Militarization of the U.S.-Mexico Border,* and Andreas, *Border Games.*

31. See Portes and Rumbaut, *Immigrant America,* 292, for example. Also, see Massey, *Beyond Smoke and Mirrors.*

Power

1. Critics may well respond that the McAllen Station was an aberration, that this case study of one station in one out of seventeen sectors cannot represent the entire organization. At the same time it is important to remember that the U.S. Border Patrol prides itself on uniformity and conformity. One station may vary in minor points from another (for example the fourth shift at the McAllen Station was relatively unique) but one station was intended, and maintained by a rigid hierarchy, as an exact replica of every other in the same fashion that military units with specific tasks, functions, training, and skills are replaceable by another military unit with the identical designation. Further, many of the agents I interviewed and observed had worked at other stations in the same sector, in other sectors in Texas, and in New Mexico, Arizona, and California. None of these agents ever suggested that, with the exceptions noted, the McAllen Station in any significant ways differed from other stations at which they had been posted. The McAllen Station employed about 300 agents, or roughly 3 percent of the total force of agents at the time. No attempt is made here to suggest that these agents were

statistically representative of the larger population of all agents; this was not a random sample. Other research should certainly follow this first study and build upon the data and analysis found here.

2. My hope is that other researchers will expand upon this research and that broader implications for public policy will then develop from that future research effort.

3. Readers are again reminded that I was never hired as a consultant by the Border Patrol but was an independent researcher.

4. Enron, for example, had Sharon Watkins to expose the criminal behavior of management at Enron. See Pamela Colloff, "The Whistle-Blower," *Texas Monthly,* Apr. 2003, 118–21, 139–42. It is interesting to note that just prior to the demise of Enron several nationally known consultants, all hired by Enron, pronounced this huge corporation to be in excellent financial shape.

5. See, for example, David A. De Cenzo and Stephen P. Robbins, *Human Resource Management,* 5th ed. I am indebted to Jacob Hochman for discussions on this topic.

6. Claire M. Renzetti and Daniel J. Curran, *Women, Men, and Society,* 4th ed., 391.

7. For example, women compose less than 6 percent of all local police departments (ibid., 242–47).

8. At this writing, the Border Patrol had still not determined the guilt or innocence of FOS Jose Monteverde.

9. Although at the McAllen Station there may be single male parents with children in their household, I never heard of nor found one. There certainly may be single male parents at other stations.

10. The only time that I ever observed agents' locking their weapons in gun lockers was when they fingerprinted undocumented workers.

11. I was impressed by the model, state-of-the-art processing facility found at the Stillwater Police Department in Stillwater, Oklahoma. The processing facility, along with the policies instituted by this municipal police department, greatly reduces risk to both suspects and officers.

12. I was shown in spring 2002 a crash site along a Hidalgo County road where an agent riding without a partner had a wreck. When he eventually was able to radio the dispatcher for help, forty-five minutes passed before he was found. Luckily the agent was not seriously injured.

13. I am not an information technology expert. These comments come from the agents themselves, my observations of the problems agents had with their computers, and my conversations with those who have expertise in computer technology.

14. Although important, this is a much more complex and tangential issue than can be discussed here. From the perspective of those involved at the McAllen Station, the debate seemed less about the efficacy of the union than budgetary concerns and ideology-based agendas.

15. Union membership is about 13 percent of the total labor force.

16. Certainly one reform objective could be to strengthen the union by encouraging it to be more responsive to the real needs of agents.

17. There is some evidence of a backlash. Several agents at the McAllen Station transferred to the Air Marshals only to find the work even less desirable, in spite of promises to the contrary, than the Border Patrol's. Critics have subsequently questioned labor practices within the Air Marshals since September 11.

18. See R. C. Trojanowicz and D. L. Carter, *The Philosophy and Role of Community Policing.*

19. Dennis J. Stevens, *Applied Community Policy in the 21st Century,* 13.

20. Ibid., 14–15. See also Herman Goldstein, *Policing a Free Society;* and P. K. Manning, *Police Work: The Social Organization of Policy;* and Kenneth J. Peak and Ronald W. Glensor, *Community Policing and Problem Solving,* 2nd ed.

21. The INS continually initiates "pilot programs" without full consideration of the political context in which the Border Patrol must function. For example, the INS began "Operation Vanguard" in the late 1990s as an experimental attempt to penalize the meatpacking industry in Nebraska for mass hiring of undocumented workers. After several task forces were formed to study the viability of the experimental program, "Operation Vanguard" was terminated. I would like to thank Lourdes Gouvea, Department of Sociology, University of Nebraska at Omaha, for her information on this and similar projects.

22. Those social scientists who worked with sensitive security data provided by the Border Patrol could be given background checks and clearances as is the case for social scientists who work with other federal agencies.

23. See Ernie J. Garrido, "Border Patrol Set to Launch Rescue Team," *The Monitor,* July 28, 2001, 1B. BORSTAR also was to work with *Grupo Beta* and other Mexican law enforcement agencies to aide undocumented workers. More recently under the Department of Homeland Security, the Border Patrol, U.S. Customs, the U.S. Coast Guard, and Mexican officials held a press conference in Matamoros to explain how they will aid illegal aliens. See Travis M. Whitehead, "Joining Forces for Safety," *The Monitor,* June 13, 2003, 1A.

24. Angeles Negrete Lares, "Eleven Found Dead in South Texas Boxcar," *The Monitor,* Oct. 16, 2002, 1A.

25. Will Weissert, "Mexico Arrests Suspects in Deaths of Immigrants," *Corpus Christi Caller-Times,* Aug. 13, 2003.

26. See, for example, Massey, *Beyond Smoke and Mirrors,* 142–64.

27. See, for example, Ryan Gabrielson, "Plan Would Allow Illegals to Stay, Work in U.S.," *The Monitor,* Jan. 14, 2004; Jessica Rocha, "United Nation's Fox Praises Bush's Immigration Reform Proposal at Summit, *The Monitor,* Jan. 14, 2004; and Molly Ivins, "Proposal Hurts U.S. Workers," *The Daily Reflector,* Jan. 5, 2004, A6.

28. In mid-October of 2002 Noelle Bush, daughter of Governor Jeb Bush and niece of President George W. Bush, was sentenced to ten days in jail for possession of cocaine. See Mike Schneider, "Noelle Bush Sentenced to Jail Time on Drug Charge," *The Monitor,* Oct. 18, 2002, 4A.

Notes

Epilogue: Drift

1. Jessica Rocha, "Diggers Reopen Mouth of Rio Grande," *The Monitor,* Oct. 10, 2002, 1A.

2. Ibid.

3. Alison Beshur, "Rio Grande Shuts Man-Made Channel," *The Monitor,* Oct. 24, 2002, 1A.

4. Ibid.

Bibliography

Aguirre, Adalberto, Jr., and Jonathan H. Turner. *American Ethnicity: The Dynamics and Consequences of Discrimination,* 3rd ed. Boston, Mass.: McGraw-Hill, 2001.

Altamirano, Adrian. "Otro Rescate de Migrantes, Abandonados por El Coyote." *El Mañana,* August 17, 2001, 1.

Amis, Martin. *The War Against Cliché.* New York: Hyperion, 2001.

Anders, Evan. *Boss Rule in South Texas.* Austin: University of Texas Press, 1986.

Anderson, Joan B., and Martin de la Rosa. "Economic Survival Strategies of Poor Families on the Mexican Border." *Journal of Borderlands Studies* 6, no. 1 (1991): 51–68.

Andreas, Peter. *Border Games: Policing the U.S.-Mexico Divide.* Ithaca, N.Y.: Cornell University Press, 2000.

Arnold, Laurence. "Bush's EPA Nominee Also Hired Immigrants." *The Monitor,* January 9, 2001, 1A.

Arrillaga, Pauline. "Officials at Odds on How to Create Safe, Orderly Border." *The Monitor,* June 18, 2001, 1A.

"As Business Scandals Mount, Both Parties Share Blame." *USA Today,* July 8, 2002, 11A.

Associated Press. "Benny the Elephant Busted After Crossing into Mexico Illegally." *North County* [California] *Times,* February 3, 2001, The Back Page.

———. "More than Three Tons of Marijuana Found during Border Inspection." *The Monitor,* April 5, 2003, 2C.

———. "One Wounded at Checkpoint." *The Monitor,* July 27, 2001, 1A.

Bibliography

Bane, Mary Jo, and David T. Ellwood. *Welfare Realities: From Rhetoric to Reform.* Cambridge: Harvard University Press, 1994.

Barrera, Mario. *Race and Class in the Southwest: A Theory of Racial Inequality.* Notre Dame, Ind.: University of Notre Dame Press, 1979.

Bedichek, Roy. *Karankaway Country.* Austin: University of Texas Press, 1974.

Bem, Sandra. *The Lenses of Gender: Transforming the Debate on Sexual Inequality.* New Haven, Conn.: Yale University Press, 1992.

Bentham, Jeremy. *Political Thought.* New York: Barnes and Noble, 1973.

Bernard, Jessie. *The Female World.* New York: Free Press, 1981.

Beshur, Alison. "Rio Grande Shuts Man-Made Channel." *The Monitor,* October 24, 2002, 1A.

Blumberg, Rea Lesser. "A General Theory of Gender Stratification." *Sociological Theory.* Ed. by Randall Collins. San Francisco: Jossey-Bass, 1984.

Booth, Britney. "Agents Seize Drug Caches Worth 7.5 Million." *The Monitor,* January 9, 2001, 1C.

Brezosky, Lynn. "Sprouting Weeds Cut Water Supply for Matamoros." *The Monitor,* May 31, 2001, 7C.

Brown, R. D. *Villa Head.* New York: Bantam Books, 1987.

Brown, Stephen, Finn-Aage Esbensen, and Gilbert Geis. *Criminology: Explaining Crime and Context,* 4th ed. Cincinnati: Anderson, 2001.

Buford, Bill. *Among the Thugs.* New York: Vintage, 1990.

Burford, Latie, and Leonardo Andreade. "Police Caught on Tape Sent on Leave." *The Monitor,* October 6, 2000, 1A.

Casares, Oscar. *Brownsville.* New York: Little, Brown, and Company, 2002.

Carl, Traci. "Fox Promises to Fire Those Responsible for Buying $400 Towels." *The Monitor,* June 24, 2001, 8A.

———. "In First U.S. Visit, Fox Looking for Investors." *The Monitor,* March 21, 2004, 6A.

Caskey, Anthony. "Border Smuggling Down, But Arrests Up." *The Monitor,* August 6, 2001, 1C.

———. "Eighteen Graduate from Latest Citizen's Academy." *Brownsville Herald,* October 9, 2001, 8C.

Castaneda, Carlos E. *Our Catholic Heritage in Texas, 1519–1936.* Austin, Texas: Von Boeckmann–Jones, 1936.

Castle, Emory N., ed. *The Changing American Countryside: Rural People and Places.* Lawrence: University Press of Kansas, 1995.

Castro, April. "Two Dead, 14 Hospitalized in Truck Carrying Immigrants." *The Monitor,* July 29, 2002, 6C.

Cavazos, R. Daniel. "The Two Sides of Brownsville's Growth." *Brownsville Herald,* March 19, 2003.

Children of the Colonias Project: Through Our Own Lenses. San Marcos: Southwest Texas State University, 1999.

Cohen, Lawrence, and Marcus Felson. "Social Change and Crime Rates: A Routine Activities Approach." *American Sociological Review* 44 (1979): 214–41.

Colloff, Pamela. "The Whistle-Blower." *Texas Monthly,* Apr. 2003, 118–21, 139–42.

Cornish, Derek, and Ronald Clarke. "Understanding Crime Displacement: An Application of Rational Choice Theory." *Criminology* 25 (1987): 933–47.

Data Services Division CoServe. "Demographic and Socio-economic Profile 2000: Cameron County." Data Services Division CoServe, University of Texas–Pan American, 2001.

Data Services Division CoServe. "Demographic and Socio-economic Profile 2000: Hidalgo County." Data Services Division CoServe, University of Texas–Pan American, 2001.

Davila, Alberto. "Immigration Reform, the INS, and the Distribution of Interior and Border Enforcement Resources." *Public Choice,* June 1999.

———, and M. T. Mora. "English Skills, Earnings, and the Occupational Sorting of Mexican Americans along the U.S.-Mexican Border." *International Migration Review* 23 (winter 2000).

———, and Robert Lee Maril. "The Socio-Economic Impact of the McAllen Sector Border Patrol." Paper, Department of Economics, University of Texas–Pan American, 2001.

Davis, Rod. "Rio Grande No Mas." *Texas Parks and Wildlife,* July 2002, 24–28, 92–101.

De Cenzo, David, and Stephen P. Robbins. *Human Resource Management,* 5th ed. New York: John Wiley & Sons, 1996.

De La Garza, Rodolpho O., and Frank D. Bean, eds. *The Mexican-American Experience: An Interdisciplinary Anthology.* Austin: University of Texas Press, 1985.

De Leon, Arnold. *Mexican Americans in Texas.* Arlington Heights, Ill.: Harlan Davidson, 1993.

———. *They Called Them Greasers.* Austin: University of Texas Press, 1983.

Del Valle, Fernando. "City Wants Second Case in 1998 Deaths Dropped." *The Monitor,* June 29, 2001, 1A.

———. "Family Loses Ground in Civil Suit." *The Monitor,* June 22, 2001, 1A.

Denzin, Norman K. *The Research Act: A Theoretical Introduction to Sociological Methods.* Englewood Cliffs, N.J.: Prentice Hall, 1989.

———, and Yvonna S. Lincoln, eds. *The Landscape of Qualitative Research.* Thousand Oaks, Calif.: Sage Publications, 1998.

DeSanto, Barbara, and D. Moss, eds. *Public Relations Cases: International Perspectives.* New York: Routledge, 2001.

Diamond, John. "Buying Own Gear is Common for Troops." *USA Today,* June 26, 2003, 6A.

Dunn, Timothy J. *The Militarization of the U.S.-Mexico Border, 1978–1992.* Austin, Tex.: CMAS Books, 1996.

Eschbach, Karl, J. M. Hagan, N. P. Rodriguez, R. Hernández-León, and S. Bailey. "Death at the Border." *International Migration Review* 33 (1999): 430–54.

Bibliography

Espinoza, J. Noel. "Cocaine Seizures in McAllen Sector of Border Patrol Most in Nation." *The Monitor,* September 22, 2002, 1A.

———. "A River in Trouble." *The Monitor,* April 12, 2003, 1A.

Faludi, Susan. *Backlash: The Undeclared War against American Women.* New York: Crown Publishers, 1991.

"Feds Undercount Illegal Aliens." NewsMax.com Wires, March 16, 2001.

Fehrenbach, T. R. *Lone Star.* New York: Macmillan Publishing Company, 1968.

Felson, Marcus. *Crime and Everyday Life: Insights and Implications for Society.* Thousand Oaks, Calif.: Pine Forge Press, 1994.

Fernandez, R. A. *The Mexican-American Border Region.* Notre Dame, Ind.: University of Notre Dame Press, 1989.

Fitchen, Janet. *Endangered Spaces, Enduring Places: Changes, Identity, and Survival in Rural America.* Boulder, Colo.: Westview Press, 1991.

Foley, Douglas E., Clarice Mota, Donald E. Fost, and Ignacio Lozano. "From Peones to Politicos: Ethnic Relations in a South Texas Town, 1900 to 1977." Monograph no. 3. Austin: University of Texas Center for Mexican American Studies, 1977.

Foley, Neil. *White Scourge: Mexicans, Blacks, and Poor Whites in Texas Cotton Culture.* Berkeley: University of California Press, 1997.

Fussell, Elizabeth. "The Effect of Tijuana's Bi-National Economy on Migration to the United States." Unpublished paper, Department of Sociology, Tulane University, 2002.

———. "Making Labor Flexible: The Recomposition of Tijuana's Female Maquiladora Labor Force." *Feminist Economics* 6 (2000): 59–79.

Gabrielson, Ryan. "Plan Would Allow Illegals to Stay, Work in U.S." *The Monitor,* January 14, 2004.

Galarza, Ernesto. *Merchants of Labor: The Mexican Bracero Story.* Santa Barbara, Calif.: McNally & Loftin, 1964.

———. *Spiders in the House and Workers in the Field.* Notre Dame, Ind.: University of Notre Dame Press, 1970.

Galliher, James M., and John F. Galliher. "A 'Commonsense' Theory of Deterrence and the 'Ideology' of Science: The New York State Death Penalty Debate." *Journal of Criminal Law and Criminology* 92, no. 2 (2002): 307–33.

Garrido, Ernie J. "Border Patrol Set to Launch Rescue Team." *The Monitor,* July 28, 2001, 1B.

Garza, Roberto. "The Pharr Riot of 1971 Thirty Years Later." Paper, Department of Sociology, University of Texas–Pan American, 2001.

Gaventa, John. *Power and Powerlessness: Quiescence and Rebellion in an Appalachian Valley.* Urbana: University of Illinois Press, 1980.

Gibson, Campbell J., and Emily Lennon. "Historical Census Statistics on the Foreign-Born Population of the United States: 1850–1990." Working Paper no. 29. Washington, D.C.: Population Division, U.S. Bureau of the Census, 1999.

Goldstein, Herman. *Policing a Free Society.* Cambridge, Mass.: Ballanger Publishing Company, 1977.

González, Genaro. *The Quixote Cult.* Houston: Arte Público Press, 1998.

Graf, Leroy P. "The Economic History of the Lower Rio Grande Valley, 1820–1875." Ph.D. diss., Harvard University, 1942.

Gramling, Robert. *Oil on the Edge: Offshore Development, Conflict, and Gridlock.* Stony Brook: State University of New York Press, 1995.

Gunther, Nancy C., and B. G. Gunther. "Domestic Division of Labor among Working Couples: Does Androgyny Make a Difference?" *Psychology of Women Quarterly* 14 (1990): 355–70.

Harper, Douglas A. *Good Company.* Chicago: University of Chicago Press, 1982.

———. *Working Knowledge: Skill and Community in a Small Shop.* Berkeley: University of California Press, 1992.

Herrera-Sobek, Maria. *Northward Bound: The Mexican Immigrant Experience in Ballad and Song.* Bloomington: Indiana University Press, 1993.

"He's Mexico's Biggest Illegal Alien." *San Antonio Express-News,* February 3, 2001, 4B.

Hester, Thomas R. "The Archaeology of the Lower Rio Grande Valley of Texas." *Proceedings, An Exploration of a Common Legacy: Conference on Border Architecture.* Austin: Texas Historical Commission, 1978.

———. *Hunters and Gatherers of the Rio Grande Plain and the Lower Coast of Texas.* San Antonio: Center for Archeological Research, University of Texas at San Antonio, 1976.

———. "Late Prehistoric Cultural Patterns along the Rio Grande of Texas." *Bulletin of the Texas Archaeological Society* 46 (1975): 106–25.

Heyman, Josiah. "Finding a Moral Heart for U.S. Immigration Policy: An Anthropological Perspective." Monographs in Human Policy Issues. Washington, D.C.: American Ethnological Society, 1998.

———. "Putting Power into the Anthropology of Bureaucracy: The Immigration and Naturalization Service at the Mexico–United States Border." *Current Anthropology* 36, no. 2 (1995): 261–87.

———. "Respect for Outsiders, Respect for the Law. The Moral Evaluation of High-Scale Issues by US Immigration Officers." *Journal of the Royal Anthropology Institute* 6, no. 4 (2000): 635–52.

———. "State Effects on Labor Exploitation: The INS and the Undocumented Immigrants at the Mexico–United States Border." *Critique of Anthropology* 18, no. 2 (1998): 157–80.

———. "United States Surveillance over Mexican Lives at the Border: Snapshots of an Emerging Regime." *Human Organization* 58, no. 4 (1999): 429–37.

———. "U.S. Immigration Officers of Mexican Ancestry as Mexican Americans, Citizens, and Immigration Police." *Current Anthropology,* June 2002, 62–79.

Bibliography

Himmel, Kelly F. *The Conquest of the Karankawas and the Tonkawas, 1821–1859.* College Station: Texas A&M University Press, 1999.

Hirschman, Charles, Josh Dewind, and Philip Kasinitz, eds. *The Handbook of International Migration: The American Experience.* New York: Russell Sage Foundation, 1999.

Horgan, Paul. *Great River.* Austin: Texas Monthly Press, 1984.

Huff, Mel. "Hydrilla Halt." *The Monitor,* January 14, 2002, 1C, 8C.

"Human Cargo." *The Monitor,* October 1, 2000, 7B.

"Informer Blows Lid off Illegal Immigration." *The Washington Post,* July 11, 2001, A16.

Ivins, Molly. "Proposal Hurts U.S. Workers." *The Daily Reflector,* January 5, 2004, A6.

Jackson, W. *Becoming Native to This Place.* Washington, D.C.: Counterpoint, 1994.

Jenkins, Perry, Brenda Seery, and Ann C. Crouter. "Linkages between Women's Provider-Role Attitudes, Psychological Well-Being, and Family Relationships." *Psychology of Women Quarterly* 16 (1992): 311–29.

Johnson, Jeffrey C. "Research Design and Research Strategies in Cultural Anthropology." *The Handbook of Method in Cultural Anthropology.* Ed. by R. Bernard. Walnut Creek, Calif.: Altimira Press, 1998.

Jones, Oakah L. *Los Paisanos: Spanish Settlers on the Northern Frontier of New Spain.* Norman: University of Oklahoma Press, 1979.

Katz, Michael B. *In the Shadow of the Poorhouse.* New York: Basic Books, 1986.

Kearney, Milo, ed. *Studies in Brownsville History.* Brownsville, Tex.: Pan American University at Brownsville, 1986.

Kidder, Tracy. *Home Town.* New York: Pocket Books, 1999.

Kondo, Dorinne E. *Crafting Selves: Power, Gender, and Discourse of Identity in a Japanese Workplace.* Chicago: University of Chicago Press, 1990.

Labor Market Information Department. "Texas Annual Employment and Earnings: 2000." Texas Workforce Commission, 2001.

Lares, Angeles Negrete. "Ashcroft Kicks off Initial Leg of Border Tour in Brownsville." *The Monitor,* May 5, 2001, 1A.

———. "Eleven Found Dead in South Texas Boxcar." *The Monitor,* October 16, 2002, 1A.

———. "President Fox's Priorities Include Immigration." *Brownsville Herald,* January 6, 2000, 1C.

———. "Retaliation Suspected in Murder of Editor." *The Monitor,* March 28, 2001, 1A.

———. "Twelve Questioned in Journalist's Death." *The Monitor,* March 29, 2001, 8A.

Larson, Jane E. "Free Markets Deep in the Heart of Texas." *The Georgetown Law Journal* 84, no. 2 (1995): 179–260.

Lea, Tom. *The King Ranch.* Boston: Little, Brown, and Company, 1957.

Levitt, Peggy. *The Transnational Villagers.* Berkeley: University of California Press, 2001.

Leyva, Yolanda Chavez. "Message Sent: INS Officers Indicted in Immigrant Death." *The Monitor,* October 20, 2002, 4D.

Lyson, Thomas A., and William W. Faulk, eds. *Forgotten Places: Uneven Development and the Loss of Opportunity in Rural America.* Lawrence: University Press of Kansas, 1993.

MacCormack, John. "Border Shooting Trial Starts Today." *The Monitor,* May 7, 2002, B1.

Malkin, Michelle. "Bush Needs to Put More Focus on Our Borders." *The Monitor,* January 26, 2003, 7D.

———. "Chicken Littles Slam Ashcroft for Illegal Immigrant Policy," *The Monitor,* May 1, 2003, 6C.

Manning, P. K. *Police Work: The Social Organization of Policy.* Prospect Heights, Ill.: Waveland Press, 1997.

Marciniak, Sean. "Agents Discover 25 Immigrants Amid Truckload of Watermelons." *The Monitor,* March 14, 2001, 8C.

———. "Authorities Seek Brother in Double Murder." *The Monitor,* August 3, 2001, 1A.

———. "Essence of Rio Grande Tarnished by Drug Problems." *The Monitor,* March 11, 2001, B1.

———. "Officials Experience Difficulties First Hand." *The Monitor,* September 23, 2001, 1A.

———. "Police Find Body of Slain Girl's Father." *The Monitor,* August 2, 2001, 1A.

———. "Smugglers Attempting to Transport Larger Groups Across Border." *The Monitor,* March 7, 2001, 7A.

———. "Unidentified Body Found on Banks of Rio Grande River." *The Monitor,* March 9, 2001, 2C.

———, and Melissa Sattley. "Man Who Switched with Cousin in Reynosa Jail Apprehended in U.S." *The Monitor,* March 22, 2001, 1A.

———, and Leonardo Andrade. "Reynosa Officials Target of Inquiry." *The Monitor,* October 27, 2001, 1A.

Maril, Robert Lee. *The Bay Shrimpers of Texas.* Lawrence: University Press of Kansas, 1995.

———. *Cannibals and Condos: Texas and Texans along the Gulf Coast.* College Station: Texas A&M University Press, 1986.

———. "Contracts for Deeds." Paper, Texas Rural Legal Aid, 1995.

———. *Living on the Edge of America.* College Station: Texas A&M University Press, 1992.

———. *Poorest of Americans.* Notre Dame, Ind.: University of Notre Dame Press, 1989.

———. *Texas Shrimpers.* College Station: Texas A&M University Press, 1983.

———. "Towards a Media Theory of the Lower Rio Grande Valley." *Borderlands Journal* 1, no. 1 (1977): 77–96.

Bibliography

———. *Waltzing with the Ghost of Tom Joad.* Norman: University of Oklahoma Press, 2000.

Martinez, Oscar J. *Border Boom Town: Ciudad Juárez Since 1848.* Austin: University of Texas Press, 1975.

Martinez, Ruben. *Crossing Over: A Mexican Family on the Migrant Trail.* New York: Metropolitan Books, 2001.

———. *The Other Side: Notes from the New L.A., Mexico City, and Beyond.* New York: Vintage, 1992.

Massey, Douglas S., Jorge Durand, and Nolan J. Malone. *Beyond Smoke and Mirrors: Mexican Immigration in an Era of Economic Integration.* New York: Russell Sage Foundation, 2002.

———. "Social Structure, Household Strategies, and the Cumulative Causation of Migration." *Population Index* 56 (1990): 3–26.

——— and Kristin E. Espinosa. "What's Driving Mexico-U.S. Migration?: A Theoretical, Empirical and Policy Analysis." *American Journal of Sociology* 102, no. 4 (1997): 939–99.

———, Joaquín Arango, Graeme Hugo, Ali Kouaouci, Adela Pellegrino, and J. Edward Taylor. *Worlds in Motion: Understanding International Migration.* Oxford: Clarendon Press, 1998.

———, Rafael Alarcón, Jorge Durand, and Humberto González. *Return to Aztlan: The Social Process of International Migration from Western Mexico.* Berkeley: University of California Press, 1987.

"McAllen's Per-Capita Income Lowest of More Than 200 Cities." *The Monitor,* September 3, 2000, 1A.

McHale-Scully, G. F. *El Cabron.* Brownsville, Tex.: El Rocinante Press, 1992.

McMurtry, Larry. *In a Narrow Grave: Essays on Texas.* New York: Simon and Schuster, 1968.

McWilliams, Carey. *North from Mexico.* New York: Greenwood Press, 1968.

Mendes, Silvia M., and Michael D. McDonald. "Putting the Severity of Punishment Back in the Deterrence Package." *Policy Studies Journal* 29, no. 4 (2001): 588–610.

Miller, Michael V. "Chicano Community Control in South Texas." *Journal of Ethnic Studies* 3 (1999): 70–89.

———. "Economic Growth and Change along the U.S.-Mexican Border." Bureau of Business Research, University of Texas at Austin, 1982.

———, and J. D. Preston. "Vertical Ties and the Redistribution of Power in Crystal City." *Social Science Quarterly* 53 (1973): 772–84.

"Mission Historical Museum Gala." *The Monitor,* March 8, 2003, 3D.

Montejano, David. *Anglos and Mexicans in the Making of Texas, 1836–1986.* Austin: University of Texas Press, 1987.

Napolitanno, Jo. "Afghans Among the Border Patrol Detainees." *The Monitor,* February 18, 2002, 1A.

Nathan, Debbie. *Women and Other Aliens.* El Paso: Cinco Puntos Press, 1991.

Navarette, Ruben, Jr. "Mexico Has What the U.S. Wants: Immigrant Laborers." *The Monitor,* July 5, 2001, 1B.

Negrete, Angeles. "President Fox's Priorities Include Immigration." *The Monitor,* January 2, 2001, 1A.

Newcomb, W. W., Jr. *The Indians of Texas.* Austin: University of Texas Press, 1961.

Newman, K. S. *No Shame in My Game.* New York: Russell Sage Foundation, 1999.

Oldenburg, Roy. *The Great Good Place.* New York: Marlowe and Company, 1999.

Oliver, Melvin L., and Thomas M. Shapiro. *Black Wealth/White Wealth: A New Perspective on Racial Inequality.* New York: Routledge, 1995.

Ordáz, Daniel Garcia. "Smoke Returns to South Texas." *The Pan American,* April 10, 2001, 1.

Ovaska, Sarah. "Groundwater Contaminated." *The Monitor,* May 7, 2003, 1A.

———. "TCEQ's $1.3M Lien on Munoz Home Dropped." *The Monitor,* April 17, 2002, 1B.

Ozuna, Juan. "Half a Ton of Pot Seized After Agents Spot Vehicles." *The Monitor,* July 12, 2000, 3C.

———. "Immigrant Smugglers Plead Guilty in Federal Court." *The Monitor,* April 4, 2002, 4C.

———. "Suspect in Double Murder Confesses." *The Monitor,* August 4, 2001, 1A;

———, and Susan Martinez. "Saharan Dust Blows Thru Valley." *The Monitor,* July 28, 2001, 1A.

Paolucci, Henry. *An Essay on Crimes and Punishments.* Indianapolis: Bobbs-Merrill, 1963.

Paredes, Américo. *George Washington Gómez.* Houston: Arte Público Press, 1990.

———. *With a Pistol in His Hand.* Austin: University of Texas Press, 1958.

Paull, Gene J. "Climatic Variations in the Lower Rio Grande Valley." *South Texas Journal of Research and the Humanities* 1, no. 1 (1977): 6–28.

Pcak, Kenneth J., and Ronald W. Glensor. *Community Policing and Problem Solving,* 2nd ed. Upper Saddle River, N.J.: Prentice Hall, 1999.

Peavcy, John R. *Echoes from the Rio Grande.* Brownsville, Tex.: Springman-King, 1963.

Pierson, Elizabeth. "Under the Seaweed." *The Monitor,* June 19, 2002, 1A, 12A.

Portes, Alejandro, ed. *The Economic Sociology of Immigration.* New York: Russell Sage Foundation, 1995.

———, and Rubén G. Rumbaut. *Immigrant America.* Berkeley: University of California Press, 1996.

Provost, Gary. *Across the Border: The True Story of the Satanic Cult Killings in Matamoros, Mexico.* New York: Pocket Books, 1989.

Rak, Mary Kidder. *The Border Patrol.* Boston: Houghton-Mifflin, 1938.

Reiser, Christa. *Reflections on Anger: Women and Men in a Changing Society.* New York: Praeger, 2001.

Bibliography

Renzetti, Claire M., and Daniel J. Curran. *Women, Men, and Society,* 4th ed. Needham Heights, Mass.: Allyn and Bacon, 1999.

Ressler, Robert K., and Tom Shachtman. *Whoever Fights Monsters.* New York: St. Martin's Paperbacks, 1992.

Rice, David. *Crazy Loco.* New York: Dial Books, 2001.

Richardson, Chad. *Batos, Bolillos, Pochos, and Pelados: Class and Culture on the South Texas Border.* Austin: University of Texas Press, 1999.

Riding, Alan. *Distant Neighbors: A Portrait of the Mexicans.* New York: Alfred Knopf, 1985.

"Rio Grande Valley of Texas: Valley Goals 2000." Rio Grande Valley Chamber of Commerce, Weslaco, Tex., 1985.

Roberts, Chris. "Officials: Smuggling on the Rise." *The Monitor,* November 2, 2001, A1.

Robertson, Brian. *Wild Horse Desert.* Edinburg, Tex.: New Santander Press, 1985.

Rocha, Jessica. "Diggers Reopen Mouth of Rio Grande." *The Monitor,* October 10, 2002, 1A.

———. "United Nation's Fox Praises Bush's Immigration Reform Proposal at Summit." *The Monitor,* January 14, 2004.

Rodriguez, Nestor. "The Social Construction of the U.S.-Mexico Border." *Immigrants Out! The New Nativism in the Late Twentieth Century.* Ed. by Juan Parea. New York: New York University Press, 1997.

Ross, H. L. *Confronting Drunk Driving: Social Policy for Saving Lives.* New Haven: Yale University Press, 1994.

———. *Deterring the Drinking Driver: Legal Policy and Social Control.* Lexington, Mass.: Lexington Books, 1983.

Ross, Sonya. "Presidents Talk Trade, Immigration." *The Monitor,* February 17, 2001, 1A.

Ross, Stanley R., ed. *Views across the Border.* Albuquerque: University of New Mexico Press, 1978.

Rotella, Sebastian. *Twilight on the Line: Underworlds and Politics at the U.S.-Mexico Border.* New York: W. W. Norton, 1998.

Rubel, Arthur J. *Across the Tracks.* Austin: University of Texas Press, 1966.

Rural Sociological Society Task Force on Persistent Rural Poverty *Persistent Poverty in Rural America.* Boulder, Colo.: Westview Press, 1993.

Rylander, Carole Keeton. *The Border: Where We Stand.* Austin: Texas Comptroller of Public Accounts, 2001.

Saenz, Rogelio, and Marie Ballejos. "Industrial Development and Persistent Poverty in the Lower Rio Grande Valley." *Forgotten Places: Uneven Development and the Loss of Opportunity in Rural America.* Ed. by T. A. Lyson and W. W. Faulk. Lawrence: University Press of Kansas, 1993.

Saldana, Rene. *The Jumping Tree.* New York: Delacorte Press, 2001.

Salinas, Vanessa. "Six People Burned in Cane Field." *The Monitor,* March 25, 2003, 1C.

Sanchez, M. L., ed. *A Shared Experience: The History, Architecture and Historic Designations of the Lower Rio Grande Heritage Corridor.* Austin: Los Caminos del Rio Heritage Project and the Texas Historical Commission, 1991.

Sassen, Saskia. "Immigration and Local Labor Markets." *The Economic Sociology of Immigration.* Ed. by Alejandro Portes. New York: Russell Sage Foundation, 1995.

Schneider, Mike. "Noelle Bush Sentenced to Jail Time on Drug Charge." *The Monitor,* October 18, 2002, 4A.

Scott, Florence Johnson. *Historical Heritage of the Lower Rio Grande.* San Antonio, Tex.: Naylor, 1937.

Seccombe, Karen. *"So You Think I Drive a Cadillac?": Welfare Recipients' Perspectives on the System and Its Reform.* Boston: Allyn and Bacon, 1999.

Sharp, J. *Bordering the Future: Challenge and Opportunity in the Texas Border Region.* Austin: Texas Comptroller of Public Accounts, 1999.

Sheridan, Molly. "The Importance of Remittances on the Honduran Economy." Master's thesis, Tulane University, 2004.

Sidor, J. *Put Up or Give Away: States, Economic Competitiveness, and Poverty.* Washington, D.C.: Council of State Community Development Agencies, 1991.

Siegel, Larry J. *Criminology,* 8th ed. Belmont, Calif.: Wadsworth Publishing, 2003.

Sissons, P. L. *The Hispanic Experience of Criminal Justice.* Bronx, N.Y.: Hispanic Research Center, Fordham University, 1979.

Skinner, Jose. *Flight and Other Stories.* Reno: University of Nevada Press, 2001.

Smiley, Jane. *Moo.* New York: Ballantine Publishing Group, 1995.

Smith, M. E. *Trade and Trade-Offs.* Prospect Heights, Ill.: Waveland Press, 2000.

Smith, Rolando Hinojosa. *The Valley.* Houston: Arte Público Press, 1983.

"Special to the Monitor." *The Monitor,* September 1, 2000.

Spivey, Stephen W. "International Link." *The Monitor,* February 15, 2001, 1, 8.

———. "McAllen Office Cannot Accommodate Agency's Growth." *The Monitor,* July 16, 2001.

———. "Monitor Parent Company Up for Sale." *The Monitor,* March 7, 2003, 1A.

Stack, Megan K. "Border D.A.s Still Unpaid for Trying Federal Cases." *The Monitor,* September 20, 2000, 1C, 12C.

Stambaugh, J. Lee, and Lillian J. Stambaugh. *The Lower Rio Grande Valley of Texas.* Austin: University of Texas Press, 1954.

Stark, O. *The Migration of Labor.* Cambridge, Mass.: Basil Blackwell, Inc., 1991.

Stevens, Dennis J. *Applied Community Policy in the 21st Century.* Boston: Allyn and Bacon, 2003.

Stoddard, E. R., ed. *Borderlands Sourcebook.* Norman: University of Oklahoma Press, 1983.

———. *Maquilla.* El Paso: Texas Western Press, 1987.

Bibliography

———. *U.S.-Mexico Borderlands Studies: Multidisciplinary Perspectives and Concepts.* El Paso: University of Texas at El Paso, 2002.

Stull, D. D., ed. *Any Way You Cut It.* Lawrence: University Press of Kansas, 1995.

Taylor, Herman S. *Mexican Labor in the U.S.: Dimmitt County, Winter Garden District, South Texas.* Berkeley: University of California Press, 1930.

Texas Workforce Commission. "Civilian Labor Force Estimates for Texas Metropolitan Statistical Areas." *Texas Labor Market Review,* 2002, 4.

Texas-Mexico Border Health Coordination Office. *Inventory of Texas-Mexico Border/South Texas Health Related Activities.* Edinburg: University of Texas–Pan American, 1999.

———. *Texas-Mexico Border Counties: 1998.* Edinburg: University of Texas–Pan American, 1998.

Thompson, Earl. *Caldo Largo.* New York: Signet, 1976.

Treat, Jonathan. "Charges of Human Rights Violations Continue to Dog INS, Border Patrol." *Borderlines* 9, no. 3 (2001): 76.

Trojanowicz, R. C., and D. L. Carter. *The Philosophy and Role of Community Policing.* East Lansing: National Neighborhood Foot Patrol Center, Michigan State University, 1988.

Tyler, Ronnie C. *The Big Bend.* Washington, D.C.: National Park Service, U.S. Department of the Interior, 1975. Reprint, College Station: Texas A&M University Press, 1996.

U.S. Department of Justice and Immigration and Naturalization Service. "INS Releases Updated Estimate of U.S. Undocumented Resident Population." Washington, D.C., 2003.

Urrea, Luis Alberto. *Across the Wire.* New York: Anchor Books, 1993.

Venecia, R. "The 1968 Edcouch-Elsa Walkout." Paper, Department of Sociology, University of Texas–Pan American, 1999.

Wallerstein, Immanuel. *The Modern World System.* New York: Academic Press, 1974.

Wambaugh, J. *Lines and Shadows.* New York: Bantam Books, 1984.

Ward, Peter M. *Colonias and Public Policy in Texas and Mexico.* Austin: University of Texas Press, 1999.

Weber, David J., ed. *New Spain's Far Northern Frontier: Essays on Spain in the American West, 1540–1821.* Albuquerque: University of New Mexico Press, 1979.

Weddle, Robert S. *Spanish Sea: The Gulf of Mexico in North American Discovery, 1500–1685.* College Station: Texas A&M University Press, 1985.

Weisman, Alan, and Jay Dusard. *La Frontera: The United States Border with Mexico.* New York: Harcourt Brace Jovanovich, 1986.

Weissert, Will. "Mexico Arrests Suspects in Deaths of Immigrants." *Corpus Christi Caller-Times,* August 13, 2003.

Wermuth, L. *Global Inequality and Human Needs.* Boston: Allyn and Bacon, 2003.

West, Cornel, ed. "Race and Social Theory." *The Cornel West Reader.* New York: Basic Civitas Books, 1999.

Whitehead, Travis M. "Border Patrol Seizes $5.8 Million in Drugs." *The Monitor,* March 12, 2003, 9C.

———. "Heat Exhaustion May Be to Blame in Death." *The Monitor,* June 17, 2002, 8C.

———. "Joining Forces for Safety." *The Monitor,* June 13, 2003, 1A.

Williams, Juan. *Thurgood Marshall: American Revolutionary.* New York: Crown, 1998.

Wilson, William Julius. *The Declining Significance of Race.* Chicago: University of Chicago Press, 1980.

———. *The Truly Disadvantaged.* Chicago: University of Chicago Press, 1987.

World Bank. *World Development Report 2000/2001: Attacking Poverty.* London: Oxford University Press, 2001.

Wright, Robert E. "La Lomita Mission." *The Handbook of Texas Online.* Texas State Historical Association, 2004. (http://www.tsha.utexas.edu/handbook/online/articles/view/LL/ugl7.html)

Zamora, Emilio. *The World of the Mexican Worker in Texas.* College Station: Texas A&M University Press, 1993.

Zimring, F. E., and G. J. Hawkins. *Deterrence: The Legal Threat in Crime Control.* Chicago: University of Chicago Press, 1973.

Index

Index

Index

Index

Index

Index

Index

Index

Index